Political Bodies

SUNY series in Contemporary Italian Philosophy

Silvia Benso and Brian Schroeder, editors

Political Bodies

Writings on
Adriana Cavarero's Political Thought

Edited by

Paula Landerreche Cardillo
and Rachel Silverbloom

Published by State University of New York Press, Albany

© 2024 State University of New York

All rights reserved

Printed in the United States of America

No part of this book may be used or reproduced in any manner whatsoever without written permission. No part of this book may be stored in a retrieval system or transmitted in any form or by any means including electronic, electrostatic, magnetic tape, mechanical, photocopying, recording, or otherwise without the prior permission in writing of the publisher.

For information, contact State University of New York Press, Albany, NY
www.sunypress.edu

Library of Congress Cataloging-in-Publication Data

Names: Landerreche Cardillo, Paula, editor. | Silverbloom, Rachel, editor.
Title: Political bodies : writings on Adriana Cavarero's political thought / edited by Paula Landerreche Cardillo and Rachel Silverbloom.
Description: Albany, NY : State University of New York Press, [2024]. | Series: SUNY series in contemporary Italian philosophy | Includes bibliographical references and index.
Identifiers: LCCN 2023029848 | ISBN 9781438497082 (hardcover : alk. paper) | ISBN 9781438497105 (ebook) | ISBN 9781438497099 (pbk. : alk. paper)
Subjects: LCSH: Cavarero, Adriana—Political and social views. | Political science—Philosophy. | Feminist theory. | Philosophical anthropology. | Philosophy, Italian.
Classification: LCC B3614.C287 P65 2024 | DDC 195—dc23/eng/20240117
LC record available at https://lccn.loc.gov/2023029848

10 9 8 7 6 5 4 3 2 1

Contents

Acknowledgments — vii

Editors' Introduction — 1
Paula Landerreche Cardillo and Rachel Silverbloom

Part One: Tracing Cavarero's Political Thought

1. Inclining toward Democracy: From Plato to Arendt — 19
   Olivia Guaraldo

2. Cavarero as an Arendtian Feminist — 37
   Julian Honkasalo

Part Two: "Who engenders politics?"

3. On the Politics of the *Who*: Cavarero, Nancy, and Rancière — 59
   Timothy J. Huzar

4. "Taking the Thread for a Walk": Feminist Resistance to the Philosophical Order in Adriana Cavarero and María Lugones — 85
   Paula Landerreche Cardillo

5. Stealing and Critical Fabulation: The Counter-Historical Methods of Adriana Cavarero and Saidiya Hartman — 109
   Rachel Silverbloom

Part Three: The Body in Politics: Conversations with Materialisms

6. One's Body in Political Engagement: Changing the Relation between Public and Private — 137
   Elisabetta Bertolino

7. Inclining toward New Forms of Life: Cavarero, Agamben, and Hartman — 155
   Rachel Jones

8. Bodies in Relation: Ontology, Ethics, and Politics in Adriana Cavarero and Giorgio Agamben — 185
   Laurie E. Naranch

Part Four: Political Violence, Voice, and Relational Selves

9. Sexual Violence as Ontological Violence: Narration, Selfhood, and the Destruction of Singularity — 211
   Fanny Söderbäck

10. Being Robbed of One's Voice: On Listening and Political Violence in Adriana Cavarero — 237
    María del Rosario Acosta López

Part Five: Uncanny Bodies

11. Elena Ferrante and the Uncanny of Motherhood — 267
    Adriana Cavarero

Appendix 1: Works by Cavarero in English — 281

Appendix 2: Secondary Bibliography on Cavarero — 283

Contributors — 287

Index — 291

Acknowledgments

Fanny Söderbäck's graduate seminar at DePaul University was, in many ways, the birthplace of this volume. It was there that we were first introduced to Adriana Cavarero—first in writing, and then later in the flesh, when she joined us in the final week of the seminar. In her classroom, Fanny facilitated our encounter with Cavarero in perhaps the most appropriate way possible: embodied, facing one another, in a space where all of our voices could be heard. When we met Adriana, we were presented with the intimidating task of telling her about the papers we were writing about her work. Our apprehension was quickly dissolved, however, when Adriana's kindness, humility, and immense intellectual generosity became apparent. We learned, there, that philosophy is best done with other people, and Fanny's classroom became a place where people wanted to gather and talk. Indeed, many of the philosophical conversations within this volume played out in real time in that space: Olivia Guaraldo and Laurie Naranch joined Adriana during her visit at the conclusion of the semester, and María del Rosario Acosta López participated throughout. We are extremely thankful for the philosophical friendships that inspired this volume and continued to grow during its production, including our very own friendships, which grew in the process of putting this project together.

Thank you to Adriana Cavarero, Elisabetta Bertolino, Fanny Söderbäck, Julian Honkasalo, Laurie Naranch, María del Rosario Acosta López, Olivia Guaraldo, Rachel Jones, and Tim Huzar for contributing your hard work and scholarship to this volume. The generosity with which you have offered your time and labor to make this volume possible, in globally and personally difficult times, means so much to us. It was a privilege to observe the conversations between papers in this volume develop and lead to the germination of new connections, dialogues, and insights. The result is a relational text of its own.

We are immensely grateful to Adriana Cavarero, not only for providing us the occasion for this book through your life's work and its contributions to philosophy and feminist thought but also for your generosity in engaging our work and contributing your time and writing to this volume.

Thank you, also, to those who offered advice, read drafts, and encouraged us from book proposal to manuscript submission. Fanny Söderbäck's mentorship extended well beyond the classroom—she always made herself available as a resource for questions and advice about the editing process, and her encouragement and support nurtured our confidence that we could, in fact, pull it off. Thank you to our colleague and friend María Victoria Londoño Becerra, who generously read drafts of the introduction and our papers for this volume and has been in conversation with our work on Cavarero since the beginning. She continues to push us to reconsider the best things Arendt's thought has to offer. Thank you to Greg Convertito for reading multiple versions of drafts and treating our work with care and for his support through this process of writing and editing.

We also want to thank everyone that participated in Fanny Söderbäck's seminar at DePaul, whose conversations inside and outside of the classroom constantly challenged and illuminated our own approach to Cavarero's work. We want to especially thank Eric Aldieri and Julian Ríos Acuña, who worked with us to bring Cavarero to SPEP in 2019; that experience laid the groundwork for what would later become this book project. Thank you to Fred Evans, who chaired our panel at SPEP and provided insightful and generous feedback.

We are grateful to Silvia Benso and Brian Schroeder, editors of the Contemporary Italian Philosophy Series to which this volume belongs, for entrusting us with this task and offering support throughout. Thank you to the Society for Italian Philosophy and the attendees of the 2021 and 2022 virtual conferences—the support and comments many of the papers and contributors in this volume received there were formative for shaping the volume as a whole. We appreciate Peg Birmingham's push for us to first take on this project when we were still graduate students and for putting us in touch with Silvia Benso. And thank you to Gavriel Wodar, Rachel's research assistant, who helped proofread final chapter drafts.

We should also acknowledge that chapter 7, María del Rosario Acosta López's "Being Robbed of One's Voice: On Listening and Political Violence in Adriana Cavarero," was originally published in Spanish in *Fuera de sí mismas: Motivos para dislocarse* by Herder Editorial in 2020. We are grateful that María made it possible for us to share a revised English translation in this volume.

Editors' Introduction

Paula Landerreche Cardillo and Rachel Silverbloom

Adriana Cavarero has been, and continues to be, one of the most innovative and influential voices in Italian political and feminist thought of the last forty years. Known widely for her departures from and challenges to the male-dominated canon of political philosophy (and philosophy more broadly construed), Cavarero has offered provocative accounts of what constitutes the political, with particular emphasis on embodiment, singularity, and relationality. Since co-founding *Diotima* in 1984, a group dedicated to feminist philosophy as political engagement, she has published several volumes that have gained critical acclaim and reached a wide audience in both the Italian- and English-speaking world and across disciplines including philosophy, political science, women's and gender studies, feminist theory, musicology, literature, modern languages, queer theory, the arts, and more.

Although much of Cavarero's work has been translated into English and discussed across disciplines, there are not many works that systematically treat her thought. At the time of writing, there is only one monograph dedicated entirely to Cavarero's thought and one edited volume that centers around her thought in conversation with Judith Butler and Bonnie Honig.[1] The aim of this volume is to join these efforts to fill this conspicuous gap in scholarship. To that end, we have gathered some of today's most prominent and well-established theorists, along with emerging scholars, to contribute their insights, questions, and concerns about Cavarero's political philosophy and to put Cavarero's work in conversation with other feminist thinkers, political theorists, queer theorists, and thinkers of race and coloniality. Particularly in this latter way, our volume features work that takes Cavarero's ideas to places they do not often go in her own writing, and as such, it is a testament to the many generative encounters that her philosophy makes possible.

Cavarero, throughout her career, has aimed to think about the singularity of the body. Perhaps it is more appropriate to say that she thinks the singularity of bodies, in plural. Sexed bodies, vocal bodies, vulnerable bodies, protesting bodies, pregnant bodies, and even dismembered bodies have a place in her thinking. The body is the place from which Cavarero thinks. One of her main challenges to the Western philosophical canon is to philosophy's claim of universality, which, as Cavarero shows throughout her career, depends upon and is deeply entangled with the repudiation of the body in philosophical thinking. She exposes the false neutrality of thought by concentrating precisely on bodies that cannot be subsumed to universal categories. Her challenge to the neutrality of thought begins from an exploration of the feminine body as a body that remains unthought in philosophy.[2] She gives us, as a result, a philosophy based on the singularity of the body. Singularity, not individuality—Cavarero sharply distinguishes these.[3] Her notion of singularity directly opposes the notion of the individual as a self-sufficient, atomistic subject in favor of a relational self that requires, constitutively and from birth, the care of others. Despite taking up a variety of themes and questions, the essays of this volume all carefully attend to and illuminate the ways in which the emphasis on embodiment in Cavarero's feminist framework challenges and transforms our very understanding of the political.

To assist the reader in locating further resources for engaging with Cavarero's philosophy, we have included two appendices in this volume. The first offers a bibliography of Cavarero's own texts that have been translated into English. The second is a selected bibliography of Anglophone engagements with her work. While by no means exhaustive, it offers a fairly comprehensive archive of scholarly engagements that may give the reader a sense of where Cavarero's work has traveled as it has been taken up by other people, cultural contexts, and disciplines.

An Unlikely Duo: Arendt and Irigaray

It is perhaps surprising to find Hannah Arendt as one of the main interlocutors of a feminist philosopher. Much of Cavarero's most explicitly political writings borrow heavily from Arendtian concepts and language: singularity and plurality, the "what" versus the "who," public happiness, and others. Cavarero also subscribes to Arendt's critique that Plato's *Republic* inaugurates political philosophy as foreclosure to politics itself.[4] Plato's desire to order the polis, they argue, comes at the expense of politics, meaning the democratic participation of all citizens. For both Arendt and Cavarero, plurality and uniqueness are fundamental aspects of politics, as politics requires the speech and action of every unique self to participate in the plural field of politics.[5] This notion of plurality, and the politics it informs, is also central to Cavarero's account of the difference between joining others in protest against forms of domination and becoming a part of totalitarian masses in her most recent book *Surging Democracy*.[6]

And yet, Cavarero is a strange Arendtian, if indeed she is one at all.[7] Her use of Arendtian concepts, taken out of context and reconsidered from a feminist lens, transforms their meaning and puts them to work in ways that Arendt, herself, did not (and perhaps *would* not). One of the most crucial disagreements between their work are their stances on the divide between the so-called private/domestic sphere and the public/political sphere; whereas Arendt is one of the division's most vocal defenders, Cavarero continually undermines and disrupts this boundary. And while she credits Arendt for challenging the conventional, masculine, philosophical obsession with death by insisting on the importance of natality, she finds that Arendt nevertheless falls short. Her writings on natality remain too abstract and are therefore insufficiently able to apprehend the body as the material site of birth.[8] In taking up (and transforming) Arendt's notion of natality, Cavarero strives to shift philosophy's orientation away from death and toward life, from disembodied eternity toward embodied finitude, and from atomistic individuality toward constitutive relationality.

Cavarero approached Arendt's work from a feminist lens to begin with. Italian Feminism generally, and the group *Diotima* that Cavarero cofounded in Verona particularly, are deeply influenced by Irigaray's philosophy of sexual difference. In fact, Irigaray's work is the starting point for a thinking that fundamentally questions the neutrality of thought and the institutions built on the structures of this thought. As Paola Bono and Sandra Kemp note, the Italian reception of Irigaray regards her "as a deeply *political* thinker, whose work—often accused by both British and American feminists of essentialism—is extremely concrete and attentive to the actual contexts of women's lives."[9] Cavarero's project begins from the desire to conceive of herself in her difference (rather than within the supposedly neutral category of Man). She understands the situated nature, and therefore the lack of stability, in Irigaray's thought and takes that to be a virtue. For her, to begin from an ontology of difference (sexual difference being the starting point) requires that our own embodied experience of the world becomes the starting point of political thought: Cavarero says "to think of ourselves as we are."[10]

From there, Cavarero takes the project of sexual difference feminism one step further. As her thought develops, she is more eager to articulate a philosophy that can give an account of each embodied singularity, which encompasses much more than sexual difference. Yet, there is something that she shares with the early work of Luce Irigaray: a desire to think from the body and bodily uniqueness in order to disrupt the symbolic order that claims neutrality precisely because it is divorced from the very bodies that conceived it. It is because Cavarero is committed to thinking from the place of the body that voice, for example, becomes a central theme in her work. In an interview with Elisabetta Bertolino, Cavarero says that she "is convinced that the best antidote to metaphysics is singing."[11] For her, the voice itself (rather than language) is the site both of our uniqueness and our openness to other beings. Insofar as we utter sounds, we do so for an other. In this way, the materiality of the resonating voice marks our relational character.[12] Thus, Cavarero's philosophy is a reevaluation of the body's place in philosophical and political thinking. In fact, the body becomes the very site that disrupts the boundaries between what is and is not political as well as the boundaries between the private and the public, the domestic and the political, and even the ethical and the political.

Cavarero's Political Bodies

From her early work on Plato up to her most recent work on pregnancy, published in this volume, Cavarero has emphasized the need for a philosophy rooted in bodily life, in contrast to the desire for abstract, universal, and eternal ideas that Western philosophical discourse has inherited from Plato. While the body is the condition of possibility for thinking (and consequently for philosophy), she identifies Western philosophy's founding gesture to be one of disembodiment, as she argues in *Stately Bodies*.[13] This contradiction is perhaps most evident in philosophical conceptions of Man: the human being, defined as first and foremost a rational agent, a thinking subject, an autonomous individual, and so on, must shed all the particularities of lived human experience in order to generate a definition that can apply to "anyone." In *Relating Narratives* Cavarero names such universals "monstrous"—they apply to everyone precisely because they apply to no one.[14] Further, while this universal notion of Man is disembodied and empty, as it must be in order to claim to be "neutral," it nevertheless conceals a quite particular notion of the human being: the masculine, adult, able body.[15] It is this very same notion of Man that structures the Western philosophical understanding of political subjectivity, and it is that political subjectivity that Cavarero, in her inextricably embodied philosophy, calls into question. Contra the erect, purely rational, autonomous, and undeniably masculine political subject, Cavarero's political bodies are constitutively relational, vulnerable, and unique. Her political bodies can, for the first time, constitute a plurality because they are permitted to be *different*.

Drawing from a story by Karen Blixen in the introduction to *Relating Narratives*, Cavarero explains that each life makes its own singular narrative possible: a unity that marks its uniqueness. It is not a unity that can be predicted or even one that guides one's life as it is lived, but is rather what is left behind.[16] For this reason, it is a shape that can only be seen by others who bear witness to that life, and it is best given expression through biographical narrative—the stories that we tell about who (not what) someone is or was.[17] She writes that "the one who walks on the ground cannot see the figure that his/her footsteps left behind, so he/she needs another perspective."[18] The *who* that is constituted in the narrative we tell about someone's life is, therefore, at once both unique and relational; it is in telling another's story that they are revealed, within and from a shared space of coappearing, as the uniqueness that they are. For Cavarero, borrowing from Arendt, this plurality—this shared space of coappearance—is what constitutes the political. And it is precisely this understanding of the political that, she argues, has been "replaced by various modes of domination" for over two-thousand years; indeed, she argues, the history of the West is "a history of depoliticization."[19] For Cavarero, to allow the uniqueness of others to appear through the act of narration is, thus, an inherently political act, and in the face of the depoliticized politics that still dominate today, it is also an act of resistance.

The constitutive relationality of political bodies thus makes possible acts of care, as can be the case in telling someone's story or protesting violence, but also renders us vulnerable to wounding. In *Horrorism*, Cavarero analyzes the ways in which bodies are exposed to a mode of ontological violence that targets the relational uniqueness of the body. Cavarero claims that horrorist violence "is an ontological crime that goes well beyond the inflicting of death" since it reduces one from vulnerable to helpless.[20] Thus, her philosophy is one that, in aiming to undo the Platonic inheritance of a depoliticized polis which depends on the vertical self-sufficient model of the individual, proposes a model of inclination as one that can account for our constitutive relationality and vulnerability, thus reevaluating the place of care in the philosophical canon.[21]

Cavarero's engagement with Plato is quite ambivalent. Although her early book suggests that she is interested in doing philosophy "in spite of Plato," as her work develops, it is clear that her dialogue with Plato is not fully negative. In fact, she finds in Plato the "seeds of [his own] self critique,"[22] which fuel productive moments of her work. As Olivia Guaraldo explains in her contribution to this volume, Cavarero is in constant dialogue with Plato from her earliest work to her latest book.[23] As she notes in her introduction to *In Spite of Plato*, her interest in Plato is in part biographical—classical philosophy is a central part of her intellectual formation—but it is also in part (and perhaps more importantly) the birthplace of the philosophy of the West. It is Plato who inaugurates Western philosophy as we know it, with its delimitations and exclusions.

Cavarero's work in *In Spite of Plato* explores the contradiction of women and Philosophy. In other words, it aims to make clear that women have no place in philosophy and that, in fact, women cannot figure in philosophy. Thus, she "steals back" the figures of women that have been used at the service of philosophy to set up this contradiction and in turn gives them shape within a "sexed" imaginary. This requires that Cavarero practice philosophy otherwise. Perhaps this "otherwise" is confusing, as what she does is not philosophy's other; rather, Cavarero opens up a different discursive universe, or perhaps pluriverse. Her early book is a working-through of the "need for a sexed thought," one that has deep implications not only for philosophy but also for politics.

Summaries of Contributions

The papers contained in this volume engage with a variety of themes and issues in Cavarero's political writings. Though we have decided to group them into sections, and did so with intention and careful thought, the reader will find that the essays mischievously spill outside of their neat categorizations and speak to one another across page borders. They simply refuse to be contained (and we would not have it otherwise). As such, the subtitled sections of this volume may provide a provisionally helpful guide to the reading of this book.

This volume begins with essays that follow the trajectory of Cavarero's political work by analyzing its engagement with two of her most persistent intellectual interlocutors—Plato and Hannah Arendt. Olivia Guaraldo's "Inclining toward Democracy" traces the "archaeology" of Cavarero's political thought from her early interest in Plato to her encounters with Arendt. The journey through Cavarero's analysis of political thought reveals Cavarero's commitment, especially in *In Spite of Plato* (1991), to countering the Platonic violence that reduces politics to order and risks both uniqueness and plurality—which are later established in *Surging Democracy* (2021) as requirements for democracy. Guaraldo argues that there is an important link between Plato's fantasy of order and totalitarian regimes of the present and past and that Cavarero's attention to uniqueness is in part motivated by a desire to reintroduce democratic possibilities in the present. While Cavarero's hesitation to think collectivity in her earlier work is perhaps related to concerns regarding totalitarian "masses," *Surging Democracy* aims to analyze and restore a notion of "the many" that has democratic potential. Thus, Guaraldo argues, Cavarero's latest work marks a turning point in her thinking of collectivity.

Julian Honkasalo's "Cavarero as an Arendtian Feminist" analyzes the way that Cavarero's feminist methodology has introduced a novel way of engaging Arendt's political philosophy. Honkasalo shows that Cavarero's distinct methodological approach, shaped in part by her engagement with Luce Irigaray's philosophy of sexual difference, offers a feminist reading of Arendt's theory of action. While other papers in this volume explore Cavarero's tactic of "stealing" primarily in relation to Plato's texts,[24] Honkasalo argues that Cavarero also applies this method in her encounters with Arendt's work; she takes Arendt's political concepts out of context, reads them from a feminist lens and in relation to themes of natality, sexual difference, and matricide, and in so doing, radically transforms their significance. This way of approaching Arendt brings into view the limitations of her (decidedly non-feminist) work from a feminist lens as well as the fruitful possibilities that are generated by reading her work in this way.

The second grouping of essays, "Who Engenders Politics?,"[25] centers around one of the meaningful ways that Cavarero's political thought critiques and departs from conventional Western political-philosophical discourse.

Specifically, these papers address some of the ways in which Cavarero's inextricably embodied, feminist framework requires a transformation of our understanding of political subjectivity and agency.

In "On the Politics of the *Who*: Cavarero, Nancy, and Rancière," Timothy J. Huzar builds upon previous writings in which he has elaborated different registers (or senses) of the political that appear in Cavarero's work: (1) a politics of indifference and (2) a poetics of politics.[26] Here, he focuses on Cavarero's "politics of the *who*." The grammar of the *who*, he argues, disrupts a conventional Western philosophical understanding of the political, wherein the singularity of actual living people is largely considered irrelevant to theorizations about justice, truth, reason, rights, and other political concepts. Huzar traces deliberations on political subjectivity and the significance of the who among the work of Jean-Luc Nancy, Hannah Arendt, and Jacques Rancière, ultimately turning back to Cavarero to emphasize the crucial contributions that her notion of the who has for transforming the landscape of political philosophy, broadly construed.

In "Taking the Thread for a Walk: Feminist Resistance to the Philosophical Order in Adriana Cavarero and María Lugones," Paula Landerreche Cardillo similarly argues that Cavarero's transformation of our notion of political subjectivity is a rich and radical one that departs meaningfully from conventional Western political discourse in ways that invite fruitful engagements with decolonial thought. She reads and weaves together Cavarero's retelling of the story of Penelope (from *In Spite of Plato*) alongside María Lugones's notion of "active subjectivity" in order to illuminate the ways that Cavarero challenges and transforms the place of bodily knowledge in philosophy. According to Landerreche Cardillo, Cavarero turns the task of philosophy upside down by retelling Penelope's story from a framework grounded in bodily knowledge rather than the conventionally abstract and universal philosophical discourse with which she is taken up in Plato's texts. Landerreche Cardillo argues that Cavarero works with Homeric and Platonic texts as if they were textiles woven with a symbolic structure that, while making apparent one pattern of cloth, conceal other possible configurations of sense and meaning. Cavarero thus works with (and against) the very texture of Platonic texts to uncover what they hide: a feminine imaginary that offers a meaningful place for bodily knowledge. In this way, Cavarero's retelling of Penelope's story not only shows that Penelope's femininity renders her alien to the masculine order but also that texture has been rendered incompatible with text. In this way, she argues, Cavarero's political writings offer meaningful and radical contributions not only to

Western feminist thought but also to explorations of embodied knowledge in transnational feminist projects.

Rachel Silverbloom picks up this thread of staging encounters between Cavarero and scholars from other discursive and global contexts by examining Cavarero's tactic of stealing alongside African American studies scholar Saidiya Hartman's methodology of critical fabulation. In her paper, "Stealing and Critical Fabulation: The Counter-Historical Methods of Adriana Cavarero and Saidiya Hartman," Silverbloom argues that the methodologies employed by both scholars offer models for how to engage with dominant archives that enact political violence (past and present), while also seeking to exceed the limits of such bodies of knowledge-production and counter their violence. By seeking to retrieve and retell the stories of women that have been silenced, discarded, or buried by the archives of philosophy and history, Cavarero and Hartman challenge notions of historical and political subjectivity that exclude such women from being understood as politico-historical agents in the first place.

Part Three, "The Body in Politics: Conversations with Materialisms," puts Cavarero's emphasis on embodiment and sexual difference in conversation with voices from materialist traditions and beyond. In particular, these three papers stage dialogues between Cavarero and other Italian thinkers who are known for having reintroduced the body and bodily figures to the discourse of philosophy, showing the radical commitment that Cavarero has to a philosophy that centers around the body.

Elisabetta Bertolino's "One's Body in Political Engagement: Changing the Relation Between Public and Private" asserts the centrality of the role that the relational and vulnerable body plays in Cavarero's notion of politics. She argues that the body, conventionally taken as the "private sphere par excellence," is shown by Cavarero to be, at the same time, constitutive of the public sphere of politics. This leaky quality of the body, contained in neither one sphere nor the other, undermines the authority with which they have been held in distinction heretofore in political philosophy. Although Cavarero is heavily influenced by Arendt, Bertolino indicates this as at least one crucial way that she nevertheless goes beyond Arendt—even as she takes up her thought. What results is a politics of care that is distributed neither in the gendered division of labor nor in the political institutions that rely on this division but, rather, that posits care and vulnerability as fundamental. Bertolino then takes up Robert Esposito's analysis of immunitary discourse and the ambivalence of the body in biopolitical discourses during the Covid-19 pandemic, considering how there is, perhaps, an agreement with Cavarero's call to rethink the abstract separation between public and private as well as the kind of political subjectivity that such a division makes possible.

Taking up this line of inquiry about how Cavarero's privileging of the body reshapes the very topography (or geometry) of the political, in "Inclining toward New Forms of Life: Cavarero, Agamben, and Hartman" Rachel Jones examines the relational ontology developed in Cavarero's work and the ways in which it transforms the scene of the ethical and political encounter. Jones traces the ways in which Cavarero's postural ethics, most explicitly developed in *Inclinations*, furthers the work that she has done to challenge masculine frameworks of upright, individuated, and autonomous subjecthood and produce a relational ontology shaped by sexual difference, motherhood, and birth. Jones puts this work into conversation with Giorgio Agamben's account of political subjectivity through his analysis of sovereign power and bare life. While both Cavarero and Agamben share the insight that the political is constituted by that which it excludes, what Cavarero's relational ontology uniquely offers is an attentiveness to the role of sexual difference in the geneaology of sovereignty. Unlike Agamben, Cavarero is able to account for how such a political genealogy is, at the same time, a genealogy of Man. Jones then turns to Saidiya Hartman in order to resituate Cavarero's ontological shift in the context of race, and specifically in relation to anti-Blackness and the transatlantic slave trade. Jones argues that the ways that Hartman challenges conventional notions of the political by attending to the fugitive and everyday forms of resistance enacted by Black women and girls offers important interventions and extensions of Cavarero's exploration of alternative political ontologies of inclined, relational, and bodily beings.

In "Bodies in Relation: Materialisms and Politics in Adriana Cavarero and Giorgio Agamben," Laurie Naranch furthers a dialogue between the work of Agamben and Cavarero to consider their philosophical treatment of the body from within, and yet also beyond, a materialist tradition that draws from Marx. While relational embodiment is central to both Cavarero's and Agamben's transformations of our understanding of political subjectivity, each approaches it in distinct ways. In contrast to Cavarero's living, sexed, and vulnerable bodies, Naranch shows that Agamben's divine, naked bodies remain somewhat disembodied. Cavarero's ethics of inclination, illustrated through her analysis of female figures, enables her to more robustly critique and displace the conventionally isolated political subject and to open possibilities for nonviolence beyond Agamben's notion of inoperativity.

Part Four, "Political Violence, Voice, and Relational Selves," features papers that take up Cavarero's notions of narratability, vocality, and uniqueness in the context of political violence and trauma. For Cavarero, the uniqueness and constitutive relationality of each person is revealed (and/or constituted, in part) by both the voice and narratability. If certain forms of violence attack precisely this ontological register of uniqueness and relationality, how might voice and narration be central to redressing and/or repairing the ways that the self is undone by violence?

Taking as a point of departure Susan Brison's testimony about her experience of sexual assault, in "Sexual Violence as Ontological Violence: Narration, Selfhood, and the Destruction of Singularity" Fanny Söderbäck engages Adriana Cavarero's work on narration to consider whether and how the self that is "undone" through traumatic violence can be "remade." For the trauma survivor who feels alienated from themselves and others, without a voice or a community of listeners, how might telling one's story aid in continued survival and healing? If certain forms of violence are, as Cavarero argues, ontological in the sense that they attack the very human condition of relationality as such, can narration offer an avenue for counteracting or responding to that destruction by putting the self back in relation? Söderbäck then explores biographical and autobiographical forms of narration in these contexts and how they might be distinct from one another.

In "Being Robbed of One's Voice: On Listening and Political Violence in Adriana Cavarero," María del Rosario Acosta López further explores the relationship of vocality, as well as audibility, to political violence in Cavarero's work. Acosta López argues that Cavarero's attention to narration and voice move away from a regime of visibility toward a regime of audibility; however, she argues that Cavarero's analysis of violence is still well inscribed in a visual regime. She explores the analysis of Medusa found in *Horrorism* to show how Cavarero ultimately ignores the regime of audibility that she carefully attends to in her other writings. Then, she provides an analysis of Ariel Dorfman's *The Death and the Maiden* to show how we might use Cavarero's own tools to think of the regime of audibility in cases of sexual violence, both from the perspective of speaking—that is, having one's own voice—and from the perspective of listening. She ends with a suggestion that Cavarero's earlier analysis of Echo provides an avenue for resistance even when one's own voice has been colonized through political violence.

We close this volume with a paper by Adriana Cavarero: "Elena Ferrante and the Uncanny of Motherhood." There, Cavarero offers a close reading of Ferrante's literary treatment of motherhood. Ferrante is able, she argues, to convey what is kept in obscurity by philosophy through its pursuit of an abstract and disembodied origin of life: the materiality and embodied experience of pregnancy and motherhood. This is significant, particularly because of the ways that such experiences and bodies have been excluded from the philosophical language of truth. Cavarero shows that Ferrante, unlike so many others, attends to the "dark side" of the maternal body—one that is so often obscured in favor of luminous and sanctified depictions of motherhood, as epitomized by Mary and baby Jesus. In contrast to the purified (indeed, sterile) depiction of the mother-son relation between Mary and Jesus, Ferrante's exploration of mothers and daughters attends to the uncanny, disorienting, and constitutively embodied relationality therein. Motherhood is uncanny, Cavarero argues, because one's experience as an embodied uniqueness (an individual self) is confronted by the rather "impersonal process" of one's body generating life from within.[27] In pregnancy and motherhood one's experience of selfhood is, at the same time, an experience of the dissolution of the individuated self—not through death, as has been theorized many times over in philosophy, but rather through the pulsing tangle of living flesh that joins (and repels) mother and daughter and that joins, in turn, the "great chain of mothers" through which life itself is generated again and again.[28] The relationship between mother and daughter is, thus, irreducible to the mother-son relation and requires special attention for both Cavarero and Ferrante (and also Clarice Lispector, who plays an important role in the paper). The mother-daughter relation is one where "repugnance and disgust for the disintegration of borders, of margins that ensure a stable form of life for the self" is at the center.[29] This instability of the bodily borders requires that we think beyond the limits of a stable ego that is the philosophical subject par excellence.

Notes

1. Timothy J. Huzar and Clare Woodford, eds., *Toward a Feminist Ethics of Nonviolence* (New York: Fordham University Press, 2021).

2. See Adriana Cavarero, "The Need for a Sexed Thought," in *Italian Feminist Thought*, ed. Paola Bono and Sandra Kemp (Oxford: Blackwell, 1991), 183.

3. See Timothy J. Huzar, "On the Politics of the *Who*: Cavarero, Nancy, and Rancière," in this volume.

4. See Hannah Arendt, *The Human Condition*, 2nd ed. (Chicago: University of Chicago Press, 1998), 220–30.

5. See Adriana Cavarero, "Politicizing Theory," *Political Theory* 30, no. 4 (2002): 506–32.

6. See Adriana Cavarero, *Surging Democracy*.

7. For a discussion of this tension, see Julian Honkasalo, "Cavarero as an Arendtian Feminist" and Elisabetta Bertolino, "One's Body in Political Engagement: Changing the Relation Between Public and Private," in this volume.

8. See Adriana Cavarero, *Inclinations*, trans. A. Minervini and A. Sitze (Stanford, CA: Stanford University Press, 2016) and "'A Child Has Been Born unto Us': Arendt on Birth," trans. Silvia Guslandi and Cosette Bruhns, *philoSOPHIA* 4, no. 1 (2014): 12–30. See also Fanny Söderbäck's critique on Cavarero and Arendt's account of birth in Fanny Söderbäck, "Natality or Birth? Arendt and Cavarero on the Human Condition of Being Born," *Hypatia* 33, no. 2 (2018): 273–88.

9. Paola Bono and Sandra Kemp, "Introduction: Coming from the South," in *Italian Feminist Thought*, ed. Paola Bono and Sandra Kemp (Oxford: Blackwell, 1991).

10. See Adriana Cavarero "The Need for a Sexed Thought," 184. See also Adriana Cavarero and Elisabetta Bertolino, "Beyond Ontology and Sexual Difference: An Interview with the Italian Feminist Philosopher Adriana Cavarero," *differences* 19, no. 1 (May 1, 2008): 128–67.

11. See Adriana Cavarero and Elisabetta Bertolino, "Beyond Ontology and Sexual Difference: An Interview with the Italian Feminist Philosopher Adriana Cavarero," *differences* 19, no. 1 (May 1, 2008): 161.

12. In *For More than One Voice*, she expands on her account of relationality. There she aims to critique the western philosophical primacy of language over voice. Whereas in other works she takes narrative to be what marks our relationality, in her work on voice Cavarero highlights that what is fundamentally relational is not language but voice. Voice leaves our bodies to be heard by an other's ear, voice resonates outside of us, and this marks our fundamental relationality. See Adriana Cavarero, *For More than One Voice: Toward a Philosophy of Vocal Expression*, trans. Paul A. Kottman (Stanford, CA: Stanford University Press, 2005).

13. See Adriana Cavarero, *Stately Bodies: Literature, Philosophy, and the Question of Gender*, trans. Robert de Lucca and Deanna Shemek (Ann Arbor: University of Michigan Press, 2002).

14. Adriana Cavarero, *Relating Narratives*, trans. Paul A. Kottman (New York: Routledge, 2000), 9.

15. Although Cavarero does not name it, it is also important to say that the idealized body, from the standpoint of Western culture, is also white and European.

16. Cavarero, *Relating Narratives*, 1.

17. For further exploration about the importance of the "who" (versus the "what") in Cavarero's philosophy, see Timothy J. Huzar, "On the Politics of the *Who*: Cavarero, Nancy, and Rancière," in this volume.

18. Cavarero, *Relating Narratives*, 3.

19. Cavarero, *Relating Narratives*, 57.

20. Adriana Cavarero, *Horrorism: Naming Contemporary Violence*, trans. William McCuaig (New York: Columbia University Press, 2011), 30.

21. She hesitates to call this a subject since the notion of the subject is a modern notion; however, she sees in Plato already the roots of the modern vertical subject that claims to be self-sufficient. See Adriana Cavarero and Lawtoo Nidesh, "Mimetic Inclinations: A Dialogue with Adriana Cavarero," in *Contemporary Italian Women Philosphers: Stretching the Art of Thinking*, ed. Silvia Benso and Elvira Roncalli (Albany: State University of New York Press, 2021), 186.

22. Adriana Cavarero, "Theory and Politics in Plato's *Republic*," trans. Paula Landerreche Cardillo, in *Contemporary Encounters with Ancient Practice*, eds. Jacob Greentine, et al. (Edinburgh: Edinburgh University Press, Forthcoming).

23. See Olivia Guaraldo, "Inclining toward Democracy: From Plato to Arendt," in this volume.

24. See Landerreche Cardillo and Silverblooms's contributions to this volume.

25. The title for this section borrows directly from Adriana Cavarero's essay, "*Who* Engenders Politics?" in *Italian Feminist Theory and Practice: Equality and Sexual Difference*, edited by Graziella Parati and Rebecca West, translated by Carmen di Cinque, 88–103. London: Associated University Presses, 2002.

26. See Timothy J. Huzar, "A Politics of Indifference: Reading Cavarero, Rancière and Arendt," *Paragraph* 42, no. 2 (2019): 205–22; and "Violence, Vulnerability, Ontology: Insurrectionary Humanism in Cavarero and Butler," in *Toward a Feminist Ethics of Nonviolence*, eds. Timothy J. Huzar and Clare Woodford (New York: Fordham University Press, 2021), 151–160.

27. Adriana Cavarero, "Elena Ferrante and the Uncanny of Motherhood," in this volume.

28. Cavarero, "Elena Ferrante and the Uncanny of Motherhood," in this volume.

29. Cavarero, "Elena Ferrante and the Uncanny of Motherhood," in this volume.

Bibliography

Arendt, Hannah. *The Human Condition*. 2nd ed. Chicago: University of Chicago Press, 1998.

Bertolino, Elisabetta R. *Adriana Cavarero: Resistance and the Voice of Law*. New York: Routledge, 2019.

Cavarero, Adriana. "'A Child Has Been Born unto Us': Arendt on Birth." Translated by Silvia Guslandi and Cosette Bruhns. *philoSOPHIA* 4, no. 1 (2014): 12–30.

———. *For More than One Voice: Toward a Philosophy of Vocal Expression*. Translated by Paul A. Kottman. Stanford, CA: Stanford University Press, 2005.

———. *Horrorism: Naming Contemporary Violence*. Translated by William McCuaig. New York: Columbia University Press, 2011.

———. *Inclinations: A Critique of Rectitude*. Translated by Adam Sitze and Amanda Minervini. Stanford, CA: Stanford University Press, 2016.

———. "The Need for a Sexed Thought." In *Italian Feminist Thought*, edited by Paola Bono and Sandra Kemp, 181–85. Oxford: Blackwell, 1991.

———. "Politicizing Theory." *Political Theory* 30, no. 4 (2002): 506–32.

———. *Relating Narratives: Storytelling and Selfhood*. Translated by Paul A. Kottman. New York: Routledge, 2000.

———. *Stately Bodies: Literature, Philosophy, and the Question of Gender*. Translated by Robert de Lucca and Deanna Shemek. Ann Arbor: University of Michigan Press, 2002.

———. *Surging Democracy: Notes on Hannah Arendt's Political Thought*. Stanford, CA: Stanford University Press, 2021.

Cavarero, Adriana, and Elisabetta Bertolino. "Beyond Ontology and Sexual Difference: An Interview with the Italian Feminist Philosopher Adriana Cavarero." *Differences* 19, no. 1 (May 1, 2008): 128–67. https://doi.org/10.1215/10407391-2007-019.

Cavarero, Adriana, and Lawtoo Nidesh. "Mimetic Inclinations: A Dialogue with Adriana Cavarero." In *Contemporary Italian Women Philosphers: Stretching the Art of Thinking*, edited by Silvia Benso and Elvira Roncalli. Albany: State University of New York Press, 2021.

Huzar, Timothy J. "A Politics of Indifference: Reading Cavarero, Rancière and Arendt." *Paragraph* 42, no. 2 (2019): 205–22. https://doi.org/10.3366/para.2019.0299.

Huzar, Timothy J., and Clare Woodford, eds. *Toward a Feminist Ethics of Nonviolence*. New York: Fordham University Press, 2021.

Söderbäck, Fanny. "Natality or Birth? Arendt and Cavarero on the Human Condition of Being Born." *Hypatia* 33, no. 2 (2018): 273–88. https://doi.org/10.1111/hypa.12403.

Part One

Tracing Cavarero's Political Thought

One

Inclining toward Democracy
From Plato to Arendt

Olivia Guaraldo

The beginning of Cavarero's intellectual trajectory coincides with the beginning of political philosophy in the sense that her authorial initial reference is Plato. In an essay published in 1973, "Platone e la democrazia," Cavarero, at the time twenty-six years old, analyzes the complex relationship of the Athenian philosopher with Athenian democracy. As it is well-known, Plato severly criticized the sophist influence on the *demos* while at the same time elaborating, in the *Republic*, an articulate philosophical formulation of the just political order. In that article, Cavarero describes the ironic fact that the authoritarian Platonic model of the perfect polis—the *kallipolis*, where a true science of the political substitutes the chaotic practice of demagogy, sustained by the public speeches of the Sophists—is far more democratic than the actual democracy of Athens.[1] Or, to put it differently, Plato's political philosophy appears here as the first intellectual attempt to contrast demagogic manipulation of the masses by virtue of a substitution of democratic practices with a political use of philosophy. This early essay, which shortly precedes Cavarero's first monograph *Dialettica e politica in Platone* (1974), is quite scholarly but already testifies to the centrality of the relationship between philosophy and politics that will be demonstrated in her further works. Her persistent interest in Plato—which is eminently represented by her 1991 renown monograph *In Spite of Plato*—mirrors a never faded philosophical interrogation of the political.

A fairly recent Italian collection of essays, written between 1973 and 2017, that Cavarero devoted to Plato, shows how her initial scholarly interest in the philosopher developed into an original elaboration, becoming, on the one hand, a severe critique of the seizure of philosophical discursive power over the practice of politics and, on the other hand, an obsessive confrontation with his polymorphous text made of myths, dialogues, images, and logic.[2] Plato—the father of Western political-philosophy and Western metaphysics and the inventor of dialectical thinking—is also an ever-Plato—the father of Western political-philosophy and Western metaphysics and the inventor of dialectical thinking—is also an ever-generative source. generative source. It is not within the scope of this article to discuss Cavarero's interrogation of Plato, yet one must start from Plato if their aim is to discuss Cavarero's notion of the political. As a matter of fact, the aforementioned collection of essays starts with the 1973 article and ends with the text of a 2017 public conference on Plato and post-truth: there, Cavarero reweaves her original interest in the Platonic critique of democracy with the current theme of post-truth. Once again, the contraposition between philosophy and politics, the status of truth in democratic regimes, comes to the fore.

In "Platone e la democrazia" (1973), Cavarero enhances a democratic aspect in Plato's critique of the Sophists, namely his denouncing the fact that the Sophists were basically working for the ruling classes while appearing democratic and egalitarian. In the 2017 text on Plato and post-truth, entitled *An Archaeology of Post-Truth* (2017), Cavarero refers to the manipulative technique that the Sophists practice and teach as a practice that does not limit itself to exploiting the people's emotional drive. Instead, it cultivates and reshapes this very drive in order to establish and implement a system of power centered on *pathos*: emotions. Cavarero calls the Sophists' system "pathological politics."[3] By criticizing the manipulative, demagogic practice of the Sophists, Plato—Cavarero claims—seems to be speaking to present post-truth debates, where politics refers to an atmosphere in which truth is irrelevant and beliefs rooted in emotions prevail: "I am [. . .] interested in his [Plato's] description of the phenomenology of pathological politics, in his anachronistic and highly polemical account of a number of features and concerns about a certain type of political pathos, whose profiles seem to converge in the current definition of post-truth."[4]

Apparently faithful to a theoretical preference expressed as far back in time as 1973, Cavarero is still attracted by Plato's critique of democracy or, to put it differently, is fascinated by the inherent tension in his work between truth and opinion, between philosophy and politics, since it is a tension that still speaks to our present: "I do think that the elitist Plato, whose anti-democratic doctrine greatly pleases far-right traditions and fascist ideologies, the execrable Plato who despises the many in the name of rational truth, helps us reflect upon the demagogic vein that runs in the body of democracy and turns it into a basically irresistible, pathological regime."[5] The "demagogic vein that runs in the body of democracy" is an eloquent metaphor that enables us to grasp, in the face of the contemporary emergence of post-truth politics, how crucial—if not prophetic—Plato's analyses are of the demagogic techniques of the Sophists. In the *Republic* VI, Plato compares the "many" of the democratic assembly to a beast whose temper the Sophist has learned to tame, feed, excite, and calm, depending on the occasion. Yet, he calls this technique "wisdom": "Good he pronounces to be that in which the beast delights and evil to be that which the beast dislikes."[6] A mighty, irrational beast is the image Plato uses to metaphorize the assembly, thereby initiating a millennial distrust in democratic politics.

Yet, while Cavarero appreciates Plato's critique of democracy as a way to discern an archeology of post-truth, she does not limit her discussion to a traditional (one might say conservative) critique of democracy. Rather, she complicates her argument by inserting Hannah Arendt's viewpoint on ancient democracy within it. It is worth noting, in fact, while proposing this brief and provisional "archaeology" of Cavarero's notion of the political, that the Arendtian perspective was absent in her 1973 essay on Plato and democracy.

Informed and inspired for much of her work since at least the late 1980s by Hannah Arendt's thought, Cavarero cannot avoid bringing Arendt into the picture when discussing and appreciating Plato. The 2017 essay put the issue at stake very bluntly: "Where Plato sees a mighty beast, Arendt sees instead an interacting plurality"[7]

Arendt's original notion of politics as a space of appearance where each individual interacts with others in their uniqueness owes much to the ancient notion of Greek democracy as it developed in the polis.[8] Plato, in this picture, figures as the champion of a tradition—that of political philosophy—which "was founded explicitly in opposition to this polis and its citizenship. The way of life chosen by the philosopher was understood in opposition to the *bios politikos*, the political way of life."[9] The trial and death of Socrates led both Plato and Aristotle, in response to this traumatic fact, to "make the world safe for philosophy"[10] by introducing—against the plural, often conflictual realm of the polis—"theoretical foundations and practical ways for an escape from politics altogether."[11] For Arendt, the conflict between politics and philosophy is at the core of our tradition of political thought. Her intention is that of contesting that tradition, especially once its thread in the twentieth century has been inexorably broken.

This is even more so in the era of post-truth, Cavarero claims; both "Plato's unpleasant image of the mighty beast and Arendt's view of an interacting plurality" must be seen as opposite poles of a fundamental tension. The tension lies at the core of "democracy as such."[12] If one had to follow the Platonic path, democratic politics should be discarded as a chaotic, senseless activity, where words and deeds are always doomed to failure insofar as they are structurally distant, alien, to the objective measures of truth that Plato locates in the realm of ideas. As Plato explains in the *Republic*, only the trained philosopher, by virtue of a selective education of his mind and senses, can eventually rule according to the right ideal measures of truth and justice. If one had to follow the Arendtian path instead, democratic politics should be radically rethought according to both an ancient recuperation of *isonomia*—namely the political experience of the polis as a public space of appearance, where words and deeds were equally shared and there was no distinction between rulers and ruled[13] and a modern rearticulation of politics as participatory action.[14] It is certain that any democratic endeavor is menaced, haunted by the populist or demagogic drive, and the "mighty beast" can always resurface in any collective dimension, as Arendt herself argues when analyzing totalitarian masses[15]. It is equally certain, however, that the way in which politics has been conceptualized by the Western tradition has been influenced by the Platonic urge to elaborate criteria for order, resolved in the task of fashioning the "just polis." Fabrication, rather than action, has been the model activity upon which the tradition of political thought has based its foundations. This is to the detriment of the plural dimension of the public sphere, where it becomes clear that, as Arendt claims, it is "worthwhile for men to live together." Organizing together in a shared, public space—the activity of this togetherness—is a source of meaning and even happiness, as we will see later.

When discussing Cavarero's notion of the political, it is therefore worth analyzing the "fundamental, if not structural, tension" that she envisages between the Platonic distrust for any collective political dimension and the Arendtian attempt at instead giving theoretical dignity to it.[16]

Since *In Spite of Plato*, Cavarero's reliance on Arendt's thought articulates itself around two main Arendtian notions: natality and uniqueness. Natality, as Arendt argues, "is the central category of political thought as opposed to mortality, which is the central category of metaphysical thought."[17] Moreover, according to the Arendtian view, each human being is from birth different from any other, unique, and irreplaceable. Yet, this uniqueness is not an inner quality of the self that can remain hidden from the world. Uniqueness, or individual difference, becomes *real* only insofar as it appears in the world to others. Only by acting in front of others and "in concert" with them—which *also* means in agonistic, controversial terms—do we disclose our unique self: "who" we are. In other words, we need others in order to appear unique, even to ourselves.[18] Uniqueness depends on plurality, or, as Arendt puts it, "[i]n man, otherness, which he shares with everything that is, and distinctness, which he shares with everything alive, becomes uniqueness, and human plurality is the *paradoxical plurality of unique beings*. Speech and action reveal this unique distinctness."[19] Birth as the inaugural scene for unpredictable, unique, yet relational beings who eventually will display themselves by appearing to each other is the frame within which Arendt locates politics, and another word for politics is freedom. Understanding freedom as the spontaneous and unpredictable coming together of unique beings who act in concert to start something new could, more or less, be a shortened formula to account for/explain Arendt's notion of politics.

By insisting on natality as the precondition of the human capacity to start something new, to act freely and spontaneously, and on uniqueness as the distinctive feature of the human being, Arendt proposes a new lexicon for political thought after the deadly outcomes of totalitarianism. Cavarero has relied on this lexicon, and the theoretical frame it opens up, since *In Spite of Plato*.[20]

Cavarero often quotes a letter Arendt wrote to her friend and former mentor Karl Jaspers where she synthetically exposed the core of her critique to the philosophical approach to politics:

> If an individual man qua man were omnipotent, then there is in fact no reason why men in the plural should exist at all—just as in monotheism it is only God's omnipotence that makes him ONE. So, in this same way, the omnipotence of an individual man would make men superfluous. [. . .]

> I suspect that philosophy is not altogether innocent in this fine how-do-you-do. Not, of course, in the sense that Hitler had anything to do with Plato. (One compelling reason why I took such trouble to isolate the elements of totalitarian governments was to show that the Western tradition from Plato up to and including Nietzsche is above any such suspicion.) Instead, perhaps in the sense that Western philosophy has never had a clear concept of what constitutes the political, and couldn't have one, because, by necessity, it spoke of man the individual and dealt with the fact of plurality tangentially.[21]

The passage reveals two things: first, that philosophy cannot—and has never been able to for Arendt, by way "of necessity"—account for the human fact of plurality since it always deals with Man in the singular and assumes that any truth about him (sic) can be told only by universalizing the features of the individual measure. It is worth noting what Arendt writes about Aristotle's *Politics*, a text that greatly inspired her notion of the political. She contests Aristotle's famous definition of Man as *zoon politikon*, a political animal, which assumes that there is a "political essence" in Man as such. She claims instead that "the *zoon politikon*: as if in Man there were a political element as part of his essence. But this is false: Man is a-political. Politics originates *among* men, therefore decisively *outside* Man. A properly political substance does not exist. Politics is born in the *in-between* and affirms itself as relation."[22]

Secondly, and consequently, discourse on philosophical truth does not take into account and is not interested in the worldly fact that each human being is different from any other by virtue of their uniqueness, which, in turn, can reveal itself only in a public context of appearance. While togetherness and company are the measures of the political actor, solitude is instead the measure of the philosopher. From the original incompatibility of philosophy and politics derives, according to Arendt, a certain blindness (or neglect) of philosophy to the fact that human beings in their plurality have been declared *superfluous* by totalitarianism; philosophy, in its lack of interest in politics, can become dangerously complacent with political authoritarianism (any reference to Martin Heidegger is obviously pertinent). The superfluity of the human, to put it differently, is a totalitarian specter that is at the core of the Arendtian ontology of natality and uniqueness.

For as much as the sentence in the letter to Jasper can appear drastic, it nevertheless summarizes how Arendt's attempt to forge her notion of the political is in specific antagonism to Plato, the philosopher who sought to overcome, with his political philosophy, exactly the excessive plurality of the public space in the polis. Cavarero follows Arendt, in this drastic enterprise, setting for herself the task of an analysis of the Platonic oeuvre in order to detect the ways in which the philosopher "by necessity" ignores or obliterates plurality. Yet, as I will argue in this essay, Cavarero's reading of Arendtian plurality is at times problematic insofar as it bears the signs of what is still an essentially Platonic distrust for "the many."

There is an interesting trajectory in Cavarero's critique of Plato via Hannah Arendt, and I would like to follow the path of how the distrust of "the many" is progressively overcome in her latest works.

In *Spite of Plato* is a work where the Arendtian categories of birth and uniqueness are central, interwoven as they are with the thought of *sexual difference*. The book marks a fundamental passage in international feminist debates insofar as it succeeds in facilitating a dialogue between the two otherwise distant fields of Arendtian studies and feminist theory. Yet, in *In Spite of Plato*, the main issue is female subjectivity and the inability of philosophical discourse to speak (of) it, since that discourse speaks "by necessity" of Man (implicitly understood as male). Here, Arendt's thinking comes to the rescue for Cavarero because its discourse on natality and uniqueness challenges the legitimacy of philosophical discourse, traditionally centered on death, allowing an innovative feminist critique of it.

In *Relating Narratives* (2000) these Arendtian categories are further thematized in relation to the narrative perspective. Following Arendt, Cavarero claims that each human being perceives (and desires) themselves as the protagonist of a unitary story, which is, in turn, a unique and irreplaceable story. In order for these perceptions to become real and tangible—and not only consciousness projections or narcissistic fantasies—Cavarero insists on the relational and reciprocal dimension of storytelling: not to tell somebody my story, but to tell somebody their story means to deliver them their identity, to respond to an impellent desire for unity that each person perceives as essential to their being. Identity in the form of a story is the outcome of a relational practice—*between* the I and the you—not an essential feature of each singularity. Identity is therefore something given to me by someone else in the form of a life story, a biography. We can easily detect, in the primacy of the relational perspective over the individual one, the echo of both Arendt's critique of Aristotle's definition of the *zoon politikon* and her letter to Jaspers: the insistence on man *qua* man does not tell us anything about people in the plural. Moreover, it can be complacent to an authoritarian, if not totalitarian, drive to discard plurality in favor of an artificially produced uniformity.

The narrative practice of telling someone their story produces, so to say, a discourse that is able to grant meaning to uniqueness: "who" somebody is. It is a discourse that allows forms of knowledge, truth, and memory around human plurality without "by necessity" subsuming it under the general concept of Man in the singular. Cavarero further weaves this perspective into the context of feminist identity debates of the '90s and, in line with *In Spite of Plato*, *Relating Narratives* intertwines Arendt's critique of philosophy with feminist theory. Is the plurality in which we can speak through narrative practice gender neutral? Or is the "paradoxical plurality of unique beings" characterized by the corporeal fact of sexuation (*sessuazione*)? As Cavarero argues:

> To use Arendt's terms, it must be decided if the fact that I am a woman and not a man belongs to the order of my qualities (what I am), rather than to my uniqueness (who I am). At the heart of the first alternative there is a subject, unique and unrepeatable, which nonetheless is born "neutral" as far as sex goes and thus can make of its feminine quality a hypostasis that can be entrusted to the realm of representation. At the heart of the second alternative there is a uniqueness, equally unique and unrepeatable; birth shows who the newborn is—namely sexed, and given over to the contextual and relational realm of expression [. . .] From birth, the uniqueness which appears, and which provokes the fundamental question "who are you?" is an embodied uniqueness and therefore sexed.[23]

This passage signals a specific time in the late '90s when, in feminist debates, the question at stake was that of "the subject" and Cavarero, in constant dialogue with Judith Butler—who discusses her narrative positions extensively in *Giving an Account of Oneself* (2005)—progressively frames this question in terms of a constitutive relationality, or relational ontology, according to which the subject is never autonomous and sovereign—as the tradition of political thought presupposes—but always dependent on and exposed to others.

Within this frame, Cavarero understands the Arendtian issue of plurality from the viewpoint of an embodied (sexed) uniqueness in its relational dimension between an "I" and a "you." It is my claim that at least until the decisive event of 9/11, Cavarero makes use of the Arendtian frame by insisting on the theme of plurality *from the side of uniqueness in relation.* There is, in other words, a certain hesitation in dealing with the theme of plurality from the side of the collective dimension. Cavarero seems reluctant to deal with the plural from the side of what Plato would call "the many." In a significant passage of *Relating Narratives*, Cavarero explains her choice clearly, drastically opposing the "you" with the "us":

> Symptomatically, the you [*tu*] is a term that is not at home (*un termine spaesante*) in modern and contemporary developments of ethics and politics. The you is ignored by the individualistic doctrines, which are too preoccupied with praising the rights of the I, and the "you" is masked by a Kantian form of ethics that is only capable of staging an I that addresses itself as a familiar "you." Neither does the "you" find a home in the schools of thought to which individualism is opposed—these schools reveal themselves for the most part to be affected by a moralistic vice, which, in order to avoid falling into the decadence of the I, avoids the contiguity of the you, and privileges collective, plural pronouns. Indeed, many "revolutionary movements" (which range from traditional communism to the feminism of sisterhood) seem to share a curious linguistic code based on the intrinsic morality of pronouns. The we is always positive, the plural you is a possible ally, the they has the face of an antagonist, the I is unseemly, and the you is, of course, superfluous.[24]

It would seem that Cavarero, in "the structural tension" between demagogy and democracy sides with Plato when it comes to the political dimension of "the mighty beast."

It must nevertheless be emphasized that in her conceptualization of relationality, Cavarero aims primarily at a severe criticism of political and ethical doctrines that have systematically neglected the relational dimension of duality while framing the human only in individual, solitary terms. Cavarero's thematization of this relationality is vast, and if in *Relating Narratives* she still conceives of it in reciprocal terms, her later work *Inclinations* (2016) provides an ethical reassessment of this dual relationship in terms of asymmetry. There, she proposes the "inclined subject," which refers to an ontological paradigm based on an ethical posture that is unbalanced and disproportionate, yet essentially relational insofar as it is exposed and extroverted toward an "outside" of the self. Also, in this proposal of an altruistic ethics of the inclined subject, Cavarero aims at criticizing the individual, autonomous subject of the modern tradition of political thought, which from Hobbes onwards conceives of Man—that Man of which philosophy spoke "by necessity" in individual terms—as "naturally" self-sufficient, sovereign, and unrelated. This critique, coupled with that of Platonic political philosophy—in which, it must be stated, individualism is not yet present, being an essentially modern invention—runs through Cavarero's entire oeuvre.[25] In *Inclinations* this critique becomes radical insofar as the relational perspective is forced, so to say, to come to terms with the possibility of an unbalanced, even excessive, inclination toward the other. Not only is the autonomous, *erect* self of traditional individualism displaced, literally, from its vertical pedestal by virtue of an ethical experiment that proposes a "postural ethics" that is spatially imagined as diagonal rather than vertical but the reciprocal relationality as it appears in *Relating Narratives* and in many feminist debates is also undone. The challenge is to imagine a self that is inclined rather than standing, given over rather than self-sufficient. Provocatively, Cavarero exemplifies this inclined subject through the figure of the mother. Maternal inclination is the specific posture of an essentially altruistic subject that is primarily extroverted toward the infant. Therefore, the privileged perspective is also in this frame of the inclined subject—even if forced toward an "outside," unbalanced, and radicalized—and it remains strictly dual.

It is at this point necessary to take a step back and recall how Cavarero elaborates such a provocative proposal in the years of the aftermath of 9/11. In constant dialogue with Butler, whose thematization of vulnerability became central for Cavarero in her 2007 book *Horrorism*, Cavarero aims at defining the new global violence after 9/11 in terms of horror rather than terror, where an instrumental use of violence for political scopes (territory, power, hegemony, etc.) is no longer at stake but is rather a violence essentially targeting human vulnerability as such. Butler, in both *Precarious Life* (2004) and *Giving an Account of Oneself* (2005) argues in favor of a radical post 9/11 move against notions of identity, sovereignty, truth, freedom, and justice conceived as fortified matters that are unquestionably yet ambiguously used to justify violence, aggression, retaliation, and preventive war.

During the decade that followed 9/11, both Butler and Cavarero were convinced that in order to come to terms with the unprecedented events of 2001 and the wars that followed it was necessary to redefine the subject in terms of a common vulnerability and from there on rethink politics in light of this new ontological paradigm.[26] While challenging the political project of modernity—especially its individualistic corollaries unrelatedness, self-sufficiency, and sovereignty—both thinkers radically rethought the human by concentrating on its essential conditions of dependency, precariousness, and vulnerability.

Their emphasis on the vulnerable subject should allow us to think of reparation and care—rather than aggression and violence—as fundamental relational dimensions, not just as altruistic exceptions. To think of the human as vulnerable, claims Cavarero, opens the possibility—not the "necessity"—of alleviating their wounds. If the human is essentially characterized by an undeniable vulnerability, it is possible to assume this condition as common and, therefore, to assume the responsibility for each other's potential wounds as equally common.

Following Cavarero's path, one can easily see how her theorizations on vulnerability, starting with *Horrorism*, have been radicalized in ethical terms in her subsequent work on *Inclinations*. The inclined subject is a response to the senseless and aimless violence of contemporary horrorism. Yet, the issue at stake after 9/11 is that vulnerability has been experienced broadly, finally hitting also the First World and displacing its privilege of apparent invulnerability, as Butler claims in *Precarious Life*. So, the question at this point is: What do we do with this socially experienced trauma? With the collective dimension of loss? Can there be a reparative and caring response that does not remain bound to the "I and you" perspective?

The dimension of corporeal vulnerability experienced dramatically by the United States with 9/11 must not, claimed Judith Butler, reinforce sovereignty discourses that justify violence and war but instead offer the occasion to reflect on our common condition, one that if it does not make us all equal it nevertheless renders us *similar*. If a certain vulnerability awareness becomes shared and acknowledged—with all its different degrees of intensity—then there is the possibility that traditional political dichotomies of friend/enemy and us/them, along with the martial and bellicose frames that sustain them can be revised, if not abandoned. So, too, can the model of the autonomous, self-sufficient individual who is independent, unrelated, and unbound and, as such, posits social bonds only as "contract" be revised or abandoned.

The experience of vulnerability, in other words, seems to carry the feminist critique of individualism that Cavarero—and Butler—had elaborated earlier a step further. To think of "the subject" as constitutively in relation to an "otherness" implies an exposure of the self to an outside that can either wound or care. If feminist discourse had previously insisted on the "caring" and relationally positive aspect of the deconstruction of individualism, the experience of 9/11 forced them to think of this relationality in negative terms, in terms of loss and mourning. Both Butler and Cavarero engage in this enterprise, which is also a theoretical and political challenge.

"Loss has made a tenuous 'we' of us all," claims Butler in reference to the shared experience of collective injury after 9/11.[27] The socially felt trauma finds, in Butler, the way to express itself in politically significant terms by way of a provocative proposal: the "us" of the community should not—cannot—be understood in terms of sovereignty or according to a supposed "fullness" of a common identity in need of restoration after the attacks. Rather, the theoretical proposal is to conceive of the community in terms of a common experience of loss: not fullness, therefore, but void. Vulnerability rather than sovereignty becomes, in Butler's terms, the source of our commonness.

In a similar vein, Cavarero reads 9/11 as an occasion to reformulate the question of the subject, this time in clear relation to the question of the political. It is my claim that Cavarero's latest book on *Surging Democracy* is inspired by the political trauma of 9/11 and seeks to respond to that trauma not in terms of a dual relationship between self and other but instead by resorting to the previously neglected collective dimension, the plurality from the side of "the many." More importantly, it aims at responding to the collapse of traditional political categories by way of a generative perspective. The "tenuous we" of which Butler speaks in *Precarious Life* becomes, in Cavarero, both the concrete evidence of a shared vulnerability and the possible site of a democratic resurgence. Arendt, after her book on the deadly outcomes of totalitarianism, explored in *The Human Condition* the possibility of a different notion of politics based on natality. In a similar vein, Cavarero moves on from the shared experience of vulnerability (which both Cavarero and Butler elaborate on in terms of exposure and relationality) to the shared experience of democracy as political participation. Loss and mourning, as experiences of shared vulnerability, make us aware of our mutual dependence, of our interrelationality. There is nevertheless *another dimension of interdependence*: one that is not based only on violence and trauma but on the common sharing of a public space, where to appear to one another and through "words and deeds" decides the modes, times, and reasons for our "assembling." Interdependence as the precondition of political action can be summarized by this famous Arendtian sentence: "No man can be sovereign because not one man, but men [sic], inhabit the earth."[28]

Judith Butler, in her 2015 work *Toward a Performative Theory of Assembly*, interestingly uses Arendtian frames to understand political movements of the present—from the *Occupy* movements to the Arab Spring, from Gezi Park protests in Turkey to Greek demonstrations against austerity measures. Butler applies Arendt's notion of "the right to have rights"—which she translates into the performative notion of "the right to appear"—to different and heterogeneous forms of political participation, stressing the crucial Arendtian idea that the basic human right is that of belonging to a political community. Cavarero dialogues with Butler also in this occasion and shares with Butler a genuine interest in new forms of political freedom as they appear on the global scene in the decade after 9/11. Yet, as it has been noted in Butler's recent reappraisal of Arendt's notion of political action, "the affective register of politics remains dominated by precariousness, loss, and lamentation, whereas public happiness and joys of action go unnoticed."[29]

Cavarero elaborates instead her notion of "surging democracy" by claiming that democracy is not only a form of government, a set of rules to rationally organize our coexistence, but an experience of joy and happiness. By borrowing extensively from Arendt's notion of public happiness developed in *On Revolution*, Cavarero argues that the concept of a surging democracy refers to "historical phenomena that regularly occur wherever people, by gathering in public spaces to protest or demonstrate, experience their ability to engender power—a diffuse, participatory, and relational power, shared equally, or better still, a power constituted by political actors that are unique and plural."[30] It is as if the experience of being exposed to others, in constant relation to them, previously considered as the source of a *reciprocity* between the I and the you or as an unbalanced postural *inclination*, now becomes the virtuous source of a collective participatory potentiality.

For Arendt, eighteenth-century revolutions were notably "the space-time in which action, with all its implications, was discovered, or rather re-discovered for the Modern age."[31] The revolutionary spirit also disclosed itself in the council moments of revolutions (theorized and promoted by a woman of action like Rosa Luxemburg), in movements of the Resistance—poet René Char, at the end of World War II, would represent it as a "lost treasure"—and the student movement of May 1968. In these contexts, Arendt insists, public happiness emerges as the spontaneous lived experience of public freedom.[32] Cavarero rereads this Arendtian conceptualization of political freedom in terms of an original democratic spring that people recognize when gathering together: if the initial move to common action is protest and fight for liberation, the subsequent and decisive political experience is instead that of tasting "a democracy-in-the-making in its nascent stage," a "distinct and thrilling experience of political freedom."[33]

As Arendt claims in *On Revolution*, while being occupied in liberating themselves from tyranny or in petitioning for "no taxation without representation," the men and women of the American Revolution, for instance, "discovered their own capacity and desires for the 'charms of liberty.'"[34] It was a sudden and communal discovery they did not expect since they thought they were fighting for liberation and instead discovered freedom: "For the acts and deeds which liberation demanded from them threw them into public business, where, intentionally or more often unexpectedly, they began to constitute that space of appearances where freedom can unfold its charms and become a visible, tangible reality."[35]

In conclusion, let us go back to the quote at the beginning of this essay: "Where Plato sees a mighty beast, Arendt sees instead an interacting plurality."[36] While reflecting on the problematic aspects of the post-truth era, Cavarero ponders not only about the pessimistic or even nihilistic trends of contemporary democracies but also about how their destinies were seemingly traced by a pathological politics Plato had already envisaged in the Sophists. To condescend to the pessimistic conservative pose of many apparently progressive intellectuals would coincide to a self-absolutory position that is, in my view, extremely distant from the ethics of responsibility that informs Cavarero's entire intellectual path. Again, in great resonance with the Arendtian spirit, which in the century of extermination camps decided to speak of the political in terms of natality, Cavarero opts for the generative frame. Even during the pandemic times of 2020 and beyond, occurrences of public freedom appeared—for example, in the BLM demonstrations for the death of George Floyd—and testified to an interacting plurality in occupying public spaces and discovering the essentially and universally human "taste for freedom."³⁷ These occurrences give us, claims Cavarero, a certain margin of political hope.³⁸

Evoking hope during the undecipherable times we are living in can seem utopian, if not naive. Yet, without at least a small margin of hope, there is no political and historical transformation but only an ever-present now, a dangerous status-quo disturbed only by recurring emergencies that just need to be "managed." Hope—and the imaginary it engenders—far from being naive is instead the necessary frame for political action and change, without which any democratic politics eventually becomes impossible.

Notes

1. All translations of this work are by the author. Adriana Cavarero, *Platone*, ed. Olivia Guaraldo (Milan: Raffaello Cortina Editore, 2018), 19–26.
2. Olivia Guaraldo, introduction to *Platone*, by Adriana Cavarero, 9–17.
3. Cavarero, *Platone*, 187.
4. Cavarero, *Platone*, 190.
5. Cavarero, *Platone*, 197.
6. Plato, *Republic*, trans. Benjamin Jowett (Project Gutenberg, 2017), 493c.
7. Cavarero, *Platone*, 198.
8. Olivia Guaraldo, "'The Political Sphere of Life, Where Speech Rules Supreme': Hannah Arendt's Imaginative Reception of Ancient Democracy," in *Brill's Companion to the Modern Reception of Ancient Democracy*, ed. Giovanni Giorgini and Dino Piovan (Leiden: Brill, 2020), 399–420.
9. Hannah Arendt, *Between Past and Future: Eight Exercises in Political Thought* (New York: Viking Press, 1968), 157.
10. Dana Villa, "The Philosopher versus the Citizen: Arendt, Strauss and Socrates," *Political Theory* 26, no. 2 (1998): 143.
11. Hannah Arendt, *The Human Condition* (Chicago: Chicago University Press, 1958), 222.
12. Cavarero, *Platone*, 198.
13. Arendt, *Human Condition*, 32; Arendt, "What Is Freedom?" in *Between Past and Future*, 142–169.
14. Arendt, *On Revolution* (New York: Viking Penguin, 1977), 30.
15. Arendt, *The Origins of Totalitarianism* (New York: Harcourt Brace, 1979).
16. Cavarero, *Platone*, 187.
17. Arendt, *Human Condition*, 9.
18. Bonnie Honig, "Arendt, Identity and Difference," *Political Theory* 16, no. 1 (1988): 88.

19. Arendt, *Human Condition*, 176 (emphasis added).

20. I have discussed elsewhere and at length Cavarero's original combination of Arendtian categories with those of the thought of *sexual difference*, a topic that informs most of her work but significantly has to do more with the question of the subject than with the issue of the political with which we are concerned here. See Olivia Guaraldo, "Figure di una relazione: Sul pensiero di Judith Butler e Adriana Cavarero," in *Differenza e relazione: L'ontologia dell'umano nel pensiero di Judith Butler e Adriana Cavarero*, ed. Olivia Guaraldo and Lorenzo Bernini (Verona: Ombre Corte, 2009), 90–121; Olivia Guaraldo, "Thinkers That Matter: On the Thought of Judith Butler and Adriana Cavarero," AG-Aboutgender 1, no. 1 (2012): 92–117; Olivia Guaraldo, "Thinking Materialistically with Locke, Lonzi, and Cavarero," in *Toward a Feminist Ethics of Nonviolence*, ed. Timothy J. Huzar and Clare Woodford (New York: Fordham University Press, 2021), 93–105.

21. Hannah Arendt and Karl Jaspers, *Correspondence 1926–1969* (New York: Mariner Books, 1993), 166.

22. Author's translation. Hannah Arendt, *Denktagebuch, 1950–1973* (Munich: Piper, 2003), 7.

23. Adriana Cavarero, *Relating Narratives* (London: Routledge, 2000), 6.

24. Cavarero, *Relating Narratives*, 90–91.

25. Adriana Cavarero, "Feminist Philosophies: A Theoretical Approach," *The Journal of Continental Philosophy* 2, no. 1 (2021): 159–201.

26. See Dominijanni, *2001: Un archivio* (Rome: Manifestolibri, 2021).

27. Judith Butler, *Precarious Life: The Powers of Mourning and Violence* (New York: Routledge, 2004), 20.

28. Arendt, *Human Condition*, 234. See also Krause, *Freedom beyond Sovereignty* (Chicago: University of Chicago Press, 2015).

29. Eri-Elmeri Hyvönen, "Arendt and 'Revolutionary Spirit' in Egypt," *Redescriptions: Political Thought, Conceptual History and Feminist Theory* 19, no. 2 (2016): 191–213.

30. Adriana Cavarero, *Surging Democracy: Notes on Hannah Arendt's Political Thought* (Stanford, CA: Stanford University Press, 2021), x.

31. Hannah Arendt, "Action and 'The Pursuit of Happiness,'" in *Thinking without a Banister: Essays in Understanding 1953–1975*, ed. Jerome Kohn (New York: Schocken Books, 2018), 201–219.

32. Arendt, *On Revolution*, 249. See also Olivia Guaraldo, "Public Happiness: Revisiting an Arendtian Hypothesis," *Philosophy Today* 62, no. 2 (2018): 395–416.

33. Cavarero, *Surging Democracy*, x.

34. Arendt, *On Revolution*, 33.

35. Arendt, *On Revolution*, 33.

36. Cavarero, *Platone*, 198.

37. Cavarero, *Surging Democracy*, xvi.

38. Hope is among the least popular items of investigation among critical scholars, yet it is worth noting that Sarah Ahmed mentions it, along with wonder,

in the introduction to her book *The Cultural Politics of Emotions*. There, she makes a claim in favor of how emotions "can work within queer and feminist politics, as a reorientation of our relation to social ideals, and the norms they elevate into social aspirations" and refers not only to feelings of "discomfort, grief, pleasure, [and] anger" but also "wonder, and hope." These feelings or emotions are affective postures that need to be activated in order to open up spaces for resistance and social transformation. Sarah Ahmed, *The Cultural Politics of Emotions* (Edinburgh: Edinburgh University Press, 2014), 16.

Bibliography

Ahmed, Sara. *The Cultural Politics of Emotions*. Edinburgh: Edinburgh University Press, 2014.
Arendt, Hannah. "Action and 'The Pursuit of Happiness.'" In *Thinking without a Banister: Essays in Understanding 1953–1975*, edited by Jerome Kohn, 201–219. New York: Schocken Books, 2018.
———. *Between Past and Future: Eight Exercises in Political Thought*. New York: Viking Press, 1968.
———. *Denktagebuch, 1950–1973*. Munich: Piper, 2003.
———. *The Human Condition*. Chicago: University of Chicago Press, 1958.
———. *On Revolution*. New York: Viking Penguin, 1977. First published 1963 by Viking Press (New York). Page references are to the 1977 edition.
———. *The Origins of Totalitarianism*. New York: Harcourt Brace, 1979. First published 1951 by Schocken Books (New York). Page references are to the 1979 edition.
Arendt, Hannah, and Karl Jaspers. *Correspondence 1926–1969*. New York: Mariner Books, 1993.
Butler, Judith. *Giving an Account of Oneself*. New York: Fordham University Press, 2005.
———. *Notes toward a Performative Theory of Assembly*. Cambridge, MA: Harvard University Press, 2015.
———. *Precarious Life: The Powers of Mourning and Violence*. New York: Routledge, 2004.
Cavarero, Adriana. "Feminist Philosophies: A Theoretical Approach." *The Journal of Continental Philosophy* 2, no. 1 (2021): 159–201.
———. *Inclinations: A Critique of Rectitude*. Translated by Adam Sitze and Amanda Minervini. Stanford, CA: Stanford University Press, 2016.
———. *In Spite of Plato: Feminist Rewriting of Ancient Philosophy*. Translated by Serena Anderlini-D'Onofrio and Áine O'Healy. Cambridge: Polity Press, 1995.
———. *Platone*. Edited by Olivia Guaraldo. Milan: Raffaello Cortina Editore, 2018.
———. *Platone e la democrazia*. Padua, IT: Cedam, 1974.

———. *Relating Narratives: Storytelling and Selfhood*. Translated by Paul A. Kottman. London: Routledge, 2000.

———. *Surging Democracy: Notes on Hannah Arendt's Political Thought*. Translated by Matthew Gervase. Stanford, CA: Stanford University Press, 2021.

Dominijanni, Ida. *2001: Un archivio*. Rome: Manifestolibri, 2021.

Guaraldo, Olivia. "Figure di una relazione: Sul pensiero di Judith Butler e Adriana Cavarero." In *Differenza e relazione: L'ontologia dell'umano nel pensiero di Judith Butler e Adriana Cavarero*, edited by Olivia Guaraldo and Lorenzo Bernini, 90–121. Verona: Ombre Corte, 2009.

———. "Introduzione." In Cavarero, *Platone*. Milan: Raffaello Cortina Editore, 2018.

———. "'The Political Sphere of Life, Where Speech Rules Supreme': Hannah Arendt's Imaginative Reception of Ancient Democracy." In *Brill's Companion to the Modern Reception of Ancient Democracy*, edited by Giovanni Giorgini and Dino Piovan, 399–420. Leiden: Brill, 2020.

———. "Public Happiness: Revisiting an Arendtian Hypothesis." *Philosophy Today* 62, no. 2 (2018): 395–416.

———. "Thinkers That Matter: On the Thought of Judith Butler and Adriana Cavarero." *AG-Aboutgender* 1, no. 1 (2012): 92–117.

———. "Thinking Materialistically with Locke, Lonzi and Cavarero." In *Toward a Feminist Ethics of Nonviolence*, edited by Timothy J. Huzar and Clare Woodford, 93–105. New York: Fordham University Press, 2021.

Honig, Bonnie. "Arendt, Identity and Difference." *Political Theory* 16, no. 1 (1988): 77–98.

Huzar, Timothy J., and Clare Woodford, eds. *Toward a Feminist Ethics of Nonviolence*. New York: Fordham University Press, 2021.

Hyvönen, Ari-Elmeri. "Arendt and 'Revolutionary Spirit' in Egypt." *Redescriptions: Political Thought, Conceptual History and Feminist Theory* 19, no. 2 (1988): 191–213.

Krause, Sharon. *Freedom beyond Sovereignty: Reconstructing Liberal Individualism*. Chicago: University of Chicago Press, 2015.

Plato. *Republic*. Translated by Benjamin Jowett. Project Gutenberg, 2017. https://www.gutenberg.org/ebooks/1497.

Villa, Dana. "The Philosopher versus the Citizen: Arendt, Strauss and Socrates." *Political Theory* 26, no. 2 (1998): 147–72.

Two

Cavarero as an Arendtian Feminist

Julian Honkasalo

Introduction

In the following essay, I will argue that although Adriana Cavarero explicitly frames and interprets Hannah Arendt's philosophy through Luce Irigaray's *An Ethics of Sexual Difference*, Cavarero's overall project is so invested in Arendt's philosophy that she can in fact be called an Arendtian feminist. In what follows, I argue that there are three particular themes that constitute the pillars of Cavarero's feminist project, namely natality, sexual difference, and the attempt to reverse matricide.[1] I seek to show that an essential characteristic of Cavarero's method is that she deliberately takes Arendt's concepts out of their context—"steals" them, to use Cavarero's own term—and then tests them in a discourse entirely foreign to them. Through this process, Cavarero establishes her own arguments as well as discloses the limits of Arendt's thinking.

Hannah Arendt (1906–1975) did not theorize gender as a political question. None of her major works deal with women's liberation, women's rights, or with gendered aspects of power. In her public life, she neither participated nor spoke up in favor of any feminist group. In fact, the single published text where Arendt explicitly reflects on the women's movement of her time is a brief book review of Alice Rühle-Gerstel's *Das Frauenproblem in der Gegenwart* (1932). Although Arendt found the book "instructive" and "stimulating," she did not see a women's political party or a women's movement as the solution to women's economic and social oppression. Instead, she proposed that women should unite with movements of other oppressed groups, such as the workers' movement, in their plight for the realization of equal political rights.[2] For these reasons, particularly US-based, second-wave feminist theorists have criticized Arendt for her disappointing, elitist arrogance and hostility toward the women's movement and feminist politics of the time. Through her conceptual, oppositional distinctions, such as the public versus the private, the political versus the social, and action versus labor, early second-wave interpreters concluded that Arendt succumbed to a male bias in her thinking.[3]

A divergent way of appropriating Arendt emerges in the context of the Continental tradition of feminist theorizing. According to scholars such as Cavarero and Julia Kristeva most notably, the theoretical implications of Arendt's failure to address gender as a political question must not be exaggerated.[4] Instead, both Cavarero and Kristeva perceive Arendt's contribution to feminist theorizing as evident in her work because her texts derive from a particular, feminine position and feminine textual style.

Cavarero is an unusual interpreter of and commentator on Arendt in the sense that she rarely explicitly refers to Arendt's texts other than the fifth chapter of *The Human Condition*, which is the most famous of Arendt's texts on action, narration, and natality. Rather than engaging in Arendtian exegeses, Cavarero uses certain Arendtian themes as stepping-stones for the articulation of her own, unique feminist project. Thus, the reader must be able to spot the intertextual references to Arendt in Cavarero's works, and they are numerous. Cavarero's feminist project, which emphasizes motherhood, corporeality, and sexual difference, may appear as standing squarely with Arendt's seemingly anti-feminist, conceptual distinctions such as the public/private and labor/action. Nevertheless, in striking contrast to American feminist critics of Arendt such as Adrienne Rich, Mary O'Brien, Hanna Pitkin, and Wendy Brown, Cavarero's reading of Arendt aims to open up a space for precisely theorizing embodiment, intimacy, motherhood, relationality, and plurality from a radically feminine and feminist perspective.[5] The conclusion that Cavarero draws from Arendt's neglect of gender is thus the complete opposite from the contention that Arendt is an elitist, misogynist, and nostalgic lover of Ancient Greek political philosophy.

For Cavarero, matricide signifies the deliberate erasure of the feminine and the maternal from the history of Western thought, and, hence, she regards matricide as historically contingent and open to reversal. One of the most important ethical tasks of Cavarero's project is to theorize the genealogy of matricide and rewrite the history of the feminine voice into Western thought. Even though Cavarero radicalizes Kristeva's notion of the "semiotic," her overall project is thus closer to Irigaray and Arendt than to Kristeva. A bit further on, I will discuss Cavarero's critique of Kristeva, which she carries out through a reading of Arendt's notion of narration, speech, and action.

As my focus is here on Cavarero's interpretation of Arendt, I will not evaluate her reading with regard to whether it is accurate or does justice to Arendt's original texts. My interest is rather in pointing out those textual passages where Cavarero's paths of thinking *need* Arendt, either as an ally or an interlocutor, in order to proceed with her own feminist project. I also do not examine and comment on her theoretical position and life work at large but focus instead on her interpretation of Arendt.

Articulating a Maternal Ontology through Arendt

In the opening pages of *The Human Condition*, Arendt prepares the setting for her conception of political action by making an analogy between birth and action. For Arendt, action means the beginning of something new. In order to illustrate this quality of action, Arendt writes that each new birth of a child represents the potential for new, unique actions and deeds. "Action has the closest connection with the human condition of *natality*; the new beginning inherent in birth can make itself felt in the world only because the newcomer possesses the capacity of beginning something anew, that is of acting."[6] Arendt thus points out that each new infant being born to this world is unique, like no one else before, and each one of us has the potential to take initiative and perform actions in a unique way. In other words, each person is a new beginning.

In this same context, Arendt links her conception of natality to the concepts of plurality as well as to spontaneity and unique distinctness. What makes new beginnings meaningful is that action always takes place in a world inhabited by others. Thus, action is always *interaction*. To live is synonymous with being among other human beings, *inter homines esse*, and to die is synonymous with to cease to be among men, *inter homines esse disenere*. Although in *The Human Condition* Arendt traces the etymology of the concept of action to the Greek term αρχειν (*archein*, to begin) and the Roman equivalent *agere* (to set in motion), what is more important with regard to the concept of natality is that Arendt credits Augustine and not Aristotle as the philosopher of beginnings and claims that the idea of action *as* beginning something new, and thus also of natality, comes originally from Augustine.[7] Arendt's notion of natality thus actually originates from the Latin concept *initium*, which for Augustine means a specific kind of beginning: that is, the beginning of time and temporality in the world through the creation of man. Augustine is credited also on the very last pages of *The Origins of Totalitarianism*, where Arendt develops for the first time the political significance of natality.[8] Hence, in a number of ways, natality is a performative concept that aims to disrupt totalitarian annihilation both in theory and in practice: "But there remains also the truth that every end in history necessarily contains a beginning; this beginning is the promise, the only 'message' which the end can ever produce. Beginning, before it becomes a historical event, is the supreme capacity of man; politically, it is identical with man's freedom. *Initium ut esset homo creates est*—'that a beginning be made man was created' said Augustine. This beginning is guaranteed by each new birth; it is indeed every man."[9]

Cavarero interprets Arendt's conception of action as beginning through the philosophy of Luce Irigaray. Resembling Simone de Beauvoir's *The Second Sex*, Irigaray's central claim is that woman has always been interpreted as the *Other* to the male subject, the *I*. Thus, Irigaray states prophetically that whereas for Martin Heidegger the fundamental question of his age was the question concerning the forgetting of being, *the* most important question of our age is the question concerning the forgetting of sexual difference. "Sexual difference is probably the issue of our time which could be our 'salvation' if we thought it through."[10]

Throughout her work—for instance in *An Ethics of Sexual Difference*—Irigaray reads the tradition of Western philosophy through the category of sexual difference. Woman is, according to Irigaray, always determined in relation to Man, never independently as an autonomous subject.[11] This is because Western philosophical, political, and religious thought, as well as writing, is grounded in the concept of the subject, which is treated as abstract and neutral. However, this concept, such as in the form Man as a universal, is in fact sexed and refers always to the male. Irigaray thus sets as her task to rewrite philosophy through the category of sexual difference, and by doing this, she aims to take us to a new era of thinking. This task involves rethinking the most elementary categories of Western metaphysics, including those of space, time, and matter.

Cavarero follows Irigaray's philosophical project and takes sexual difference as one of her two axes of interpretation. The other axis is Arendt's philosophy of natality. Writing about sexual difference and birth, Cavarero states:

> Here the revolution in perspective is of a particularly female, feminine sort. It appears to the basic realism when a woman observes her individual embodiment [. . .] This name [woman] must resonate within the kind of symbolic order where birth, the act by which embodied individuals are born and actualized, will also restore meaning for everyone, female and male. Humans always come to this world in this way, never otherwise [. . .] Here in the new philosophical horizon of sexual difference, the basic element of philosophy is a *two*, not a *one*. [. . .] All persons, male and female are inevitably born from their mother's womb as finite beings. In my desire to disinvest myself from the existing context, I found the second axis of my theoretical approach in Hannah Arendt's category of *birth*. The central position of birth within her work brings about a subversive shift in perspective with regard to the patriarchal tradition that has always thrived on the category of death.[12]

We can see from the passage above how Arendt functions as a Trojan horse against the Western patriarchal tradition of thinking. Birth and its connection to the maternal carry, according to Cavarero, great potential for feminist thinking because, as an existential concept, natality ("being-from-birth") problematizes traditional male conceptualizations of human existence such as Martin Heidegger's notion of "being-toward-death" (*Sein zum Tode*). Cavarero thus shares the Anglophone critique of patriarchy that Rich, O'Brien, Pitkin, and Brown promote.[13] However, Cavarero views the problem of male domination as a philosophical, ontological question, not exclusively a socioeconomic and political problem.

Undoing Matricide

Cavarero's reconceptualization of human existence as originating in birth and the body of the mother provides her with a new, feminine way to think about corporeality, materiality, and relationality. The mother-child relation provides an ontological foundation for a philosophy that begins with the intersubjective relation between two. Furthermore, natality functions as the ontological foundation of plurality. The miraculous event of birth is the precondition for the appearing of new individuals, beginnings, actions, and narrations in this world.

In order to articulate this feminine symbolic order, Cavarero elaborates on the metaphor of weaving. Her feminist task of rewriting history as a process "embraces the gestures of other female weavers."[14] The metaphor of weaving refers back to Homer's *The Odyssey*, in which Queen Penelope is described as weaving a cloth while waiting for Odysseus to return home. In order to keep competing suitors away, each night Penelope undoes what she has weaved the day before. She tells her suitors, who assume Odysseus to be dead, that once she is finished with the cloth, she will choose a suitor and remarry. This never happens and Penelope is finally reunited with Odysseus. In her retelling of the story of Penelope, Cavarero describes Penelope in the weaving room after Odysseus's return, sharing her story with other female weavers. They laugh in amusement at Penelope's strategy of keeping the suitors away.[15]

When Cavarero states that her own method is related and indebted to Arendt's method, she is intertextually alluding to the process of dismantling and recontextualizing that Arendt formulates in her last work, *The Life of the Mind*. In the first part of this trilogy, Arendt also refers to Penelope and elaborates that "the business of thinking is like Penelope's web; it undoes every morning what it has finished the night before."[16] The idea here is that thinking produces no tangible end results. Instead, the products of thought must be spoken in words or recorded in writing, which is not always an easy task. Let me elaborate on this connection briefly since it is a significant element in Cavarero's interpretation.

In her last work, which is one of the few places where she explicitly reflects on her own philosophical way of thinking, Arendt claims that her aim is to show how our use of language and its concepts affects our philosophical thinking. In order to show this, she uses both grammatical and etymological analysis. Arendt stresses the importance of interpretation and narration as constitutive of contemporary philosophy and, like Irigaray, expresses skepticism toward projects that seek to disclose an original beginning ἀρχή (*arche*) within history. For Arendt, history is a form of storytelling that consists of several different interpretations based on historical practices and events.[17] Arendt reflects on her own philosophical thinking and then clarifies her position in an often-quoted passage: "I have clearly joined the ranks of those who for some time now have been attempting to dismantle metaphysics, and philosophy with all its categories, as we have known them from Greek until today."[18]

For Arendt, so-called metaphysical fallacies and erroneous strands of thought must not be denied, but neither can they be solved. Instead, they must be located and exposed.[19] The practice of dismantling thus focuses on the implicit presuppositions that philosophers inevitably make in their research and thinking. Since thinking produces no tangible end products, not everything is recorded in the written texts. Equally important is to pay attention to what is left unsaid. By following the philosophical argumentation of a chosen philosopher or philosophical doctrine to its limits, Arendt claims to be able to reveal strands of thought that are not visible to the author. This opens up a space for a critical dialogue between the author and the reader.

I argue that Cavarero follows the Arendtian technique of dismantling and finds that natality is a forgotten theme in the textual tradition of Western philosophy.[20]

> In her work, she [Arendt] focuses on the site [birth] that the gaze of men has long sought to avoid for fear of staring death in the face as the yardstick of human existence. This anxiety is what gives rise to the symbolic event that constitutes the original act of matricide [the erasure of the Great Mother]. It is also the basis of the obsessive desire to endure, to survive, which leads men to entrust eternal objects of thought with the task of "saving" them from the selfsame death they chose as the locus of meaning when they decided, not by chance, to call themselves *mortals*.[21]

To clarify, for Cavarero, the study of metaphysics—from the Greek τὰ μετὰ τὰ φυσικά (*ta meta ta physica*, beyond physics)—isolates human existence from its origins in physical nature. She argues that, from Parmenides on, true Being has been conceived as that which is everlasting and unchanging, while the cycle of life, on the other hand, has been degraded as belonging to the perishable and merely apparent world. Cavarero sees here the traces of "the original act of matricide," in other words, the "erasure of the Great

Mother."²² Whereas Heidegger saw the forgetting of the meaning of being as the most important philosophical question of our time and whereas Irigaray translated Heidegger's project in her own quest for the meaning of sexual difference, Cavarero argues that the most fundamental question of our time is the forgetting of natality.

For Cavarero, this erasure does not come without a price. The neglect of maternal embodiment as the site of life's origin as well as the symbolic order elevates death as the center of meaning. Now, the soul is regarded as eternal and immortal, whereas the body, which is born out of a woman, is shunned as perishable, continuously and slowly dying until it finally decomposes and vanishes back into nothingness. According to Cavarero, the masculine obsession with immortality comes from the dread of both death and the maternal. Death is so powerful that it can negate life whereas the maternal is so powerful that it can generate new life. By placing the achievement of immortality through contemplation as a central task of philosophical reason, masculinity attempts (according to Cavarero) to overcome what makes us all human: temporality and finitude.

Sexed Natality

In her work *In Spite of Plato*, Cavarero sets out to unravel the symbolic order that underlies Western metaphysics from Parmenides on. Whereas Irigaray commits herself to a feminist deconstruction of canonical philosophical texts, Cavarero focuses on figures in ancient mythology. For Irigaray, as for Cavarero, the Western tradition is characterized by a phallic symbolic order, in which "a male subject claiming to be neutral/universal declares his central position, disseminating a sense of the world cut to his own measure and revealed in his own mythic figures."²³ Consequently, all feminine representations are a creation of the masculine and receive their meaning in relation to Man as omnipotent and universal. Given this situation, mythic heroines that would express female subjectivity in an adequate way are nonexistent.

Cavarero develops her position by asking what kind of possibilities for identification or illumination of the "embodied existence as a woman" figures such as Oedipus, Prometheus, or Don Juan provide for women and the "female intellectual worker." She then states that a woman asking this question always runs up against the image created by Man and can therefore only find "an essential image of otherness."[24] This is because even figures such as Diotima and Penelope, for instance, are a creation and fantasy of male authors. Attempting to identify with these figures is pointless, claims Cavarero.

The condition for the possibility of this "patriarchal *basso continuo*" in the history of Western thought is, according to Cavarero, an "original act of erasure" of the culture of the archaic Great Mother, a maternal deity that represents feminine infinity as the origin of all life.[25] This deity threatens the masculine fantasy of self-generation and eternity, since She establishes life's precondition of natality as a corporeal and sexed event. We are all born from the womb of a mother who was also born from a mother and who is, as such, part of an entire female genealogy. "Sexual difference is a *fact* that marks humans from the outset, since one *always* enters the world as *either* man *or* woman."[26] This maternal alternative to the patriarchic tradition is something that Cavarero wants to reawaken: "My starting point is the feminine philosophy of our time that is founded on a maternal figure. From there we women search for, and ultimately find, the ancient figuration of the Mother surrounded by daughters and sisters."[27]

I argue that in order to establish a connection between maternity and materiality, Cavarero engages in a kind of a Heideggerian praxis of etymology by stating that the symbolic figure of the Great Mother is rooted in nature, in accordance with the Greek word φύσις (*physis*), which she takes to originate in the verb φύειν (*phyein*), and which she translates as meaning "to be born."[28] It goes without saying then, that in Cavarero's "yearning for a radical, woman-centered definition of the human" *birth* is one of her most crucial conceptual tools, and it is here that Hannah Arendt's philosophy enters the scene.[29]

Cavarero is well aware that Arendt does not theorize birth "as coming from a mother's womb." Quite the contrary, in *The Human Condition* and in *The Life of the Mind*, Arendt theorizes birth as being generated from nowhere: "In this world which we enter, *appearing from a nowhere*, and from which we disappear into a nowhere, Being and Appearing coincide."[30] I want to highlight here that there is a notable difference between Arendt's formulation of birth in relation to unique distinctness and Cavarero's interpretation of these terms, and this is important for Cavarero. In *The Human Condition* Arendt writes that it is our "second birth" through speech and action, not our birth from the womb, that enables us to enact our individual distinctness:

> Human plurality is the paradoxical plurality of unique beings. Speech and action reveal this unique distinctness. Through them, men distinguish themselves instead of being merely distinct; they are the modes by which human beings appear to each other, not indeed as physical objects but qua men [Mensch].³¹ With word and deed we insert ourselves into the human world and this insertion *is like a second birth,* in which we confirm and take ourselves the *naked fact* of our *original physical* appearance.³²

On the contrary, for Cavarero already the "naked fact of our original physical appearance" makes us unique and distinct. According to her, Arendt theorized birth without conceptually relating the event to sexual difference, motherhood, or the feminine because she did not regard feminism as a philosophically relevant question. However, through Irigaray's framework of sexual difference, Arendt's concept of natality can, according to Cavarero, be interpreted so that it refers back to the original act of birth from the womb of the mother: "In its singularity the newborn is a 'beginning' found already 'started' inside the mother: it is generated by the female who has been generated by a m/other, and so ad infinitum in a sequence (*theoria*) of past mothers."³³ Natality as a new beginning is thus begun already before the event of actual birth giving. In *Relating Narratives*, Cavarero elaborates further on her Irigarayan reading of Arendt's natality: "The newborn—unique and immediately expressive in the fragile totality of her exposure—has her unity precisely in this totally nude self-exposure. This unity is already a physical identity, visibly sexed, and even more perfect in so far as she is not yet qualifiable."³⁴ Cavarero shares the common feminist concern according to which Arendt's rigid distinctions risk excluding women from the political sphere altogether. By interpreting the event of physical birth as always and already indicating uniqueness and distinctness, Cavarero aims to develop Arendt's notions of "speech" and "action" in ways that expand our understanding of the political. The central task of *Relating Narratives* is to locate and understand forms of narration that have traditionally been excluded from what is conceived as the political realm, and see that these narrations can be conceived as political. An example is the self-narration of women in households, such as in the story of Penelope. Cavarero argues that when the disclosure of uniqueness and distinctness is theorized as a necessary element of birth, then the disclosure of the "who" is not an event exclusive to the public realm of speech and action. Because Cavarero understands self-narration as a deeply unique and personal form of disclosure, the personal can, according to her, be understood as having political significance.

Throughout her reading, Cavarero operates with fairly straightforward, binary notions of femininity and masculinity as each other's polar opposites. Femininity is here associated with embodiment, birth, finitude, and materiality, whereas masculinity is seen as resting on notions of heroism, risk, dominance, omnipotence, and violence. Cavarero argues, for instance, that epic drama (one of her favorite literature genres) presents masculinity as being constructed through the heroic male figure, who defies death by risking his life for his cause, such as the life of the city. For Cavarero, this is the main narrative format of all war stories and histories of great battles. In this type of format for writing history, it becomes difficult, if not impossible, to envision feminine narratives of agency.[35]

Femininity and the Philosophy of Voice

In order to fill the void in history and reverse the matricide, Cavarero confronts the patriarchic, symbolic order by restoring the meaning of human existence as first and foremost natal and sexed.[36] However, unlike Irigaray, Cavarero is not interested in establishing an ontology based on an amorous and/or erotic relationality between the feminine and the masculine.[37] Instead, she places the mother-child relation as the basis of her ontology of sexual difference. This relation functions also as the ontological threshold toward theorizing a new feminine and maternal philosophy of the voice. Here, Cavarero's Arendtian philosophy of the voice directly confronts Kristeva's Lacanian-inspired philosophy of the semiotic and the symbolic as well as her psychoanalytic theorization of matricide.

On the surface, Kristeva's reading of Arendt resembles Cavarero's interpretation in many ways. Natality, the maternal, the material, as well as the valuing of a life-centered philosophy over death are also crucial to Kristeva's reading of Arendt. However, upon closer examination, it becomes evident that Kristeva uses these terms often in an opposite way to Cavarero. For instance, she regards matricide as a necessary element of subject formation and holds natality to be inherently violent. Most importantly, Kristeva's relationship to feminist theory is highly ambivalent, whereas Cavarero clearly self-identifies as a feminist philosopher. In Kristeva's reading, Arendt becomes an ally both for criticizing standpoint feminism as well as for articulating a radically feminine, political conception of birth.

In two chapters in *For More than One Voice*, titled "The Maternal *Chora*; or, The Voice of the Poetic Text" and "A Vocal Ontology of Uniqueness," Cavarero both elaborates on Kristeva's psychoanalytic theorization of the semiotic and takes distance from Kristeva. Contrary to Kristeva, for Cavarero, voice and language are theorized as being intimately connected. This means that the relationship between the mother and the child does *not* need to be broken through psychic matricide in order for the infant to enter into the realm of the symbolic, the social, and the linguistic. The development is more gradual. Commenting on Kristeva, Cavarero affirms some of her key ideas:

> The "semiotic *chora*": [is for Kristeva] the preverbal and unconscious sphere, not yet inhabited by the law of the sign, where rhythmic and vocalic drives reign. This semiotic *chora* has a profound bodily root and is linked to the indistinct totality of mother and child. It precedes the symbolic system of language, or the sphere of the semantic where syntax and the concept rule—the paternal order of separation between the self and the other, between mother and child, and between signifier and signified.[38]

Cavarero affirms Kristeva's notion of the *chora*. However, due to their different readings of Arendt's conception of natality and uniqueness, Cavarero claims that "before communicating 'merely something—thirst or hunger, affection or hostility or fear,' the human voice communicates itself, its uniqueness. Without this communication, the scene of infancy and the relation of the infant to the mother is reduced to a mere semiosis of needs."[39] By elaborating on Arendt, Cavarero questions psychoanalytic theories according to which the vocal utterings of a baby, as something oral, belong to the *mere* "semiotic," pre-linguistic realm. Because Cavarero theorizes sexual difference, uniqueness, and distinctness as inherent aspects of the event of physical birth, the shift from oral vocalizations to speech is gradual in her philosophy. I will quote Cavarero at length in order to clarify her conception of the uniqueness and distinctness of the voice:

> Already in utero, an internal musicality wraps the unborn in the rhythms of the maternal body; it envelopes the baby in its sonorous texture [. . .] Precisely because the mother [not the father] gives language to the infant, there is no rupture between this music and speech. The lullaby, or the song of words that

rocks the baby to sleep with rhythmical movements, is perhaps the clearest example of the absence of such a rupture [. . .] The maternal figure is precisely the conduit that, in all our lives, embodies this link—to which, as it were, metaphysics reacts in the name of the father. She is voice *and* speech; or better, she is the originary sense of voice, insofar as the voice is destined to give speech its essential sense. Instead of transmitting speech as something that can be taught and learned—a system, a language— the maternal voice transmits to speech the primary sense of the vocalic, the sonorous self-expression of *uniqueness* and relation, the self-invocation of embodied singularities through spontaneous resonance. This resonance, begun by the duet between mother and infant, is not simply music—it is *the* music of speech, the specific mode for which speech sings musically.[40]

Arendt's notions of natality, speech, and action and their relation to unique distinctness are thus quite literally *fleshed* out by Cavarero. Unlike for Kristeva, language is not theorized primarily as text. Instead, Cavarero emphasizes the maternal and material element at the root of all human communication, including the self-expression of infants. As I have argued above, in order to carry out her philosophical project that radicalizes Kristeva's notion of the "semiotic" and "the chora," Cavarero utilizes Arendt. Hence, even though Arendt never theorized natality as sexed or even maternal, her philosophy of natality becomes the bedrock for both Cavarero's and Kristeva's feminist projects.

Conclusion

To conclude, my discussion of Cavarero's interpretations of Arendt, Irigaray, and Kristeva has sought to establish that, in contrast to feminist critiques that view Arendt as an anti-feminist, Cavarero focuses on natality, birth, life, the feminine, and the maternal to construct Arendt as a *female* philosopher with a uniquely *feminine* textual style. The lack of a political philosophy of gender and sexuality in Arendt's oeuvre does not constitute an obstacle for Cavarero's theorization of the feminine and maternal. Quite the contrary; as I have argued, Cavarero's philosophical method consists in "stealing," that is, taking Arendt's concepts out of their context. Whether or not Arendt herself would have agreed with this, Cavarero establishes natality as the concept through which the tradition of Western philosophy can, according to her, be reframed into a feminine and maternal path of thinking and speaking. By doing this, Cavarero's project is so invested in Arendt's philosophy that Cavarero can be rightfully termed an Arendtian feminist.

Notes

1. For the purpose of my analysis, I use the term *sexual difference* quite freely and broadly. I interpret it as a deconstructive concept in both Irigaray's and Cavarero's philosophy. Italian and French feminist critiques of Western philosophy have traditionally focused on disclosing an inherent normative and hierarchical symbolic order in classic texts of philosophy, particularly in ontology and metaphysics. Some examples are the oppositions between mind and body, reason and nature, as well as emotions and language. According to feminist philosophers such as Irigaray and Cavarero, these juxtaposed concepts have contributed to a sexual hierarchy in which femininity, womanhood, and nature are subordinate to masculinity, manhood, and reason. Both Irigaray and Cavarero aim to revitalize sexual difference as a non-hierarchical concept. In an interview from 2008, titled "Beyond Ontology and Sexual Difference: An Interview with the Italian Feminist Philosopher Adriana Cavarero," Cavarero states that sexual difference is a morphological, biological, and anthropological fact. And yet, she denies being an essentialist: "I affirm, for example, that feminine sexual difference is a corporeal difference. In saying that, I am asserting a banality, because this is not just confirmed by biology, medicine, and anthropology, but it is also evident when a baby is born; one can see immediately if it is a boy or a girl, with the exception of rare cases. Consequently, I maintain that sexual difference is a corporeal given (banality). The corporeal given asks for a meaning, the returning of a meaning. To say that the corporeal given of the vagina is lack or the absence of the phallus is the winning way the Western tradition addresses the problem. Yet, I do not feel like an essentialist in stating this banality, that there is a corporeal morphology in the feminine and in the masculine" (143–44). It is beyond the scope of this essay to elaborate in detail on whether Cavarero is a reductionist and an essentialist in terms of sexual difference and whether her stance on sexed dimorphism and biological/genetic motherhood has cisnormative or intersex and trans exclusive implications. Cavarero's use of the term *banality* in this context of the interview does not seem to be related to Arendt and her use of the term *banality* in her analysis of evil and Adolf Eichmann. In my reading of Cavarero's interpretation of Arendt, I interpret Cavarero's philosophy as deconstructive and certainly more post-structuralist, in Derrida's and Foucault's sense, than what Cavarero herself would perhaps be willing to support. For a queer and intersex elaboration and critique of Cavarero's notion of sexual difference, see Kevin Ryan's "Thinking Sexual Difference with (and Against) Adriana Cavarero:

On the Ethics and Politics of Care." (2019). For a detailed account of the meaning of sexual difference in Simone de Beauvoir and Luce Irigaray, see Sara Heinämaa's *Toward a Phenomenology of Sexual Difference* (2003). For an analysis of the multiple meanings and historical usages of sexual difference within Francophone and Anglophone feminist theorizing, see Anne-Emanuelle Berger's "The Ends of an Idiom, or Sexual Difference in Translation" (2014) and Paola Bono and Sandra Kemp's *The Lonely Mirror: Italian Perspectives on Feminist Theory* (1993). For a critical analysis of Cavarero's ontological notion of motherhood, see "The Ontology of the Maternal: A Response to Adriana Cavarero" by Allison Stone (2010).

2. Hannah Arendt, "On the Emancipation of Women," in *Essays in Understanding 1930–1954: Formation, Exile, and Totalitarianism*, ed. Jerome Kohn (New York: Shocken Books, 1994), 67–68.

3. Julian Honkasalo, "Arendt and Feminism," in *The Bloomsbury Companion to Hannah Arendt*, ed. Peter Gratton and Yasemin Sari (London: Bloomsbury, 2020).

4. Adriana Cavarero, *In Spite of Plato: A Feminist Rewriting of Ancient Philosophy* (Cambridge: Polity Press, 1995); Julia Kristeva, *Hannah Arendt*, trans. Ross Guberman (New York: Columbia University Press, 2001).

5. Adrienne Rich, "Conditions for Work: The Common World of Women," in *Lies, Secrets and Silence* (New York: Norton, 1979); Mary O'Brien, *The Politics of Reproduction* (Boston: Routledge and Kegan Paul, 1981); Hanna Pitkin, *The Attack of the Blob: Hannah Arendt's Concept of the Social* (Chicago: University of Chicago Press, 1998); Wendy Brown, *Manhood and Politics: A Feminist Reading in Political Theory* (Totowa, NJ: Rowman and Littlefield, 1998).

6. Hannah Arendt, *The Human Condition* (Chicago: University of Chicago Press, 1998), 8 (emphasis added).

7. Arendt, *The Human Condition*, 8, 177, 189; In *The Human Condition*, Arendt traces the idea of action as beginning something new to the twelfth book (chapter 20) of St. Augustine's *De Civitate Dei* (City of God) and interprets it in a secular ways as stating that what is unique about this type of a beginning is that it is "the beginning of somebody [. . .] who is a beginner himself." (8n1; 177n2). For an extensive analysis of Arendt's reading of St. Augustine, see Stephan Kampowski's *Arendt, Augustine, and the New Beginning* (2008) and Miguel Vatter's "Natality and Biopolitics in Hannah Arendt" (2006).

8. Hannah Arendt, *The Origins of Totalitarianism* (New York: Harcourt Brace Jovanovich, 1973), 478–79.

9. Arendt's original footnote in the text refers here to the same book and chapter of *City of God* as in *The Human Condition*, namely book 12, chapter 20. Although Arendt does not yet use the concept of natality in *The Origins*, it is clear that the conception of natality in *The Human Condition* is Arendt's political response to totalitarian annihilation and that the idea of action as beginning something new is developed already in *The Origins*. For more on the appearance of the concept of natality in Arendt's thinking, see Vatter, "Natality and Biopolitics in Hannah Arendt"; and Kampowski, *Arendt, Augustine, and the New Beginning*.

10. Luce Irigaray, *An Ethics of Sexual Difference*, trans. Carolyn Burke and Gillian C. Gill (Ithaca, NY: Cornell University Press, 1993), 5.

11. Irigaray, *An Ethics of Sexual Difference*, 8–11; cf. Luce Irigaray, *To Be Two*, trans. Monique M. Rhodes and Marco F. Cocito-Monoc (London: Routledge, 2001).

12. Adriana Cavarero, *In Spite of Plato*, 6.

13. Rich, "Conditions for Work: The Common World of Women"; O'Brien, *The Politics of Reproduction*; Pitkin, *The Attack of the Blob: Hannah Arendt's Concept of the Social*; Brown, *Manhood and Politics: A Feminist Reading in Political Theory*.

14. Cavarero, *In Spite of Plato*, 8.

15. Cavarero, *In Spite of Plato*, 17–18; cf. Adriana Cavarero, *Relating Narratives: Storytelling and Selfhood*, trans. Paul A. Kottman (New York: Routledge, 2000), 59.

16. Hannah Arendt, *The Life of the Mind: Volume One, Thinking* (New York: Harcourt Brace Jovanovich, 1978), 77.

17. Arendt, *The Human Condition*, 273; Hannah Arendt, *Between Past and Future: Eight Exercises in Political Thought*, ed. Kohn Jerome (New York: Viking Press, 1968), 42–43.

18. Arendt, *The Life of the Mind: Volume One*, 212.

19. Hannah Aredndt, *The Life of the Mind: Volume Two, Willing* (New York: Harcourt Brace Jovanovich, 1978), 55; Kristeva, *Hannah Arendt*, 172; Jacques Taminiaux, *The Thracian Maid and the Professional Thinker: Arendt and Heidegger*, ed. and trans. Michael Gendre (Albany: State University of New York Press, 1997), 125, 140.

20. Cavarero, *In Spite of Plato*, 6–7.

21. Cavarero, *In Spite of Plato*, 7.

22. Cavarero, *In Spite of Plato*, 3.

23. Cavarero, *In Spite of Plato*, 2.

24. Cavarero, *In Spite of Plato*, 3.

25. Cavarero, *In Spite of Plato*, 5.

26. Cavarero, *In Spite of Plato*, 3 (emphasis added).

27. Cavarero, *In Spite of Plato*, 5.

28. Cavarero, *In Spite of* Plato, 57–59. The original meaning of the term is actually not "to be born," but "to grow." The first occurrence of the term is in Homer's *Odyssey*, referring to a plant. In *Introduction to Metaphysics*, Heidegger traces the etymology of the terms *phainesthai* and *phyein* as referring to the becoming of phenomena (Steiner 1999, 47–48). Cavarero seems to follow Heidegger here, whereas Arendt does not follow Heidegger in her formulation of natality. For Heidegger and Arendt on birth, see Vatter, "Natality and Biopolitics in Hannah Arendt," 138–39.

29. Rosi Braidotti, foreword to *In Spite of Plato: A Feminist Rewriting of Ancient Philosophy*, by Adriana Cavarero (Cambridge: Polity Press, 1995), ix. See also Söderbäck, 2018.

30. Arendt, *The Life of the Mind: Volume One*, 19 (emphasis added).

31. In German, *Mensch* refers to all genders, whereas the English *men* can mean either human beings in general, or men as in males. According to Jerome

Kohn (personal conversation), Arendt uses the term *Mensh* to designate the gender-neutral use of the term.

32. Arendt, *The Human Condition*, 176 (emphasis added).
33. Cavarero, *In Spite of Plato*, 82.
34. Cavarero, *Relating Narratives*, 38.
35. Cavarero, *Relating Narratives*, 23–24.
36. Tuija Pulkkinen, "Vulnerability and the Human in Judith Butler's and Adriana Cavarero's Feminist Thought: A Politics of Philosophy Point of View," *Redescriptions: Political Thought, Conceptual History and Feminist Theory* 23, no. 2 (2020): 151–64.
37. E.g., Luce Irigaray, *An Ethics of Sexual Difference*, *Democracy Begins Between Two*, and *To Be Two*.
38. Adriana Cavarero, *For More than One Voice: Toward a Philosophy of Vocal Expression*, trans. Paul A. Kottman (Stanford, CA: Stanford University Press, 2005), 133.
39. Adriana Cavarero, *For More than One Voice*, 181; See also: Hannah Arendt, *The Human Condition*, 176.
40. Cavarero, *For More than One Voice*, 179–80 (emphasis original).

Bibliography

Arendt, Hannah. *Between Past and Future: Eight Exercises in Political Thought*. New York: Viking Press, 1968.
———. *The Human Condition*. Chicago: University of Chicago Press, 1998.
———. *The Life of the Mind: Volume One, Thinking*. New York: Harcourt Brace Jovanovich, 1978.
———. *The Life of the Mind: Volume Two, Willing*. New York: Harcourt Brace Jovanovich, 1978.
———. "On the Emancipation of Women." In *Essays in Understanding 1930–1954: Formation, Exile, and Totalitarianism*, edited by Jerome Kohn, 66–68. New York: Shocken Books, 1994.
———. *The Origins of Totalitarianism*. New York: Harcourt Brace Jovanovich, 1973.
Berger, Anne-Emanuelle. "The Ends of an Idiom, or Sexual Difference in Translation." *Redescriptions: Political Thought, Conceptual History and Feminist Theory* 17, no. 1 (Spring 2014): 44–67.
Bono, Paola, and Sandra Kemp. *The Lonely Mirror: Italian Perspectives on Feminist Theory*. London: Routledge, 1993.
Braidotti, Rosi. Foreword to *In Spite of Plato: A Feminist Rewriting of Ancient Philosophy*, by Adriana Cavarero, vii–xix. Translated by Serena Anderlini-D'Onofrio and Áine O'Healy. Cambridge: Polity Press, 1995.
Brown, Wendy. *Manhood and Politics: A Feminist Reading in Political Theory*. Totowa, NJ: Rowman and Littlefield, 1998.

Cavarero, Adriana. "'A Child has Been Born unto Us': Arendt on Birth." Translated by Silvia Guslandi and Cosette Bruhns. *philoSOPHIA* 4, no. 1 (2014): 12–30.
———. *For More than One Voice: Toward a Philosophy of Vocal Expression*. Translated by Paul A. Kottman. Stanford, CA: Stanford University Press, 2005.
———. *In Spite of Plato: A Feminist Rewriting of Ancient Philosophy*. Cambridge: Polity Press, 1995.
———. *Relating Narratives: Storytelling and Selfhood*. Translated by Paul A. Kottman. New York: Routledge, 2000.
Cavarero, Adriana, and Elisabetta Bertolino. "Beyond Ontology and Sexual Difference: An Interview with the Italian Feminist Philosopher Adriana Cavarero." *differences* 19, no. 1 (2008): 128–67.
Heinämaa, Sara. *Toward a Phenomenology of Sexual Difference*. Lanham, MD: Rowman and Littlefield, 2003.
Honkasalo, Julian. "Arendt and Feminism." In *The Bloomsbury Companion to Hannah Arendt*, edited by Gratton Peter and Yasemin Sari, 583–94. London: Bloomsbury, 2020.
Irigaray, Luce. *An Ethics of Sexual Difference*. Translated by Carolyn Burke and Gillian C. Gill. Ithaca, NY: Cornell University Press, 1993.
———. *Democracy Begins between Two*. Translated by Kirsteen Anderson. London: Routledge, 2001.
———. *To Be Two*. Translated by Monique M. Rhodes and Marco F. Cocito-Monoc. London: Routledge, 2001.
Kampowski, Stephan. *Arendt, Augustine, and the New Beginning: The Action Theory and Moral Thought of Hannah Arendt in the Light of Her Dissertation on St. Augustine*. Grand Rapids, MI: Eerdmans Publishing, 2008.
Kristeva, Julia. *Black Sun: Depression and Melancholia*. Translated by Leon S. Roudiez. New York: Columbia University Press, 1987.
———. *Colette*. Translated by Jane Marie Todd. New York: Columbia University Press, 2004.
———. *Hannah Arendt*. Translated by Ross Guberman. New York: Columbia University Press, 2001.
———. "Hannah Arendt on Refoundation as Survival." Hannah Arendt Prize for Political Thought acceptance speech, December 15–16, 2006. http://www.kristeva.fr/Arendt_en.html.
———. *Powers of Horror: An Essay on Abjection*. Translated by Leon S. Roudiez. New York: Columbia University Press, 1982.
O'Brien, Mary. *The Politics of Reproduction*. Boston: Routledge and Kegan Paul, 1981.
Pitkin, Hanna. *The Attack of the Blob: Hannah Arendt's Concept of the Social*. Chicago: University of Chicago Press, 1998.
Pulkkinen, Tuija. "Vulnerability and the Human in Judith Butler's and Adriana Cavarero's Feminist Thought: A Politics of Philosophy Point of View." *Redescriptions: Political Thought, Conceptual History and Feminist Theory* 23, no. 2 (2020): 151–64.

Rich, Adrienne. "Conditions for Work: The Common World of Women." In *Lies, Secrets and Silence*. New York: Norton, 1979.
Ryan, Kevin. "Thinking Sexual Difference with (and Against) Adriana Cavarero: On the Ethics and Politics of Care." *Hypatia: A Journal of Feminist Philosophy* 34, no. 2 (2019): 222–41.
Söderbäck, Fanny. "Natality or Birth? Arendt and Cavarero on the Human Condition of Being Born." *Hypatia* 33, no. 2 (2018): 273–288.
Steiner, George. *Heidegger: An Introduction*. Ithaca, NY: Cornell University Press, 1999.
Stone, Allison. "The Ontology of the Maternal: A Response to Adriana Cavarero." *Studies in the Maternal* 2, no. 1 (2010): 1–7. https://doi.org/10.16995/sim.94.
Taminiaux, Jacques. *The Thracian Maid and the Professional Thinker: Arendt and Heidegger*. Edited and translated by Michael Gendre. Albany: State University of New York Press, 1997.
Vatter, Miguel. "Natality and Biopolitics in Hannah Arendt." *Revista De Ciencia Politica* 26 no. 2 (2006): 137–59.

Part Two

"*Who* engenders politics?"

Three

On the Politics of the *Who*

Cavarero, Nancy, and Rancière

Timothy J. Huzar

> It is the *existent* (and not the existence *of* the existent).
> With this in mind, the question asks "who?"
>
> —Jean-Luc Nancy, *Who Comes after the Subject?*[1]
>
> The question of the who remains without an answer.
> And it is right that it should be so.
>
> —Adriana Cavarero, "*Who* Engenders Politics?"[2]
>
> Egalitarian society is only ever the set of egalitarian relations that are traced here and now through singular and precarious acts.
>
> —Jacques Rancière, *Hatred of Democracy*[3]

There are multiple registers of the political in the work of Adriana Cavarero. Previously I have identified a politics of indifference, seen in Cavarero's reading of Penelope, marooned on Ithaca with her handmaids, unweaving and reweaving a funeral shroud that maintains the anomalous space shared between her and her handmaids; and I have argued for a poetics of politics in Cavarero's work, exemplified in the ontology of vulnerability that she and Judith Butler, among other recent feminist scholars, position as an insurrection of autarchic, masculinist sovereignty.[4] Meanwhile Bonnie Honig has identified a heterotopian politics of refusal in Cavarero's account of inclination, while Cavarero herself closely aligns her politics with the influential account offered by Hannah Arendt, whereby politics is first the public expression of one's uniqueness.[5] This latter politics has most recently been formulated by Cavarero in *Surging Democracy* and, as Olivia Guaraldo notes in this volume, demonstrates a transition from Cavarero's earlier focus on an interpersonal politics—a "dyadic encounter" in Butler's words—to a politics primarily concerned with collective action: "to act in concert," as Arendt says.[6]

In this chapter, I develop another politics that can be found in Cavarero's work: the curious politics of the *who*. The who, indicating the uniqueness of each singular existent, already plays a role in Cavarero's Arendtian politics to the extent that politics for Arendt concerns the public disclosure of uniqueness. Arendt says, "This disclosure of 'who' in contradistinction to 'what' somebody is—his qualities, gifts, talents, and shortcomings, which he may display or hide—is implicit in everything somebody says and does. It can be hidden only in complete silence and perfect passivity, but its disclosure can almost never be achieved as a willful purpose, as though one possessed and could dispose of this 'who' in the same manner he has and can dispose of his qualities."[7] Rather than rehashing Arendt's account of action, which has already been well articulated by Arendt, Cavarero, and many other scholars, here I instead want to consider the politicity implicit in the upending of the metaphysics of European modernity that the grammar of the who enacts. Following Arendt, but also significantly expanding her thought, Cavarero insists that philosophy has a problem with singularity, with being able to think and talk about who a person is. Philosophy's temptation is to consider what people are to the detriment of actual people living their lives in the past, and present, and on into the future. Who a person is—the fact that they are a unique existent—is for philosophy superfluous to considerations of justice, truth, reason, rights, the organization of the community, and everything else that accounts for politics in the Western tradition. Cavarero's work points out that this failure to apprehend who a person is is a monumental epistemic error, often prejudiced along the lines of dominant, inaugural, and ongoing exclusions within European modernity—primarily, for Cavarero, the exclusion of women.[8] Instead, Cavarero makes the topic of unique singularity central to her work. By training her attention steadfastly on who people are, Cavarero offers a generative philosophical imaginary at odds with much theoretical scholarship.

However, speaking in the grammar of the singular *who* makes it difficult to speak about politics. Politics conventionally operates through the what, grounding itself in an abstract subject that is either discrete, collective, or fragmented. As Cavarero notes, "The question of the what determines [. . .] the plane on which the modern West constructs its political model and legitimizes its own contradictions."[9] With its focus on the singular existent that I am and that you are, one might assume that Cavarero's insistence on uniqueness is apolitical or antipolitical from the get go. This reading of the dyadic encounter—whereby my uniqueness is revealed in the relation sustained between myself and another—disqualifies a consideration of collective action, which is intimately tied to politicity in many traditions of political thought. This is not the case for Cavarero, since a plurality is necessary for uniqueness to be both apparent and to maintain its political qualities. This plurality encompasses the immediate relation not only between myself and another but also between innumerable other people in what Arendt called the "'web' of human relationships."[10] In either case, one need not get caught in the binary of the dyad and the collective. I argue that what is political about the who is its "methodological impropriety," its short-circuiting of the ways of thinking about politics—and existence in general—that are central to the Western tradition.[11] Making this argument requires moving beyond the resources provided by Cavarero and borrowing those of Jacques Rancière. For Rancière, as I will demonstrate, politics is first the refusal of the proper theoretical determination of politics. To focus on the singular who, as Cavarero's work does, necessitates the relinquishing of properly articulated accounts of politics.

At the heart of this politics is a question of representation: not the representation of political institutions, but rather how another is represented, made sense of, or accounted for. However even here, representation is not quite the right word. The representative traditions of European modernity do a bad job of capturing uniqueness; or, perhaps, they do too good a job, capturing, hiding, and ultimately nullifying uniqueness. Representation too often foregrounds a particular type of relation whereby the person who knows has the capacity to represent another but is only tangentially affected in this process, if at all. In this instance, uniqueness slips through the fingers of representation, just as it does when I try to name my uniqueness and inevitably offer a list not of who I am but of what I am.[12] Instead, I suggest we should think about how one *apprehends* uniqueness, emphasizing the inclination at the heart of apprehension as one person reaches out toward another—something like a complicated mode of touch—sustaining a relation that reveals not just the uniqueness of the one apprehended but also the uniqueness of the one apprehending. Apprehension is always, when it comes down to it, a type of comprehension: a sharing with others as much as a unidirectional accounting of another. How does one apprehend the singularity of another? How is my singularity also celebrated in this moment? What does apprehending singularity have to do with this thing called politics?

The politics of the who might be understood as a different account of the subject: an alternative ontology of what it is to be political that is concerned with the qualities or capacities one should possess or the activities one should be enacting. This *is* a key contribution of Cavarero's work and other feminist theories of vulnerability. However, the politics of the who that I draw attention to is different, albeit related. As I argue, the subject, constituted in the abstract, is anathema to the who. What is political about the who—about attending to the banal fact of the here-and-nowness of all existents—can be thought of at the same level as these ontological questions of subjectivity. But rather than offering an alternative ontology, attending to uniqueness involves a deconstruction of abstracted conceptions of subjectivity. Focusing on the particularity of this existent, here, whom I apprehend and am apprehended by in turn, provides generative resources for articulating other forms of existence or, better, other ways of approaching existence as a proximal, intimate, and motile process. Cavarero's attention to the who and the philosophical imaginary she articulates around it is, then, a refusal of traditions of thought that sustain the abstract subject. This is a deeply political maneuver both in its disruptive mode *and* in the space it makes for new forms of existence not to be represented but to be apprehended.

I begin by detailing Cavarero's discussion of the who in her chapter "*Who* Engenders Politics?" While uniqueness and the question of the who is central to all of Cavarero's work, this chapter is notable both because it explicitly links the who with issues of politics and because it is one of the lesser-studied texts of Cavarero's oeuvre. I then turn to Jean-Luc Nancy's landmark question of who comes after the subject, which in part prompts Cavarero's own reflections in "*Who* Engenders Politics?" Nancy's question, and the controversy it has provoked, enables us to appreciate the radicality of the who, the specificity of its appeal to singularity, and how the politics it maintains takes a different tack to the public happiness of acting in concert that is Cavarero's primary focus in her most recent work. I then analyze a critique of Nancy and Arendt's account of the who mounted by Christian Haines and Sean Grattan in their introduction to a special issue of the journal *Cultural Critique* titled "What Comes after the Subject?" I resist Haines and Grattan's refusal of the who in favor of the what and appraise Rancière's relation to the who, whom Haines and Grattan lean on in their critique of Nancy and Arendt. Rancière is the subject of a brief consideration by Cavarero in *Surging Democracy*; turning to Rancière's work in the context of a discussion of the singular who offers a chance to expand on Cavarero's cursory engagement with his idiosyncratic understanding of politics and to develop Rancière and Cavarero's political thought in the process.[13] Finally, I return to Cavarero, whom Haines and Grattan do not consider and who has contributed more than anyone else to articulating a mode of thought oriented around singular uniqueness. I emphasize the politics of the who that is a vital source of all of Cavarero's scholarship.

Who Engenders Politics?

In her chapter "*Who* Engenders Politics?," published in a 2002 collected volume, Cavarero reorients the philosophical stakes of the who that she discussed extensively in her seminal *Relating Narratives*, shifting these philosophical stakes toward questions of politics. An intervention in contemporary debates on feminist theory, Cavarero argues for an alternative to her polemically exaggerated binary, which consists of continental postmodern feminism on the one hand—championing a deconstructed and, consequently, fragmented subjecthood—and analytic metaphysical feminism grounded in a discrete and essential conception of womanhood on the other. While sympathetic to currents of continental poststructural thought, for Cavarero, both traditions miss the uniqueness of the women that are ultimately at the heart of feminist movements; that is, who they are. Rather than being some kind of quality hidden within a person, for Cavarero "the who is not a substance at all: he or she is simply someone that always has a face and a name. It is someone who consists of his/her life and his/her story. He or she is an unrepeatable existing being whose identity coincides perfectly with that lived life that is his/her story."[14] Uniqueness is not something that needs to be proven. Uniqueness simply *is*, and the onus is on us to consider what is stopping us from apprehending it. Cavarero says:

> No demonstrations or logical rationalizations are necessary to argue that each human being is a unique being with a face, a name, a story. It is enough to see the reality of who appear[s] just as he or she is. It is enough to trust the everyday wisdom that assures us that whomever we encounter is different from all those who live, who lived, and who will live. It is enough, then, to conform to the familiar sense of an appearance that is not mere semblance, not superficial expression, and not an external phenomenon of a truer, hidden, and more profound being.[15]

It is this mundane fact that is, for Cavarero, overlooked in debates within contemporary feminist theory. Whether the subject is understood as fragmented or essential, the subject is in either case abstract. Cavarero's thought is in this way at odds with "the presumed universality of the metaphysical subject and the obligatory fragmentariness of the postmodernist subject."[16] It follows an idiosyncratic path, one that disarms both traditions with its patient insistence on the necessity of operating in a philosophical imaginary that accounts for the singularity of each existent: that is, who they are.

This is not to say that Cavarero is unaware of the significance of what people are, particularly for various forms of political mobilization that operate around identity. By focusing on the who over the what, Cavarero is not concerned with doing away with issues of identity but with freeing them from the dominion of what people are so that who a person is can come to the fore, revitalizing identity. She notes the significance of the various forms of identity that can be summated into what we are and the value of these multiple and at times contradictory identities in staging forms of politics. Further, she says that the hard distinction between who and what—with the latter typically privileged—ultimately needs to be declined, creating an opportunity to enliven what we are by revealing the inevitable proximity of who and what. For Cavarero, "The *who* is never without the *what*. Indeed, the who is not an originating substance, a pure reality, to which is added, in the course of life, the variable multiplicity of the what. [. . .] [P]recisely in this mixture of the *who* with the *what* lies that so very familiar enigma that every life story tells."[17] The who, Cavarero says, is not an "adversative" to the what.[18] She insists that we instead shift our focus—which is inexorably drawn to what people are thanks to our millennia-old philosophical traditions—and first look at who people are. This is a gentle shifting of our gaze but one that is potent, with the potential to ensure that our claims to identity do not become rigid but remain supple and more powerful as a consequence. Cavarero's focus on uniqueness, on who a person is, can then be seen as a supplement to other forms of political mobilization that are oriented around the what of identity. For Cavarero, "It is left up to the contextualizing relationship itself to demonstrate whether being lesbian, philosopher, or communist is a quality, a thing, or, rather, a way inscribed in the very expressivity of the embodiments of uniqueness that are here exposed"[19]—what Cavarero has elsewhere described as "the spiritual matter of [an existent's] uniqueness."[20] Uniqueness is indifferent to these aspects of selfhood as *qualities* but not indifferent to them per se since to be indifferent to them per se would be to be indifferent to something that is always at play in who a person is. Freed from the stricture of what we are and put in contact with who we are, these qualities become self-apparently integral to our ontopolitical articulations and upend the binary of either what or who.

By parochializing the what and centralizing the who, in the process destabilizing the what/who binary, Cavarero bypasses considerations of recognition, representation, and normativity, not because these are unimportant—they are always attendant to any discursively constituted community, which is to say all community, and necessarily make up a central concern of political activism—but because they do not exhaust what constitutes politics and do not render the mundane, banal, and vulgar fact that I am here and you are there, here and now, superfluous to discussions of the political. Instead, for Cavarero, it is the who that carries the weight of her political intervention, which is inspired by Jean-Luc Nancy's earlier question of who comes after the subject. For Cavarero, her and Nancy's questions are important not only because feminist political debates have overlooked uniqueness but also because broader Western formations of politics are unable to account for who a person is, in their flesh, engendered in a specific way. Politics, in its liberal democratic variant, situates itself around the locus of a subject who is free and equal; but, for Cavarero, free and equal also means equivalent, substitutable, and fungible—the singular life of this free and equal person being superfluous to the oligarchy of representative systems and periodic elections. To emphasize the who is to fundamentally shift the political terrain on which we are walking. For Cavarero,

> The strange question that I formulated above, "*who* engenders politics?," had then a clear polemical intention. In its usual system, politics never has anything to do with the *who*, because it concerns itself instead with the *what*. Politics always thinks

> on a grand scale: through universal concepts, general categories, collective identities, specific cultures, communities, memberships, and groups. Politics never looks its subjects in the face. For if it looked them in the face, if it took an interest in that spectacular ontology where existing beings appear face-to-face, it would have to renounce a language that, with infinite internal variations, goes back to the "whatifying" foundation of its own disciplinary statute.[21]

Cavarero's response to this "whatifying" politics is to consider the politics of Italian feminist consciousness raising groups, where the who of each woman is revealed in their reciprocal apprehension of one another. This does not mean that for Cavarero politics can only be understood as this type of activity, or even that Cavarero believes this type of activity is a particularly efficacious type of politics. Rather, it is simply an example of a politics that does not nullify singularity but celebrates it. There is in Cavarero a primary politics of the who that I am drawing attention to, detected prior to any particular historical instantiation. This can be seen in the maneuver that begins by insisting on the self-evident meaningfulness of singular lives, that de-emphasizes what we are without renouncing our identities, that affirms difference as the "spiritual matter" of our uniqueness, and that refuses the fantasy of abstract subjects imbued with abstract qualities and capacities that can properly determine their politicity.

Who Comes after the Subject?

What, then, would be a politics that looked its subjects in the face? If we redact the question mark from Cavarero's question, we could say that *who* engenders politics; and when Jean-Luc Nancy asked his colleagues to consider "Who comes after the subject?," his own answer might best be understood by simply removing the question mark from his provocation.[22] Who comes after the subject? *Who* comes after the subject. Not "X comes after the subject, whom we might approach through the grammar of the who" but the somewhat cumbersome "after the subject comes *who*." If we can endure this phrasing, then it can help us see something important in not only Nancy's response but also in the responses of other scholars who have foregrounded the who as integral to the ethico-political reimagining of existence, prime among them Cavarero. If it is *who* that comes after the subject, then, in a sense, the who is a stand-in for myriad singular existents, each unique. But, in another sense, none of these singular existents would satisfy the philosophical stakes of Nancy's initial question in that no single *one* can function as the representation, or the representative, of all the others. Perhaps capitalization would make the claim clearer: after the subject comes Who. But the capital, with its gesture toward the abstract universal, is never appropriate for the who, which signifies precisely and nothing more than the here-and-now singularity of any one existent. There is no Who, only a plethora of *whos*; a fullness that is an overabundance or an overflowingness, escaping the proper political articulation of the state of the world (or the world as a state).

Nancy's response, embedded in the question, renders both the question and his answer inoperative, which is another way of saying it refuses to play the game of philosophy. Maybe Nancy's provocation was a trick question then, a riddle that could never adequately be answered by the philosophical tradition and its continued commitment to abstraction.

"What has four legs in the morning, two in the day, and three in the evening?" asks the Sphinx in an inaugural moment of philosophical speculation, according to Cavarero.

And Oedipus the philosopher, beloved of riddles, replies, "Man"—the monstrous response that signifies everyone (badly) and so no one.[23]

But we could imagine that the Sphinx did not ask *what* comports itself in this way but *who*, further highlighting the failure of Oedipus's response. To ask *who* would be to turn from philosophy toward narrative: the story of Oedipus "himself, he himself, in the hiddenness of his being."[24] For Cavarero, there is here a "confrontation between two discursive registers that manifest opposite characteristics. One, that of philosophy, has the form of a definitory knowledge that regards the universality of Man. The other, that of narration, has the form of a biographical knowledge that regards the unrepeatable identity of someone. The questions that sustain the two discursive styles are equally diverse. One asks '*what* is Man?' The second asks instead of someone '*who* he or she is.'"[25] The riddle, notes Cavarero, is "the very form of philosophy."[26] The Sphinx's riddle is "a philosophical discourse in reverse," beginning with the definition of Man and seeking the referent, but it is no less philosophical because of this. "Philosophy asks after man as a universal," says Cavarero. "The definition, which functions as a necessary response to the question, can be more or less refined, and is almost always inadequate or even wrong, but the *correct* approach to the problem, its epistemic form, does not change."[27] But Nancy's riddle, like our reimagining of the Sphinx's riddle, is more like a Trojan Horse, appearing as a philosophical conundrum but containing, if not the destruction of philosophy, then at least resources to celebrate a place apart from philosophy. When who comes after the subject, philosophy's failure to comprehend this grammar becomes apparent. For Philippe Lacou-Labarthe, concluding his response to Nancy's question, "Perhaps, then, one should leave to 'literature' (I would willingly say: to writings, with no more identification than that) the effort of sounding that call: 'Who?'—the effort of giving itself up to that call and of being summoned by it—so that the feeling 'that there is someone' can tremble again, even if it were anonymous, and that from this *lethargy* there might arise the admiration for existence."[28]

It is only natural that, from the perspective of the discipline of philosophy, one might be drawn not to the who but to the seemingly inevitable figure that the who merely gestures toward. Who comes after the subject? Give me your best bets, you shining stars of French philosophy, and we will see. The temporality embedded in Nancy's question does not help, but this is a minor point. As Nancy says, "What is posed here as the question of an 'after' (in history) is just as much a question of the 'before.'"[29] Or as Lacou-Labarthe notes, "*Who* therefore cannot come after the subject. *Who*, enigmatically (and always according to the same enigma), is ceaselessly prior to what philosophical questioning installs as a presence under the name of subject."[30] Even if we take Nancy's question as a genuine search for the figure that would supersede the subject rather than a provocation to his colleagues that secretly contains its own answer, Nancy's phrasing suggests that a different philosophical imaginary will be necessary to make sense of his question since the who can neither be a subject in the abstract, nor can the singularity of any one be the representative who of all others. There is a necessary equality to the who, one based not on equivalence and fungibility but rather on the who's incapacity to fulfill the theoretical articulation of the political community.

The figure superseding the subject will be known by who they are, not what they are. They will be known in their singular particularity. They will be known in a manner alien to philosophy. And of course, they will already have been here. This last point matters, since it would be understandable if one were to get caught up in the "after" of Nancy's question. The after, as Jacques Rancière intimates in his response to Nancy's question, presumes that the present way of understanding the world and inhabiting it is inadequate. Philosophers are required to articulate an alternative. Like the schoolmaster who first teaches his students that they do not know as much as him, to philosophize in this way, for Rancière, is to stultify people—the opposite of emancipation.[31] In his response to Nancy's question, Rancière says that focusing on the after places a gap between the night watchmen—intellectuals of both right and left, qualified to know what is best for the political community—and the slumbering masses whom they overlook. These night watchmen, for Rancière, have a self-recognized capacity—and with it a responsibility—to identify an epoch that the slumbering masses did not know they were living in and have unwittingly outgrown: an eternal, stultifying gap that will never be overcome.[32] But it is not clear why asking who it is that comes after the subject necessarily presumes, in Rancière's words, "the schema of the beginning of the end and that of the supposed naïveté of the other."[33] For sure, one could take Nancy's question in this direction, as many of the respondents to his provocation did. But one could just as easily imagine the question of "after" asking not what follows a dominant way of life, or even a dominant mode of subjecthood, but a dominant mode of thought, a dominant "philosophical imaginary," one that has failed to represent the majority of those who exist and even did a bad job of representing the people who deviated the least from its supposedly universal figuration.[34] Not, "Who comes after the subject now that the subject that the foolish masses were in thrall to has been revealed to always already contain the seeds of its own demise?" but rather, "Who comes after the subject now that our naming of the subject has been shown to be a failure, not least by those who never recognized themselves in its representation to begin with?" The question is not, "What comes after the subject?" with the implication that "the subject" fails to account for the way people are now. Here, the distance maintained between the knowledgeable ones and the ignorant masses would be blatant. Nancy is not asking for a new figure who more closely matches the activities of the current generation or a figure that adequately represents them in their abstractness. In Nancy's words,

> "Before/after the subject": *who*. This is first of all an affirmation: the being is *who* . . . But this is also a question: *who* is *who*? It is not "What is who?"—it is not a question of essence, but one of identity (as when one asks before a photograph of a group of people whose names you know but not the faces: "Who is who?"—is this one Kant, is that one Heidegger, and this other one beside him? . . .). That is to say, a question of presence: Who is *there*? Who is present there?[35]

To ask "Who comes after the subject?" is, through the distinction between the what and the who, to return being to each existent, to be present to each one, to "presence" who they are, to apprehend their life not as a vibrant vitalism but as a narrative told by a "pluriphony," sometimes via the reason of speech, but also sometimes via the sonority of voice, while at other times in a manner that refuses the Aristotelian binary to begin with.[36]

To ask who is to work in a manner that refuses the question's proper theoretical articulation. As Cavarero says, "Uniqueness is epistemologically inappropriate."[37] The who is not a better representation of the subject. The who renders inoperative its representative role. It begs a question that it cannot answer. It in this way bears some resemblance to Rancière's insistence that the political subject is the one who refuses the terms that would enable the proper identification of the political subject. In *Surging Democracy* Cavarero focuses on comments Rancière makes in his *Hatred of Democracy*, emphasizing Rancière's anarcho-Marxist credentials to demonstrate a distinction between an antagonistic politics—seen in radical democratic traditions—and her focus on the Arendtian interactive plurality that does not assume conflict but a public happiness in democracy's inaugural surging.[38] However, one can draw a connection between Cavarero's understanding of uniqueness as "epistemologically inappropriate" and what Rancière describes as the "impropriety pertaining to the very principle of politics."[39] One cannot approach Rancière's political subject through the whatness that political philosophy provides. But one might approach this political subject by asking who they are, given that the who, like Rancière's political subject, also disarms us, short-circuiting the circularity whereby Being maintains the sole capacity to recognize and therefore name Being, just as those who are political, for Rancière, maintain the sole capacity to recognize and therefore name politicity. This is a maneuver that Rancière says is a form of "policing" at odds with what he would otherwise valorize as "the anarchic principle of political singularity,"[40] or "the set of egalitarian relations that are traced here and now through singular and precarious acts."[41] Who comes after the subject? The surplus of anyone, of any one; the reality of equality "that is constantly and everywhere attested to"; an equality at the heart of every order that can only be verified and never proven.[42] So, too, the who is never proven and is continually verified in the mundane givenness of the existent, "constantly and everywhere attested to." That is, *you* come after the subject—just you, in the here and now, in your "flesh," and in your banality.[43] In this sense, the *you* can do more work than the who in that the you gestures toward a relation that the who is at risk of obscuring. You in your singularity are constituted in a relation to me that precedes both of us and, in fact, extends infinitely beyond the dyad that once more risks foregrounding the individual. Nonetheless, to the extent that we are to be apprehended in our particularity and not in our abstractness—which is to say also in our obscurity, our opacity, neither of which belie the knowledge you have of who I am—the you, and even the who, will do better than the what. We can, as Édouard Glissant says, "agree not merely to the right to difference but, carrying this further, agree also to the right to opacity that is not enclosure within an impenetrable autarchy but subsistence within an irreducible singularity. Opacities can coexist and converge, weaving fabrics."[44] And it is not for nothing that Cavarero—following Nancy, but more so Arendt—combines both the who and the you in the question "Who are you?"[45] To ask this question is to "focus on the texture of the weave and not on the nature of its components," to borrow Glissant's words.[46] It is to apprehend "individual uniqueness [. . .] individual differences not as detracting from each piece but as enriching the whole quilt," as Patricia Hill Collins says.[47] To operate at the level of the who—to celebrate singularity rather than balking at its uncouthness—is to interrupt an epistemology of those who know and those who do not, of those who understand and those others who, thus understood, are rendered "transparent."[48]

What Subject?

In his response to Nancy's question, Rancière does not reflect on the possible resonances between the who and his emerging account of politics. Drawing on Rancière, Christian Haines and Sean Grattan—writing the introduction to a special issue of the journal *Cultural Critique* entitled "What Comes after the Subject?"—also call into question the political value of the who. For Haines and Grattan, Nancy's mobilization of the who is a hindrance to articulating forms of resistant life lived in the present. Instead, they suggest that asking what comes after the subject better accounts for these forms of life. Drawing on Rancière, Haines and Grattan suggest that Nancy proposes "a *who* of subjectivity"; that within his designation of *some one* "lurk myriad specters: the conflation of liberal personhood with subjectivity *tout court*, the delineation of the social in terms of possessive individualism, the opposition between man and animal, and the reduction of the political to the question of identity"; and that "the 'who' risks sliding into a latent anthropocentrism, one that causes the subject to be reborn from its own ashes."[49] They then suggest that "the 'what' entails a reclaiming of the present as a fecund time for politics, as a time in which productive struggles can occur over what it means to be, over who/what counts, and over how matter comes to matter."[50] Haines and Grattan's charge extends beyond Nancy, encompassing Arendt and, by proxy, any scholar who approaches political thinking through the who, not least Cavarero. But why does switching *what* for *who*—while retaining *after*—retrain our gaze on the present rather than the future? On what basis is the designation of *who* responsible for revitalizing not simply the subject per se but the anthropocentric subject of possessive liberal individualism? Is Nancy's who really a who "of subjectivity"?

The who is imputed with a temporal and restrictive force that, I would suggest, is beyond its powers. By asking who comes after the subject, Nancy was not of necessity committed to an anthropocentric subjecthood because he was not searching for another subjecthood better able to approximate the reality of subjectivity within the contemporary conjuncture. As Nancy makes clear in *The Inoperative Community*, an early and foundational text in his thought, the dispossessive, ecstatic relationality that interrupts any coincidence between the community and itself—or the individual and itself, or the community and the individual—also interrupts the proper separation of Man and animal.[51] And it is in this text that Nancy offers a riposte to Bataille, whose passionate refusal of the subject, Nancy argues, is enacted in a sovereign mode.[52] We do not need to agree with Nancy to see that his thought is not simply the rehabilitation of an anthropocentric subjecthood. Nancy was not seeking a who of subjectivity, an upgraded who, and his use of who was not an unfortunate, restrictive grammatical error. Nancy's question was a challenge to the tradition of Western philosophy being adequate to make sense of key ethico-politico-ontological questions that can only be approached from the givenness of existence: its hereness, its banality. As Cavarero has made clear, to continue the philosophical project would be to continue to search for that form of subjecthood that would unlock radical, emancipatory futures; it would continue to be posed through the grammar of the what—which previously would have asked "What is Man, the Individual, the Human, the Subject?"—and now might overcome these figures through a whatness that is placed after those of the present. It would continue to sustain the stultifying gap between those who know (that is, those who have the capacity to know and to recognize knowledge) and those who lack this knowledge or lack the capacity for this knowledge: the animal, the object, the thing—and the enslaved, who throws these nominations into crisis in their escape from them.[53] It would continue to instill mastery, which is what Haines and Grattan go on to do, despite their imputation of Nancy doing the same.

For Haines and Grattan, their question "What comes after the subject?" might provoke "a thinking that maps emergent forms of life, or singular entities, through the analysis of transformations in the *whatness* of contemporary subjectivities."[54] The respondents to the question would then be cartographers, "surveying emergent modes of subjectivity" to identify moments when the whatness of subjectivities is transformed, producing maps that can account for the radicalness of what they are seeing.[55] These modes of subjectivity emerge from the "long nineties" and its de-territorialized, immaterial labor, as do the critical theories mapping these subjectivities.[56] Haines and Grattan distance themselves from previous theory in their insistence on following the lead of those who are living their lives apart from a proper way of being—"an immersion of theoretical *praxis* in ontology"—while nonetheless not abandoning critique; their question "therefore tries to reinvigorate critique not simply by coupling to the affirmation of new forms of life but also by framing this *praxis* in historico-political terms."[57] Yet, despite following the lead of those forms of life living their negotiation of the contemporary conjuncture, in seeking a whatness of the present (despite being couched in the grammar of the after) and in playing the role of cartographers who map those forms of life and reflect back their proper philosophical articulation, Haines and Grattan retain more of a proximity to Rancière's night watchmen than Nancy does. Perhaps this is unfair, however. The stultifying pedagogic gap that Rancière imputes to much modern political thought is difficult to throw off, although it may be negotiated in more ways than Rancière appreciates. The answer is not, as Rancière himself makes clear in his discussion of Antonin Artaud's theater of cruelty in *The Emancipated Spectator*, the collapsing of the distinction between the ones who know with the ones who do not, which once again reinstates that distinction as quickly as it is disavowed.[58] There is a place for theory that, following the lead of those living their lives in the midst of the world (which includes, after all, those doing the theory, no matter how tall and impregnable their ivory towers), proposes new ways of being as a performative, polemical intervention in otherwise anemic dominant theoretical imaginaries, even if this might catch in the throat of Rancière. Those living their lives (which again, is everyone) can, after all, take the theory or leave it and are unlikely to be duped by it; they may repurpose it in ways that they should not (or should not be capable of). What is less important is condemning a way of doing theory and instead exploring how Haines and Grattan miss the radicality of the who and its potential to disarm the grandstanding of philosophy in the name of those who simply *are*, here and now.

Haines and Grattan's imputation of the who as bearing an anthropocentric posture takes its lead less from Nancy's thought and more from another major thinker of the who: Hannah Arendt. Arendt is certainly crucial to any exploration of the stakes of the distinction between who and what, making it central to her magnum opus *The Human Condition* via the category of uniqueness. Haines and Grattan highlight that Arendt's linking of the who to glorious action and the what to the drudgery of labor delimits the scope of who can be a who to begin with; in their words, "Action safeguards the gap separating the 'who' from the 'what,' which is to say that it protects human civilization from devolving into mere nature."[59] As they point out, while on the one hand Arendt insightfully identifies the outlines of the biopolitical conjuncture—the prioritization of the management of life over the plurality of unique existents—she also, as has been noted in a plethora of critical scholarship, does so via a schema that cannot hide its privileging of action as the highest realization of human life, despite attenuations from later scholarship that draw out the subtleties in her account of the *vita activa* and the arguable porosity of its component categories: labor, work, and action. We know that the rearticulation of Greek and Roman distinctions between the public and the private that subtend much of Arendt's argument are closely linked to her privileging of action. Arendt makes it too easy to reinforce a masculinist understanding of politics whereby the public sphere is the condition for action, the necessities of life taken care of by an absent other. Further, she outright rejects the possibility of the Black Power movements of her time fulfilling her definition of action; rather than acting, one could say that for Arendt they were *acting out* a kind of unhelpful social negotiation that ultimately served only to sully proper political expression free of "identity." For Haines and Grattan, then, Arendt's distinction between who and what correctly identifies the biopolitical turn—the management of life in its whatness and the obfuscation of the who—but also fetishizes a particular who: a who who acts, a who constituted in his action with others in the public realm, a who who can only be recognized in his proximity to those who are not. As a consequence, for Haines and Grattan the who should be abandoned, and the what resignified for the purpose of articulating novel forms of resistant subjectivity.

However, this reading of Arendt overlooks another aspect of her who/what distinction, one further from the paradigm of biopolitics and closer to Nancy's mobilization of the who in the phrasing of his question, and one powerfully articulated by Cavarero throughout her work. The biopolitical split of what from who is not the focus of Nancy's reflections. Rather, it is philosophy's fetishization of the abstract universal—the what signifying anyone and so no one—that Nancy as well as Arendt and Cavarero admonish. No doubt, for Arendt, there is a relation between these two readings, one crystallized in Cavarero's account of "horrorism" that describes a violence that targets a person's uniqueness, reducing them to what they are.[60] Nonetheless, a difference of emphasis is evident, one that does not focus on whatness as first the production of "bare life" and instead understands whatness as the fulcrum of Western metaphysics, archetypically seen, in Cavarero's words, in the "universalizing arrogance of anonymous categories" that are dear to the disciplines of philosophy and political theory: Man, the Human, the Individual, the Citizen, and the Subject.[61] Within these disciplines, the singular lives of men, women, and nonbinary existents are superfluous, an unhelpful remainder, an irritant. And it is these singular lives who are signified in Arendt, Nancy, and Cavarero's mobilizations of the who. Philosophy founders when thinking these existents, which is why Nancy's question disarms itself in its asking. The who is not an empty signifier but is overflowing, resplendent, a surplus that demonstrates that in front of us is not abstract Man, or the undifferentiated mass, or the fungible "speck of capital" but this singular existent, in their flesh and in their banality.[62] By reading Arendt's who/what distinction through a biopolitical lens, Haines and Grattan are able to rethink whatness as the excessive potentiality of "life itself," a force flowing through both human and non-human forms of life as well as the non-sentient matter that all life exists in intimate relation to. For them, the what can be—and has been—recuperated to articulate the myriad forms of life cast out from the who: what they describe as "the ambivalence of the 'what.'"[63] And yet, doing so misses the force of the who in confronting the absolute difference of singular particularity while also not heeding the dangers that even a reconstructed whatness still harbors: namely, a proximity to the abstract, to the disciplining of philosophy, to the pedagogic masteries concomitant with the discipline, and to the instantiation of the gap between the ones who know and the ones who do not. To ask not what these forms of life are but *who* they are is not necessarily to resurrect an anthropocentrism; it is to say that life can only be known in its singular particularity—*this* life, *here*—which is to say in its fundamental imbrication with the plurality of all forms of life. Because to work through the prism of the who is always to open a relation sustained by the question "Who are you?" which reveals not only *who* is asked the question but also *who* is doing the asking.

A Politics of *Who*

For both Cavarero and Butler, a contestation of Arendt's public/private divide is required if it is to be mobilized for emancipatory political ends.[64] However, while this contestation may be necessary for Cavarero, it does not form the basis of politics, which Cavarero would instead locate in the moments of public happiness palpably seen in democracy's surging, germinal state.[65] Rancière also insists on the contestation of the public/private divide, making this central to his understanding of democracy and, with it, politics: within democracy is a "movement that ceaselessly displaces the limits of the public and the private, of the political and the social."[66] But more pertinently for an analysis that centralizes the who, as Cavarero's work powerfully does, is the publicity this who would otherwise require—this unique, singular, particular existent—without which their life fails to be marked by politicity. Rancière sidesteps this issue by insisting that politics is the polemical claiming of the universal in any moment of particularized exclusion.[67] However, even on Rancière's terms, the political subject is caught in an account of politics that fuses politicity with polemical claiming, revealing the equality that any justification of inequality depends on. Not only does this risk overlooking those who act politically through fugitivity, waywardness, and refusal—central themes in recent Black feminist scholarship in the United States and elsewhere—but further, the singular particularity of the who—of this existent, here, apparent to me, and revealing me in their apparition—is swallowed in the abstraction of a proper articulation of the political. This is despite "the displacement inherent to politics" that otherwise marks Rancière's groundbreaking and idiosyncratic interventions in the last forty years of conceptual political debate.[68]

Earlier, following Cavarero, I asked what a politics would be that looked its subjects in the face. This is a politics that would apprehend who each existent is and return their singularity to them (as if they had lost it), revitalizing "the spiritual matter of [their] uniqueness" that is sullied when *what a person is* becomes the fulcrum of politics. Perhaps this politics would look something like Rancière's idiosyncratic account of politics, if we uncouple Rancière's account from the examples he uses to illustrate it, emphasizing "the displacement inherent to politics" that is crucial to his political thought. For Rancière, politics cannot be accounted for in the abstract in advance—properly recognized and, ultimately, policed. Politics is the breaking of any proprietorial account of politics. I would add that this always happens not by a "subject" but by particular, singular existents, which is a metaphysically extravagant way of saying just you or me, she, he, or they. My point is not that we need to find appropriate "real world" examples to exemplify a politics of the who; the singular can never be the representative or the representation of other singularities. Cavarero focuses on the Italian feminist consciousness raising groups in her early works such as "*Who* Engenders Politics?" and focuses on collective political action in her most recent work. While both of these may be moments of politics, what makes them political is not that they respect the uniqueness of those who take part. "Respecting uniqueness" would then become the rule for an activity to qualify as political. Instead, to consider uniqueness is to abandon a way of thinking about politics that tolerates qualifications for being political because uniqueness—or respect for it—cannot be properly generalized. The politics of the who is not about finding the appropriate example that could then be abstracted to all other activity that we wish to determine the politicity of. It is political in the curious way that Rancière speaks of politics in that it is faithful to the refusal of proper, abstracted theories of politics emerging out of the irrefutable equality of any and all people. This does not mean that there is always politics but, rather, that politics is to be made sense of in its particular occasions and cannot be judged based on abstract, universal principles. There is no yardstick to measure politicity; politics is the refusal of the validity of the yardstick, or the authority of the one wielding it, or the tradition that renders the yardstick intelligible. And if politics is this refusal of the yardstick—a refusal of the proper judgement of what constitutes politics (and a refusal of the authority that would elevate some as capable of making this judgement, relegating others)—then this itself cannot properly be declared. The refusal of the yardstick can be declared, but the power of its declaration—if it contains any power—emerges in the moment of its declaration, its enactment, or its verification and is not grounded or legitimized in theory. We may generalize—"all are unique," or "politics is the refusal of proper accounts of politics"—but we never do so properly. Rancière returns our gaze to the "epistemologically inappropriate" moment of politics' verification, which of course is being verified by particular people.[69] To this extent, we can and should speak about Rancière's politics through the grammar of the who and consider the politics of Cavarero's who through the indecorum of Rancière's politics.

For Rancière, politics might be apprehended in a variety of settings. Nonetheless, he stresses that

> In a theatre, in front of a performance, just as in a museum, school or street, there are only ever individuals plotting their own paths in the forest of things, acts and signs that confront or surround them. The collective power shared by spectators does not stem from the fact that they are members of a collective body or from some specific form of interactivity. It is the power each of them has to translate what she perceives in her own way, to link it to the unique intellectual adventure that makes her similar to all the rest in as much as this adventure is not like any other.[70]

On the one hand, we can see a rejoinder Rancière might pose to Arendt and, consequently, Cavarero concerning the grounding of politics in "some specific form of interactivity." For both Arendt and Cavarero, politics stems from the interactions of a plurality. On the other hand, we can see a sensitivity that Rancière maintains to the singular, apparent not only in his insistence that "there are only ever individuals" that embark on a "unique intellectual adventure" but also, and more significantly, in his recourse to the singular pronoun *she*. There are only ever specific people—apparent to anyone who cares to look, listen, or feel—verifying their intellectual equality. This is the basis of the refusal of the proprietorial, stultifying declaration of what politics is—that is, the basis of emancipation.[71] This refusal, for Rancière, is the only thing that can go by the name of politics. And while Rancière's rejoinder to the Arendtian plurality carries some weight, it is also crucial that this plurality is nothing more than the collective noun of singular, unique existents, separated by "irreducible distances" that do not belie their imbrication.[72]

This politics of the who is central to Cavarero's work, and it is radical despite its banality. It is different to a heterotopian politics of refusal or indifference, different to a politics of fugitivity, different to the "insurrectionary humanism" of Cavarero and Butler's ontology of vulnerability, and different also to primary moments of public happiness cognate with the surging moments of democracy's formation, even if it is never entirely separate from these types of politics either.[73] Each draws its vitality from

Cavarero's insistence on a philosophical imaginary that can account for who each person is, but the politicity of this imaginary—trained at the level of *this* existent, *here*—is nonetheless distinct. To apprehend who another is and to find oneself apprehended in this moment—in an intimacy that we could think of as a form of "touch" in Nancy's words, or "hapticality" in Harney and Moten's, or a refusal or mockery of "every internal distinction between [. . .] flesh and spirit" in Cavarero's words—is to be curiously political, anomalous, and indecorous as the foundations of the proper, proprietorial edifice of the traditions of European modernity are shaken.[74]

Notes

1. Jean-Luc Nancy, introduction to *Who Comes after the Subject?* ed. Eduardo Cadava, Peter Connor, and Jean-Luc Nancy (New York: Routledge, 1991), 6.

2. Adriana Cavarero, "Who Engenders Politics?" in *Italian Feminist Theory and Practice: Equality and Sexual Difference*, ed. Graziella Parati and Rebecca West, trans. Carmen di Cinque (London: Associated University Presses, 2002), 93.

3. Jacques Rancière, *Hatred of Democracy*, trans. Steve Corcoran (London: Verso, 2006), 96–97.

4. See Timothy J. Huzar, "A Politics of Indifference: Reading Cavarero, Rancière and Arendt," *Paragraph* 42, no. 2 (2019): 205–22, https://doi.org/10.3366/para.2019.0299; and "Violence, Vulnerability, Ontology: Insurrectionary Humanism in Cavarero and Butler," in *Toward a Feminist Ethics of Nonviolence*, ed. Timothy J. Huzar and Clare Woodford (New York: Fordham University Press, 2021), 151–60.

5. Bonnie Honig, *A Feminist Theory of Refusal* (Cambridge, MA: Harvard University Press, 2021), 45–71. Adriana Cavarero, *Surging Democracy: Notes on Hannah Arendt's Political Thought*, trans. Matthew Gervase (Stanford, CA: Stanford University Press, 2021).

6. Judith Butler, *Giving an Account of Oneself* (New York: Fordham University Press, 2005), 32. Hannah Arendt, *The Human Condition* (Chicago: University of Chicago, 1998), 179.

7. Arendt, *The Human Condition*, 179. Who I am is not something I possess; more strongly, one could say a reflection on the who—on one's uniqueness—may reveal the limits of the possessive traditions of European modernity, where my sovereignty is grounded in my body, extending to all that I affect through my laboring. See John Locke, *Second Treatise of Government* (South Bend: Infomotions, 2000), ProQuest Ebook Central, chapter 5, section 27.

8. The exclusion of Black life should also be recognized within these inaugural exclusions, stemming from the legacies of colonialism and the transatlantic slave trade and the consequent anti-Blackness that pervades the contemporary Western

world, cf. Timothy J. Huzar, "Apprehending Care in the Flesh: Reading Cavarero with Spillers," *Diacritics* 49, no. 3 (2021): 6–27, https://doi.org/10.1353/dia.2021.0027.

9. Cavarero, *"Who Engenders Politics?"* 98.

10. Arendt, *The Human Condition*, 183.

11. Timothy J. Huzar, "The Public Library, Democracy and Rancière's Poetics of Politics," *Information Research* 18, no. 3 (September 2013), http://www.informationr.net/ir/18-3/colis/paperC15.html#.YW0vsXUecUE.

12. Arendt, *The Human Condition*, 181; Cavarero, *"Who Engenders Politics?"* 92–93.

13. Cavarero, *Surging Democracy*, 10–11.

14. Cavarero, *"Who Engenders Politics?"* 91.

15. Cavarero, *"Who Engenders Politics?"* 94.

16. Cavarero, *"Who Engenders Politics?"* 91.

17. Cavarero, *"Who Engenders Politics?"* 100.

18. Cavarero, *"Who Engenders Politics?"* 100.

19. Cavarero, *"Who Engenders Politics?"* 101.

20. Adriana Cavarero, *Relating Narratives: Storytelling and Selfhood*, trans. Paul A. Kottman (New York: Routledge, 2000), 111.

21. Cavarero, *"Who Engenders Politics?"* 98.

22. Jean-Luc Nancy, "Introduction," *Topoi: An International Review of Philosophy* 7, no. 2 (September, 1988): 87–92, https://link.springer.com/journal/11245/7/2.

23. "The true mark of the monster lies, rather, in Man, as Oedipus had the occasion to learn," notes Cavarero. *Relating Narratives*, 9.

24. Maria Zabrano, *Chiari del Bosco*, quoted in Cavarero, *Relating Narratives*, 7.

25. Cavarero, *Relating Narratives*, 13.

26. Cavarero, *Relating Narratives*, 7.

27. Cavarero, *Relating Narratives*, 8.

28. Philippe Lacoue-Labarthe, "The Response of Ulysses," in *Who Comes after the Subject?* 205.

29. Jean-Luc Nancy, introduction to *Who Comes after the* Subject, 6.

30. Philippe Lacoue-Labarthe, "The Response of Ulysses," 202.

31. Jacques Rancière, *The Ignorant Schoolmaster: Five Lessons in Intellectual Emancipation*, trans. Kristin Ross (Stanford, CA: Stanford University Press, 1991), 7.

32. Jacques Rancière, "After What?" in *Who Comes after the Subject?* 248, 251.

33. Rancière, "After What?" 251.

34. Michèle Le Dœuff, *The Philosophical Imaginary*, trans. Collin Gordon (Stanford, CA: Stanford University Press, 1989).

35. Nancy, introduction to *Who Comes after the Subject*, 7.

36. On "presence" see Gail Lewis, "Questions of Presence," *Feminist Review* 117, no. 1 (2017): 1–19, https://doi.org/10.1057%2Fs41305-017-0088-1. On "pluriphony" see Cavarero, *Surging Democracy*, 75. On the speech/voice distinction see Cavarero, *For More than One Voice: Toward a Philosophy of Vocal Expression*, trans. Paul A. Kottman (Stanford, CA: Stanford University Press, 2005).

37. Cavarero, *For More than One Voice*, 9.
38. Cavarero, *Surging Democracy*, 10–11.
39. Rancière, *Hatred of Democracy*, 37.
40. Rancière, *Hatred of Democracy*, 76.
41. Rancière, *Hatred of Democracy*, 96.
42. Rancière, *Hatred of Democracy*, 48.
43. Hortense Spillers, "Mama's Baby, Papa's Maybe: An American Grammar Book." *Diacritics* 17, no. 2 (Summer 1987): 65–81. "Banality" comes from the French *banal*, signifying the holding of something in common within a feudal order, itself emerging from the Latin *bannālis*: to be subject to feudal authority. In this way the "banality" of existence is held in common, under a feudal order that depends upon this commonality for its existence.
44. Édouard Glissant, *Poetics of Relation*, trans. Betsy Wing (Ann Arbor: University of Michigan Press, 1997), 190.
45. Arendt, *The Human Condition*, 178; Cavarero, *Relating Narratives*, 20.
46. Glissant, *Poetics of Relation*, 190.
47. Patricia Hill Collins, *Black Feminist Thought: Knowledge, Consciousness, and the Politics of Empowerment* (New York: Routledge, 2000), 263.
48. Glissant, *Poetics of Relation*, 189. This is an epistemology that has its origins in the colonialism of European modernity, saturating contemporary intellectual and institutional articulations of politics. This is reflected in Nancy's narrowing of his question at the beginning of *The Birth to Presence*, where Nancy is in particular interested in who comes after the subject of the West: "this coming of another that the West always demands, and always forecloses." *The Birth to Presence*, trans. Brian Holmes and others (Stanford, CA: Stanford University Press, 1993), 2.
49. Christian P. Haines and Sean Grattan, "Life after the Subject," *Cultural Critique* 96, no. 36 (Spring 2017): 1–2, https://muse.jhu.edu/article/669098.
50. Haines and Grattan, "Life after the Subject," 3.
51. Jean-Luc Nancy, *The Inoperative Community*, trans. Peter Connor, Lisa Garbus, Michael Holland, and Simona Sawhney (Minneapolis: University of Minnesota Press, 1991), 2.
52. Nancy, *The Inoperative Community*, 23.
53. Fred Moten, *The Universal Machine* (Durham, NC: Duke University Press, 2018), 16.
54. Haines and Grattan, "Life after the Subject," 4.
55. Haines and Grattan, "Life after the Subject," 5.
56. Phillip Wegner, quoted in Haines and Grattan, "Life after the Subject," 4.
57. Phillip Wegner, quoted in Haines and Grattan, "Life after the Subject," 5, 6.
58. "Distance is not an evil to be abolished, but the normal condition of any communication," says Rancière. He continues: "could we not invert the terms of the problem by asking if it is not precisely the desire to abolish the distance that creates it?" *The Emancipated Spectator*, trans. Gregory Elliott (London: Verso, 2011), 10, 12.

59. Haines and Grattan, "Life after the Subject," 7.

60. Adriana Cavarero, *Horrorism: Naming Contemporary Violence*, trans. William McCuaig (New York: Columbia University Press, 2011).

61. Giorgio Agamben, *Homo Sacer: Sovereign Power and Bare Life* (Stanford, CA: Stanford University Press, 1998), 8. Cavarero, *For More than One Voice*, 26.

62. Wendy Brown, "Sacrificial Citizenship: Neoliberalism, Human Capital, and Austerity Politics," *Constellations* 23, no. 1 (2016): 3, https://doi.org/10.1111/1467-8675.12166.

63. Haines and Grattan, "Life After the Subject," 19.

64. Cavarero, *Surging Democracy*, 49–50. Judith Butler, *Notes toward a Performative Theory of Assembly* (Cambridge, MA: Harvard University Press, 2015), 75–76.

65. Cavarero, *Surging Democracy*, 30–44.

66. Rancière, *Hatred of Democracy*, 62.

67. Rancière, *Hatred of Democracy*, 60.

68. Rancière, *Hatred of Democracy*, 62. On the limits of Arendt and Rancière's thought for understanding the politics of fugitivity, see Timothy J. Huzar, "Toward a Fugitive Politics: Arendt Rancière, Hartman," *Cultural Critique* 110 (Winter 2021): 1–48, https://doi.org/10.5749/culturalcritique.110.2021.0001.

69. Cavarero, *For More than One Voice*, 9.

70. Rancière, *The Emancipated Spectator*, 17.

71. Rancière, *The Ignorant Schoolmaster*, 13.

72. Rancière, *The Ignorant Schoolmaster*, 17.

73. Huzar, "Violence, Vulnerability, Ontology."

74. Jean-Luc Nancy, *Corpus*, trans. Richard A. Rand (New York: Fordham University Press, 2008). Stefano Harney and Fred Moten, *The Undercommons: Fugitive Planning and Black Study* (New York: Minor Compositions, 2013), 97–99. Cavarero, *Relating Narratives*, 111.

Bibliography

Arendt, Hannah. *The Human Condition*. Chicago: University of Chicago Press, 1998.

Brown, Wendy. "Sacrificial Citizenship: Neoliberalism, Human Capital, and Austerity Politics." *Constellations* 23, no. 1 (2016): 3–14. https://doi.org/10.1111/1467-8675.12166.

Butler, Judith. *Giving an Account of Oneself*. New York: Fordham University Press, 2005.

———. *Notes toward a Performative Theory of Assembly*. Cambridge, MA: Harvard University Press, 2015.

Cavarero, Adriana. *For More than One Voice: Toward a Philosophy of Vocal Expression*. Translated by Paul A. Kottman. Stanford, CA: Stanford University Press, 2005.

———. *Horrorism: Naming Contemporary Violence*. Translated by William McCuaig.

New York: Columbia University Press, 2011.
———. *Relating Narratives: Storytelling and Selfhood*. Translated by Paul A. Kottman. New York: Routledge, 2000.
———. *Surging Democracy: Notes on Hannah Arendt's Political Thought*. Translated by Matthew Gervase. Stanford, CA: Stanford University Press, 2021.
———. "Who Engenders Politics?" In *Italian Feminist Theory and Practice: Equality and Sexual Difference*, edited by Graziella Parati and Rebecca West, translated by Carmen di Cinque, 88–103. London: Associated University Presses, 2002.
Collins, Patricia Hill. *Black Feminist Thought: Knowledge, Consciousness, and the Politics of Empowerment*. New York: Routledge, 2000.
Glissant, Édouard. *Poetics of Relation*. Translated by Betsy Wing. Ann Arbor: University of Michigan Press, 1997.
Haines, Christian P., and Sean Grattan. "Life After the Subject." *Cultural Critique* 96, no. 36 (Spring 2017): 1–36. https://muse.jhu.edu/article/669098.
Harney, Stefano, and Fred Moten. *The Undercommons: Fugitive Planning and Black Study*. New York: Minor Compositions, 2013.
Honig, Bonnie. *A Feminist Theory of Refusal*. Cambridge, MA: Harvard University Press, 2021.
Huzar, Timothy J. "A Politics of Indifference: Reading Cavarero, Rancière and Arendt." *Paragraph* 42, no. 2 (2019): 205–22. https://doi.org/10.3366/para.2019.0299.
———. "Apprehending Care in the Flesh: Reading Cavarero with Spillers." *Diacritics* 49, no. 3 (2021): 6–27. https://doi.org/10.1353/dia.2021.0027.
———. "The Public Library, Democracy and Rancière's Poetics of Politics." *Information Research* 18, no. 3 (2013). http://www.informationr.net/ir/18-3/colis/paperC15.html#.YW0vsXUecUE.
———. "Toward a Fugitive Politics: Arendt Rancière, Hartman." *Cultural Critique* 110 (Winter 2021): 1–48. https://doi.org/10.5749/culturalcritique.110.2021.0001.
———. "Violence, Vulnerability, Ontology: Insurrectionary Humanism in Cavarero and Butler." In *Toward a Feminist Ethics of Nonviolence*, edited by Timothy J. Huzar and Clare Woodford, 151–160. New York: Fordham University Press, 2021.
Lacoue-Labarthe, Philippe. "The Response of Ulysses." In *Who Comes after the Subject?* edited by Eduardo Cadava, Peter Connor, and Jean-Luc Nancy. New York: Routledge, 1991.
Le Dœuff, Michèle. *The Philosophical Imaginary*. Translated by Collin Gordon. Stanford, CA: Stanford University Press, 1989.
Lewis, Gail. "Questions of Presence." *Feminist Review* 117, no. 1 (2017): 1–19. https://doi.org/10.1057%2Fs41305-017-0088-1.
Locke, John. *Second Treatise of Government*. South Bend: Infomotions, 2000. ProQuest Ebook Central.
Moten, Fred. *The Universal Machine*. Durham, NC: Duke University Press, 2018.

Nancy, Jean-Luc. *The Birth to Presence*. Translated by Brian Holmes and others. Stanford, CA: Stanford University Press, 1993.

———. *Corpus*. Translated by Richard A. Rand. New York: Fordham University Press, 2008.

———. *The Inoperative Community*. Translated by Peter Connor, Lisa Garbus, Michael Holland, and Simona Sawhney. Minneapolis: University of Minnesota Press, 1991.

———. "Introduction." *Topoi: An International Review of Philosophy* 7, no. 2 (September 1988): 87–92. https://link.springer.com/journal/11245/7/2.

———. Introduction to *Who Comes after the Subject?* edited by Eduardo Cadava, Peter Connor, and Jean-Luc Nancy, 1–8. New York: Routledge, 1991.

Rancière, Jacques. "After What?" In *Who Comes after the Subject?* edited by Eduardo Cadava, Peter Connor, and Jean-Luc Nancy, 246–252. New York: Routledge, 1991.

———. *The Emancipated Spectator*. Translated by Gregory Elliott. London: Verso, 2011.

———. *Hatred of Democracy*. Translated by Steve Corcoran. London: Verso, 2006.

———. *The Ignorant Schoolmaster: Five Lessons in Intellectual Emancipation*. Translated by Kristin Ross. Stanford, CA: Stanford University Press, 1991.

Spillers, Hortense. "Mama's Baby, Papa's Maybe: An American Grammar Book." *Diacritics* 17, no. 2 (Summer 1987): 65–81.

Four

"Taking the Thread for a Walk"[1]

Feminist Resistance to the Philosophical Order in Adriana Cavarero and María Lugones

Paula Landerreche Cardillo

> Emphasizing the craft of weaving bears a political weight, insofar as it becomes necessary to grant that thinking indeed emerges within manual practices, within labor. Perhaps craft and labor are not about turning off the brain but about reactivating different centers. As the weavers' writings and textiles show, ideas became manifest in their physical manipulation of the loom—either unwittingly or with a bit of savvy.
>
> —T'ai Smith[2]

> Skill is the most complete embodiment of craft as an active, relational concept rather than a fixed category.
>
> —Glenn Adamson[3]

Silvia Rivera Cusicanqui gives us the tools to understand the interwoven nature of distinct feminist fights—fights that can extend beyond continental barriers through the notion of *chi'ixi*.[4] This notion refers to a kind of weave whose elements seem disordered and whose combination of different colored strings create a color that is only visible from a distance; but, upon closer look, the different threads that make up the color are revealed as singular and distinct. These differences become a productive force.

In the chapter titled "Oralidad, mirada y memorias del cuerpo en los Andes," Rivera Cusicanqui starts from a double meaning of the notion of thought in *Aymara*. The first meaning is associated with a clear head, which comes from a notion of the sun as clarity. The second meaning is more closely associated with thinking with the heart, although she clarifies that the heart in this case includes the guts and the lungs—understood here as the loci for the bodily functions of absorption and purification. She talks about the second meaning of thought as "the thought of walking, the thought of ritual, the thought of song and dance. And that thought/thinking has to do with memory, or better yet, with the multiple memories that inhabit (post) colonial subjectivities in our area of the Andes."[5] This second form of thought involves memory because it inhabits a form of space that is "inside us," that inhabits us. This already weaves a fabric that is not the space of colonialism and coloniality. I want to dwell on this second form of thought that Rivera Cusicanqui explains, as it resembles Cavarero's reformulation of the task of philosophy through her analysis of Penelope's bodily knowledge in *In Spite of Plato*. What is curious is that although these two accounts were never in conversation with one another, both relate embodied knowledge with practices of weaving, and both accounts require that we conceive of space in different terms.

Rivera Cusicanqui suggests that to think of space differently, we must shift away from thinking of space as a map and, rather, start thinking of it through the texture of cloth.[6] I want to take her suggestion to think space through textile seriously, as I tie it to Cavarero's analysis of Penelope's weaving and unweaving, in which, as I will argue, she seeks to carve out a counter-hegemonic space in which female agency and temporality can unfold in their own terms. My aim is to find other ways to think of space beyond strict boundaries and to look at the ways in which manual practices, such as weaving, but also embodied practices more broadly, such as walking, shape the ways in which we inhabit and share space. Understanding the world through weaving opens up possibilities for political projects that defy the established order inherited from Western categories.

Weaving is often devalorized, left outside narratives of art, and classified as a craft. Craft is oftentimes "coded as feminine or even as 'ethnic.' "[7] This carries with it a devalorization of the work not only of weaving itself but of domestic work, broadly construed. Thus, the activity of weaving, "taking a thread for a walk" in a cyclical loop, is rendered futile and unworthy of any attention in a masculine economy. Furthermore, the labor of weaving, an embodied practice that requires a profound bodily awareness and tacticity, is rendered invisible under the logic that can only apprehend it as an endless cycle of walking the thread.

The knowledge of the craft, what Glenn Adamson calls "skill,"[8] is thus reduced to the reproduction of life rather than to a meaning-making practice. Smith claims, "This is important, for while the field of fine art has a longstanding connection to 'concepts' or 'intellectual labor' in Western culture dating back to the Renaissance (in treatises like Alberti's on architecture or Leonardo's on painting), craft's relationship to 'theory' and 'thinking' in that context has been a bit more tenuous. Craft, it seems, is by definition not an 'intellectual exercise.'"[9] The distinction between craft and intellectual labor is one that has held true for centuries. For example, in Plato we find the expulsion—or perhaps the stark opposition—of the labor of weaving from the labor of philosophy; in the *Phaedo*, Socrates famously compares the work that Penelope, in Homer's *Odyssey*, performs—weaving— to the unphilosophical attitude of the men that are crying upon Socrates's inevitable death. The expulsion of weaving from the work of philosophy in the *Phaedo* comes immediately after the expulsion of women from the room. Socrates asks that his wife, Xanthippe, be removed from the premises so that the properly philosophical conversation can begin,[10] a gesture that is common in Platonic dialogues.[11] And this moment inaugurates in the history of philosophy a devalorization of skill, of what Cavarero will call *metis*.

The exclusion of women and weaving from philosophy and art have ramifications beyond disciplinary boundaries. This exclusion extends to Western political thinking itself. As Cavarero analyzes throughout her work, Plato is not only the "father of philosophy," but he is also the father of political theory, who gives shape to politics in his image.[12] Thus, an exclusion from the task of philosophy also means exclusion from the very way in which the space of politics is constituted, such that any political work—for example, that which Cavarero's Penelope does—is rendered unintelligible. This is even more prominent when the philosophy inherited from Greece becomes the only legitimate form of thinking and thus of shaping the space of political appearance. In this chapter, I want to claim that the exclusion of women in philosophy cannot simply be solved by allowing women to enter the public sphere or spaces of philosophical reflection. Rather, I call into question the very operations that rendered women incapable of examining the modes of producing meaningful knowledge. Cavarero takes on this task systematically throughout her work, beginning in her early book *In Spite of Plato*, which I will focus on here.

In what follows, I will engage in depth with Cavarero's reading of the figure of Penelope within the context of Homer's *Odyssey* and Plato's *Phaedo*. In her reading, weaving takes an important role, and it helps illuminate the exclusion of the practice and the knowledge it produces from the realm of philosophy. Cavarero's reading is indeed the analysis of a figure who weaves (and that, perhaps even more characteristically, unweaves), but it is also a reading that enacts and highlights the practice of weaving as a productive practice. Cavarero turns the task of philosophy upside down through a reading of Penelope that is grounded—perhaps rooted—in bodily knowledge rather than in the Platonic mode of philosophizing that aims to go above our heads to reach the disembodied world of ideas (*eidos*). Cavarero works with the Homeric and Platonic texts as fabrics woven within a symbolic structure that is incapable of understanding the work of Penelope, and, instead, she looks at the texture of the fabric to uncover what it hides: a feminine imaginary that resists the place that was given to women including Penelope but, more importantly, to bodily knowledge. Thus, Cavarero's reading reveals not only Penelope's alien—to the masculine order—imaginary but also the alienness of texture to text.

I will first offer an exegesis of Cavarero's chapter on Penelope in *In Spite of Plato* and explain her methodology and commitment to sexual difference within this chapter as central to understanding her project. I dwell on the closing of the chapter, as I find it shows an important limitation of Cavarero's work. I bring in María Lugones's notion of "active subjectivity" to better understand the shift required to render Cavarero's reading of Penelope intelligible and to reevaluate the place of bodily knowledge in philosophy. I take this reading of Cavarero with Lugones as an encounter that already takes a step back to see Cavarero's work within the cloth of a transnational feminist project rather than enclosed within the symbolic constellation of Western thought.

Cavarero's Penelope

In Homer's *Odyssey*, Penelope plays a rather minor role: she is the wife of the main character, Odysseus, who was left behind when Odysseus went to war. While he remains away, she is harassed by suitors who want to take her hand in marriage. To keep the suitors at bay, Penelope claims that she must first weave a burial cloth for Odysseus's father and that when she finishes that task, she will choose a suitor to marry. Famously, she unweaves at night what she has woven during the day, day by day delaying her delivery to the suitors. This story is often read as Penelope's unending fidelity to Odysseus—for she refused to marry someone else—yet she does not recognize Odysseus when he finally comes back. Thus, her task is rendered futile, for she does not even recognize the man that she was waiting for.

In the *Phaedo*, Plato mentions Penelope's task of weaving and unweaving as "turning the task of Philosophy upside down."[13] The use of this metaphor, according to Cavarero, is misleading. It does not account for the rhythm, bodily knowledge, and design of Penelope's work. Plato takes Penelope as a weaver, never as a philosopher. Furthermore, he takes her to be undoing all the work that the philosopher accomplishes. She weaves: she reestablishes the soul's ties to the body and, in doing so, undoes the task of unweaving from the body that the philosopher does. Thus, Plato encloses Penelope in her room, where she cannot access philosophy. But Penelope does not weave back what the philosophers have unwoven because the task of that philosopher is already displaced from the world that Penelope inhabits. That is Plato's mistake.

Cavarero takes Plato's mention of Penelope in the *Phaedo* as an entry point to a reformulation of the task of philosophy. It is in that quoted fragment that Socrates talks explicitly about the task of philosophy. His analogy with Penelope's task of weaving is highly questionable and opens up a space to undo Plato's formulation:

> The soul of a philosophic man will reason as follows: if it is the task of philosophy to untie the soul from the body, then the soul itself, untied from the body, should not return to prior pleasures and pains, nor deliver itself to their chains, thereby doing Penelope's endless task, as she weaves and unweaves her cloth. Rather, it should secure protection from these, by following discourse [*logismos*] and always keeping within it, by contemplating truth, the divine and what is not appearance, and being nurtured by it. The soul thus believes that it should live for as long as life lasts, and, when life finally comes to an end, the soul goes towards that which is naturally similar to it, free of any human evil.[14]

Here, the task of weaving is equated to that of tying the soul back to the body, delivering oneself into the chains of the body. The task of philosophy according to Plato should be to undo the weaving, to untie, and to strive to untie until the soul can ultimately be delivered to its home, to the eternal truths. Penelope is charged with the mistake of reweaving what she had already unwoven.

Plato takes Penelope as a weaver. He, along with Homer, expels her from the masculine place of the public and writes about her as belonging to a private room, where she is supposed to weave. Penelope is not and does not belong to the space where the philosophers think. Yet, Plato claims that her action of weaving—or rather, reweaving what she had already unwoven—is turning the task of philosophy upside down. He likens those who cry at Socrates's death to Penelope who reweaves. It is the task of the philosopher to untie his soul from the body and return to the eternal truth; crying for Socrates's death is like undoing all the work he had accomplished as a philosopher.

Let me first note that the task that Penelope was given was to weave. The absurdity in her case was to unweave what she had done. Plato's mention of weaving as Penelope's characteristic task is, thus, strange. The second curious thing that Cavarero notes about the mention of Penelope in the *Phaedo* is that her work of weaving and unweaving seems to be incommensurable with the task of untying the soul from the body, yet Plato compares bad philosophers to Penelope. Her work is not important because she weaves or even because she unweaves, for she unweaves in her room, not in the public space of the philosopher who thinks in the *agora*. Rather, it is important that she weaves and unweaves as a rhythmic task, with cadence and a "precise intention."[15] In this sense, Penelope doesn't quite turn the task of philosophy upside down, but rather, she does something that has its own, and altogether different, logic.

Let me take a step back to explain why this is significant for Cavarero. Her methodology, following Luce Irigaray's philosophy of sexual difference, is precisely to show that the form of thinking that takes itself to be universal and (sexually) neutral, is actually localized and sexed. For Cavarero, we cannot take thought outside of the conditions of its productions and its localized character. Additionally, as Cavarero and Irigaray both have shown, philosophical thinking originates from a division of the sexes where only one (the masculine) has the right to practice philosophy. Furthermore, the place of philosophy is the masculine space of the *agora*. For Plato and for Socrates, Penelope could never be a philosopher; it is even comical to think she could (thus, Socrates's dismissal of crying upon his death as a womanly action) since it would represent a contradiction in philosophical thought.[16] But philosophy, despite being localized and sexed, takes itself to be neutral precisely because, since Plato, it begins from a separation of the body and the soul and, therefore, from its own sexed roots. From that moment on, philosophy has inherited more than two millennia of thought that takes itself to be divorced from the conditions of its production, including sexed bodies. This is Cavarero's starting point in criticizing the absurdity of taking up Penelope as the one who turns the task of philosophy upside down, as her own existence within the philosophical world is itself a contradiction.

Cavarero then proceeds to read Penelope within her own logic. Within the Platonic symbolic framework, the philosopher, much like Penelope, is trapped. While Penelope is trapped in the weaving room, the philosopher is trapped in the body. In contrast, what will "free" Penelope from the room is weaving, for she is to weave a cloth that will deliver her to one of her suitors, while the philosopher escapes the body by untying his soul from it. In this sense, Penelope stands opposite of the philosopher; the philosopher, in company, gives speeches, thinks, and in doing so, he slowly unties and unweaves his soul from his body. The woman (Penelope) stays in the home, she weaves, and she lives as a slave to her body. Thus, for Plato, to cry over Socrates's death is "to deliver [your]self to the chains [of the body]," much like for Penelope to finish her weaving would be to deliver herself to her suitor. Thus, she unweaves every night.

For Cavarero, Penelope has to be taken out of the frame of reference from which Plato reads her. In that sense, she is "stealing" Penelope away from Plato. Penelope performs an act of resistance by unweaving, she refuses to deliver herself to the order provided for her. But the work of unweaving and reweaving is more than just resistance to being delivered to her suitors. Cavarero notes that in Homer's tale, Penelope fails to recognize Odysseus upon his return. This illuminates her interpretation of Penelope's endless work. In a first reading, it seems like Homer writes the tale of Penelope to make Odysseus's return more memorable. After all, Penelope had been waiting for him. She had undone all her day's work by night to delay her delivery to another suitor. However, upon Odysseus's return, Penelope claims to not recognize him. This makes it look as though Penelope's unending work was more than just a strategy for delay.

Cavarero tells the reader that Penelope's work appears to nullify any usefulness, including within this usefulness allowing her to wait for Odysseus. She writes that "if measured against the action of the hero, Penelope's time is empty."[17] Her task of weaving and unweaving marks a temporality that does not correspond to that of the epic tale and is not intelligible by its logic. It is not a strategy for delay but rather a rhythm that produces its own temporality. In the same way, the weaving room that Penelope inhabits is not the weaving room that was assigned to her by the patriarchal order that confines her within the borders of the home but, rather, one in which she carves out a space for herself.

It is worth noting that Penelope is not alone in the weaving room. In fact, it is important to Cavarero that she weaves in the company of other women. Penelope and her fellow weavers spend every day in the weaving room that she keeps open through the task of unweaving at night what she had woven in the day. The seemingly endless task of weaving and unweaving is precisely what keeps the weaving room open. It is what has prevented a new patriarch from coming to interrupt the gatherings of these women that weave every day. The weaving room is their space, the space of the weavers' relationality. And the usefulness of Penelope's task is revealed if we understand that she is opening a time and space that allows for possibilities that are different from those assigned to her.[18]

Penelope's rhythmic time/space is impenetrable by the order of the tale, to the point that Odysseus stands outside it. Penelope does not recognize him upon his return because he does not belong to the space she has carved out through her rhythmic task. Ultimately, Penelope does not belong to the private realm of the home that is put in contrast with the public realm of the epic tale. Rather, she belongs to a space that does not correspond to the dichotomy set out by the Homeric epic.

Cavarero reads Penelope's impenetrable time alongside the impenetrable time to which the philosopher tries to ascend. The time of the philosopher is solemn and immobile and, in its own way, impenetrable. It is also not the time of the epic tale but stands beyond in death and, thus, eternity. For Odysseus as well as for the philosopher, death is the goal; it is the entry to eternity. According to Cavarero, for the male philosopher and for the epic hero, death is "an abode, which is immobile."[19]

The epic hero reaches immortality with death through the epic tale; the philosopher reaches immortality with death by reaching the forms. Eternity is the ultimate home. Cavarero claims that the philosopher splits in two, in body and in soul, and preserves only the soul. He thus displaces life from the realm of bodily life. Cavarero positions herself as a reader of Hannah Arendt, who distances herself from a tradition that neglects the fact of birth. For Cavarero, as for Arendt, we cannot speak of life if we do not speak of birth. Their argument is that, by splitting into two, life is neglected for the sake of death and death for so-called eternal life or, rather, an abstraction of life. In this sense, for the philosopher, the body "does not possess a living dimension."[20] For Arendt and for Cavarero, action is rooted in birth and life. However, action for Arendt does not belong in the home but takes place in public. Cavarero takes up Arendt's rescue of birth but reformulates it in her own way. By reading the tale of Penelope differently, she speaks of a different notion of the home, one that does not stand over and against the world of the hero or the philosopher but that gives itself its own conditions for existence. It is marked by its own spatial and temporal logics, embodied in the rhythmic task of weaving and unweaving.

In contrast to the male philosopher or the epic hero, the weaver is tied to finitude. In the Greek world and its inheritors, finitude is undesirable. For that world and its legacy, the finite world is a prison, not a home. But Penelope makes her own home through her rhythmic work. She gives herself the conditions for her existence, belonging neither to the order of the private space nor to the order of the public space. Her action has a purpose, but her purpose is not given by any outside rules. It is given through the action itself, through the weaving and the unweaving, which opens up a space/time of its own that is impenetrable by the order established for her. She is not split in two but rather she has an intelligence that is whole.

Penelope Trapped in the Weaving Room

I want to pause to examine the closing scene of Cavarero's chapter. She ends by remarking that "in the weaving room, these women neither separate their philosophy from the body to grant it eternal duration nor entrust their experience of finitude to death in an arrogant desire for immortality. Having let the men go forth to their adventures at sea, they stay together quietly, exchanging looks and words rooted in the individual wholeness of their existence."[21] It is unsettling that Penelope remains enclosed within the walls of the weaving room. In part, this is a problem of the example used by Cavarero. While this example gives us a way to read Penelope differently and to rescue her from Plato's ridiculing, such that the Platonic view of the task of philosophy simultaneously can be complicated, the tale of Penelope told by Homer nevertheless does leave her in the room while Odysseus travels the world, participates in glorious adventures, and ultimately dies in battle. Cavarero's aim is not to change the story but rather to steal

Penelope from the male imaginary and read her otherwise. This means that Penelope lives the same fate that Homer assigned to her, but the way in which she lives this fate is inscribed within a different framework given by Cavarero's feminist reading—a feminist one that gives a different meaning and purpose to her seemingly meaningless work. However, Cavarero closes the door on Penelope and reinforces her place in the weaving room with the other women "weaving and laughing in their quiet abode."[22]

Clearly, this image we are left with seems all too limited as a model for feminist agency. Yet, I nevertheless want to argue that if we read Cavarero carefully and listen to her philosophical work, not only her rhetorical devices, the fate of Penelope is not to stay enclosed in her room but rather to create her own home. The importance of her work lies not in the place where she weaves, or even in the work of weaving and unweaving, but in her disruption of the order set in place. The importance of her work is that she opens a time/space that does not belong to the preestablished order, that gives itself its own conditions.

Timothy J. Huzar reads the time/space that Cavarero's Penelope inaugurates within the framework of a politics of indifference.[23] Huzar explains that Cavarero's Penelope is indifferent to the symbolic order that encloses her in the weaving room. Thus, the place of weaving is already transformed into a fugitive space of indifference, where Penelope, along with the women in the weaving room, live "in the undercommons of Ithaca."[24] Although I agree with Huzar that we must read the weaving room as a space not apprehended by the symbolic order that encloses Penelope to the private, I propose that we read her as actively resisting, rather than as being indifferent to, the symbolic order that encloses her. Although this shift from indifference to active resistance is small, a reformulation of the notion of activity—which is not opposed to passivity but, rather, has its own logic—can help us understand the ways in which a philosophy of sexual difference already resists the logic of patriarchy. To use Bonnie Honig's conceptualization of *feminist refusal*, where Cavarero is an important figure, I take Cavarero's reading of Penelope to be an "entry into a contest over meaning, a bid for the posterity that might make a past episode into the start of a feminist future."[25] Here, I take María Lugones's conceptualization of *active subjectivity* to be crucial in understanding this shift.

I must first explain that *active subjectivity* is a term that, for Lugones, comes from a mode of relationality, an encounter. *Encounter* is a technical term that Sara Ahmed develops in *Strange Encounters: Embodied Others in Postcoloniality*. For Ahmed, an encounter is the process in which two or more bodies come into contact, such that their coming into contact reconfigures the bodies. Thus, an encounter requires a shift away from the familiar but *not* toward the recognition of the other as not familiar (and therefore stranger). Rather, it is a complete shift, where one is no longer in a space of familiarity. In that sense, the encounter is a shift of the boundaries that make us feel at home (in our bodies and in the world). It is for this reason that Ahmed thinks of the encounter through the skin—that which delimits our bodies at the same time that it opens them up to affective encounters with other bodies.[26] The encounter shapes space and time insofar as it allows us to inhabit the space that is only opened by the encounter itself. Ahmed is clear that although the encounter might involve facing someone—that is, an encounter might come from a face-to-face meeting that allows for the opening of the space that brings us closer—facing each other is not a necessary condition. Likewise, an encounter does not presuppose the category of a person but "suggests a coming together of *at least two elements*."[27] Reading is an example of an encounter that comes up multiple times throughout the text.

To take the reading of a text as an encounter, we must analyze how the encounter between text and reader comes to be; that is, we must analyze the encounter as prior to the reader and the text. Ahmed clarifies that this does not mean that neither the reader nor the text existed before the encounter, but it forces us to recognize that the encounter between any given text and any given reader gives life to the text.[28] Yet, if the encounter is that which changes the boundaries of the elements involved, it seems like the encounter between reader and text is one-sided, as the text cannot be changed by the encounter, at least not what has already been written and fixed in print. But to think of a text as that which has already been set in print, unchangeable in its fixity, is a reductive way to think of texts. To begin with, texts become important in their circulation and their place in history. They are as much what they contain as what use has been given to them, how they have been read, who they have influenced, and how their meanings have changed over time. In other words, texts are a part of history, and, just like bodies, they have been inscribed and reinscribed with meaning in their multiple encounters with readers. Thus, to encounter a text is never only to encounter the materiality of the printed text but to encounter the text as it has become materialized through history. Ahmed speaks of the skin in similar ways: "The skin is not simply matter in place but rather it involves a process of materialization."[29] The encounter between reader and text thus changes the boundaries of the skin of the reader and the skin of the text as that which has been materialized in history but not fully determined by it. This encounter, then, allows for the surprise that comes from the lack of full determination.

The encounter between reader and text is that which allows for a productive reading. Thus, I take this notion of encounter to illuminate Lugones's reading of the Chicana thinker and writer Gloria Anzaldúa. This concept can also help illuminate Cavarero's reading of Penelope. I will explain the relationship between these two encounters, as well as their profound differences, in the following section. I will also explain Lugones's notion of "active subjectivity" as a way to illuminate my reading of Cavarero's chapter on Penelope specifically and her contribution to a reformulation of the task of philosophy more generally.

Active Subjectivity and Sense Making

In her paper titled "From within Germinative Stasis: Creating Active Subjectivity, Resistant Agency," María Lugones engages in an encounter with the work of Anzaldúa. Lugones's encounter with Anzaldúa, much like Cavarero's encounter with Penelope, allows her to see the resistance that has been invisibilized by a framework that sees their actions as nonsensical. Here, I read Cavarero with Huzar. As he beautifully puts it, "Penelope is sensed—Cavarero receives a flavour (*un sapore*) of this Penelope—in a way that, presumably, she was not before, and if she is apprehended by Cavarero then perhaps she is not also captured."[30] Cavarero's reading already produces a space where her encounter with Penelope can happen without apprehending her but, rather, by writing and theorizing with her. In a similar way, Lugones explicitly describes her reading of Anzaldúa as carefully avoiding appropriating Anzaldúa's path, instead attempting to "try to take lessons from her inhabitation of space; her complex incarnate memory; her brooding her self into being; her isolating her self from the pulls toward normalcy, passivity, subordination."[31]

Lugones's encounter with Anzaldúa helps her get closer to her text, to inhabit the space that her text opens up, while opening herself up to it. She sees the ways in which Anzaldúa's text is productive, where it produces a resisting subjectivity and not only an oppressed one, and she sees the ways in which Anzaldúa opens up possibilities not only for herself as a resistant agent but also for her readers. Lugones claims that "Anzaldúa recognizes here that the possibility of resistance depends on this creation of a new identity, a new world of sense, in the borders."³² Lugones becomes this self in the borders by allowing herself to be touched by Anzaldúa's text and open up a new world of sense.

Similarly, I take Cavarero to see a place of resistance in her reading of Penelope. She opens up a reading that takes the decisive moment when Odysseus comes back home, when Penelope does not recognize him, as her final act of resistance. This moment in the story allows for a reading of Penelope that inhabits a different symbolic universe, where her action of weaving can be read by a logic that does not reduce her to the space the masculine imaginary has designated for her but by a logic that is able to see the resisting strategy that she embodies in her tale. Cavarero occupies this position with Penelope, which allows her to see Penelope through another logic and to open other possibilities.

This step is crucial to understanding the possibilities of active resistance that I want to highlight in contrast to Huzar's reading. I want to be cautious when I make this distinction because I understand the politics of indifference and the notion of the undercommons to be in themselves resistant to the logic of oppression, which is close to my reading. However, I think Cavarero aims to go one step further and claim that Penelope already threatens that logic. Her engagements with Plato—from her reading of Penelope in *In Spite of Plato* to the later ones (including the untranslated and recently published *Platone*)—aim to pull the thread that threatens the patriarchal logic that structures the Platonic system the West inherited.³³ Pulling this thread already reformulates the task of philosophy into a form of thinking that is rooted in embodied knowledge rather than abstract ideas. Cavarero's irreverence, as Huzar puts it,³⁴ becomes her strategy of sense-making that allows her to make Penelope, and herself in the process of reading, a resistant actor.

Lugones, with Anzaldúa, sees the possibility of sense-making as an active resistance against logics of oppression. She writes, "From within this position [her personal engagement with Anzaldúa's text] I learned to block the effectiveness of oppressive meanings and logics. This blocking is a *constant, recurrent, first gesture* in coming to understand the limits of the possible. The inhabitation of this place/vantage enables me to withdraw my energies from cementing and contributing to the relations of power that define me as servile or as nonsensical."³⁵ This kind of reading is a productive sense-making practice in that it uncovers in the reading itself something that was made unintelligible by the framework that enclosed the text. Lugones reads in Anzaldúa a notion of resistance that can only be made intelligible through a shift in sense-making practices. This is similar to what Cavarero does through the theft of Penelope, which illuminates how the Platonic framework is insufficient to make sense of Penelope's practice of weaving and unweaving.

For Lugones, it is imperative that we leave to the side the modern conception of agency and instead start to think about a notion of resistance that can account for "a making of oneself against the logic, the sense, the weight of oppressions."[36] She explains that the modern notion of agency, rooted in individuality, "presupposes *ready-made hierarchical worlds of sense* in which individuals form intentions, make choices, and carry out actions in the ready-made terms of those worlds."[37] And it is because agency is well-embedded in the modern colonial universe of sense and its hierarchy of values that it is not a useful concept to think possibilities of liberation. Instead, Lugones proposes that we think of what she calls an "active subjectivity." The active subject, she claims, "concocts sense away from the encasement of dominant sense."[38] This is precisely what Cavarero reads as Penelope's activity of weaving and unweaving: it is a mode of sense-making that does not correspond to the one she has been encapsulated within, and she, along with her fellow weavers, creates a space of resistance that moves away from a logic of individuality to a logic of relationality. Lugones calls this space of resistance a "germinative stasis," and it is curious that Cavarero, in her most recent work, uses the language of germination as well. *Democrazia Sorgiva*, translated as *Surging Democracy* but carrying connotations of the process of germination, explores the notion of democracy specifically but of politics more generally sprouting out of a moment of relationality, much like the weaving room of Penelope. To Cavarero, "surging democracy" is also a break, a stasis, that breaks open the system of domination and allows for a contest over meaning and the space of politics to take place.[39] From within germinative stasis, one resists the systems of meaning that encase them through a development of alternative meaning systems.

Let me take the time now to explain what I see as the crucial differences between Cavarero's encounter with Penelope and Lugones's encounter with Anzaldúa. For starters, and perhaps most importantly, Cavarero's encounter with Penelope takes place through her reading of an ancient text, written—and read for millennia—within a distinctly masculine imaginary. Although Cavarero's reading is decidedly irreverent, it is nonetheless a reading of a fictional text produced by a man (or maybe multiple men, as Homer's authorship of the *Odyssey* is contested). In contrast, Lugones's encounter with Anzaldúa is an encounter with what Anzaldúa herself refers to as her *autohistoria/teoría*, which is a writing that comes from a living, embodied person who has suffered the effects of oppression in ways similar to Lugones's own lived experience. Thus, a comparison seems almost out of place. However, I take Cavarero's task of reading to be a practice that very much makes a text come to life.[40]

Yet, a limitation of Cavarero's work (and this extends far beyond her reading of *The Odyssey*) is that she consistently uses literary examples as her basis for theorization. This brings with it some problems: the first and most obvious one in the case I am exploring is that the outcome of Penelope's story will always remain the same, regardless of any reframing that we might perform. In this sense, Cavarero's is not a literary experiment of changing a story but, rather, a philosophical encounter with a text that produces with it a different meaning. The second problem is that the texts Cavarero often rereads are among those most read in the Western tradition. Given this, producing a rereading, as liberatory as this might be, already reinforces their place in the canon.[41] Finally and most importantly, Cavarero's use of literary examples keeps her from speaking to actual, living cases of oppression and their effects. Instead, she explores abstract examples that seem to universalize the very experiences of oppression, something that she explicitly aims to resist. In contrast, Lugones inserts her own experience into the text, although sometimes it becomes imperceptible, as she adds out of context windows into her life and her relations to other women in footnotes and floating paragraphs throughout her work, most prominently in her book *Pilgrimages/Peregrinajes*, where she often inserts such passages in Spanish.[42]

Just as Cavarero does not tire from pointing to the ways Plato's texts are plagued with a metaphorical use of the body/corporeality that he cannot escape,[43] it is important for me, at this point, to talk about the ways in which Cavarero's own analysis of bodily knowledge and the importance of physicality comes from the use of textual examples that are more often than not metaphorical. Such is the case of Penelope for Cavarero. In the example of weaving, one to which she often turns,[44] bodily knowledge is situated within a literary example, which obscures the ways in which the actual practices of weaving have been marginalized and reduced to nothing but the cyclical futility of feminine work, not to mention the broader ways in which a marginalization of bodily knowledge and embodied forms of resistance operate in the actual world. I want to be cautious because, although Cavarero often writes within the canon of Western philosophy, she is clear that this is in and of itself a necessary strategy to change structures of oppression. In *Conceiving Life*, Patrick Hanafin makes a compelling argument as to why a book like *In Spite of Plato* is necessary for the liberation of women from patriarchal structures that limit our (reproductive) possibilities in the world. For Cavarero, Hanafin argues, an activist practice that secures the right of women to decide to have an abortion has to be accompanied by a change in the symbolic structure that renders women as incapable of self-determination.[45] Furthermore, I want to argue that the driving argument of *In Spite of Plato* is that the bodies of women—and not so much of women, but of bodies capable of gestating—cannot figure in the Western political and philosophical canon; therefore, politics cannot account/make space for and, thus, legislate about gestating bodies. Here, Cavarero's commitment to a feminism of sexual difference is evident; she takes from Irigaray the insight that "in order to make possible to think through, and live, this difference, we must reconsider the whole problematic of *space* and *time*"[46] and that a feminist project requires that we fundamentally question the shape of the world, the figures that make it up, and what they allow.

Part of Cavarero's insistence on going back to ancient philosophy in general, and to Plato in particular, is that she sees there the birthing moment of Western thinking, where some of the original tensions, buried in patriarchal theoretical thinking, show themselves to be constitutive of philosophical and political thinking. She claims that "the philosophy of antiquity posits itself at the onset of our history, making its mark on the destiny of the so-called West."[47] Thus, her work of "stealing back" Penelope relies on the work of unweaving the fabric that makes up the beginning of the Western tradition and looking at the very threads that constitute the fabric of theory it has handed down. Cavarero is also clear that there is an intricate co-constitution between the sphere of philosophy and the sphere of politics.

And yet, reading Cavarero through Lugones's notion of active subjectivity allows us to see her recounting of Penelope's story as one that fundamentally challenges not only the task of philosophy but also the ways in which the symbolic structures make certain forms of political resistance, namely those that arise at the margins, unintelligible, or render them as apolitical—to use Huzar's term, indifferent. If we take Cavarero's claim that the philosopher created the space of politics in his own image, it is important that we see the profound challenge her reading of Penelope poses not only to the order of philosophy but also to the order of politics. We must, in other words, reconceive of the place of politics as well as the place of philosophy. Here, Lugones's work is illuminating.

On Walking

Lugones begins the introduction to her book *Pilgrimages/Peregrinajes* by defining what she means by *pilgrimage*. This term has a strange status, as it serves as a methodological description of the book rather than a thematic one. The book, as well as the concept of pilgrimage, "moves through different levels of liberatory work in company forged through a practice of *tantear* for meaning, for the limits of possibility."[48] As a practice of circulation, of movement—be it as an offering or as an attempt to look for something different, something better—pilgrimage is thought by Lugones through a way of knowing that requires feeling the very boundaries of the space of possibilities and, with it, the very boundaries of ourselves and our relations with others. She locates the possibilities of pilgrimage not only in the open spaces where hundreds of bodies can come together, as Cavarero does in *Surging Democracy*, but also in those spaces that seem enclosed, guarded, normed, or repressive.[49] She practices the task of tantear to "accommodate different levels of comprehension and incomprehension"[50] that in turn determine what counts as political.[51]

Lugones sees the possibility to find means of liberations even through the confined spaces that have been assigned to the oppressed. She disregards the dichotomy, exemplified in the tale of Penelope, between the public open space of the epic hero and the private closed space of the weaver. And she also resists the impulse to call one of these a political form of resisting and the other non-political, fundamentally questioning what constitutes the boundaries between public and private, political and non-political.

Unlike for Cavarero, whose analysis takes place in the philosophical imaginary of Plato, Lugones is clear that the act of resisting is one that is placed in history, in the concrete situations we face, with particular histories of fragmentation, exclusion, enclosures. Pilgrimage is, then, what allows Lugones to move between levels of intelligibility, between senses of what counts as politics, and beyond oppressive structures. Lugones's encounter with Anzaldúa is important because she takes from it a notion of resistance, namely active subjectivity. There is a second encounter that Lugones cites that prompts a discussion of an active form of subjectivity that resists oppressive structures and, at the same time, conceptualizes the space of resistance beyond the enclosure of a place like Penelope's weaving room.

In a long footnote to the last chapter of *Pilgrimages/Peregrinajes* titled "The Tactical Strategies of the Streetwalker/*Estrategias Tácticas de la Callejera*," she recounts her encounter with a woman that worked at the mental institution where she had been held against her will.[52] She describes having found company with a young woman who worked as a sex worker and as a housekeeper in the mental institution; they shared with each other the violence they had endured in the enclosed spaces that, in some way or another, they called home. The unnamed woman, Lugones explains, had no home; she occupied other people's homes, police stations, and other spaces. Lugones, on the other hand, did have a home (although her home was the asylum, and her home before that also represented a space of violence for her). Given their complex relationships to home, both found "freer" motility in the street.[53]

Throughout the chapter she moves thinking to the street, or rather, thinks at "street level" as a way to destabilize the distinction between the private and the public, between places of safety and places of violence that women know all too well can never be easily parsed out. This move allows her to explore other practices of sense-making. She develops the notion of the streetwalker as a woman who is not at ease at home. She must, therefore, make a home for herself, and she does so in streetwalking, in leaving the "home" that confined her to a determined space. The streetwalker is a tactical thinker and an active subject. In her walking, she undoes the static notions of space confining by the dominating order. In the street, she finds spaces for gathering, movable spaces that perform a germinative stasis in their coming into being as relational spaces. She calls these movable spaces "hangouts," which are "spaces that cannot be kept captive by the public/private split. They are worldly, contestatory, concrete spaces within geographies sieged by and in defiance of logics and structures of domination."[54] Lugones writes of the tactical thinker in opposition to the strategist, who views the world from above, as a map, to use Rivera Cusicanqui's words. The strategist assumes total knowledge of the world, as opposed to the localized knowledge of the streetwalker, who understands—at street level—the world through the tactile practice of tantear, through her bodily knowledge that carries with her memory.

We can think of Penelope and the weavers as streetwalkers. Under the Platonic view, their task is senseless. The Platonic view is the strategists' view, which distributes tasks and spaces from above, incapable of seeing the internal movements of the tactical thinker. To understand this, we have to shift levels of intelligibility and sensibility to uncover new "senses of the possible."[55] To think tactically requires that we understand bodily knowledge as legitimate knowledge, that we understand that walking and "taking the thread for a walk" are those practices that open up space for these forms of resistance and refusal of the established order. It also requires that we understand the "agential" beyond an individualist logic of autonomy, instead learning to see active subjectivities in the weaver and the walker who act in common, not reactively, to establish the parameters for their own activities.

Conclusion

Throughout this chapter, I argued that Cavarero's reading of Penelope aims to fundamentally question and undo the philosophical framework that reduces the task of philosophy to disembodied knowledge. This reduced notion of the task of philosophy is also an exclusion of certain bodies and certain practices from the activity of philosophizing. Reading Cavarero with Lugones allows me to show that Penelope's activity gains political force as it disrupts the framework that encloses her body and her work in a room with seemingly no political significance. Rather, Penelope disrupts the notion of a political agent (one that aims to maintain the exclusion and hierarchy that enclosed her in the weaving room in the first place) and the time and space of politics and philosophy.

Lugones's notion of the streetwalker is an important addition to Cavarero's reading of Penelope because she highlights the mobility of relational spaces and places for political resistance. In reading the streetwalker next to the weaver, we can understand both as tactical thinkers that create their own homes and spaces for political action, spaces that are situated and embodied and that ultimately challenge the age-long distinction between a non-political private sphere and a political public sphere. Reading Cavarero after Lugones shows that Cavarero did not close the door to Penelope after all. We can read Cavarero's Penelope as being situated not enclosed in a room but, rather, as an active subject who encounters others in the world and who, by the tactile practice of tantear, creates meaning with those around her.

Notes

1. The title of this chapter refers to the 2019 title of the exhibit on Anni Albers's work at the Modern Museum of Art, New York, which is a play on Paul Klee's description of drawing as "taking a line for a walk." In this reformulation of Klee's definition, weaving (instead of drawing) is to take the thread for a walk.

2. T'ai Smith, *Bauhaus Weaving Theory: From Feminine Craft to Mode of Design* (Minneapolis: University of Minnesota Press, 2014), xxvi.

3. Glenn Adamson, *Thinking Through Craft* (London: Berg Publishers, 2007), 4.

4. See Silvia Rivera Cusicanqui, *Un Mundo Ch'ixi Es Posible* (Buenos Aires: Tinta Limón, 2018).

5. Rivera Cusicanqui, *Un Mundo Ch'ixi*, 121. All translations of this text are by the author.

6. Rivera Cusicanqui, *Un Mundo Ch'ixi*, 126.

7. Adamson, *Thinking Through Craft*, 5.

8. Adamson, *Thinking Through Craft*, 4.

9. Smith, *Bauhaus Weaving Theory*, xxi.

10. Plato, *Phaedo*, 60a.

11. This is the case in the *Symposium*, for example, when the flute player (a woman) is excused from her duties before the series of speeches commence. Plato, *Symposium*, 176e.

12. See Adriana Cavarero, "Theory and Politics in Plato's *Republic*," in *Contemporary Encounters with Ancient Practice*, ed. Jacob Greentine and David Messing, trans. Paula Landerreche Cardillo (Edinburgh: Edinburgh University Press, Forthcoming).

13. Plato cited in Adriana Cavarero, *In Spite of Plato: Feminist Rewriting of Ancient Philosophy*, trans. Serena Anderlini-D'Onofrio and Áine O'Healy (New York: Routledge, 1995), 23. My references to Plato's text are from Cavarero's *In Spite of Plato*. The translations of Plato in the book are from Cavarero's Italian rendering of the Greek text, not an English translation. No English translation maps well onto the quoted passages in Cavarero's book.

14. *Phaedo*, 84a–b, as quoted in Cavarero, *In Spite of Plato*, 11.

15. Cavarero, *In Spite of Plato*, 28.

16. See Adriana Cavarero, "The Need for a Sexed Thought" in *Italian Feminist Thought*, ed. Paola Bono and Sandra Kemp (Oxford: Blackwell, 1991), 181–85.

17. Cavarero, *In Spite of Plato*, 17.

18. In *What's the Use? On the Uses of Use*, Sara Ahmed describes the scene of a postbox that was "put out of use" when a bird put its nest inside it. She explains that the postbox has been put out of use because it has been occupied by the bird: "it is providing a home for nesting birds." Although the postbox is out of use for sending mail, it is clearly in use by the birds. She explains, however, that the intended user and intended use have changed. In the eyes of the postal service, the box is now useless; it cannot aid in the transportations of letters, but for the birds, the postbox has provided a refuge, just as the weaving room provided a relational space for Penelope and the weavers. Although her task appears useless for Plato and Homer, in fact, her task has use in that it provides a relational space that could not exist without Penelope unweaving at night what she wove during the day. See Sara Ahmed, *What's the Use? On the Uses of Use* (Durham, NC: Duke University Press, 2019), 33.

19. Cavarero, *In Spite of Plato*, 23.
20. Cavarero, *In Spite of Plato*, 26.
21. Cavarero, *In Spite of Plato*, 30.
22. Cavarero, *In Spite of Plato*, 30.
23. Timothy J. Huzar, "A Politics of Indifference: Reading Cavarero, Rancière and Arendt," *Paragraph* 42, no. 2 (2019): 205–22.
24. Huzar, "A Politics of Indifference," 218.
25. Bonnie Honig, *A Feminist Theory of Refusal* (Cambridge, MA: Harvard University Press, 2021), xiv. Although this formulation corresponds more directly to Honig's discussion of Saidiya Hartman, I am convinced by Rachel Silverbloom's and Rachel Jones's readings of Cavarero—in particular, the claim that Cavarero's chapter on Penelope enacts a methodology, the practice of "stealing," which like critical fabulation confronts the hegemonic meaning of colonial hetero-patriarchy. See Rachel Silverbloom, "Stealing and Critical Fabulation: The Counter-Historical Methods of Adriana Cavarero and Saidiya Hartman"; and Rachel Jones "Inclining toward New Forms of Life: Cavarero, Agamben, and Hartman," both in this volume.
26. Sara Ahmed, *Strange Encounters: Embodied Others in Postcoloniality* (New York: Routledge, 2000), 45. See also the skin of the community essay.
27. Ahmed, *Strange Encounters*, 7.
28. Ahmed, *Strange Encounters*, 7.
29. Ahmed, *Strange Encounters*, 45. Ahmed borrows the language of *materialization* from Judith Butler. See Judith Butler, *Bodies That Matter: On the Discursive Limits of Sex* (New York: Routledge, 1993).
30. Huzar, "A Politics of Indifference," 217.
31. María Lugones, "From within Germinative Stasis: Creating Active Subjectivity, Resistant Agency," in *Entre Mundos/Among Worlds: New Perspectives in Gloria E. Anzaldúa*, ed. Ana Louise Keating (New York: Palgrave Macmillan, 2005), 85.
32. María Lugones, "On Borderlands/La Frontera: An Interpretative Essay," *Hypatia* 7, no. 4 (1992): 31.
33. Adriana Cavarero, *Platone*, ed. Olivia Guaraldo (Milan: Raffaello Cortina Editore, 2018).
34. Huzar, "A Politics of Indifference," 213.
35. Lugones, "Germinative Stasis," 85 (emphasis original).
36. Lugones, "Germinative Stasis," 86.
37. Lugones, "Germinative Stasis," 86 (emphasis original).
38. Lugones, "Germinative Stasis," 86–87.
39. Adriana Cavarero, *Surging Democracy: Notes on Hannah Arendt's Political Thought*, trans. Matthew Gervase (Stanford, CA: Stanford University Press, 2021).
40. In fact, Andrea J. Pitts's reading of Anzaldúa, although centered on *autohistoria/teoría* as a bodily form of writing, argues that reading for Anzaldúa is itself also embodied. They write, in reference to Anzaldúa's claim that different readers will find different "entradas" to her work, that "this spatial metaphor, in addition to presenting writing as a sensuously embodied act, also supports an

embodied account of reading, that is, a view that works against the image of a solitary reader who attempts to encounter a text abstractly. Prominent theorists of Spanish-language Latin American literature also defend such a view of reading. For example, both Sylvia Molloy and Doris Sommer have argued in their respective works that cultural and historical trajectories that bring a reader to a text will shape how a reader encounters the possibilities for meanings in a text." Andrea J. Pitts, "Gloria E. Anzaldúa's Autohistoria-Teoría as an Epistemology of Self-Knowledge/Ignorance," *Hypatia* 31, no. 2 (2016): 360–61, https://doi.org/10.1111/hypa.12235; Gloria Anzaldua, "To(o) Queer the Writer—Loca, Escritora y Chicana," in *The Gloria Anzaldúa Reader*, ed. Ana Louise Keating (Durham, NC: Duke University Press Books, 2009), 174.

41. There are, however, exceptions to this. For example, in *Relating Narratives* Cavarero reads Gertrude Stein's *The Autobiography of Alice Toklas* in an engagement that stands close to Lugones's own engagement with Anzaldúa. Another example is the chapter titled "The Hurricane Does Not Roar in Pantameter" in *For More than One Voice*, a chapter dedicated to Kamau Brathwaite.

42. Lugones's use of both Spanish and explanation is in itself a mode of resisting. She often leaves these notes out of context precisely as a way to resist discursive modes that privilege clarity and purity. This is clear in chapter 6, "Purity, Impurity and Separation," where she narrates the process of her mother's cooking and remarks that her mother will make sure you get to the end of the puzzle "because she hasn't stored that much resistance." The explanation of her mother's cooking becomes a mirror of the structure of Lugones's writing. In María Lugones, *Pilgrimages/Peregrinajes: Theorizing Coalition Against Multiple Oppressions* (New York: Rowman and Littlefield, 2003), 124.

43. See Adriana Cavarero, *Stately Bodies: Literature, Philosophy, and the Question of Gender*, trans. Robert de Lucca and Deanna Shemek (Ann Arbor: University of Michigan Press, 2002).

44. See, for example, Adriana Cavarero, *In Spite of Plato*; *Stately Bodies*; and "Theory and Politics in Plato's *Republic*."

45. Patrick Hanafin, *Conceiving Life: Reproductive Politics and the Law in Contemporary Italy* (Abingdon, OX: Routledge, 2007), 41–43. I want to make clear that use of the language *woman* to refer to people who can get pregnant is Hanafin and Cavarero's. It is important to note that not all women and not only women are capable of getting pregnant. I believe Cavarero's analysis can account for this and, in fact, that her work allows us to understand all of the different ways in which bodies that are capable of gestating have not figured in political, legal, and philosophical frameworks.

46. Luce Irigaray, "Sexual Difference," in *An Ethics of Sexual Difference*, trans. Carolyn Burke and Gillian C. Gill (Ithaca, NY: Cornell University Press, 1993), 7.

47. Cavarero, *In Spite of Plato*, 4.

48. Lugones, *Pilgrimages/Peregrinajes*, 1. *Tantear* means to hold one's hands out to measure, with the body, the space, around us. It is what we do when we

are trying to orient ourselves in a dark room. It is also how we negotiate borders, limits. Lugones says, "I use the Spanish word 'tantear' both in the sense of exploring someone's inclinations about a particular issue and in the sense of 'tantear en la oscuridad.'" Tantear is a tactile practice of orientation and negotiation.

49. Lugones, *Pilgrimages/Peregrinajes*, 1.
50. Lugones, *Pilgrimages/Peregrinajes*, 1.
51. Lugones, *Pilgrimages/Peregrinajes*, 2.
52. Claudia Acuña recounts Lugones's story from "the scene of the crime," where Lugones was first confined to a small house until she finally managed to escape, was caught, and then put in a "manicomnio" or "insane asylum" by her parents, as she describes in *Pilgrimages*. See "Hasta siempre, maestra," *lavaca* (blog), July 14, 2020, https://www.lavaca.org/notas/hasta-siempre-maestra/.
53. Lugones, *Pilgrimages/Peregrinajes*, 209 unnumbered footnote.
54. Lugones, *Pilgrimages/Peregrinajes*, 221.
55. Lugones, *Pilgrimages/Peregrinajes*, 1.

Bibliography

Acuña, Claudia. "Hasta siempre, maestra." *lavaca* (blog), July 14, 2020. https://www.lavaca.org/notas/hasta-siempre-maestra/.

Adamson, Glenn. *Thinking Through Craft*. London: Bloomsbury Visual Arts, 2019.

Ahmed, Sara. *Strange Encounters: Embodied Others in Post-Coloniality*. New York: Routledge, 2000.

———. *What's the Use? On the Uses of Use*. Durham, NC: Duke University Press, 2019.

Anzaldúa, Gloria. "To(o) Queer the Writer—Loca, Escritora y Chicana." In *The Gloria Anzaldúa Reader*, edited by AnaLouise Keating, 163–75. Durham, NC: Duke University Press, 2009.

Butler, Judith. *Bodies That Matter: On the Discursive Limits of Sex*. New York: Routledge, 2011.

Cavarero, Adriana. *For More than One Voice: Toward a Philosophy of Vocal Expression*. Translated by Paul A. Kottman. Stanford, CA: Stanford University Press, 2005.

———. "The Need for a Sexed Thought." In *Italian Feminist Thought*, edited by Paola Bono and Sandra Kemp, 181–85. Oxford: Blackwell, 1991.

———. *Platone*. Edited by Olivia Guaraldo. Milan: Raffaello Cortina Editore, 2018.

———. *In Spite of Plato: Feminist Rewriting of Ancient Philosophy*. Translated by Serena Anderlini-D'Onofrio and Áine O'Healy. Cambridge: Polity Press, 1995.

———. *Stately Bodies: Literature, Philosophy, and the Question of Gender*. Translated by Robert de Lucca and Deanna Shemek. Ann Arbor: University of Michigan Press, 2002.

———. *Surging Democracy: Notes on Hannah Arendt's Political Thought*. Stanford, CA: Stanford University Press, 2021.

———. "Theory and Politics in Plato's Republic." In *Contemporary Encounters with Ancient Practice*, edited by Jacob Greentine and David Messing. Translated by Paula Landerreche Cardillo. Edinburgh: Edinburgh University Press, Forthcoming.

Hanafin, Patrick. *Conceiving Life: Reproductive Politics and the Law in Contemporary Italy*. Abingdon, OX: Routledge, 2007.

Honig, Bonnie. *A Feminist Theory of Refusal*. Cambridge, MA: Harvard University Press, 2021.

Huzar, Timothy J. "A Politics of Indifference: Reading Cavarero, Rancière and Arendt." *Paragraph* 42, no. 2 (2019): 205–22.

Irigaray, Luce. *An Ethics of Sexual Difference*. Translated by Carolyn Burke and Gillian Gill. Ithaca, NY: Cornell University Press, 1993.

Lugones, María. "From within Germinative Stasis: Creating Active Subjectivity, Resistant Agency." In *EntreMundos/AmongWorlds: New Perspectives on Gloria E. Anzaldúa*, edited by AnaLouise Keating, 85–99. New York: Palgrave Macmillan US, 2005.

———. "On Borderlands/La Frontera: An Interpretive Essay." *Hypatia* 7, no. 4 (1992): 31–37.

———. *Pilgrimages/Peregrinajes: Theorizing Coalition Against Multiple Oppressions*. Lanham, MD: Rowman and Littlefield Publishers, 2003.

Pitts, Andrea J. "Gloria E. Anzaldúa's Autohistoria-Teoría as an Epistemology of Self-Knowledge/Ignorance." *Hypatia* 31, no. 2 (2016): 352–69. https://doi.org/10.1111/hypa.12235.

Rivera Cusicanqui, Silvia. *Ch'ixinakax Utxiwa: On Decolonising Practices and Discourses*. Translated by Molly Geidel. Cambridge: Polity, 2020.

———. *Un mundo ch'ixi es posible*. Buenos Aires: Tinta Limón, 2014.

Smith, T'ai. *Bauhaus Weaving Theory: From Feminine Craft to Mode of Design*. Illustrated edition. Minneapolis: University of Minnesota Press, 2014.

Five

Stealing and Critical Fabulation

The Counter-Historical Methods of
Adriana Cavarero and Saidiya Hartman

Rachel Silverbloom

Introduction

Archives, as Stephanie Smallwood has said, are "a domain of power."[1] The practice of archiving "expresses a particular way of knowing that gives structure and meaning to its enunciations" and, in so doing, sets the terms for what is knowable in history and, indeed, what counts as history at all.[2] For those whose work necessitates engaging archives that have been produced and shaped by racial and gendered violence (among other forms of violence), one must grapple with the question of how to utilize such archives while also attempting to challenge and exceed the histories that they constitute and legitimate. If, as Michel-Rolph Trouillot has said, each historical narrative is made possible through a particular "bundle of silences," then how might one take up those silences in order to tell history otherwise?[3] And how does undermining dominant historical discourses also entail reimagining who counts as a historical and political agent—who can be not only subjects of history but also generators of histories?

In this chapter, I will stage an encounter between two scholars and methodologies that generate counter-histories from and against violent and annihilating archives: Adriana Cavarero's "stealing" and Saidiya Hartman's "critical fabulation." Cavarero's tactic of stealing generates intentionally unfaithful yet richer narratives of both straightforwardly fictive and more ambiguously mythical women (such as Homer's Penelope and Plato's Diotima), who have served only as minor figures in the history of the West and who have been taken up in the Western philosophical tradition in order to inscribe and enact the exclusion and subordination of women.[4] Stealing is a methodology that resists the ways that feminine subjectivity is buried in those mythic and philosophical archives that constitute, in turn, discourses of knowledge about women and their relation to the political and historical realm.

Saidiya Hartman's methodology of critical fabulation seeks to "exhume the lives" of the Black women and girls who have been buried by the archives of slavery, and whose silencing has served as the ground of dominant historical narratives of transatlantic slavery.[5] Hartman frames this methodology as an attempt to "throw into crisis" the authority of those narratives (and the linear-progressive temporality that organizes them).[6] Further, her work strives to generate narratives that counter and exceed the violent limits of the archive, and that engage our present by attending to the "past that is not past" (to borrow Christina Sharpe's phrase) and the "detritus of lives with which we have yet to attend."[7]

The counter-histories that they each produce are, as Hartman has said of her work, "histories of the present"; they begin from a recognition that our present is subtended and interrupted by the past and, therefore, exist in an intimate relationship with it.[8] Whereas Cavarero's tactic of stealing reappropriates mythic figures and their use in the philosophical canon, Hartman's critical fabulation takes up and challenges the production of historical "Truth" within slavery's archives and exposes the ways in which that truth is, in fact, the product of slanted narratives, violent imaginations, and suppressed voices.

What is required to work with and against archives built upon the burial or erasure of women if the desired outcome is to tell their stories otherwise? Can such women be "recuperated" at all, if their stories are "entangled with and impossible to differentiate from the terrible utterances that condemned them to death?"[9] Referring to the complex set of ethical issues involved in Hartman's engagement with slavery's archives, Brian Connolly and Marisa Fuentes ask: "If re-telling their stories requires, to some degree, working with the very archives that condemned them (since this is how they 'enter history' in the first place, as Hartman says), what kind of relation to those archives does that task require?"[10] These questions of how to (or if one even can) work within and against violent cultural materials and narratives give rise to the methodologies developed and deployed by Cavarero and Hartman in their work. Both are strategic modes of engaging with dominant histories in order to undermine their power, but as we will see, they do so in distinct ways that correspond to the irreducible contexts and archives they engage. The women that Cavarero steals from Ancient Greek myths and Platonic dialogues have already, in a sense, had their stories told—meager or degrading though they are. For her, then, the task is not to reinvent the stories whole cloth but, rather, to skew their perspectives to generate different meanings. For Hartman, on the other hand, the material of slavery's archives is much more limited, and the risk of imposing further violence is much higher; after all, the women and girls she narrates were real people (despite the fact that they were systematically stripped of their singularity when they entered the archive). Sometimes, the women she seeks to retrieve appear only as a name and description on a ship's manifest, an observation made by a doctor, or an obscene description from a legal proceeding. As such, the work of critical fabulation does not only skew perspective but must also generate new descriptions and fill in some gaps with imaginings (leaving others still in place), while avoiding romanticizing those lives or overly instrumentalizing them for our purposes today.

In what follows, I will outline each scholar's methodology and attempt to stage an encounter between their works. Despite the important and irreducible differences between them, my focus here is to consider what Cavarero's stealing and Hartman's critical fabulation share in common, in the hope that something might be gleaned from these attempts to simultaneously engage and refuse violent archives in order to generate different social meanings and futures. I will especially emphasize what I understand to be a resonant temporal structure of their work, which takes up the archival materials and narratives of the past in order to transform the present and generate different possibilities for the future. I will also show how their work is shaped by a shared emphasis on the constitutive relationality of our lives and their meanings, as well as the possibilities of both wounding and care inherent in our implications with one another.

Cavarero Steals Penelope

Cavarero lays out her tactic of stealing in the introduction to *In Spite of Plato*. After critiquing the supposed universality of mythic figures that, in fact, turn out to be engendered and constrained by masculine subjectivity, she describes her methodology: "My hermeneutical project consists of investigating the traces of the original act of erasure contained in the patriarchal order, the act upon which this order was first constructed and then continued to display itself. This is how my technique of theft works: I will steal feminine figures from their context, allowing the torn-up fabric to show the knots that hold together the conceptual canvas that hides the original crime."[11] Cavarero makes explicit that her aim in reappropriating feminine figures from their masculine contexts is not to tell a "truer" story, nor will she try to be faithful to their original representation. Instead, the stories she weaves about women like the *Odyssey*'s Penelope have "already decided the symbolic twist" that will transform their cultural significance; namely, their narratives are reshaped by the lens of sexuate difference. She positions this tactic of stealing as "outside and against" the masculine narratives that repeat their logic again and again, never allowing actual difference to emerge but only appearing to do so under the guise of universal human nature.[12] And while her work is "outside and against" that context, it nevertheless takes up its stories and figures in order to disfigure and refigure them from the lens of sexuate difference. "It involves working with the studied naivete of someone who patiently attempts to displace the very same language that squeezes her inside her own prison, without the omnipotent claim of being able to fly freely through the air. Rather, my tactic has the explicit intention to steal by leaning on theoretical axes that have already sought to dislodge themselves from their context through a radical shift in perspective."[13] This methodology of taking up the same discourse that has sought to imprison and bury female subjectivity, subverting it through a shift in perspective, and, in so doing, generating different meanings is a transformative repetition. It is a return that makes something different possible.[14] If history is a canvas that is "so thick as to be almost perfectly capable of concealing its secrets," then Cavarero's "needle turns in the opposite direction" so that the canvas "easily unravels."[15] It produces something different not by setting aside or ignoring the tradition that has excluded women but by returning to it and undermining its authority through the mischievous act of theft, organizing a revolt of meaning from the inside.

 It is clear from her description of this method that Cavarero identifies with Penelope, the weaver and unweaver, who "unties the matted threads of the father's tapestry."[16] Or, rather, she identifies with the version of Penelope that she makes possible by stealing her from Homer and Plato's texts. While Penelope's defiant activity is more traditionally seen as evidence of her undying devotion to her husband, for whom she waits obediently and faithfully, Cavarero steals her and transforms her into a feminist figure bent on generating a political space of revolt where she is shielded from the masculine order, where she can scheme against patriarchal power with her handmaidens. She suggests that Penelope's unending work of doing and undoing not only fends off the unwelcome marriage, thus displacing and negating the patriarchal power that seeks to define her place, but also generates a time and space of her own.[17] Penelope's rhythmic and unending work produces an "impenetrable time" closed off from the masculine temporality that urges her toward completion and marriage.[18] Her "absurd" tempo secures, at the same time, a site where her life can have a place and a meaning other than one prescribed by oppressive masculine logic.[19] As Cavarero writes, "[Penelope's] space is anomalous according to the patriarchal symbolic order that sets up a particular place for her: her place as a woman, and most of all as wife. But even though Penelope lives in a royal palace, by endlessly weaving and unraveling she defines her own place, where she is the wife of no one."[20]

This dimension of self-belonging is generated not through the linear-progressive action of the masculine Homeric hero, but through the parodying of its opposite—the repetitive sameness of cyclical time. It is a parody because Penelope's absurd tempo does not remain a simple repeating and regurgitating, as it might be viewed from the perspective of linearity; Penelope's futility is a form of refusal that is highly generative. Through the "endless, cadenced sameness" of weaving and unweaving—an activity associated with the domestic labor of women, no less—Penelope opens a space of refusal in spite of (and perhaps inside of) oppressive circumstances that render political action, in the conventional sense, impossible for a woman. The displacement enacted by her generative repetition exposes the fragility of the reigning linear-progressive order and defies the reductive conception of cyclical, embodied activity that such a framework espouses. As Rachel Jones puts it, "It is as if the inclined, asymmetrical postures that can be sites of resistant care, even as they manifest an unavoidable potential for wounding, are accompanied by a subversive, sideways glance that steals away from the imposing forms of Man to disclose other possibilities of being and relating, not only in a future yet to arrive but also already here, been and gone, still with us, and yet to be."[21] Penelope thus performs through her weaving and unweaving the same temporal structure that guides Cavarero's methodology of stealing: it is a repetition that displaces a dominant order in order to generate new possibilities and meanings. While the tempo of linear-progressive action believes itself to be the source of novelty and spontaneity, Cavarero reminds us that "this action is the consummation of pressing events following one after the other," each one ephemeral and passing away into oblivion. As such, "the time of action needs to preserve itself in a culture's memory so as not to disappear with the unrepeatable moment of its enactment."[22] Penelope's absurd tempo utterly disrupts this attempt at preservation through the act of unweaving and seals off a time and space that is "impenetrable" to the masculine order. Paradoxically and cunningly, she achieves this in and through the role that has been assigned to her by the patriarchal order; her deception is "rooted significantly in the womanly experience of weaving, and transforms a role into its own liberating rejection."[23] Just as Cavarero has described her tactic of stealing, Penelope takes up the very thing that was meant to "squeeze her inside her own prison" in order to render it impotent.[24]

Cavarero also makes clear the crucial role of the body for the radical potential of this work of repetition, whether in the methodology of stealing or in the story of Penelope. In a sense, Cavarero steals feminine figures in order to put the body back into their stories, to generate the appearance of a singularity that can only be grounded in embodiment and, for Cavarero, sexuate difference. Penelope's body and its movements are integral to the opening of this site of not only resistance but of generativity; her body, bent over at the loom, strains in its effort to create its time and place of belonging in "the dimension that comes out of her hands."[25] Her temporal-spatiality of self-belonging is thus produced *in and through* her body's movements and cannot be untied from them. Penelope's *metis* (cunning, skill, craft),[26] Cavarero explains, "cannot be separated from her body, and its object is not an eternal essence positioned outside this world, outside the weaving room where she sits with her handmaids. On the contrary, Penelope weaves a time of cadenced repetition where, day after day, *metis* is actualized in the work of her hands [. . .] and earns the weaver her own place of signification."[27] The transgressive work of unweaving lies in the embodied activity of pulling apart the threads, within the weaving room alongside Penelope's accomplices. Grounding her time and space in the movements of her body flies in the face of linear-progressive temporality and the masculine understanding of political subjectivity that it constitutes. It makes possible a place of signification that is not sourced in the eternal and unmoving forms or ideas but in the dynamic and living flesh of the body.

This temporality and its space is, as such, a tenuous and fragile one, despite its power to generate possibilities, "for in Penelope's *metis* there is no everlasting comfort from the eternal, there is rather a repetition that risks breaking its ongoing rhythm in the attention of every gesture, in the complicitous gaze of every handmaid."²⁸ It is here that Cavarero hints at a fundamental premise of her work: that our self-belonging and unrepeatable uniqueness is intricately and inextricably tied up with others. While Penelope's defiance of the men who seek to define her place produces a space of "self-belonging," it would be wrong to conclude that such a space is as unequivocally "impenetrable" as Cavarero, at times, describes it. Such a space of uniqueness requires, for its persistence, those "complicitous gazes" of Penelope's handmaidens. Indeed, it is the community created among those women that makes Penelope's story one of political resistance. In *Relating Narratives*, Cavarero defines the political as "a shared, contextual, relational space [. . .] created by some women who exhibit *who* they are to one another," adding that "this *who* is precisely an unrepeatable uniqueness which, in order to appear to others, needs first of all a plural—and therefore political—space of interaction."²⁹ The space of self-belonging is always, necessarily, a space of coappearing for Cavarero. Following Arendt, this is what constitutes the political in Cavarero's work rather than some autonomous, individualized notion of the sovereign political subject.

It is worth mentioning, however, that Cavarero's renarration of Penelope's story does not attend to the dynamics of class in the weaving room. The women who make Penelope's space of self-belonging possible are not her friends or comrades but her servants. There is, thus, a subtle erasure of the verticality (complicit with patriarchal power) that remains in the weaving room; an intersectional feminist reading of Penelope's story might attend to its uncanny and unsettling resonance with the living history (in the United States and globally) of white privileged women's liberation movements standing on the backs of the women of color they employ in their homes as care workers so that they could be "free."³⁰ Such a reading would complicate Cavarero's claim that Penelope's weaving room is one of coappearance and the suspension of patriarchal logics. Perhaps a reading of the reading, a theft of the theft, is necessary to generate not only a feminist narrative of Penelope but also an *intersectional* feminist narrative.

Despite the limitations of Cavarero's theft of Penelope in *In Spite of Plato*, what remains nevertheless crucial for feminist politics (and is resonant with many Black and decolonial feminisms) is Cavarero's insistence on disrupting the conventional separation and polarization of the domestic/private and the political/public spheres, a disruption which departs significantly from the political philosophy of Hannah Arendt. In the story of

Penelope, we find a political space of resistance that is generated precisely in and through the repetitive, cadenced, and collective domestic activity of weaving and unweaving. It is precisely through Penelope's defiance of linear-progressive, masculine action that she inscribes her own space, where she is able to be something other than the role prescribed for her by patriarchal power. It is in that very same space where she belongs to herself, in her uniqueness; there, she can show *who* she truly is (not just *what*), in and through the weaving room's community of women. So, too, by stealing Penelope from Plato and telling her story otherwise, Cavarero attempts to inscribe a place for women in the political realm and in the archives of Western philosophy and culture.

Hartman Fabulates Venus

Whereas the Black women and girls who enter History through the archives of transatlantic slavery were, unlike Penelope, flesh and blood, when they do appear, they still do so as mythic figures, stereotypes, and abstractions. Hartman begins "Venus in Two Acts" by reflecting on the ubiquity of the name *Venus* in the archives of slavery and the anonymity and erasure that such ubiquity, paradoxically, comes with. While the women called *Venus* appear everywhere, they are in fact, nowhere to be found (at least, not truly).[31] "Variously named Harriot, Phibba, Sara, Joanna, Rachel, Linda and Sally, she is found everywhere in the Atlantic world. The barracoon, the hollow of the slave ship, the pest-house, the brothel, the cage, the surgeon's laboratory, the prison, the cane-field, the kitchen, the master's bedroom—turn out to be exactly the same place and in all of them she is called Venus."[32] This is a different sort of disappearing act than the one that buries Penelope beneath masculine subjectivity. It involves real women and girls who have been reduced to the anonymity of myth, denied the dignity and singularity marked by their proper names, and tossed carelessly into the archives as throwaway lives (or not even acknowledged as human lives and reduced to the status of objects). This stripping away of their singularity makes attempts to retell their stories an otherwise difficult, perhaps impossible, task: "We only know what can be extrapolated from an analysis of the ledger or borrowed from the world of her captors and masters and applied to her."[33]

In *Relating Narratives* Cavarero remarks upon the significance of the proper name, which she calls "a sort of 'vocative' unity" of "uniqueness."[34]

Paradoxically, while thousands may share the same proper name, it signifies one's singularity: it is what one says when asked *"who* are you?"[35] In this sense, the proper name is a mark of one's humanity within a shared and relational context. Names, therefore, hold tremendous power either to show care or to harm.[36] If, for Cavarero, narratives ought to tell a story of "who" not "what" someone is, for Hartman, this "who" is precisely what is rendered absent in Venus's appearances throughout slavery's archives.[37] Hartman explains, "One cannot ask 'Who is Venus?' because it would be impossible to answer such a question. There are hundreds of thousands of other girls who share her circumstances and these circumstances have generated few stories. And the stories that exist are not about them, but rather about the violence, excess, mendacity, and reason that seized hold of their lives, transformed them into commodities and corpses, and identified them with names tossed-off as insults and crass jokes."[38] The particular incarnation of Venus that occasions Hartman's essay appears in a legal indictment against a slave ship captain who is accused of murdering her and another enslaved girl. She is described in that document simply as a "dead girl."[39] Hartman remarks, "Hers is the same fate as every other Black Venus: no one remembered her name or recorded the things she said, or observed that she refused to say anything at all. Hers is an untimely story told by a failed witness."[40] The fact that she appears at all, that she enters history and is recorded even in this meager and degrading way, is "an aberration from the expected and usual course of invisibility" that has "catapulted her from the underground to the surface of discourse."[41] What appears of her is nevertheless fleeting, and it does not indicate anything of the human reality and the depth of her: what she thought, what she hoped for, or how/if she knew the other slain girl. Despite the fact that it is impossible to give an account of who she truly was, or how she might have been "in a free state," Hartman expresses a wish to tell a story about Venus and the other girls and women buried by History, that can do more than simply "recount the violence that deposited these traces in the archive."[42] She wants to tell a story that exceeds that violence, perhaps one that can even restore some "beauty" to the lives of those girls, out of not only a care for their lives but also in response to the demand that they place upon us in the present.[43] She takes up the archival remains of the past in order to imagine what stories can be told that might exceed its frame. What possibilities can such narratives generate, and how can they rupture the archive's hold to open different futures?[44]

Her attempt to meet these demands informs a methodology that she names *critical fabulation*, which she has also called *close narration* in later iterations of the method (as in her 2019 book *Wayward Lives, Beautiful Experiments*).[45] *Fabula*, she explains, refers to the elements or building blocks of narrative that are set in motion by the story's agents (which, quoting Mieke Bal, she notes are "not necessarily human").[46] Critical fabulation rearranges those narrative elements, playing with their temporal sequence and producing "divergent stories" that emerge from "contested points of view."[47] In so doing, Hartman attempts to undermine the authority with which dominant history and its archival materials record and proliferate the "facts" by introducing competing narratives and accounts of what might have happened and what could have been. She explains,

> By throwing into crisis "what happened when" and by exploiting the "transparency of sources" as fictions of history, I wanted to make visible the production of disposable lives (in the Atlantic slave trade and, as well, in the discipline of history), to describe "the resistance of the object," if only by first imagining it, and to listen for the mutters and oaths and cries of the commodity. By flattening the levels of narrative discourse and confusing narrator and speakers, I hoped to illuminate the contested character of history, narrative, event, and fact, to topple the hierarchy of discourse, and to engulf authorized speech in the clash of voices.[48]

This mode of narration requires pulling the threads of history retrieved from the archives and weaving some of them back together (perhaps, as Cavarero said, with the needle moving in the opposite direction), while leaving others untied. Hartman describes the outcome of this method in the language of weaving and unweaving not only the elements of the story but also the temporal order that renders them coherent or incoherent. She calls it "a 'recombinant narrative,' which 'loops the strands' of incommensurate accounts and which weaves present, past, and future in retelling the girl's story and in narrating the time of slavery as our present."[49] Like Penelope's activity of weaving and unweaving, Hartman's recombinant narratives transform sedimented historical and political meanings prescribed to (or denied to) women and generate a time and space where they can appear as something other than what they have been reduced to within the archives.

And yet, despite the radical potential it offers to generate narratives of care, in "Venus in Two Acts" Hartman frames critical fabulation as, ultimately, an "impossible" writing. While Hartman's relationship with critical fabulation changes somewhat in her later work *Wayward Lives*, in "Venus in Two Acts" she has a more tenuous and even ambivalent relationship to the practice, and its potential hazards.

> I want to tell a story about two girls capable of retrieving what remains dormant—the purchase or claim of their lives on the present—without committing further violence in my own act of narration. It is a story predicated upon impossibility—listening for the unsaid, translating misconstrued words, and refashioning disfigured lives—and intent on achieving an impossible goal: redressing the violence that produced numbers, ciphers, and fragments of discourse, which is as close as we come to a biography of the captive and the enslaved.[50]

Hartman also expresses concern about romanticizing and further objectifying the lives of the women she narrates otherwise; she does not want to produce a narrative that merely consoles and tries to "resolve" the violence of the archive. This risk of romanticization is further compounded by the risk of instrumentalization, or what we might call teleological violence. In a way, Hartman explains, her attempt to take up the story of Venus in order to generate something instructive and meaningful for the present "replicates the very order of the violence that it writes against by placing yet another demand upon the girl, by requiring that her life be made useful or instructive, by finding in it a lesson for our future or a hope for history."[51] Thus, if the aim of critical fabulation is to redress (or, more modestly, counter or resist) historical violence by telling the stories of those it has silenced, then it is clear that, for Hartman, it must inevitably fail to achieve that aim. No attempt at narration could ever truly "represent" those women, and what's more, those narratives that are produced have not and do not successfully "install themselves as history, but are rather insurgent, disruptive narratives that are marginalized and derailed before they ever gain a footing."[52] After all, as Connolly and Fuentes explain, "even as we formulate new methods that challenge archival power, some things remain unrecoverable, silent."[53]

However, if we read Hartman carefully, it becomes clear that redemption through resurrection is not the aim of critical fabulation after all. What is exhumed from the archives through close narration are not the women themselves or some facts about their lives; rather, it is the demand that their lives place upon us in the present. As she says, what is dormant and must be activated is "the purchase or claim of their lives on the present."[54] To attempt to give voice to those who have been silenced, in Hartman's work, is not to give a content to their speech that must be decoded but rather to place a demand upon the present to *listen*—to bear the ethical responsibility of attending to their lives and the historical conditions that led to their erasure with care, especially because those historical conditions persist as the ground of our present. This very act of care and attention, this reorientation toward those lives that have been rendered the silent and invisible ground of our present, is a transformative reorientation of the dominant historical and political framework whereby what is past is understood as, at the same time, absent and disposable.

Generative Failures, Radical Futilities

Hartman and Cavarero converge here in the following way: they both insist, in the end, that the failure to adequately "resurrect" or give voice to the lives we first encounter through violent archives is productive. Attempts at narration achieve the following, despite (and, indeed, because of) their inevitable failure. First, they resist the dissolution of those buried by History into the silence of oblivion; indeed, for both scholars it is the lesser of two evils, in a sense, to try and fail to tell their stories out of an orientation of care for the subjects' lives rather than allow them to sink beneath the waves of History once and for all.[55] The care with which these lives are attended to counters the disregard with which history has discarded them as illegible and disposable. Hartman asks, "By retreating from the story of these two girls, was I simply upholding the rules of the historical guild and the 'manufactured certainties' of their killers, and by doing so, hadn't I sealed their fate? Hadn't I too consigned them to oblivion? In the end, was it better to leave them as I found them?"[56] Similarly, in "Narrative Against Destruction" Cavarero considers the demand for and dangers of narrating the lives of those killed during the Holocaust, who also face the threat of further extinction through the erasure of the historical traces of that genocide. She, like Hartman, suggests that telling their stories is an important way to resist their violent and intentional erasure. She writes, "The aim is, on one hand, to contrast and to preserve the unspeakable horror of the perpetrated destruction that, precisely because of its excess, risks escaping the tangles of history as the storybook of mankind. On the other hand, the aim is to recover individual stories from silence, stories that otherwise would risk remaining meaningless."[57] This demand placed upon the present to interrupt the silences perpetuated by dominant discourses must, however, be held in tenuous balance with the simultaneous imperative to stave off the deceptive feeling of closure and redemption that might result from filling all of the gaps. In "Venus in Two Acts" Hartman asserts that "narrative restraint, the refusal to fill in the gaps and provide closure, is a requirement" of her method."[58] Cavarero echoes this sentiment in "Narrative Against Destruction." In her analysis of the biographical writings of W. G. Sebald, she insists that engaging with what is irreducibly inexplicable about those lives under threat of erasure—what narration cannot give expression to and what must always exceed its frame—is powerful precisely because it is inexplicable. The failure to adequately narrate those lives, and to expose and make explicit that failure, is a crucial element of its resistance against the totalizing forces that seek to absorb and dissolve them. "Far from explaining the inexplicable, running the risk of dissolving it, absolving it, and normalizing it, this capacity instead leaves the inexplicable open as an inextinguishable scandal: like an infinite task or a warning that only the narration of injured vulnerable lives can pronounce and signal, or as an ethical and political necessity—shared also by Arendt—to radically rethink the human in light of its unspeakable destruction."[59] Cavarero also praises Sebald's biographies for their use of literary narrative elements that "break the barriers between a realistic account and fiction, between documentation and invention."[60] In fact, she describes his narrative as "fundamentally choral and multiperspectival," given how it interweaves "singular lives pulled out of the complicity between destruction and oblivion."[61] Indeed, much of how she describes Sebald's narratives resonates with Hartman's methodology of critical fabulation. These similarities are confirmed by Hartman, who credits Sebald, among others, for offering a "model of possibility" for how to "*creatively disorder* the institutional fictions and the violent abstractions authorized as fact and truth" in the archives.[62]

For Hartman and, it seems, for Cavarero, attempting to tell the stories of those who face historical erasure otherwise, while simultaneously rendering explicit the impossibility of truly redeeming them or redressing the violence that sought to erase them in the process, exposes the limits of history and of narration as well as impresses upon us the ways in which our present is "tethered" to those pasts we seek to retell otherwise.[63] In this way, the failure itself is necessary in order to expose and undermine such violence. By wondering about their lives, without pretending to ever exhaustively (or even "factually") represent them, one both resists inexplicability and amplifies its presence, keeping in "productive tension" what must not be resolved in their telling.[64] Hartman writes, "The intention here isn't anything as miraculous as recovering the lives of the enslaved or redeeming the dead, but rather laboring to paint as full a picture of the lives of the captives as possible. This double gesture can be described as straining against the limits of the archive to write a cultural history of the captive, and, at the same time, enacting the impossibility of representing the lives of the captives precisely through the process of narration."[65]

And yet, while Hartman's concerns about "the risk involved in exceeding the limits of the archive" places certain limitations on the kind of story she could tell about Venus, *Wayward Lives, Beautiful Experiments* takes on that risk in order to generate "new narratives" that are "untethered or indifferent to the rules of the historical guild."[66] Hartman situates the book as an attempt to "explore" rather than "answer or resolve" the "set of questions about writing, genre, fabulation, and historiography" that she raised in "Venus in Two Acts."[67] As with "Venus," it is a text that begins with the time and space of the erased and silenced, and she describes the book as "written from nowhere, from the nowhere of the ghetto and the nowhere of utopia."[68] In it, she writes creatively and imaginatively, with and against the archives, to tell stories of the radical possibilities and beauty generated by the lives of Black women and girls in the ghettos of New York and Philadelphia at the turn of the twentieth century. *Wayward Lives*, she explains, turned out to be somewhat of an "unanticipated departure and experiment with method."[69] In "Intimate History, Radical Narrative" she describes the way in which she "lived with" the material for the book for seven years and in the "raucous company" of the women whose lives she tried to narrate otherwise, even "listening to them and speaking with them daily."[70] The experience of living with "Mattie and Esther and Mabel and Gladys and Loretta and Edna [. . .] sustained" her, she says.[71] In them, she "saw all of those [she] loved," and in their radical modes of living, she saw "a blueprint for another set of arrangements."[72] The intimacy with which she describes living with and sitting alongside the historical remnants of those women "enabled [her] to hear *something else* in the compelled biographies and meager stories of the case file and the state archives," to sense and recreate something of the "ambient sound and minor music of Black life, a composition of shared utterance" that exceeds the frames of life produced in history's books.[73] In listening to the ways that Hartman describes working within and against the archives for *Wayward Lives* as a mode of living with the women whose stories she retells otherwise, I am reminded of Christina Sharpe's description of what she calls *wake work* in *In the Wake: On Blackness and Being*—a careful practice of sitting-with the Black dead, dying, and still living (in a state of social death) in the wake of slavery. Hartman's *Wayward Lives* is one attempt at wake work, at sitting-with and alongside, as keeping watch over the dead and dying, in the (hesitant) hopes of generating "possibilities for rupture."[74] I think also of Cavarero's Penelope, in a sewing circle with other women, unweaving together so that they might continually rupture the patriarchal order that confines them and weave a time and space where they can generate new possibilities, new meanings for their lives. Similarly, Hartman describes *Wayward Lives* as a "love-letter" that "endeavored to regard Black life from inside the circle and to recapture the wild thought and the beautiful recklessness capable of imagining the *with* and the *us* and the *we*."[75]

Unlike in "Venus in Two Acts," where Hartman treads more carefully among the boundaries of history and fiction, in *Wayward Lives, Beautiful Experiments*, Hartman employs a modification of critical fabulation that she calls *close narration*. It is a method "for engaging and remaking the document, for assembling and composing alternative narratives of Black existence," in order to tell stories that breathe new life into the Black women and girls that appear only as "minor figures" in archival sources like police reports, news articles, notes from orphanages, sociological surveys, and others.[76] The aim of the book is to "illuminate the radical imagination" that is activated by tending to those women with care, such that a different story—a different history—emerges.[77] She explains, "For the most part, the history and the potentiality of their life-world has remained unthought because no one could conceive of young black women as social visionaries and innovators in the world in which these acts took place."[78] Like Cavarero's investment in troubling conventional public/private distinctions that have historically rendered the "domestic sphere" of women unintelligible as political, in *Wayward Lives* Hartman attends to the erasure of the rich political lives and imaginations of Black women. Whereas many, particularly white, outsiders look at the ghetto and "see only the disorder," Hartman's "counter-narrative" aims to illustrate "all the ways black folks create life and make bare need into an arena of elaboration."[79] Like her other work, it is a project driven by an orientation of care for those "minor lives" and from a positionality of identification with those whom have been rendered unidentifiable by how they have been recorded/discarded.[80] She explains, "It was my way of redressing the violence of history, crafting a love letter to all those who had been harmed, and, without my being fully aware of it, reckoning with the inevitable disappearance that awaited me."[81]

In the chapter "Minor Figure" Hartman employs critical fabulation/ close narration to imagine and narrate the story of a young Black girl, photographed nude and reclined on an arabesque sofa.[82] The photograph is perhaps the only trace she left behind—there is no name on an inscription, no description of who she might have been, no explanation for why the photograph was taken, nor by whom. If the photographers had bothered to record her name, Hartman explains, she might have been able to find her in the 1900 census, or discover if she lived in an orphan house, or if she danced at the Lafayette Theatre. The girl's anonymity imposes the risk of her erasure: "Without a name, there is the risk that she might never escape the oblivion that is the fate of minor lives and be condemned to the pose for the rest of her existence."[83] Despite this, Hartman does not give the girl a name. "The fiction of a proper name would evade the dilemma, not resolve it."[84] Instead, she weaves a story into the girl's anonymity and transforms it into an act of defiance, one that puts her in relation with the other Black women and girls who have faced similar erasures. "In being denied a name, or perhaps, in refusing to give one, she represents all the other girls who follow in her path."[85]

With only a photograph to go on, Hartman weaves a story. She conjures a tale where the girl is surrounded by other characters: friends, housekeepers, and cooks. And while she does not give the girl a name, she inscribes words on her image. Pages 26 and 27 of *Wayward Lives* have Hartman's words superimposed over the photograph of the girl, almost so faint as to be unnoticeable. Hartman asks, at the top of page 26, her words brushing the girl's hair, "Was it possible to annotate the image? To make my words into a shield that might protect her, a barricade to deflect the gaze and to cloak what had been exposed?"[86] The words covering the girl's exposed form pose a series of questions about her experience while her photograph was taken: what she thought or felt, how she moved, what she smelled. Hartman describes her leaving the studio where she was photographed, through a garden, passing by a water hydrant, cats, and dogs. In imagining her this way, in wondering about what might have been, Hartman attempts to restore some depth to this girl who has been flattened and turned into "public property" by the photograph and the normalized "regime of brutality" that made it possible; she speculates about *who* she was, not merely *what* she has been reduced to by the photographer's gaze.[87] She wonders, "How might this still life yield a latent image capable of articulating another kind of existence, a runaway image that conveys the riot inside?"[88]

It is that image of the reclined girl that Hartman seems to credit for the impetus to write *Wayward Lives*. She explains that after a year of looking at the photo, she "decided to retrace her steps through the city and imagine her many lives" as well as follow in the footsteps of the many other Black women and girls who lived in Philadelphia and New York City. "In the end," she explains, "it became not the story of one girl, but a serial biography of a generation, a portrait of the chorus, a moving picture of the wayward."[89] It is not only a portrait *of* the chorus but one that is, in turn, made possible *by* the chorus, given that "making new narratives entails a creative practice untethered to the rules of the historical guild, and directed by the assembly, the ensemble, the multitude, the chorus."[90]

Conclusion

Early in the essay about Venus, Hartman wonders about whether narration is, itself, a gift and if so, for whom? Are the stories she conjures up really *for* the girls they are about, if "overcoming the past and redeeming the dead" is not possible?[91] Or, what's different, are they *with* them but *for* "us?"[92] In Cavarero's *In Spite of Plato*, she makes it clear that the aim of her methodology is not for the sake of the mythic figures she steals but, rather, for the sake of women in the present so that when they look to myth and literature, they can recognize something of themselves within it, rather than only men and the monstrosity of universal Man. Cavarero and Hartman recognize that writing a history of the present and striving to generate a different future is predicated on wrestling with the past and the stories we tell about it. For both, the "now" is continually "interrupted by [the] past," which must be revisited in order to generate new possibilities for living otherwise.[93] Hartman has explained that the "free state" that she imagines and conjures for the Black women of slavery's archives is not one that exists, nostalgically, prior to capture and enslavement but is rather the "anticipated future" of her writing.[94] As such, this work is driven by a recognition that "the deathly implications of the past have similar consequences for the present and future."[95] Or, as Smallwood has said,

> The colonial archive's silences and disavowals are themselves an active epistemological gesture that leaves in its wake a trace of its own processes and maneuvers. Our task, then, is to tell the stories that bring the ghostly outline of that tracing fully into view. I understand what is possible as counter-history by way of metahistorical analysis to be politically necessary, not because it can ever fully recuperate the subaltern, but rather because by its

critique it reveals the otherwise naturalized and taken-for-granted structures of power that produce subaltern figures as such.[96]

Counter-histories cannot resurrect or redeem the dead—Hartman has made it clear that this is the "impossible" task that critical fabulation must try and fail to achieve. They can, however, trouble our relation to the past by telling the stories that would otherwise sink into oblivion and activate the power that such stories have to trouble the authority of the hegemonic discourses of history and of Truth that would see them buried. If mainstream historical writing "assumes the bourgeois white male as the citizen-subject whose consciousness of the past it narrates and naturalizes the ideologies and structures of power that have produced him and the global order of the sovereign nation-states he inhabits," it is no wonder that disrupting such discourse and generating other imaginaries is crucial to contemporary attempts to counter the ways in which the present reproduces the violence of the past.[97]

To attempt this task, Cavarero and Hartman have created distinctive methodologies for generating counter-histories from the very materials that render them illegitimate and unauthorized. This labor, while it works on "the past," disrupts the ordinary ways that the past is partitioned from our present and rendered as something distant and/or absent. For both scholars, this work of countering erasure through narration is an act of care—not only for those women buried by the archives but also for those in the present who still live in a world predicated on their invisibility. As Cavarero remarks in *Relating Narratives*, "Rather than salvation, the accidental needs care. To tell the story that every existence leaves behind itself is perhaps the oldest act of such care."[98]

For Cavarero, our constitutive relationality entails the possibility of both care *and* wounding: to be relational is to be vulnerable. In stealing Penelope from Homer and Plato, Cavarero practices care by imagining other possibilities for female subjectivity, both in the archives of philosophy's past and for the present and future. This gesture of care, enacted through narration and Cavarero's feminist theft, is not without its own dangers of wounding (as I tried to show by attending to the invisibilization of class hierarchies in Cavarero's Penelope). Concerns about the thin edge between wounding and care are echoed in Hartman's description of critical fabulation as an act of care that nevertheless risks replicating the violence of romanticization and instrumentalization. To take on and acknowledge, without resolving, the inevitable risks of wounding entailed in the work of unraveling the threads of History, of turning the needle in another direction as Cavarero and Hartman have done, is to labor with care to "transform the terms of the possible."[99]

Notes

1. Stephanie Smallwood, "The Politics of the Archive and History's Accountability to the Enslaved," *History of the Present* 6, no. 2 (October 1, 2016): 124, https://doi.org/10.5406/historypresent.6.2.0117.

2. Smallwood, "The Politics of the Archive," 124.

3. Michel-Rolph Trouillot, *Silencing the Past: Power and the Production of History* (Boston: Beacon Press, 1995), 49.

4. As Fanny Söderbäck and Paula Landerreche Cardillo have helpfully pointed out to me, whereas Penelope is a more straightforward example of a fictional character from Homer's *Odyssey*, the other figures that Cavarero "steals" in her work occupy a more ambiguous space between the fictive and the real, and their usage by Cavarero works, in part, to trouble that distinction. There is debate, for example, about whether Diotima was a purely fictional character or a pseudonym used in Plato's dialogues to refer to a person who may have lived around 440 BCE. To complicate things further, some of these fictive characters, like Diotima, have been utilized in the history of philosophy in order to proliferate discourse about (and purportedly grounded in) truth/Truth. As such, Cavarero's engagement with these figures troubles those claims to truth and blurs the boundaries between the fictive and the real. After all, as she explains, the work of narration, unlike philosophy, is not interested in "capturing the universal in the trap of a definition" but in telling a story that "reveals the finite in its fragile uniqueness." Cavarero, *Relating Narratives*, trans. Paul A. Kottman (New York: Routledge, 2000), 3. As I will show, this challenge to the authority of discourses of Truth that characterize both mainstream philosophy and history is also central to Hartman's methodology.

5. Christina Sharpe, *In the Wake: On Blackness and Being* (Durham, NC: Duke University Press, 2016), 9; Saidiya Hartman, "Venus in Two Acts," *Small Axe* 12, no. 2 (June 2008): 6, https://doi.org/10.1215/-12-2-1.

6. Hartman, "Venus in Two Acts," 12.

7. Sharpe, *In the Wake: On Blackness and Being*, 9; Hartman, "Venus in Two Acts," 13.

8. Hartman, "Venus in Two Acts," 4.

9. Brian Connolly and Marisa Fuentes, "Introduction: From Archives of Slavery to Liberated Futures?" *History of the Present* 6, no. 2 (Fall 2016): 3, https://doi.org/10.5406/historypresent.6.2.0105.

10. Connolly and Fuentes, "Introduction," 6.

11. Adriana Cavarero, *In Spite of Plato: Feminist Rewriting of Ancient Philosophy*, trans. Serena Anderlini D'Onfrio and Áine O'Healy (New York: Routledge, 1995), 5. It is worth noting that both Hartman and Cavarero use metaphors of weaving

in describing their methodologies for working with(in) and against dominant discourses and the social "fabrics" they generate and maintain. There is much more to explore regarding the significance of weaving and textiles (including hair) in the context of gendered and racialized oppressions, but I will not be able to do justice to it here. See Tanisha Ford, *Liberated Threads: Black Women, Style, and the Global Politics of Soul* (Chapel Hill: University of North Carolina Press, 2015); and Adriana Michelle Burkins, "Strands of Power, Tools of Resistance: Black Hair and Consciousness as Concept and Medium" (PhD diss., University of North Carolina at Chapel Hill, 2019), ProQuest, https://doi.org/10.17615/7288-9704. See also Sonya Clark, "Sculptural Headdresses" *Ornament: The Art of Personal Adornment* 20, no. 3 (Spring 1997); and Leda Cempellin, "Sonya Clark: Hair as Collective Identity," *Juliet Art Magazine*, no. 181 (February–March 2017): 91.

12. Cavarero, *In Spite of Plato*, 5.

13. Cavarero, *In Spite of Plato*, 5–6.

14. While I do not have the space to develop it explicitly here, my approach to reading the temporality of Cavarero's methodology is strongly influenced by Fanny Söderbäck's *Revolutionary Time* (Albany: State University of New York Press, 2019). I am especially drawing from her engagement with Luce Irigaray's work in order to explain how the temporality of mimesis is a repetition that transforms (rather than being "merely" cyclical or "merely" redundant, as repetition is so often understood from the standpoint of masculine linear-progressive temporality). I develop this connection explicitly in my dissertation, *Nonlinearity as Care: Black, Feminist, and Queer Temporalities of History* (DePaul University, 2022).

15. I see particular resonance with these words and American artist Sonya Clark's performance and textile pieces, *Unravelling* (2015) and *these days, this history, this country* (2019).

16. Cavarero, *In Spite of Plato*, 7. For other generative engagements with Cavarero's theft of Penelope, see Paula Landerreche Cardillo, "Taking the Thread for a Walk: Feminist Resistance to the Philosophical Order in Adriana Cavarero and María Lugones," in this volume; and Rachel Jones, "Inclining toward New Forms of Life: Cavarero, Agamben, and Hartman," in this volume.

17. Cavarero, *In Spite of Plato*, 11.

18. Cavarero, *In Spite of Plato*, 14.

19. Cavarero, *In Spite of Plato*, 17.

20. Cavarero, *In Spite of Plato*, 12.

21. Jones, "Inclining toward New Forms of Life," in this volume.

22. Cavarero, *In Spite of Plato*, 14.

23. Cavarero, *In Spite of Plato*, 18.

24. Cavarero, *In Spite of Plato*, 5–6.

25. Cavarero, *In Spite of Plato*, 14.

26. See further discussion of the significance of Cavarero's use of *metis* in Paula Landerreche Cardillo's "Taking the Thread for a Walk" and Rachel Jones's "Inclining toward New Forms of Life," in this volume.

27. Cavarero, *In Spite of Plato*, 19.
28. Cavarero, *In Spite of Plato*, 19.
29. Adriana Cavarero, *Relating Narratives*, trans. Paul A. Kottman (New York: Routledge, 2000), 58.
30. For an incisive and illuminating analysis of the long-standing and still-contemporary appropriation, exploitation, and invisibilization of the labor of women of color for white women's liberation, see Françoise Vergès, "Capitalocene, Waste, Race, and Gender," *e-flux* 100 (May 2019), https://www.e-flux.com/journal/100/269165/capitalocene-waste-race-and-gender/. For an analysis of this same dynamic in the particular context of Black women's care, labor in the context of slavery, and its afterlives, see Saidiya Hartman, "The Belly of the World: A Note on Black Women's Labors," *Souls* 18, no. 1 (2016): 166–73. See also Rachel Jones's rich engagement with Hartman's "The Belly of the World" in conversation with Cavarero's work in "Inclining toward New Forms of Life," in this volume.
31. Thanks to Fanny Söderbäck for drawing my attention to a similar remark that Cavarero makes in *Relating Narratives* about the discourse of Man, which applies to no one in particular because it claims to apply universally to everyone. It is this monstrous universality that Cavarero seeks to disrupt in her methodology of stealing. She writes, "'Man' is a universal that applies to everyone precisely because it is no one. It disincarnates itself from the living singularity of each one, while claiming to substantiate it. It is at once masculine and neuter, a hybrid creature generated by thought, a fantastic universal produced by the mind. It is invisible and intangible, while nevertheless declaring itself to be the only thing 'sayable' in true discourse." Cavarero, *Relating Narratives*, 9.
32. Hartman, "Venus in Two Acts," 1.
33. Hartman, "Venus in Two Acts," 2.
34. Cavarero, *Relating Narratives*, 18.
35. Cavarero, *Relating Narratives*, 18.
36. As Fanny Söderbäck describes in an essay that puts Cavarero's philosophy of singularity into conversation with Alex Haley's *Roots*, "Names have this strange feature of singling out the one who has been named in their utmost singularity [. . .] while, simultaneously, reducing what ultimately cannot be captured by a proper name to, precisely, that. This explains why naming can be both an act that affirms our singularity [. . .] and, when used to label someone, an act of destruction of that same singularity (forcing a slave to go by the name of Toby, or even the rendering of human beings into 'slaves')." Fanny Söderbäck, "Singularity in the Wake of Slavery: Adriana Cavarero's Ontology of Uniqueness and Alex Haley's *Roots*," *Philosophy Compass* 15, no. 7 (July 2020): 4, https://doi.org/10.1111/phc3.12685.
37. For a more thorough analysis of the "who" versus the "what" in Cavarero's thought, see Timothy J. Huzar's "On the Politics of the *Who*: Cavarero, Nancy, and Rancière," in this volume.
38. Hartman, "Venus in Two Acts," 2.

39. Hartman, "Venus in Two Acts," 1.
40. Hartman, "Venus in Two Acts," 1.
41. Hartman, "Venus in Two Acts," 2.
42. Michel Foucault, "Lives of Infamous Men," quoted in Hartman, "Venus in Two Acts," 2.
43. The role of beauty in Hartman's work and, especially, her method of critical fabulation is interesting and complex; I will not be able to do justice to it here. It does seem to me, however, that when Hartman invokes "beauty" both in "Venus in Two Acts" and in other works like *Wayward Lives, Beautiful Experiments* (New York: Serpent's Tail, 2019) it is connected to something like restored possibilities, especially possibilities that are generated through returning to and taking up the stories of Black women and girls for the sake of expressing their demand upon our present. Later in "Venus in Two Acts," she considers how one might imagine the two girls offering "the glimpse of beauty, the instant of possibility" in their possible friendship with one another (Hartman, "Venus in Two Acts," 8). Beauty is also invoked on pages 3 and 4 of the essay as well as several times in *Wayward Lives* (including in the title). Bonnie Honig suggests that Hartman transforms beauty from "something to be seen into something to be done." Bonnie Honig, *A Feminist Theory of Refusal* (Cambridge, MA: Harvard University Press, 2021), 76.
44. As Bonnie Honig puts it, "Hartman seeks to hold and distort the archives on behalf of a future, rather than allow them to endlessly hold us in relation to a distorted past" (*A Feminist Theory of Refusal*, 75). Though, I would caution against an overemphasis on futurity at the cost of acknowledging the inextricability of the relation between the past and present. The aim, for Hartman, is not to sever the relation between past and present in order to move toward a possible future (there is, perhaps, in this sense, no absolute "break" from the past and the "hold" it has on us); rather, futures are made possible through caring for and tarrying with the past from within the present. While Hartman wants to tell narratives that exceed the violent logics that dominate the past/present, her solution is not quite to sever such ties, but to transform them through working with/on/against them.
45. Hartman, "Venus in Two Acts," 11; Saidiya Hartman, "Intimate History, Radical Narrative," *Journal of African American History* 106, no. 1 (Winter 2021): 127, https://doi.org/10.1086/712019.
46. Hartman, "Venus in Two Acts," 11.
47. Hartman, "Venus in Two Acts," 11.
48. Hartman, "Venus in Two Acts," 12.
49. Hartman, "Venus in Two Acts," 12.
50. Hartman, "Venus in Two Acts," 2–3.
51. Hartman, "Venus in Two Acts," 14.
52. Hartman, "Venus in Two Acts," 12–13.
53. Connolly, Fuentes, "Introduction," 105.
54. Hartman, "Venus in Two Acts," 2.

55. With this language, I have in mind Derek Walcott's poem, "The Sea is History," *The Paris Review* 74 (Fall–Winter 1978), https://www.theparisreview.org/poetry/7020/the-sea-is-history-derek-walcott.

56. Hartman, "Venus in Two Acts," 10.

57. Adriana Cavarero, "Narrative Against Destruction," *New Literary History* 46, no. 1 (Winter 2015): 7, https://www.jstor.org/stable/24542656.

58. Hartman, "Venus in Two Acts," 12.

59. Cavarero, "Narrative Against Destruction," 11.

60. Cavarero, "Narrative Against Destruction," 11.

61. Cavarero, "Narrative Against Destruction," 11.

62. Hartman, "Intimate History, Radical Narrative," 129 (emphasis original).

63. Hartman, "Venus in Two Acts," 13.

64. Hartman, "Venus in Two Acts," 12.

65. Hartman, "Venus in Two Acts," 11.

66. Hartman, "Intimate History, Radical Narrative," 130.

67. Hartman, "Intimate History, Radical Narrative," 130.

68. Hartman, *Wayward Lives, Beautiful Experiments*, xiii. Theorizing radical, political possibilities from the spaces that have been explicitly excluded from the linear realm of politics is shared with Cavarero's work, not only in the example of Penelope in the weaving room but also in the way that she describes the collectives of Italian feminists in *Relating Narratives* and the kinds of important political work that takes place in kitchens, hallways, and other "domestic" scenes that are conventionally devalued as potential political spaces. And, of course, recognizing the radical feminist work that takes place in the kitchen is also central in the writings of Audre Lorde, who was a cofounder of Kitchen Table: Women of Color Press around precisely this insight.

69. Hartman, "Intimate History, Radical Narrative," 130.

70. Hartman, "Intimate History, Radical Narrative," 128.

71. Hartman, "Intimate History, Radical Narrative," 128.

72. Hartman, "Intimate History, Radical Narrative," 128.

73. Hartman, "Intimate History, Radical Narrative," 129.

74. Sharpe, *In the Wake*, 7.

75. Hartman, "Intimate History, Radical Narrative," 131. I do not want to overstate the resonances between Hartman's project in *Wayward Lives* and Cavarero's engagement with Penelope, however. While Cavarero's retelling of Penelope's story emphasizes the communality and relationality of the women co-conspiring to rupture patriarchal power from within, it is worth remembering the hierarchical class dynamics that operate in the weaving room. After all, the other women are not Penelope's friends and equals but her handmaidens, whose job is explicitly to care for Penelope. This is perhaps especially relevant given the racial dynamics that overlap with the labor of care in the United States (past and present).

76. Hartman, "Intimate History, Radical Narrative," 127.

77. Hartman, *Wayward Lives*, 4.
78. Hartman, *Wayward Lives*, xv.
79. Hartman, *Wayward Lives*, 5–6.
80. Hartman, *Wayward Lives*, 31.
81. Hartman, *Wayward Lives*, 31.
82. She also implements Christina Sharpe's methodology of annotation, as described in *In the Wake*, which I do not have the space here to describe in detail, though I do so in my dissertation, *Nonlinearity as Care: Black, Feminist, and Queer Temporalities of History* (DePaul University, 2022).
83. Hartman, *Wayward Lives*, 15.
84. Hartman, *Wayward Lives*, 14.
85. Hartman, *Wayward Lives*, 14.
86. Hartman, *Wayward Lives*, 26.
87. Hartman, *Wayward Lives*, 27.
88. Hartman, *Wayward Lives*, 30.
89. Hartman, *Wayward Lives*, 31.
90. Hartman, "Intimate History, Radical Narrative," 130.
91. Hartman, "Venus in Two Acts," 3.
92. Hartman, "Venus in Two Acts," 3. The content of that *us* does not necessarily include every reader of Hartman's work (including me). I take it that the *us* she speaks of is more likely the Black women and girls of the present. She does not make this explicit in the part of the text that is quoted. However, she does indicate more about the content of the *we* and the *us* in "Intimate History, Radical Narrative" when she describes her methodology as an attempt to "regard Black life from inside the circle and to recapture the wild thought and beautiful recklessness capable of imagining the *with* and the *us* and the *we*." Hartman, "Intimate History, Radical Narrative," 131.
93. Hartman, "Venus in Two Acts," 4.
94. Hartman, "Venus in Two Acts," 4.
95. Connolly, Fuentes, "Introduction: From Archives of Slavery to Liberated Futures?" 106.
96. Smallwood, "The Politics of the Archive," 126–27.
97. Smallwood, "The Politics of the Archive," 126.
98. Cavarero, *Relating Narratives*, 53.
99. Hartman, *Wayward Lives, Beautiful Experiments*, 349.

Bibliography

Burkins, Adriana Michelle. "Strands of Power, Tools of Resistance: Black Hair and Consciousness as Concept and Medium." PhD diss., University of North Carolina at Chapel Hill, 2019. ProQuest. https://doi.org/10.17615/7288-9704.

Cavarero, Adriana. *For More than One Voice: Toward a Philosophy of Vocal Expression*. Translated by Paul A. Kottman. Stanford, CA: Stanford University Press, 2005.

———. *Inclinations: A Critique of Rectitude*. Stanford, CA: Stanford University Press, 2016.

———. *In Spite of Plato: Feminist Rewriting of Ancient Philosophy*. Translated by Serena Anderlini D'Onfrio and Áine O'Healy. New York: Routledge, 1995.

———. "Narrative Against Destruction." *New Literary History* 46, no. 1 (Winter 2015): 1–16. https://www.jstor.org/stable/24542656.

———. *Relating Narratives*. Translated by Paul A. Kottman. New York: Routledge, 2000.

Cempellin, Leda. "Sonya Clark: Hair as Collective Identity." *Juliet Art Magazine*, no. 181 (February–March 2017): 91.

Clark, Sonya. "Sculptural Headdresses." *Ornament: The Art of Personal Adornment* 20, no. 3 (Spring 1997): 33–37.

Connolly, Brian, and Marisa Fuentes, "Introduction: From Archives of Slavery to Liberated Futures?" *History of the Present* 6, no. 2 (Fall 2016):105–16. https://doi.org/10.5406/historypresent.6.2.0105.

Ford, Tanisha. *Liberated Threads: Black Women, Style, and the Global Politics of Soul*. Chapel Hill: University of North Carolina Press, 2015.

Freeman, Elizabeth. *Beside You in Time: Sense Methods and Queer Sociabilities in the American 19th Century*. Durham, NC: Duke University Press, 2019.

Hartman, Saidiya V. "The Belly of the World: A Note on Black Women's Labors." *Souls* 18, no. 1 (January–March 2016): 166–73. https://doi.org/10.1080/10999949.2016.1162596.

———. "Intimate History, Radical Narrative." *Journal of African American History* 106, no. 1 (Winter 2021): 127–35. https://doi.org/10.1086/712019.

———. *Lose Your Mother: A Journey along the Atlantic Slave Route*. New York: Farrar, Straus, and Giroux, 2007.

———. *Scenes of Subjection: Terror, Slavery, and Self-Making in 19th-Century America*. New York: Oxford University Press, 1997.

———. "Venus in Two Acts." *Small Axe* 12, no. 2 (June 2008): 1–14. https://doi.org/10.1215/-12-2-1.

———. *Wayward Lives, Beautiful Experiments*. New York: Serpent's Tail, 2019.

Honig, Bonnie. *A Feminist Theory of Refusal*. Cambridge, MA: Harvard University Press, 2021.

Jones, Rachel. "Inclining toward New Forms of Life: Cavarero, Agamben, and Hartman." In *Political Bodies: Writings on Adriana Cavarero's Political Thought*, edited by Paula Landerreche Cardillo and Rachel Silverbloom, 155–184. Albany: State University of New York Press, 2024.

Landerreche Cardillo, Paula. "'Taking the Thread for a Walk': Feminist Resistance to the Philosophical Order in Adriana Cavarero and María Lugones." In *Political Bodies: Writings on Adriana Cavarero's Political Thought*, edited by

Paula Landerreche Cardillo and Rachel Silverbloom, 85–108. Albany: State University of New York Press, 2024.

Sharpe, Christina. *In the Wake: On Blackness and Being*. Durham, NC: Duke University Press, 2016.

Smallwood, Stephanie. "The Politics of the Archive and History's Accountability to the Enslaved," *History of the Present* 6, no. 2 (October 1, 2016): 117–32. https://doi.org/10.5406/historypresent.6.2.0117.

Söderbäck, Fanny. *Revolutionary Time*. Albany: State University of New York Press, 2019.

———. "Singularity in the Wake of Slavery: Adriana Cavarero's Ontology of Uniqueness and Alex Haley's Roots." *Philosophy Compass* 15, no. 7 (July 2020). https://doi.org/10.1111/phc3.12685.

Trouillot, Michel-Rolph. *Silencing the Past: Power and the Production of History*. Boston: Beacon Press, 1995.

Vergès, Françoise. "Capitalocene, Waste, Race, and Gender." *e-flux* 100 (May 2019). https://www.e-flux.com/journal/100/269165/capitalocene-waste-race-and-gender/.

Walcott, Derek. "The Sea Is History." *The Paris Review* 74 (Fall–Winter 1978). https://www.theparisreview.org/poetry/7020/the-sea-is-history-derek-walcott.

Part Three
The Body in Politics: Comversations with Materialisms

Six

One's Body in Political Engagement
Changing the Relation between Public and Private

Elisabetta Bertolino

Introduction

For the philosopher Adriana Cavarero, body politics requires an ontological rethinking of body and self in the world: asking who one is and who speaks, questioning what constitutes politics, and considering how one's private interiority and unique body-self can engage as a whole in the public space of politics. In this paper, I consider the vulnerable body—as Cavarero intends—in terms of relationality and as the ground of politics. In other words, the body, as the private sphere par excellence, comes to be constitutive of the public sphere of politics, orienting politics by transforming the traditional vertical approach into a bending and inclining approach. The body becomes both a radical space of resistance for and beyond politics and a trigger element for political institutions.

In Cavarero's perspective, there is an attempt to politicize the body by rethinking it ontologically, politicizing the whole understanding of politics, and ultimately orienting politics via the body. The traditional, nonpolitical, biological position of the body can be seen as a source of knowledge and power, capable of reversing the body's position in politics and changing politics itself. In her view, the body is not a general entity separated from the self. Rather, the body is part of the self, together with the soul and the mind, and involves vulnerability. One's vulnerability is revealed when one speaks, suffers, takes care, interacts with others.

In her book *Stately Bodies*, Cavarero talks about the strange relationship between the body and politics.[1] The body, for Cavarero, has been expelled from the founding categories of politics, if only through its use as a metaphor. *Stately Bodies* explores the curious prevalence of bodily metaphors in conceptions of incorporeal institutions. Cavarero revisits *Antigone* as the tragedy in which a displaced body allows for the disruption of a misogynous political order. In *Antigone*, the incorporeal institutions of the polis, founded on reason, fight the impulses and weaknesses of the body in order to achieve power.[2] The polis, as the locus of male reason par excellence (Creon), is confronted with a body (Antigone) that insists on another passionate and carnal order.

For Cavarero, the masculine and logocentric character of the body in politics began with the Greeks and was entrusted to a tradition that endures today in the opposition between female and male subjectivity, where the banished body is seen as female.[3] Since the Greeks, the corporeal has been considered nonpolitical. The body that appears in politics in no way resembles the banished private and biological body since the body of the political metaphor is thought of as already adult, perfect, and vigorous, fit for display in the public sphere; neither infancy nor old age, nor sickness, nor disability debilitate its flesh. Consequently, the real body is believed to be the opposite of the logos as the fleshy component of existence; it is construed as a female body that is nonpolitical and constrained to biological life and, thus, ontologically separated and split.

Contrary to Cavarero's ontological rethinking of the body, feminists have generally attempted to politicize the nonpolitical body by publicly foregrounding it. Yet, this requires shifting the body—still private, split, and construed as a detached biological animality—to the logos of the public sphere. By doing this, current feminist politics appears to politicize the body, but the body remains separated from itself, unable to speak in a relational context, and thus disengaged from politics.

The separation of the ontological body becomes evident during medical emergencies, when the body enters politics by necessity due to the danger of diseases, with the body becoming both the subject and the object of politics. The role of the body in such biopolitical contexts—as in the Covid-19 pandemic—has been analyzed by Robert Esposito, who has reflected on immunitary discourses and the ambivalence of the body in biopolitical contexts. Even in Hannah Arendt's perspective on body politics—in which Cavarero's political thought is rooted—there appears to be some kind of ontological fracture in engaging the body in politics. In Arendt, the body that participates in the agora and acts anew through plurality needs, in some ways, to retreat from the burden of its physical necessity and center more on public freedom.

This paper focuses on the political engagement of the body in Adriana Cavarero's thought through her ontological rethinking of the body as a whole. I will also discuss the ambivalence and separation of the body that occurs when the body is engaged in biopolitics—as in Esposito's analysis—or when the body needs to go beyond its private necessity to exercise freedom in terms of plurality—as in Hannah Arendt's political vision. Despite their diverging understandings of body politics, in the work of Cavarero, Esposito, and Arendt there is a common need to overcome the abstract individuality of the political subject and rethink public and private spaces of body politics.

When Body Politics Becomes Necessity and Security

For Hannah Arendt, freedom, as opposed to necessity, is the main characteristic of politics.[4] Such a division implies Arendt's refusal of a politics focused on the maintenance of life and security. For Arendt, when the goal of politics consists of safeguarding life—as in liberalism—politics becomes directed by necessity, and the body's engagement in politics remains trapped in the private sphere.[5]

Foucault understood well that politics' behavior can be inextricably focused on the dimension of *bios*. When life takes charge of politics, the biological and corporeal are politicized, merging public with private.[6] Law and medicine work together, and a new rationality arises centered on the question of life and its conservation, development, and management.[7] When political practice is directed toward life and its processes rather than toward freedom, the body gets involved in politics, but only in terms of necessity and security. The body seems right at the center of politics but is actually socially unimportant; this happens probably because the body is ontologically separated from itself and from its constitutive paradigm.

In the wake of Foucault, Roberto Esposito explains how biopolitics relates to politics' dependence on, and affirmation of, life and the body. Biopolitics is the politics of (or over) life/body; it objectifies its subject.[8]

Biopolitics for Roberto Esposito, in fact, contains a riddle: that is, life/body and politics seem to almost oppose one another.[9] In biopolitics, politics must satisfy all corporeal requests and, at the same time, exercise control over bodies. Therefore, for Esposito, politics not only moves vertically—from the top down, from state to individuals—but also horizontally in the sense that it improves performance, maximizes life, guarantees happiness, and also strengthens the state by expanding life.[10]

Moreover, Esposito notes how within a politics of life, a sort of immunity politics has arisen. The coronavirus, for instance, attacks our bodies through the air we breathe; it proliferates in the respiratory tract, where there is a passage of air. Emissions by the breath and voice need to be restricted because they can become a means of contagion. During a pandemic emergency, it becomes important to render individuals immune to contagions and for them to acquire herd immunity. Conversely, in a condition of normality, one's breath and voice allow them to relate in community and reveal intimate aspects of themselves with others.

Being immune, explains Esposito, implies both an exemption from obligation and a privilege.[11] Immunity infers two different trajectories.[12] The first trajectory consists of the fact that immunity refers to something proper: belonging to something uncommon and thus noncommunal. Immunity can thus be understood in opposition to community, as immunity interrupts the communal circuit of gift-giving.[13] Gift-giving is a social activity that confirms communal relationships and social interactions. Early studies in the fields of anthropology and sociology emphasize the importance of gift-giving and reciprocity in social relations.[14]

The second trajectory refers to a more biomedical aspect with a political application: the resistance of an organism to a virus or bacteria. The resistance/immunity of the organism is often actively induced (for example, a vaccine), stemming from the idea that an attenuated form of infection can protect against a more harmful infection.[15] The inoculation of less harmful quantities of a virus encourages the development of antibodies capable of fighting the virus at an early stage.[16] This biomedical trajectory of the immunitary paradigm also has a political implication, suggesting that politics do not operate through action but, rather, through reaction.[17] Immunity politics such as social distancing imply privatizing the body's relational function.

A context such as the Covid pandemic aligns precisely with the biopolitical contexts analyzed by Esposito, where immunity politics constitutes and reconstitutes the body and engages with the body by negating the body itself. Bodily violence and separation appear to be incorporated inside politics. Antibodies protect the body by assimilating a foreign substance, which induces an immune response in the body, creating antigens in order to avoid strong reactions to the disease. To preserve itself in the short term, the body objectifies itself by introducing the foreign substance to create antibodies, though in the long term those antibodies protect the body by providing immunity from the contagion.

Similarly, within biopolitics, the body enters politics but is made immune from the contagion of the community and considered only from the point of view of disease. As a matter of fact, if the body is at the center of politics, the potential for disease is at the center of the body.[18] Therefore—as Cavarero suggests—the body enters politics as separated from its constitutive relationality, uniqueness, and vulnerabilities and is imagined only in terms of life necessity and security, in terms of physical life to be both defended and controlled. The immunitary significance of body politics is that the body becomes the ultimate criterion for legitimating political power, and an antidote is needed to avoid dissolving the possibilities of the body itself. As Esposito has underlined, there are aporias and paradoxes in such an engagement of politics with the body.

Donatella Di Cesare has also underlined how coronavirus increased the aspects of immunity and *bios* already intertwined with current politics.[19] The self-centered individual of liberalism expels the other and the body to feel secure. Di Cesare underlines a series of measures that politics adopts to safeguard body and life.[20] First, politics grounds itself on the exception; executive power prevails over the power of parliament, and politics becomes more about excluding, separating, and distancing the individual self and body from other bodies. Fear of the breath and voice of other bodies, the outside, and immigrants makes the emergence of discrimination against the other even more apparent. The ways in which the discourse of the virus emphasizes bodily boundaries and the expulsion of germs is also reflected in how national borders are discussed in relation to foreign invaders or immigrants. Thus, it is also the national body that is managed through body politics.

Political priorities shift from the external to the internal-private. As Arendt explains, such an approach is typical of certain liberal philosophies and politics grounded on the identity of the individual, which were present well before the time of the coronavirus pandemic.[21] As social and physical distancing became the most important measure to prevent contamination, the engagement of the body in politics became that of a body already split and separated from itself. There was a shift of interests and boundaries from public to private, as if political power was not governed from above but inscribed in the lives and bodies of citizens and so enjoyed more power in order to satisfy all the requests coming from the body.

These ideas concerning the politics of life and the body are reflected in today's politics. This was especially true during the Covid emergency, when, more than before, politics was revealed to be intersected with the life and security of the self-individual. In the time of Covid, some of those mechanisms of engaging the body in politics were, in fact, amplified. Suddenly, politics had discovered the banished body to be vulnerable and focused mainly on guaranteeing the security of life and immunity of the body.

In such a context, as Arendt has envisioned, political freedom gets linked with life processes and necessity and, consequently, politics is unable to maintain a space of plurality; instead, politics becomes a way for the liberal individual to interact with themselves.[22] For Arendt, liberalism separates the subject-individual from emotions—from nonrational and physical aspects—by focusing precisely on an abstract subject capable of "will power."[23] This causes the same self-centered and sovereign individual to be unable to act.[24] We can derive from this that in such a politics, the focus on the physical body remains a non-engagement with the body.[25]

When politics is regulated by necessity rather than freedom, as Arendt suggests, life and the body, generally excluded from politics, enter politics. The question is whether the body can engage in politics in a horizon that is not determined by the immunization of biopolitics—whether the body can be engaged in politics without being split and separated. In the next section, I explore ways of engaging the body in politics differently by comparing Cavarero with Arendt.

Hannah Arendt's Idea of Body Politics

In *The Human Condition*, Arendt distinguishes between three fundamental human activities: labor, work, and action.[26] While *labor* is, for Arendt, the activity that corresponds to the biological processes of the human body and *work* is an artificial activity, only *action* is an activity that allows plurality, and she views it as the functioning condition of politics. Arendt divides public life from labor and the necessities of the body, as the private sphere and the body become hidden in such a framework. Consequently, at first glance, one could assume that there is an underlying message in Arendt's political understanding that contrasts with the conception of labor in modern times.

Nowadays, many feminists believe that bodily functions and material concerns should not be hidden and that there is a need to make the body and its necessities public. Feminism can even be interpreted as a fight to get the body, and women, into the public realm, bringing in the body and its necessities as principles of reality. Thus, the modern emancipation of women seems to subvert Hannah Arendt's political approach.

However, even though Arendt's distinctions between labor, work, and action—as well as her distinctions between public and private, freedom and necessity—appear as aporias between the sphere of politics and the body, we can understand that Arendtian politics requires the body to act in plurality; the body is part of her understanding of politics. Arendt explains later in *The Human Condition* that these three activities are connected with the condition of human existence and, in particular, with natality as the capacity for beginning something new.[27]

As Arendt grounds politics on birth and natality—that is, on the body—we can deduce that the body and the material conditions of human existence are the basis for political action in Arendt's body politics. Yet, for Arendt, politics happens when we can act in a situation of plurality rather than being trapped in necessity. The political sphere is generated by sharing the words and deeds of unique human beings. For Arendt, then, the political lies in the relational space between human beings, and in acting together and revealing their uniqueness, people make a political space.[28]

Cavarero suggests that the way to understand politics in Arendt is as a pure concept outside traditional understandings of institutional politics, where natality is politics' most important material condition.[29] The fact that Arendt speaks of unique human beings in plurality, which is different from speaking of citizens or a mass of people, is important to Cavarero. Plurality is the specific characteristic of human beings to be individually unique. The uniqueness of one (body-mind-soul) and the community in which one can express their uniqueness are common points in Cavarero's political thinking.

For Cavarero, there are spatial, corporeal, and material dimensions in Arendt's politics.[30] Arendt's politics, in fact, needs a plurality of flesh-and-bone actors to physically interact.[31] We can say that there is a body in her conception of politics, as Arendt's politics implies a shared space between the actors, where each can appear, speak, and act. Politics happens between a plurality of unique material and corporeal beings, face to face, in a material and concrete space, here and now. Politics is, in fact, a space where one's material and corporeal uniqueness appears with others.[32] Those aspects are developed by Cavarero in more radical and material ways.

Consequently, the unique and private body in Arendt is to be considered political, despite the distinctions she makes between labor, work, and action. Therefore, in both Arendt and Cavarero, there is a political possibility for unique, private bodies to have plural and relational interactions in public spaces where the private uniqueness of the body is valued and constitutive of the plurality itself. Such an interconnection between public and private in Arendt's body politics allows fundamental rights to be exercised, not as ideals but as ways of acting. We can even say that, for Arendt, both the material and physical private dimension and plurality are fundamental conditions of politics.

There is an aspect of political performativity reflected in Arendt's ideas of actions and plurality. Such performativity changes the relationship between public and private. While the individual of liberalism necessitates a private sphere to exist outside politics, and politics is dealt with in abstract ways—that is, in forms where the public *agora* remains abstract and hidden, without material interconnection of bodies—in Arendt (and in Cavarero) there is a corporeal and unique human being, in flesh and bones, whose private aspects of uniqueness and materiality appear during their public, physical interactions in a material *agora*.

To understand Arendt's view for Cavarero, one has to refer especially to her analysis of totalitarianism.[33] Totalitarianism seems to compress people together until they are formed into one. By contrast, a public space emerges whenever people act together in concert. For Arendt, a political space is not a space in any topographical or institutional sense, and there is no division between public and private spaces. In such a political vision, even a home, a private space par excellence, can become a public space whenever there is action in concert. Any location becomes public space in that it becomes the site of common action, a type of political power where freedom is possible.

For Arendt, the distinction between public and private, or body and politics, coincides with the opposition of necessity and freedom. Yet—I want to emphasize again with Cavarero—Arendt's move is not to refuse the body but to call for body politics as an expression of freedom rather than necessity. Arendt talks of the power that emanates from acting in plurality, where the private uniqueness of the body appears in that liberatory space that is politics. Arendt's political vision is grounded in the polis as a space where freedom can appear through words and deeds and where it is possible to act and begin something anew. We find a similar political space in the concept of relationality in Cavarero, where one's uniqueness is revealed by speaking in one's voice, yet Cavarero focuses more radically on the body, with further consequences for body politics.

Engaging One's Vulnerable Body in Cavarero's Political Vision

Cavarero's ontological body paradigm disorients both Arendt's conception of body politics and the division between public and private. In Cavarero's way of envisioning politics, one's body and its vulnerabilities are central. Cavarero engages the body in politics by making it an indissoluble part of the political self: avoiding divisions and separations between the self and the nonpolitical body or between the body and itself. The self is a unique body, mind, and soul that speaks in its own voice—a voice that starts from the body and continues through the air that one's body breathes. In breathing and speaking together in community, one's uniqueness and vulnerabilities are revealed.[34] All this works against the *bios* and immunity politics of social distancing, antibodies, and understanding life as security and necessity, which are grounded on an ontological separation of the body and the self.

Contrastingly, Cavarero's political vision is grounded on community: unique bodies and selves being together, aware of their vulnerability, and opting to ethically take care of those who are more vulnerable. In such a perspective, temporary physical distancing or administering vaccines for immunity against Covid-19 may be understood as part of a protocol of care for the community rather than as individual immunity from the community and its voices.

One's voice participates in the communal production of words and language. Speaking is always to another in a polyphonic community of voices. Such a conceptualization of the voice—as coming from one's corporeal body to produce language in community—exemplifies how the body engages with the political system. Language, in fact, represents the crossing point between the body and political institutions.

Saying—for Cavarero—is more important than the said. Selves are political because they speak to one another in their corporeal voices and, in doing so, reveal their uniqueness and fragilities, not because they speak of political things. What is important in her political understanding is the quality of the community's relations and actions; temporary distancing and immunity measures can be seen precisely as such a quality action when positioned in terms of community. One's voice and the vulnerability of the body in relationality represent the energy charge for politics and language. Beginning from this understanding, Cavarero criticizes the vertical posture of the political subject as the abstract individual that stands upright in isolation from other individuals. In Cavarero's ontological frame of uniqueness, relationality, and vulnerability, the body-self loses the vertical position of an isolated subject of rights in an abstract, political, and public space.[35]

As a matter of fact, for Cavarero, one's body can deconstruct the traditional philosophical link between politics and verticality. A politics of verticality is a politics of institutions, systemic language, and predetermined subjects, where there is a "structural complicity between the various systems of truth constructed by philosophers."[36] The subject of a vertical politics is "steadily balanced on its vertical posture, does not lean, does not bend, does not incline and does not become old or vulnerable; it stands upright, very confident."[37]

Thus, for Cavarero, it is not only a matter of unmasking the notorious exclusion of the body from politics, politicizing the body by making it public, or focusing on the necessity and security of the body to control itself. The question for Cavarero is more complicated. It is about rethinking the body, who one is, and who speaks to make politics a real engagement with one's unique, corporeal, and vulnerable body. Politics for Cavarero happens precisely when we relate with our vulnerable bodies, when we deal with our wounds and frailties, and thus choose to bend and incline toward others. Speaking in a political community also implies dealing with the vulnerability of oneself and others around us. Such vulnerability appears and is revealed if we focus on the body.

Cavarero grounds politics on the body's relationality, and such a body reveals all her fragility. Vulnerability is revealed to us and others continuously when speaking and acting together with other bodies. Aware of vulnerability, the corporeal self inclines toward others, resisting the arrogant uprightness of the subject of traditional politics. Thus, there are two political scenarios for Cavarero: "The free and rational individual who stands upright and whose correspondent political model postulates the natural symmetry between equally autarkic individuals standing upright [. . .]. The second scenario presents us with the issue of a relational subjectivity, structurally asymmetrical and unbalanced, consisting of the paradigmatic exposure of the human as vulnerable to the inclined posture of the other who bends over him or her."[38]

We can suppose that the first political scenario is the one grounded on the traditional liberal philosophy, where the subject is constructed in abstract and general ways as a self-referential subject and where body and vulnerability are excluded from politics or can enter politics only peripherally through reforms or processes of body objectification. In such a political context, what is vulnerable is private and can be admitted into the public sphere—and consequently into politics—through the ontological exclusion of the body operated in traditional liberal political philosophy in the first place.

In contrast, the second political scenario envisaged by Cavarero rejoins the ontological fracture operated by traditional political liberal ideology by allowing one's material body in relationality to be itself political. Consequently, in being a newborn baby, a disabled person, an old person, a woman, or a man, a vulnerable body-self becomes constitutive of politics. Politics is no longer made of abstract significations or vague communications. Rather, what makes and orients politics is precisely the relationality between vulnerable bodies and the uniqueness of the speakers. For Cavarero: "The political valence of signifying is [. . .] shifted from speech—and from language as a system of signification—to the speaker. The speakers are not political because of what they say, but because they say it to others who share an interactive space of reciprocal exposure. To speak to one another is to communicate to one another the unrepeatable uniqueness of each speaker."[39] In Arendt we see that what counts for politics is the freedom of unique selves to act in plurality. Arendt's conception of politics can happen regardless of the space (public agora or private home), as Arendt talks of a sort of public happiness, that of acting in plurality, and it is precisely this specific public aspect of life that is political.[40] Politics is experiencing public freedom in plurality, acting together in a shared public space.[41] Politics consists of a common space of visibility where every*body* can reveal their uniqueness and thus enjoy being together, being happy in discussing and participating politically.[42] To do this, Arendt's politics goes beyond any division and shows itself to be a pure idea of politics.

Like Arendt, Cavarero focuses on a unique, relational body-self. Here, too, the self enjoys participation, and in relationality one's uniqueness is revealed. And yet, in Cavarero, there is a radical perspective of vulnerability with a body that exposes its vulnerability in relationality to also experience the vulnerability of other bodies. There is, in Cavarero's political philosophy, an ontology that is deeply aware of the reality of the human condition. Our dependent body makes freedom conditional because this is our possibility of being. Politics is made by non-sovereign subjects that are dependent on one another.

In line with Cavarero's philosophical ontology, Luigina Mortari explains how, as corporeal beings, it is impossible to escape fragility and that awareness of this constraint makes us understand the reality of being.[43] It becomes paramount to be aware of the reality of the body and not to lose track of such a reality. Lack of sovereignty and the weakness of our condition lead to both Cavarero and Mortari choosing care as political action. If for Arendt, in some ways, we need to go beyond necessity to act, participate, and enjoy freedom, for Cavarero, participatory actions and freedom are made possible by remaining radically anchored to the ontological understanding of beings conditioned by necessity.

In Cavarero, politics happens precisely in such a moment of ethical relationality, where one can speak and reveal one's vulnerability. Such an exposure of uniqueness and vulnerability needs politics to take account of dependence, asymmetry, and hospitality, to be a public space of reciprocal interaction where bodies can incline toward others. And I think that it is precisely the action of inclining, bending, and choosing politically and ethically to care for others that generates happiness in Cavarero's political vision.

From this perspective, taking care of the body in the context of a pandemic can be understood as a moment in which one becomes more aware of vulnerability and where necessity is not intended as separation from the body or as a limit but rather as part of the body and body politics. For Cavarero, freedom happens at the same time as we are dependent bodies and selves in necessity, as this is the condition of our life and thus the condition of politics. Political happiness is experienced through awareness of the limits of the body and the ethical and political action of inclining in relationality. The body, with its necessity and vulnerability, engages in politics and constitutes politics. Thus, for Cavarero, the public moment of politics does not exclude the private, inner space of the body's vulnerability. Taking care of the sphere of necessity—that is, vulnerability—is part of who we are, our uniqueness, and orients participatory politics. Cavarero's political perspective connects public and private spheres through the vulnerability of the body in a way that supersedes dichotomies.

On the contrary, the traditional philosophical tendency of thinking about a political subject in terms of identity, which are foreign to the body, creates cuts, splits, and separations in the construction of the subject and in the way it intends politics. Politics needs to give shape to life without losing the connection to materiality and the body. Such a political shape has to take into account our ontological weakness, our corporeal fragility and vulnerability.

Thus, even though Cavarero starts from the Arendtian image of natality and from the mother and the newborn, Cavarero connects deeply the body to politics. More than focusing on the newborn as a new beginning in life and a new possibility for action, Cavarero focuses her political approach on the relational inclination between the mother and the newborn. To the Arendtian political vision, Cavarero adds the ethical relationality connected to the vulnerability of one's body-self, meaning that political participation implies consigning one's vulnerable body to the other and calling for a political ability to incline and bend over to others.

We can say that Cavarero emphasizes the quality of relationality in Arendtian participatory plurality. What Cavarero does is a demolition of the political subject in its verticality and a rethinking of the political subject ontologically, grounding the self in the body and the body in vulnerability within a relational public context. On the contrary, the verticality of the political subject, its invulnerability and egocentricity, emerges from the division of public and private and the exclusion of the private body, which are often reflected in actions of discrimination, racism, and homophobia. This emphasis on the quality of relationality and vulnerability in Cavarero is precisely political.[44] In the sense that politics springs from the relationality and vulnerability of concrete and unique bodies, it is not based on free and autonomous individuals but on vulnerable bodies and selves in relationality.

The subject of Kant is exemplary of the division between public and private in politics, and Cavarero uses him to show the traditional political scenario.[45] Cavarero underlines that Kant does not love children as, for him, children are deficient in reason and intellect and instead communicate through noise, songs, and crying; they are thus disturbing thinking subjects.[46] Kant does not allow the self-referential subject to bend; the subject can only be upright, rational, and public. The austere and vertical subject of Kant does not bend, even into himself, and overall does not incline toward others. Consequently, the relation between mother and child is seen as incomplete, as inclining in an asymmetrical way—which is not the way of the vertical and balanced subject—is not political according to Kant's view.

On the contrary, in Cavarero's view, the asymmetrical relationship of caring between bodies-selves is political. There is thus an ontological rethinking of the body-self, of who one is and what speaking politically implies. The banished body is not simply brought to the public space and made political but rethought ontologically within a dimension of uniqueness, vulnerability, and relationality. The intimate power of the state over the body becomes the power of the state that aligns with the intimate body.

Conclusion

In conclusion, Cavarero appears to change how she engages the body in politics. Cavarero maintains—as does Arendt—the idea of politics as a liberatory public moment when she talks of relationality and a polyphonic community of voices. However, this does not mean to retreat from our material roots and bodies. It seems that Cavarero's ontological view of the body intersects deeply with her political view. The result is a connection of the body with politics that deals in some ways with the tensions between freedom and necessity and the public and private spheres.

In addition, politics happens for Cavarero in a community where one can speak to others beginning with one's body and voice. Such public communication is penetrated continuously by the private sphere, as uniqueness and body-related aspects appear in public, resulting in a revelation of intimate features. And, in turn, the appearance of private intimate aspects promotes the awareness of responsibility for actions in public and in the community. Precisely, awareness of vulnerability might bring one to see social distancing and immunity as necessary actions that may cut relationality in the short term but that, in the long term, protect and restore the community. Awareness of the body and its vulnerability is the key element for differently understanding political limits. Temporary mechanisms of separation, physical distancing, and immunization—as during the Covid-19 pandemic—may then be seen in terms of taking care and safeguarding vulnerability.

Politics becomes the capacity for taking care of the uniqueness of each body, the plurality of the community, and the diverse vulnerability of bodies. Acting politically results in searching for a good life for both oneself and the other, enabled by the capacity for bending and choosing ethically to care about life and the body. There is a need to act and speak from the relationships between our bodies, which confront us with fragility and vulnerability. Bending and caring are political actions, ethically connected to our relational bodies by flesh and bones, and they are also the foundation for political participation.

By focusing on the body, Cavarero also goes beyond the dichotomized gender and hierarchically ordered logics of identity at the basis of traditional political institutions. As dichotomies are not neutral and are grounded on the exclusion of the body, Cavarero rethinks the aporias of the body. In her ontological understanding of the body, one's body—with its necessities and frailties—is no longer seen as superfluous and is no longer associated only with women. The body is a necessary part of life, and the body is thought of as belonging to everyone, man and woman.

From what has been discussed, Cavarero's political philosophy could be considered as a pure political thought and a radical political space outside political institutions; it is a liberatory space where one can speak in one's voice, from inside out, against the existing political and symbolic order. Yet, in Cavarero's political vision, I also appreciate the potentiality for revitalizing current political institutions, as institutions are relevant in defining, orienting, and transforming political agendas, and they can move away from a vertical conception. Political order is often imagined as verticality; the homo erectus is the main referent for politics, where head, heart, and stomach indicate verticality within the body itself.[47]

Following Cavarero's insights, political institutions need instead to disrupt such a verticality and engage with the uniqueness and vulnerability of every*body* in the plurality of the community. If institutions contain tensions between inside and out, private and public, body and abstract political subject, one's physical body no longer has to be included in politics. Rather, it needs to become constitutive of politics and be thought from inside politics itself. While the logic of inclusion implies politics is an already existent thing in which to locate the banished body, focusing on the exposure of bodies—that is, revealing one's uniqueness and vulnerabilities—reverses the logic of political institutions from the inside.

The relationality of bodies moves institutional politics from being centered on a generic, self-sufficient, and divided subject of rightness to an open and relational corporeal self that is aware of vulnerability. Infancy, old age, sickness, disabilities, and other vulnerable life events connected to the body show the illusion of the self-referential subject of traditional political institutions. By reframing political institutions from the perspective of the body and life, politics is regenerated. Cavarero seems to suggest that without the pain of a body that gets wounded, sick, and ages, there would be no limit from which to orient politics; there would only be an illusory politics that suffocates life and no real happiness. She makes us reflect on the fact that it is precisely the body that saves us from an unhappy politics built on a constructed and split subjectivity that excludes and separates the body from the self and the community.

Notes

1. Adriana Cavarero, *Stately Bodies: Literature, Philosophy and the Question of Gender*, trans. Robert de Lucca and Deanna Shemek (Ann Arbor: University of Michigan Press, 2002).
2. Cavarero, "On the Body of Antigone," in *Stately Bodies*, 13–97.
3. Cavarero, *Stately Bodies*, 18.
4. Hannah Arendt, *The Human Condition* (Chicago: University of Chicago Press, 1958), 7.
5. Hannah Arendt, "What Is Freedom?" in *Between Past and Future* (New York: Penguin Books, 2006).
6. Michael Foucault, "The Birth of Social Medicine," in *Power: Essential Works of Foucault 1954–1984, Volume 3* (London: Penguin Books, 2002), 134–56.
7. Foucault, "The Birth of Social Medicine," 134–56.
8. Roberto Esposito, *Bios: Biopolitica e filosofia* (Turin: Einaudi, 2004), 25.
9. Esposito, *Bios*, 25.
10. Esposito, *Bios*, 30.
11. Roberto Esposito, *Immunitas: The Protection and Negation of Life*, trans. Zakiya Hanafi (Cambridge: Polity Press, 2011), 5.
12. Esposito, *Immunitas*, 5.
13. Esposito, *Immunitas*, 6.
14. Marcel Mauss, *The Gift: The Form and Reason for Exchange in Archaic Society* (London: Cohen and West, 1954).
15. Esposito, *Immunitas*, 7.
16. Esposito, *Immunitas*, 7.
17. Esposito, *Immunitas*, 8.
18. Esposto, *Immunitas*, 15.
19. Donatella Di Cesare, *Virus sovrano? L'asfissia capitalistica* (Turin: Bollati Boringhieri, 2020).
20. Di Cesare, *Virus*.
21. Arendt, "What Is Freedom?" 155–63.
22. Arendt, "What Is Freedom?" 155.
23. Arendt, "What Is Freedom?" 157–63.
24. Arendt, "What Is Freedom?" 157–63.
25. The body has been already split and banished from the subject of liberalism.

26. Hannah Arendt, *The Human Condition* (Chicago: University of Chicago Press, 1958).
27. Arendt, *The Human Condition*, 8.
28. On this, see generally: Adriana Cavarero, *Democrazia sorgiva: Note sul pensiero politico di Hannah Arendt* (Milan: Raffaello Cortina Editore, 2019).
29. Cavarero, *Democrazia sorgiva*, 38.
30. Cavarero, *Democrazia sorgiva*, 38.
31. Cavarero, *Democrazia sorgiva*, 39.
32. Cavarero, *Democrazia sorgiva*, 38.
33. Hannah Arendt, *The Origins of Totalitarianism* (New York: Schoen Books, 1951).
34. On the voice and Adriana Cavarero, see Elisabetta Bertolino, *Adriana Cavarero: Resistance and the Voice of Law* (London: Routledge, 2018).
35. Adriana Cavarero, "Recritude: Reflections on Postural Ontology," *Journal of Speculative Philosophy* 27, no. 3 (2013): 220–35.
36. Cavarero, "Recritude," 221.
37. Cavarero, "Rectitude," 221.
38. Cavarero, "Recritute," 229.
39. Cavarero, *For More than One Voice: Toward a Philosophy of Vocal Expression*, trans. Paul A. Kottman (Stanford, CA: Stanford University Press, 2005), 190.
40. Cavarero, *Democrazia sorgiva*, 55–58.
41. Cavarero, *Democrazia sorgiva*, 58.
42. Cavarero, *Democrazia sorgiva*, 59.
43. Luigina Mortari, *Politica della cura: Prendere a cuore la vita* (Milan: Raffaello Cortina Editore, 2021); see also Luigina Mortari, *Filosofia della cura* (Milan: Raffaello Cortina Editore, 2015).
44. Adriana Cavarero, *Inclinazioni: Critica della rettitudine* (Milan: Raffaello Cortina Editore, 2013), 23.
45. Cavarero, *Inclinazioni*, 37–63.
46. Immanuel Kant, *Scritti Politici*, ed. Roberto Bobbio (Turin: Utet, 2010), 197.
47. Cavarero, *Inclinazioni*, 109–10.

Bibliography

Arendt, Hannah. *The Human Condition*. Chicago: University of Chicago Press, 1958.
———. *The Origins of Totalitarianism*. New York: Schoen Books, 1951.
———. "What Is Freedom?" In *Between Past and Future*. New York: Penguin Books, 2006.
Bertolino, Elisabetta. *Adriana Cavarero: Resistance and the Voice of Law*. New York: Routledge, 2018.
Cavarero, Adriana. *Democrazia sorgiva: Note sul pensiero politico di Hannah Arendt*. Milan: Raffaello Cortina Editore, 2019.

———. *For More than One Voice: Towards a Philosophy of Vocal Expression*. Translated by Paul A. Kottman. Stanford, CA: Stanford University Press, 2005.

———. *Inclinazioni: Critica della rettitudine*. Milan: Raffaello Cortina Editore, 2013.

———. "Rectitude: Reflections on Postural Ontology." *Journal of Speculative Philosophy* 27, no. 3 (2013): 220–35.

———. *Stately Bodies: Literature, Philosophy and the Question of Gender*. Translated by Robert de Lucca and Deanna Shemek. Ann Arbor: University of Michigan Press, 2002.

Di Cesare, Donatella. *Virus sovrano? L'asfissia capitalistica*. Turin: Bollati Boringhieri, 2020.

Esposito, Roberto. *Bios: Biopolitica e filosofia*. Turin: Einaudi, 2004.

———. *Immunitas: The Protection and Negation of Life*. Translated by Zakiya Hanafi. Cambridge: Polity Press, 2011.

Foucault, Michael "The Birth of Social Medicine." In *Power: Essential Works of Foucault 1954–1984, Volume 3*. London: Penguin Books, 2002.

Kant, Immanuel. *Scritti Politici*. Edited by Norberto Bobbio. Turin: Utet, 2010.

Mauss, Marcel. *The Gift: The Form and Reason for Exchange in Archaic Society*. London: Cohen and West, 1954.

Mortari, Luigina. *Filosofia della cura*. Milan: Raffaello Cortina Editore, 2015.

———. *Politica della cura: Prendere a cuore la vita*. Milan: Raffaello Cortina Editore, 2021.

Seven

Inclining toward New Forms of Life
Cavarero, Agamben, and Hartman[1]

Rachel Jones

Between the gestures of Penelope's hands and the figure of "the mother bent over her child," Cavarero's work displaces the abstract universality and fantasized self-sufficiency of Man and offers us a "new postural geometry" for orienting ourselves in the world and toward others.[2] This reconfigured corporeal geometry—which transforms the scene of the ethical and political encounter—is rooted in a relational ontology that takes sexual difference and birth as its orienting horizons and that discloses uniqueness, relationality, and vulnerability (or, as they are also rendered, singularity, plurality, and exposure) as mutually constitutive of the human condition.[3] If, in *Horrorism*, Cavarero foregrounds the violence against this condition that she calls an "ontological crime," *Inclinations* can be read as disinterring the potential for an ethical reorientation rooted in an attentiveness to the human condition as it is incarnated in a plurality of singular beings, each "consigned to one another" in a web of asymmetrical exposures.[4]

In so doing, *Inclinations* furthers Cavarero's project of articulating a relational ontology that counters "the violent practices of domination, exclusion, and devastation of which the subject itself is an accomplice."[5] By making relationality ontologically constitutive, rather than merely "correcting" individualist ontologies via a greater emphasis on relations,

Cavarero does not simply oppose these "violent practices" as if they were an empirical given.[6] Rather, her work transforms our understanding of the violation that such violences perpetrate. It does so by offering an ontological register through which to transform the terms of shared life and reimagine the "postural geometry" of the human condition. As Cavarero suggests, what is at stake in "the effort of thinking a relational ontology where the figure of the mother, and the scenario of birth it evokes, works as a key issue" is nothing less than "re-signify[ing] the concept of the human together with that of politics."[7]

This chapter follows an interpretative thread through several of Cavarero's key texts so as to tease out the profound shift in perspective involved in this relational ontology and the ethico-political reorientation it implies. To help bring out its distinctiveness and significance, I will juxtapose Cavarero's work with key aspects of Giorgio Agamben's, drawing in particular on his essay "Form-of-Life" and his writings on *Homo sacer*.[8] Cavarero and Agamben each offer incisive accounts of the ways in which, in the Western tradition, the political has been constituted by that which it excludes: Agamben through his analysis of sovereign power, bare life, and inclusive exclusion, and Cavarero by disclosing the disavowed dependence of the political order on an apolitical material life that is identified with the feminine, maternal, and animal. For both thinkers, the Nazi death camps are emblematic of the violence that characterizes the internal logic of Western political modernity. Yet, because Cavarero attends to the role of sexual difference in the genealogy of sovereignty and understands the latter more specifically as the political genealogy of Man—that supposedly universal yet archetypally male figure that disowns the corporeality on which human beings depend—her work allows for "a radical shift in perspective": a view from elsewhere that is able to register that which the polis excludes in terms *other than those* that the polis permits.[9]

While the work of both Cavarero and Agamben opens onto the question of racialization, the constitutive role of race and colonialism in Western modernity is not central to their analyses.[10] The concluding section of this chapter will turn to Saidiya Hartman to resituate the "ontological crime" of which Cavarero writes in the context of the invention of race and, more specifically, of anti-Blackness and the transatlantic slave trade.[11] Hartman's work asks us to begin again with the contested question of "life" in the context of the "afterlife of slavery"[12] and turns to the "wayward lives" of Black women and girls to recover a lexicon for rethinking what "counts" as political.[13] Her claiming of Black women's "brilliant and formidable labor of care" as a mode of fugitive resistance can be read as amplifying—and complicating—the possibilities that Cavarero explores for an alternative political ontology of inclined, relational, and always bodily beings.[14]

Cavarero's *schielende Blick*

As Laurie Naranch helps us to appreciate, the relationship between Cavarero's and Agamben's work is neither one of simple consensus nor of straightforward opposition.[15] Their concerns overlap in important ways, and where Cavarero differs, this is not so much a matter of proving Agamben wrong as seeing what escapes his analytical frame through a different lens.[16] Cavarero's texts cast what Sigrid Weigel calls a *schielende Blick* at Agamben's project—a sideways, indirect glance that allows for a double focus, capable of looking "in two diverging directions simultaneously."[17] Never fully taking an eye off "the pattern set by the dominant images," this sideways glance is able to discern an alternate weave shimmering beneath the contours of sovereignty and bare life.[18] In keeping with the hermeneutical tactics Cavarero theorizes in the introduction to *In Spite of Plato*, her attentiveness to sexual difference allows her to cast the violence of this sovereign gesture in sharp relief while simultaneously working "*outside* and *against*" its grip.[19] It is as if the inclined, asymmetrical postures that can be sites of resistant care, even as they manifest an unavoidable potential for wounding, are accompanied by a subversive, sideways glance that steals away from the imposing forms of Man to disclose other possibilities of being and relating, not only in a future yet to arrive but also already here, been and gone, still with us, and yet to be.

This seems to me to be one of the crucial differences between the perspectives that Cavarero and Agamben open up. Both thinkers seek ways of being—and in particular, being together, living in community—that are no longer subject to the violence of sovereignty; and both strive to make a place for uniqueness or singularity that is irreducible to identity particularly insofar as the latter is secured by the ascription of properties.[20] The "coming" of Agamben's "coming community" is thus not simply temporal or futural but signals the way that singularity is always coming-to-be in an ecstatic haecceity that ruptures the grip of sovereignty. Nonetheless, tending to singularity also displaces the logic of sovereignty in ways that are figured by Agamben in historico-temporal terms as a "completely new politics [. . .] no longer founded on the *exceptio* of bare life"[21] as well as something humanity has yet to learn, and that requires knowing and unknowing midwives.[22] For Cavarero (and also, I would suggest, for Hartman and other Black feminists), such possibilities for being and living otherwise already exist, woven into submerged pasts and fugitive presents that thread speculative futures through time and place.

For Agamben, the global political present is the inheritance of a founding divide between *zoe* and *bios*, from which, perversely, a generalized and undifferentiated concept of life has emerged. This is life understood as "that naked [bare] presupposed common element that it is always possible to isolate in each of the numerous forms of life."[23] Bare life is produced by the gesture of sovereignty understood as the power to decide on the state of exception—that is, to decide under what conditions or to whom the law does not apply. Sovereign power thus produces a mode of belonging to the political qua those from whom the law is withdrawn in a founding gesture of inclusive exclusion. To exist in a state of exception produced by the suspension of the law is to be stripped of the forms of social and political life and abandoned to bare life in a zone of indistinction where "everything is possible."[24] Thus, the concentration camp is the *nomos* of the modern, not only because it materializes and makes visible the production of bare life and its concomitant violence as the "hidden foundation of sovereignty" but also because it exemplifies and totalizes the state of exception that—as the constituting function of sovereign power—is always and everywhere in play, actualizing an onto-political structure (the camp) where the exception is the norm.[25]

On this account, bare life is not exactly identical with *zoe*, understood as "the simple fact of living common to all living beings."[26] Rather, bare life is produced when *bios*, formed life, is stripped of its form via the suspension of the law, allowing *zoe* to enter "into the sphere of politics" through this gesture of subtraction or abandonment.[27] As Ewa Ziarek puts it, "Bare life, wounded, expendable, and endangered, is not the same as biological *zoe*, but rather the remainder of the destroyed political *bios*."[28] Bare life is both the necessary condition and the constitutive manifestation of sovereign power that, by withdrawing the law, "isolates" a supposedly generalized "life" that is retroactively presupposed as the "common element" on which political power operates: "Life—in its state of exception that has now become the norm—is the naked [bare] life that in every context separates the forms of life from their cohering into a form-of-life."[29] The hyphenated term *form-of-life* embodies the life of a "coming politics" that would no longer be constituted by sovereign power: "a life that cannot be separated from its form" and for which "what is at stake in its way of living is living itself," that is, a life in which the "ways, acts, and processes of living are never simply *facts* [*zoe* sequestered from *bios*] but always and above all *possibilities* of life, always and above all power [as potentiality, *potenza*]."[30] The "intimacy of this inseparable life" is irreducible to the logic of universals and particulars in which specific forms of life are always reducible to so many common properties of a generalizable identity.[31] In contrast, the irreducible as-suchness of "singularities" are "the exemplars of the coming community."[32]

Cavarero, too, seeks "to rethink the very core of community"[33] in ways that revolve around corporeal uniqueness and the "living singularity" of each human being as an irreplaceable "who" rather than a "what" that can be defined in terms of its qualities.[34] In their commitment to reorienting ethics toward singular beings constituted wholly in exposure, Cavarero and Agamben both resist the weight of the Western metaphysical tradition and its investment in essence as well as in subject-predicate logic.[35] Cavarero, however, also centers the singular-relational scene of originary exposure found in human beings' beginnings in birth. Thus, rather than seeking a power that "incessantly reunites life to its form or prevents it from being dissociated from its form,"[36] her work inclines instead toward a power of bearing life—maternal generative power—that (ontologically, and not merely temporally) precedes and undercuts the *zoe*/*bios* distinction (which, as Agamben indicates, maps onto the nature/culture distinction).[37] In her insistence that this, too, is a power that is irreducible to "life" in its sequestered biological sense, Cavarero reclaims maternal generative power as a capacity to bear life as possibility as well as "possibilities of life": "there is another path that could be taken, one that crucially challenges the long-established conviction that female bodies belong solely to the sphere of 'life' intended in its biological dimension."[38] Cavarero's approach involves rethinking the relation between form and life in ways that allow "the *meaning* of human life to exist outside the confines of the *polis*," not so much as life that cannot be separated from its form as a plurality of singular-relational lives that are each the manifestation of a life-forming-power.[39] This means, I think, that the hyphens that reunite life with form, whether as form-of-life or life-forming-power, mark not an absolute inseparability but a more ambiguous, vulnerable relation that allows for severing and violation as well as the intimacy between a life and its forms;[40] or, to borrow from Cavarero's relational ontology, life's always hyphenated forms unavoidably allow for both wounding and care. As will be discussed further below, it is because Cavarero insists on holding the uniqueness of singular beings together with the mutually constitutive role of vulnerability and relationality that she provides a different perspective on the violation that takes place wherever bare life is produced.[41]

The roots of this alternative perspective are found in the *schielende Blick* with which Cavarero approaches *zoe*—that apparently "simple fact of living" that seems to shadow "bare life" while receding from political life altogether via the instituting divide between *zoe* and *bios*. Indeed, *zoe* seems to retain an ambiguous quality within the logic of sovereign power. On the one hand, insofar as both *zoe* and bare life are constituted as such by the gesture of inclusive exclusion, they appear almost identical, as if superimposed on one another, as when Agamben writes of "an inclusive exclusion (an *exceptio*) of *zoe* in the *polis, almost as if* politics were the place in which life had to transform itself into good life and in which what had to be politicized were *always already* bare life."[42] Yet, this apparent identification is undercut by that "almost as if," reminding us that, in Agamben's account of the classical schema that underpins the Western political tradition, *zoe* is also that "natural sweetness" of "the simple fact of living"[43] that differs both from *bios* as "qualified life" or "the form or manner of living peculiar to a single individual or group"[44] and from the bare life that is produced by the withdrawal of the law. Thus, elsewhere in Agamben's work, *zoe* is more firmly distinguished not only from *bios* but also from "the bare life of *Homo sacer*": while the latter is akin to social death, *zoe* is identified with "simply natural reproductive life."[45] Birth as "bare *natural* life" is therefore distinguished from the way it can be taken up as a marker of nationality and citizenship, which in turn can be stripped to produce bare political life.[46]

In this identification of *zoe* with the "simply natural" and the reproductive, the schema of sovereign power repeats a tradition that "considers the female body as a pre-political, nature-driven, and nature-oriented entity," even if the determination of *zoe* as "pre-political" is itself a founding political gesture.[47] Zoe is thereby linked to unformed (unqualified) and (from the point of view of the polis) threateningly wild life, which is in turn recouped via the regulatory figure of *physis*, understood as the laws of nature (which the ancient Greeks saw as the laws of the gods). *Physis* allows a potentially wild *zoe* to be folded back into the operations of sovereign power in a gesture that appears as a decisive separation—of *physis* from *nomos*, or the laws of the polis—but that, in fact, institutes an inclusive exclusion; *physis* is included in the operations of sovereign power by being determined as the realm where the laws of the polis do not apply. Moreover, the identification of *zoe* as *physis* paves the way for it to be further tamed and appropriated as the reproductive labor (what Cavarero calls the "work for life") that sustains the life of the city and that can be turned into the basis for citizenship.⁴⁸ Zoe stands for that which not only allows for these founding gestures of inclusive exclusion but which cannot be countenanced—or even thought—by sovereign power *except* through the gesture of inclusive exclusion. By naming that which both allows for and can only be approached via this gesture, the ambiguous figure of *zoe* carries with it the almost neutralized trace of that which, from the perspective of sovereign power, must always already be foreclosed.

One of Cavarero's distinctive contributions is to disinter this structure of foreclosure and reanimate *zoe*'s disruptive trace as a life-forming, generative power that gives birth to unique beings always already linked in a weave of relations that are not merely "natural"⁴⁹ but sites of shared sense-making through the inclined gestures of wounding and care. This relational weave refuses capture not only by the *physis/nomos* divide but also by the founding distinction between *zoe* and *bios*. For this reason, Cavarero's work does not so much negate Agamben's as constitute an oblique but sustained displacement of its analytical lens. As I will discuss in the next section, her reading of Sophocles's *Antigone* is exemplary of this work to disinter that which remains unthought within the logic of sovereign power.⁵⁰

Antigone and the Foreclosure of Life-Forming Power

As Cavarero reminds us, *Antigone* centers on a body: the corpse of Polynices. Cast outside the city walls and abandoned to the birds, in a zone of indistinction where neither the laws of the polis nor religious rites apply, Polynices seems to be the epitome of *Homo sacer*. In stealing out to cover his body with "thirsty dust," Antigone seeks to restore him to human community and reclaim him from an exposure that constitutes a total abandonment.⁵¹ As Cavarero notes, in ways that are integral to the play but consolidated in its interpretation in the modern Western tradition, Antigone operates as a double figure of radical, non-political otherness.⁵² First, as Hegel's reading emphasizes and as feminist responses have more critically examined, Antigone is aligned with a distinctively female realm whose allotted purpose is to tend to the body and the rites that care for the blood relations of kinship.⁵³ Such corporeal, affective labor is essential to the city, even as those who undertake it are excluded from the polis as specifically *political* life in an originary inclusive exclusion. And second, in her alignment with the laws of the gods and "the ancient law of relation by birth," Antigone also counters the more specifically tyrannical face of political power that Creon represents, which threatens the city from within.[54]

In response, Antigone performs the rites that reassert the claims of kinship and reclaims Polynices's body from the overreach of Creon's tyrannical power. In so doing, she can read as a reminder of the potentially dangerous (for the polis) slippage between the domesticated forms of bodily life that are assigned to women's care and the realm of *zoe*, the non-political life beyond the city walls: "a naked life, a wild corporeity and carnal profundity."[55] But it is here that things get interesting: for Cavarero, this wild life is neither harmonious sweetness, nor unformed and inhuman, nor "incommunicable and mute,"[56] and neither does it require regulation by the gods. Rather, it manifests a "female generative potency" that has its own formative power and from which springs relations of care, love, and affection as well as the terrible possibilities for violence that engender anguish and mourning.[57] Thus, while Cavarero restores to *physis* its link to *phyein* (to be born), she also emphasizes the ambiguity of "maternal generation, on which singularity is based and into which it is submerged."[58] As Antigone's incestuous blood line demonstrates in its "carnal implosion," this transindividual generative life poses a particular threat to daughters, who may find themselves rendered indistinguishable from their mothers and wholly submerged in "the life of blood kin, symbiotically becoming one substance with them."[59] Here, the daughter is reduced to "a bare life" produced not by the stripping of the law but by total absorption in "the horizon of antiegoistic blood kinship," whose only purpose is the conservation of "the corporeal blood-line."[60] Yet, in ways that do not simply negate these risks, the generative potency of birth also provides an alternative perspective from which to judge both the constitution and the actions of the polis.

Cavarero leans on Sophocles's image of Antigone responding to the sight of Polynices's exposed and abandoned body by "lament[ing] with the strident voice of an anguished bird at seeing the empty nest that has been robbed of its young."[61] In her alignment with the mother bird, Antigone stands against the polis as a reminder of "the corporeal materiality of existence" in ways that are reinforced by the incestuous bloodline of the house of Oedipus.[62] This overdetermined reminder that "one is born of a woman's body, of a maternal blood that generates and encloses" is without doubt "a terrifying and uncanny fact from the perspective of the polis's virile logocentrism."[63] From this perspective, Antigone is aligned with a terrifying return of *zoe* as the non-political that must be excluded from the polis in its founding gesture. But from another perspective, Antigone's insistence on burying "my mother's son" and honoring the irreplaceability of her brother can be seen as attesting to maternal generative power,[64] as can her lament for the tragic transgression of generational relations epitomized in another brother who is also her father.[65] Thus, what links Antigone to the grieving mother bird is an entirely different order of things: one that comes with its own risks, as seen in the potential for a symbiotic collapse of mother and daughter, but which is shaped not by god-given laws of nature but by the contingent patterns of attachment and loss through which life is shared between singular-relational beings.

From this perspective, it is not the animals who tear at the flesh of the body, who are inhuman. Rather, in ways that prefigure Cavarero's later work in *Horrorism*, the "horrible feasting on the body of Polynices" reveals the non-coincidence of the human and the political, insofar as it is the tyranny that the polis makes possible that dehumanizes and desecrates.[66] Antigone's gesture of covering the body with earth might be read as an attempt to make it less appetizing to the hungry animals who disfigure its form, "shredding that precise configuration which renders it a unique body."[67] Yet, the alignment of Antigone with the mother bird refuses any simple opposition between humans and animals and reminds us that both participate in what Cavarero elsewhere describes as an impersonal life that simultaneously exceeds and makes possible each unique existence.[68]

This is reinforced by the way that Antigone's actions as she defies Creon for a second time are shielded by a dust-storm that suddenly springs up from the earth, "a trouble [*akhos*, pain, grief, or distress] in the air."[69] Rather than reading this as a simple anthropomorphism, we might instead take it as a reminder of the intimate connections between human and non-human beings and the elemental materialities of the cosmos. From this perspective, death is not the opposite of life but the counterpart of birth that folds all bodily beings, human and other animals alike, into "the unending metamorphosis of impersonal life,"[70] as signaled by the ancient custom Cavarero references of offering the body of the dead to the birds and burying only the bones.[71] It is only Man whose tyrannical power condemns the body to disfigurement solely for the purposes of dehumanizing, in a totalizing gesture of violation, because it is only from the perspective of the polis, given its founding division between *bios* and *zoe*, that to be consigned to life (or death) outside the city walls is to be condemned to the inhuman and unformed.

What Cavarero's work makes it possible to see is that the very visibility of the constitutive gesture that divides *bios* from *zoe* (even, and perhaps especially, where this is understood as producing an *inclusive* exclusion) conceals another, more primary gesture of exclusion that cannot even be seen as such. This primary exclusion forecloses the possibility that what is captured as *zoe* is neither simply *un*formed life in contrast to *bios* nor already governed life ruled by the natural laws of *physis* but a life-forming, sense-making power that shapes a complex weave of living-dying relations in patterns of generation and loss where living is never reducible to the merely biological.[72] It is this life-forming power and the maternal generativity in which it both manifests and renews itself whose violation cannot be seen through the paradigm of sovereign power, which depends on simultaneously appropriating and obscuring this "forbidden weft of life"[73] in a (necessarily repressed) act of primitive accumulation that provides the material for the gestures of inclusive exclusion. As Cavarero's work suggests, presenting the distinction between *bios* and *zoe* as the founding gesture of the political makes it impossible to register this more primary act of appropriation/obliteration that has always already happened as the condition of this particular world-making narrative. Hence, the *schielende Blick* that Cavarero has to employ to disinter this primary foreclosure[74] and reveal that Antigone is not just non-political—insofar as she is aligned with the domestic order of state-sanctioned kinship—or apolitical—to the extent that she is allied with "simple" natural life in contradistinction to the polis. Rather, in Cavarero's approach, Antigone is *apolis* in a more radical, disruptive, and potentially generative sense. Her "crime" is to remain connected to another order of being rooted in an insurgent, life-forming power that the polis violently denies[75] in ways that—as Sophocles shows—only confirm the deathliness of its operations.[76]

From Maternal Generative Power to a Relational Ontology

It is thus not by chance that Cavarero presents the myth of Demeter as revealing "*a sovereign figure* of female subjectivity who decides, in the concrete singularity of every woman, whether or not to generate."[77] Cavarero steals back the alternative to sovereign power that is embodied in maternal generative power by working the Demeter-Kore myth against the weave. Through the hermeneutical gestures made possible by an orientation toward sexual difference and birth, Cavarero unties "the matted threads" of a patriarchal tapestry—a canvas "so thick as to be almost perfectly capable of concealing its secrets"—so as to compose "the different figures of a feminine symbolic order."[78] According to the myth, after her daughter's abduction by Hades, Demeter withdraws fertility from the earth and agrees to restore it only in exchange for Kore's periodic return. Henceforth, the earth will be barren and fecund by turns, mirroring the separation and reunification of mother and daughter. As Cavarero shows, Demeter's compromise structures a mythic account of the inauguration of the seasons that mimetically binds women and the earth together in generative cycles ("simply natural reproductive life") whose supposed inevitability springs from the laws of the gods. Followed through to its intended conclusion, the myth naturalizes the capacity to birth as normal and necessary such that it becomes defining of women and prescribes their social role. In this way, maternal generative power is captured and reduced to a socially regulated (but divinely sanctioned) reproductive function.

In Cavarero's deft unravelling of this myth, what is crucial—and what must remain crucially unthematized for the myth's instituting power to remain intact—is that before the abduction of Kore, a reciprocal gaze already existed between mother and daughter. This "interweaving" of gazes[79] structures a relational, earthly existence that precedes the ordering power of the polis without needing to look up toward either the edicts of the gods or the eternal realm that orients the theorizing of the philosopher. Instead, in the glance shared between Demeter and Kore, the daughter "looks in the direction from which she came" in a gesture that implies "an infinite series of the engendered, of new beginnings unfolding in reverse progression."[80] This shared glance depends on a spacing between mother and daughter that prevents the symbiotic collapse with which Antigone is threatened. At the same time, as each newborn "is a 'beginning' found already 'started' inside the mother," the Demeter-Kore myth points back to a structuring temporality incarnated in gestational rhythms that allow natal beings "to take root and find meaning" *prior* to the daughter's abduction and the subsequent naturalization of birth as a reproductive function in service of the polis.[81]

Cavarero's analysis again seeks to reclaim the etymological and ontological links between *physis* and birth that are distorted once *physis* is understood as the province of natural law that regulates the generative powers of both women and the earth,[82] prescribing the "marginal but necessary" social role of women and schematizing the earth's rhythms in ways that lend themselves to agricultural management by the polis.[83] In contrast, by reclaiming *physis* as "the world's act of constituting itself," including through maternal generative power, Cavarero insists that the relational web of human (and more-than-human) lives already *makes sense*, "outside the confines of the polis," in "a space where the rules of common living are found through the concrete matter that concerns it."[84] As she reminds us both in her reading of *Antigone* and in the final chapter of *In Spite of Plato*, this space is co-constituted in a continuum with the animal lives and elemental materialities with which human beings share the earth.

One of the key, if backgrounded, aspects of Cavarero's analysis of the Demeter-Kore myth—which tends to emphasize the reciprocity of their shared gaze—is that it embodies a relationship between unequals.[85] It is this imbalance, epitomized in the relation between a mother and her newborn, that becomes paradigmatic for the relational ontology that is more fully developed in Cavarero's later work. Here, in contrast to the upright lines that characterize the geometries of Man and his celebrated autonomy,[86] human beings are conceptualized in terms of asymmetrical relations between bodily beings inclined toward one another in gestures of wounding and care. The always present ambiguity of inclination springs from the ontological indeterminacy of the *vulnus*, the vulnerability to wounding that can elicit either violence or care in response.[87] If uniqueness and relationality are woven into Cavarero's work from the start, embodied in the gestational relations that bring each human being into the world in their unsubstitutable uniqueness, the language of vulnerability comes to the fore in her more recent texts, where it becomes the third term of the relational ontology she develops. Rather than supplanting the concept of exposure, vulnerability allows Cavarero to more fully bring out its ambiguous complexities. In ways that are informed by Butler's meditations on precarious life[88]—an alternative to "bare life" that better captures the differential distribution of vulnerability and violence—Cavarero foregrounds vulnerability to emphasize the precarious relationality of an exposure *to* others that always affords asymmetrical possibilities of wounding and care *by* others. Thus, each singular being finds themselves "irremediably open" to either care or abandonment: "the vulnerable one exists totally in the tension generated by this alternative."[89]

As is searingly disclosed in *Horrorism*, it is this constitutive tension that also makes possible the "ontological crime" perpetrated by the Nazi death camps. For Cavarero, attending to the co-constituting terms of the human condition—uniqueness, relationality, and vulnerability—reveals that the category of bare life is insufficient to do justice to the violation that takes place wherever bare life is produced. In systematically destroying uniqueness and relationality (destroying each by destroying the other)[90] and fabricating "helpless beings [who are] paradoxically no longer vulnerable," pushed beyond the point where they can register either wounding or care, the camps perpetrate an ontological crime that not only "exceeds death" but goes beyond the production of bare life to violate the human condition itself, as incarnated in the vulnerability of each singular-relational being.[91] Indeed, Cavarero suggests that reducing human beings to a state of bare need and survival—to "absolute hunger"—does not disclose a generalized or common element "that it is always possible to isolate in each of the numerous forms of life."[92] If bare life endures in the zone of indistinction where "the essential boundary between living and dying has been erased," this is clearly not the vibrant impersonal life that Cavarero links to maternal generative power, where birth and death are the "rhythm and cadence" situating singular lives in an always relational weave.[93] The violence of the camps obliterates this "rhythm and cadence," disfiguring the human condition by "nullifying any possible relations [. . .] including [. . .] the solidarity of the oppressed" and producing "a degenerated helpless one," "who is as indifferent to others as he is to himself."[94] Cavarero thereby transforms our understanding of the violation that such violence perpetrates, locating this violation not simply in the production of bare life but in the "killing of uniqueness": the "ontological crime" that results from systematically destroying the co-constituting matrix of relationality, singularity, and vulnerability.[95] Yet, it is because the camps are understood in this way that it also becomes possible to see that this matrix holds out the possibility of articulating the terms of shared life otherwise—in ways that can neither compensate for the violence of the camps nor render such violence an impossibility but that might, nonetheless, bypass the logic of sovereign power altogether.

It is by attending to this co-constituting matrix and its rootedness in the scenario of birth that Cavarero retrieves a perspective from which to reimagine the entire "postural geometry" of the human condition. The maternal relation as it is thematized throughout her work—that is, as a generative life-forming and sense-making power—orients us toward a world in which interdependencies are the norm and the singularly plural lives of natal beings take shape "along multiple coexisting lines, which may be contingent and intermittent and at times even random."[96] In *Inclinations*, Cavarero thus risks the stereotypical figure of a mother leaning toward their child to show how the oblique lines of inclination cut across the moral uprightness of the supposedly autonomous subject and provide an alternative ethical paradigm. From this perspective, our actions and the relations in which they are embedded are evaluated according to the degree to which they incline toward the always-present alternatives of wounding or care.[97] In the asymmetries of inclination, Cavarero finds "a new fundamental schematism [. . .] for evaluating the terrain of the encounter" and rethinking "the core of community."[98]

By drawing attention to the morphological resonances between the "oblique" and "slanted" lines of inclination and "queer" contestations of "straightness,"[99] Cavarero makes it clear that this reimagining of community is no longer governed by a heteronormative logic, offsetting one of the risks incurred by her "exaggerated" method of reclaiming maternal inclination.[100] Such passages invite reading alongside Sara Ahmed's analysis of the alignment of moral rectitude and compulsory heterosexuality.[101] By attending to the "everyday negotiation" of "inhabiting the queer slant,"[102] Ahmed counters the diagnosis of the queer body as a "failed orientation" and explores the possibilities for reconfiguring "the sociality of being 'with' others" via "queer orientations."[103] Equally, we might read Cavarero's reminder of the intimacy between inclination and the swerve of the *clinamen* with Emanuela Bianchi's invitation to "tarry with the aleatory," which she painstakingly disinters from Aristotle in an alternative to *bios* and *zoe* that lends itself to an interruptive, anti-patriarchal politics that "thrives in lively collectivities."[104] Or, we could allow Cavarero's invocation of the "deep quiver" and ekstatic swerve of sexual inclination to resonate alongside Lynne Huffer's queer feminist ethics of eros, which listens for that which "makes the 'I' strange to itself [. . .] in ways that can suspend and transform everyday practices of living."[105]

Cavarero finds one such suspension in the figure of Penelope. In the first chapter of *In Spite of Plato*, Cavarero teases out the ways in which Penelope's ruse of unravelling by night what she has woven by day allows her to resist capture by a patriarchal order twice over, temporarily holding off her suitors while subverting the productivity of domestic labor.[106] Penelope has no need of the deathly horizons of action, against which Man measures himself in terms of his capacity to win immortality, or of the philosopher's (perhaps equally cunning) ruse of overcoming anxiety about death by turning toward the eternal (while even more firmly displacing the ontological significance of birth). Cavarero depicts Penelope as weaving an "anomalous" space and time where women belong to themselves, working and laughing together in a "disinvestment" from the polis[107]—a withdrawal that not only preempts the withdrawal of the law that produces bare life but also nullifies the more originary withdrawal of the very possibility of sense-making from a bodily realm that the polis consigns to "simple reproductive life." In this "liberating rejection," Penelope "simply allows the polis to be elsewhere."[108] Yet, Cavarero's initial portrayal of Penelope ends with the note, "We women will have to leave Penelope's Ithaca" and go back into the world.[109] The question is, which world?

It is Cavarero's painstaking work to reclaim a "home of the living" where meaning is returned to birth and natality that unfolds into the relational ontology of singularity, plurality, and vulnerability, thereby offering "a way of rethinking the entire world, including the category of communal living."[110] Here, we might read the knowing gestures of Penelope's *metis*, which bind together the movements of undoing and remaking, as prefiguring the alternatives of wounding and care that provide this reoriented world with its ethical valence. Turning back to Agamben one last time, we might note his reclamation of gesture as distinguished from both acting (as itself an end) and making (as a means to an end). Drawing on Varro, Agamben suggests that in gesture "nothing is being produced or acted, but rather something is being endured and supported" and that "the gesture, in other words, opens the sphere of *ethos* as the more proper sphere of that which is human."[111] In the "cadenced repetition"[112] of Penelope's gestures, too, "something is being endured and supported," both because they allow her to endure within deathly horizons and because, through them, an anomalous space is "being en-dured" in the sense of being given duration, being spun out through time, in ways that hold open possibilities for existing otherwise.

For Agamben, intellectuality and thought hold open the way to a "coming politics" no longer governed by sovereign power and that, rather than being "form[s] of life among others," comprise "*the unitary power that constitutes the multiple forms of life as form-of-life.*"[113] Although he allows that thought can appear in "the materiality of corporeal processes and of habitual ways of life no less than in theory," Cavarero makes a more decisive turn away from *theoria*, whose reduction of the political to a question of law and order—and concomitant complicity with sovereign power—she takes Arendt to decisively reveal.[114] Instead, Cavarero points us to the gestures of wounding and care prefigured in Penelope's metis as a mode of knowing that refuses to sever body from thought or corporeality from sense-making right from the start.[115] It is these gestures that allow Penelope's "disinvestment" from the polis, revealing that what sovereign power forgets as it decides on the withdrawal of the law is the possibility that others may have already withdrawn from its totalizing grip, not only in acts of resistance but also by orienting themselves otherwise: through a generative, life-forming-power that refuses to separate a generalized "life" of mere biological survival from the vibrant processes of relational sense-making and the ambiguities of vulnerability that shape the "warp and weft" of ethical conviviality.[116] Thus, for Cavarero, it is the "rhythm and cadence" of Penelope's gestures that open the way to an ethos of inclination as "the more proper sphere of that which is human."

Wayward Gestures of Living

Of course, one cannot simply "escape" the grip of sovereign power, so this withdrawal that is both made possible by and makes possible a different orienting perspective takes place always *in the midst*—not just by slipping away, sidling out, but by allowing other ways of being and relating to endure through gestures that remain illegible to sovereign eyes. If Cavarero is able to register the life-forming-power that the polis excludes in terms other than those that the polis permits, then it is indeed "possible that this force will take on the task of redefining the polis," though I read Cavarero as also suggesting that we may need terms other than "the political" for this reinvention of shared living.[117] As I hope to have shown, her relational ontology does crucial work to provide those terms while not simply withdrawing from the necessity of contesting the political as it is (and has been) lived and endured.

It is in the quest for ways of thinking and living otherwise that we might generatively read Cavarero alongside Saidiya Hartman, as she recovers the chorus of "ordinary colored girls" who "tirelessly imagined other ways to live and never failed to consider how the world might be otherwise."[118] Noting the etymology linking the Greek word for chorus to "*danc[ing] within an enclosure*,"[119] Hartman attends to the "waywardness" of young Black women finding ways to live "otherwise" in early twentieth-century New York and Philadelphia, whose experiments in living "articulate the paradox of cramped creation, the entanglement of escape and confinement, flight and captivity."[120] These "wayward lives," Hartman suggests, provide a lexicon for the transformation that can take place through "acts of collaboration and improvisation that unfold within the space of enclosure," generating forms of life that cannot be unambiguously separated from the violent encroachment of sovereign power yet refuse to be governed by its terms.[121]

Reading Cavarero with Hartman, we might see both thinkers as seeking to amplify "moments of withholding, escape and possibility" by reclaiming figures of women and girls who "elude the law and transform the terms of the possible."[122] One opening to this juxtapositional reading is found in Cavarero's attention to "the spaces where we are cared for because we are so exposed to violence," as Laurie Naranch beautifully puts it.[123] We might read this alongside Hartman's invocation of Black women's "brilliant and formidable labor of care, [that] paradoxically, has been produced through violent structures of slavery, anti-black racism, virulent sexism, and disposability."[124] Another is found in Cavarero's note that, in the ancient polis, work for life was "reserved to un-political beings who are not-fully or less-than-human: women and slaves in the Greek world."[125] In the modern transatlantic world, as Hartman shows, the mutually constitutive categories of the political and the (less-than-)human are racialized via captive Black flesh in ways that depend on the expropriation and violation of Black women's reproductive capacities.[126] If Cavarero casts a sideways glance toward the relational life-giving capacities of maternal generative power that are not only excluded and appropriated but also withdraw from the polis, Hartman attends to the "fugitive gestures"[127] of Black maternity in "the afterlife of slavery" to insist that these "forms of care, intimacy, and sustenance exploited by racial capitalism, most importantly, are not reducible to or exhausted by it."[128] Noting that the labors of Black women have typically remained "marginal or neglected in the narratives of black insurgency, resistance, and refusal,"[129] Hartman sets out to reimagine Black radicalism in ways that refuse to oppose insurgency and care,[130] attending to the entwining of waywardness with gestures of welcome, tenderness, and sustenance and emphasizing the "mutual aid [that] provides the resource for collective action."[131]

Nonetheless, to read these two thinkers together is to risk obscuring the critical difference made by the invention of race and the emergence of anti-Black racism, as well as the particular context of the Black Atlantic in which Hartman's work is situated, and thereby to repeat the gesture of foreclosure by erasing the specificity of the forms of capture and inventiveness that manifest in the lives of Black women and girls contending with "the afterlife of slavery" in the transatlantic world. In ways that point to the larger project of rethinking sexual difference through the lens of race and colonialism, the asymmetries between Cavarero's and Hartman's projects need to be attended to even—or exactly—where they might seem most tightly connected. To read Cavarero's texts with and through Hartman means transposing Cavarero's analysis of the forgetting of birth and its ancient transformation into a passage toward death[132] and taking it up again in the context of the Middle Passage and a trade in human commodities that relied on the expropriation of the children of African mothers,[133] the natal alienation of the enslaved,[134] and the capture of Black female flesh that turns the mother's body into a passageway to social death, transforming children into property and birth into "reproducible kinlessness."[135]

Thus, I want to resist my own (potentially wounding) inclination to read Penelope's "cramped creation" too quickly together with Hartman's account of the wayward practice of "making and relation that enfolds within the policed boundaries of the dark ghetto." If waywardness is "an improvisation with the terms of social existence, when the terms have already been dictated, when there is little room to breathe," taking it up as a generalized figure for women's resistance to social confinement—as epitomized by Penelope—erases the specificity of the racialized policing and carceral regimes that suffocate Black life, as well as the specific modes of expropriation and violence that structure Black women's relations to the domestic sphere, both during and in the afterlife of slavery, to which Hartman asks us to attend.[136] Building on the work of other Black feminist scholars such as Hortense Spillers and Hazel Carby,[137] Hartman explores the ways in which, for Black women, the issue is not so much confinement within the home as the relentless extraction of labor and care to "tend the white household [. . .] at the cost of [their] own."[138] Unlike Penelope and at least some—largely middle class—white women in the transatlantic world for whom the home could function as a retreat as well as a trap, for Black women and girls "the domestic offers no refuge"; and yet, Hartman attests to the inventive care with which, again and again, they transformed shared spaces "into places of refuge that welcomed all."[139]

As Hartman shows, if enslaved Black women existed "out of the world and outside the house,"[140] domestic labor in the privatized white household in the afterlives of slavery continued to expose Black women and girls to racial-sexual violence, while "the black interior" becomes a site of policing and surveillance, pathologized as a "moral hazard."[141] *Wayward Lives* painstakingly charts the ways in which Black women and girls in early twentieth-century New York and Philadelphia were criminalized, commodified, and rendered disposable in both public and private spaces and how they responded by improvising possibilities for intimacy and attachment in the liminal zones of hallways and stairwells, alleys and rooftops, clubs and cabarets.[142] Hartman's reconstructed portraits of Edna Thomas, Gladys Bentley, Eva Perkins, and Mabel Hampton show how they took up the "lexical gap between black female and woman" to turn ungendering into riotous invention.¹⁴³ Ungovernable: not only because of a "refusal to be governed" but also thanks to a creative errancy that lives by its own "rhythm and cadence."¹⁴⁴ If the transgenerational legacy of slavery is "wounded kinship" and maternal dispossession,¹⁴⁵ Hartman suggests that "the gender non-conformity of the black community, its supple and extended modes of kinship, its queer domesticity, promiscuous sociality and loose intimacy" are the site of a wayward inventiveness and insurgent care that "enable those 'who were never meant to survive' to sometimes do just that."¹⁴⁶

Perhaps here we might, after all, bring the gestures that manifest Black women's "brilliant and formidable labor of care" together with the knowing metis through which Penelope navigates "the paradox of cramped creation."¹⁴⁷ As Detienne and Vernant note, the ancient Greek art of *metis* is a "cunning intelligence" that combines "flair, wisdom, forethought, subtlety of mind, deception, resourcefulness, vigilance [and] opportunism."¹⁴⁸ With its "resourceful ploys and stratagems" and "chancey inspiration[s]," metis is at odds with "the picture of thought and intelligence presented by the philosophers."¹⁴⁹ Deployed in situations that are "transient, shifting, disconcerting and ambiguous," metis offers a way to reclaim the gestures of manual labor and fugitive care as modes of resistant knowing and knowing inventiveness, providing an ancient register for the new political lexicon created by hands "cracked and swollen [. . .] burnt taking the pies out of the oven [. . .] stiff and disfigured from wringing cold sheets and towels outside in winter."¹⁵⁰ Hartman's evocation of these gestures provides us with figures for "another kind of story, not of the great man[,] or the tragic hero," or the sovereign power but woven from the insurgent care whose existential and political dimensions are underscored by Hartman's account of "creat[ing] possibility in the space of enclosure."¹⁵¹

Perhaps, then, we might follow Cavarero's lead and steal Penelope all over again, bypassing her place in the classical imaginary of the West and connecting the threads of her story to what Danielle Skeehan calls the "tactile literacies" through which captive Black women in the transatlantic world shared knowledge, forged intimacies, and crafted strategies of survival.¹⁵² Skeehan tells of an enslaved seamstress, Coobah, who, on the first of October 1768, was tasked with mending clothes on a Jamaican plantation and who stitches the letters *D T S J H* onto the smock of another enslaved woman, Silvia. The plantation owner, Englishman Thomas Thistlewood, who is better known for his unrelenting brutality, notes in his journal that this stands "for Dago, her [Coobah's] husband; Mr. Meyler's Tom, her sweetheart; and John Hart[nol]e, who she is supposed to love best."[153] In describing her as "Phibbah's Coobah,"[154] Thistlewood invokes a maternal relation overwritten by the laws determining that the enslaved status of a child was inherited from their mother[155] and provides a fragment—freighted with the weight of dispossessed maternity—through which we might also recall irretrievable intimacies and tender attachments.

As Skeehan suggests, by recording Coobah's actions, Thistlewood briefly acknowledges her authorship and agency, while in her subversive stitching, Coobah "converts the very tools of her labor as an enslaved seamstress into a medium through which she can tell stories of love and kinship, as well as sexual exploitation and loss."[156] What Thistlewood doesn't comment on is the significance of the central S in Coobah's embroidered message. Following Skeehan, who notes "the bonds between women that are gestured to in the smock but that are not made legible or translated into print in Thistlewood's journal,"[157] we might speculate that S stands for "Silvia," centering an alliance or friendship forged under conditions of oppression and perhaps even suggesting that it is Silvia who she "loves best." Coobah's skillful gestures add another metis to "the practice of the social otherwise."[158] Indeed, by tracking the connections between Coobah and S, we find that Thistlewood owned another enslaved woman called Coobah, whose infant daughter—also named Silvia—died in March 1768, a few months before the stitching of the smock.[159] After her daughter's death, this Coobah became a persistent runaway, despite Thistlewood's appalling punishments, until he eventually sold her on.[160] The embroidered S thus acts as a vector recalling loss and resistance along with suppressed maternal genealogies and intimate relationships that endured in the midst of a rupturing violence.

If Cavarero reminds us that when life is reduced to mere survival what is violated is the ethos of inclination that springs from maternal generative power and allows meaningful lives to take shape amidst relations of wounding and care, Hartman and Skeehan remind us that when birth is disfigured into "reproducible kinlessness," survival and enduring can themselves become meaningful acts of resistance, while gestures of insurgent care and intimacy become part of "the untiring practice of trying to live when you were never meant to survive."[161] This, too, is a mode of living that "surpasses the distinction between *zoe* and *bios*"[162] and that attests to "all the ways black folks create life and make bare need into an arena of elaboration," as Hartman shows in her vigilant retrieval of what she calls an "*everyday choreography of the possible.*"[163] Between Penelope and Coobah, Hartman and Cavarero, "the gestures disclose what is at stake—the matter of life returns as an open question."[164]

Notes

1. The author would like to thank the editors of this volume for their extremely helpful feedback and comments on drafts of this chapter.

2. Adriana Cavarero, *Inclinations*, trans. Adam Sitze and Amanda Minervini (Stanford, CA: Stanford University Press, 2016), 129.

3. Singularity, plurality, and exposure belong to registers informed by Cavarero's sustained engagement with Arendt as well as her more intermittent dialogue with Nancy. Although it seems to me that Cavarero leans toward uniqueness and relationality (as perhaps less abstract and more readily corporeal), for the purposes of this chapter, I will use these terms as roughly synonymous with singularity and plurality, respectively.

4. Cavarero, *Inclinations*, 13.

5. Cavarero, *Inclinations*, 12.

6. Cavarero, *Inclinations*, 13.

7. Cavarero, "Violent Female Bodies: Questioning Thanatopolitics," *Graduate Faculty Philosophy Journal* 36, no. 1 (2015): 129–44; 129.

8. Giorgio Agamben, "Form-of-Life," in *Means without End: Notes on Politics*, trans. V. Binetti and C. Casarino (Minneapolis: University of Minnesota Press, 2000); *Homo Sacer: Sovereign Power and Bare Life*, trans. D. Heller-Roazen (Stanford, CA: Stanford University Press, 1998).

9. Cavarero, *In Spite of Plato: A Feminist Rewriting of Ancient Philosophy*, trans. Serena Anderlini-D'Onofrio and Áine O'Healy (Cambridge: Polity Press, 1995), 6.

10. As others have suggested, taking the Nazi death camps as the culminating instance of modern political violence both points to and occludes the colonial, racialized genealogies of sovereign power; see, for example, Achille Mbembe, *Necropolitics*, trans. S. Corcoran (Durham, NC: Duke University Press, 2019). For a direct connection to the Black Atlantic context in which Hartman writes, see Cavarero's engagement with Edward Kamau Brathwaite in *For More Than Once Voice*, trans. P. A. Kottman (Stanford, CA: Stanford University Press, 2005), 146–51.

11. Cavarero, *Horrorism: Naming Contemporary Violence*, trans. W. McCuaig (New York: Columbia University Press, 2009), 16, 29.

12. Saidiya Hartman, *Lose Your Mother: A Journey Along the Atlantic Slave Route* (New York: Farrar, Straus, and Giroux, 2007), 6.

13. Hartman, *Wayward Lives, Beautiful Experiments* (New York: Norton, 2019). For a generative conjoined reading of Cavarero and Hartman, see Rachel Silverbloom, "Stealing and Critical Fabulation: The Counter-Historical Methods of Adriana Cavarero and Saidiya Hartman," in this volume.

14. Hartman, "The Belly of the World: A Note on Black Women's Labors," *Souls* 18, no. 1 (2016): 166–73; 171.

15. Laurie Naranch, "Bodies in Relation: Materialisms and Politics in Adriana Cavarero and Giorgio Agamben," in this volume.

16. For direct discussions of Agamben's work by Cavarero, see *Horrorism*, 39, 43; Cavarero, "Violent Female Bodies"; and Cavarero and Angelo Scola, *Thou Shalt Not Kill*, trans. M. Adams Groesbeck and A. Sitze (New York: Fordham University Press, 2015), 70–74. For other feminist critiques of Agamben directly relevant to this chapter, see also: Tina Chanter, *Whose Antigone? The Tragic Marginalization of Slavery* (Albany: State University of New York Press, 2011), 119–32; and Ewa Ziarek, "Bare Life," in *Impasses of the Post-Global: Theory in the Era of Climate Change*, vol. 2, ed. H. Sussman (Ann Arbor: Open Humanities Press, 2012).

17. Sigrid Weigel, "Double Focus: On the History of Women's Writing," in *Feminist Aesthetics*, ed. G. Ecker (Boston: Beacon Press, 1986), 59–80; 73.

18. Weigel, "Double Focus," 71.

19. Cavarero, *In Spite of Plato*, 5 (emphasis original).

20. See Agamben, *The Coming Community*, trans. M. Hardt (Minneapolis: University of Minnesota Press, 1993), 1–2, 9–11; and Cavarero's crucial deployment of the distinction between the "what" and the "who," as explored in *Relating Narratives*, trans. P. A. Kottman (New York: Routledge, 2000). For an in-depth discussion of a potential politics of the "who," see Timothy J. Huzar, "On the Politics of the *Who*: Cavarero, Nancy, and Rancière," in this volume. Cavarero's and Agamben's resistance to the logic of properties might be allied with Hartman's critique of fungibility in the context of slavery and racial capitalism; see Hartman, *Scenes of Subjection* (Oxford: Oxford University Press, 1997).

21. Agamben, *Homo Sacer*, 11.

22. Agamben, *The Coming Community*, 50. This knowing echo of Plato's image of Socrates continues a long-standing philosophical appropriation of the metaphorics of birth while absenting the ontological significance of birth from a human mother; see Cavarero, *In Spite of Plato*, 91–107.

23. Agamben, *Means without End*, 3.

24. Agamben, citing Arendt, *Homo Sacer*, 170.

25. Agamben, *Means without End*, 6; *Homo Sacer*, 9.

26. Agamben, *Means without End*, 3.

27. Agamben, *Homo Sacer*, 4. Cavarero also emphasizes the non-identity of *zoe* and bare life; see "Violent Female Bodies," 140.

28. Ziarek, "Bare Life," 195.

29. Agamben, *Means without End*, 3, 6.

30. Agamben, *Means without End*, 4, 11–12. See also *Homo Sacer*, 188.

31. Agamben, *Means without End*, 12.

32. Agamben, *The Coming Community*, 11.

33. Cavarero, *Inclinations*, 131.

34. Cavarero, *Relating Narratives*, 9. Crucially, even when it first appears in the world in the "absolute nudity" of the newborn, the singular "who" that Cavarero contrasts with the categorizable "what" is equivalent to neither bare life, stripped of form, nor *zoe* understood as unqualified life. Not only is the uniqueness of the

newborn always embodied as a sexuate being (where sexual difference is a mode of ontological orientation, not a categorizable property that defines *what* one is) but its natal appearing also forms the beginning of the story that will be composed by the pattern that takes shape as this singular being exposes itself to a plurality of others (*Relating Narratives*, 38–39). The *bios* of biography thus seems to qualify as a form-of-life insofar as the narratable self is inseparable from the story that constitutes its unity; nonetheless, here too, things are not so unambiguous, for singular beings remain vulnerable to harm through the unfaithful telling of their story.

35. See Agamben, *The Coming Community*, 43, 96–97; Cavarero, *Relating Narratives*, 20–21.

36. Agamben, *Means without End*, 11.

37. Agamben, *Homo Sacer*, 181.

38. Cavarero, "Violent Female Bodies," 129.

39. Cavarero, *In Spite of Plato*, 84 (emphasis added). I thank Allie Edwards for her insightful work on Irigaray's articulation of the feminine as life in the forming in an unpublished paper (2021) that informs my thinking here.

40. My analysis here and throughout is informed by Lisa Guenther's account of an ethics of feminine welcome that is similarly ambiguous, in that it gives an Other a place in the world only by withdrawing in a gesture of "nonreciprocal, asymmetrical generosity" that unavoidably allows the possibility of being forgotten, taken for granted, or exploited. Guenther, *The Gift of the Other* (Albany: State University of New York Press, 2006), 72–73.

41. In contrast, as Naranch suggests ("Bodies in Relation"), the bodies through which Agamben seeks to reclaim nudity and grace remain too glorious and erect, as if untouched by corporeal vulnerability or dependencies.

42. Agamben, *Homo Sacer*, 7 (emphasis added).

43. Agamben, *Homo Sacer*, 2, 11.

44. Agamben, *Homo Sacer*, 1; *Means without End*, 3.

45. Agamben, *Homo Sacer*, 109. On social death, see Orlando Patterson, *Slavery and Social Death* (Cambridge, MA: Harvard University Press, 1982).

46. Agamben, *Homo Sacer*, 128 (emphasis added).

47. Cavarero, "Violent Female Bodies," 129. See also 136.

48. Cavarero, "Violent Female Bodies," 136.

49. This is the case whether nature is seen as governed by the laws of the gods (as per the ancient Greeks) or by the de-godded laws of Western scientific modernity.

50. Cavarero, *Stately Bodies, Literature, Philosophy, and the Question of Gender*, trans. R. de Lucca and D. Shemek (Ann Arbor: University of Michigan Press, 2002), 13–53. For important engagements with *Antigone* that intersect with Cavarero's, see Judith Butler, *Antigone's Claim* (New York: Columbia University Press, 2000) and Fanny Söderbäck, ed., *Feminist Readings of Antigone* (Albany: State University of New York Press, 2010), as well as Chanter, *Whose Antigone?* Chanter's attentiveness

to Antigone as disclosing the politics of disavowal and of "excluded yet constitutive others" has been particularly important for my own thinking (Chanter, in *Feminist Readings of Antigone*, ed. Söderbäck, 83–98; Chanter, *Whose Antigone?* 57–86). *Whose Antigone?* argues that the focus on kinship and gender in modern Western (including feminist) interpretations of *Antigone* has occluded the significance of slavery within Sophocles's original text. In response, Chanter attends to the way that this aspect of the play animates reappropriations of *Antigone* in contexts of colonialism and racialization.

51. Sophocles, *Antigone*, in *Sophocles I*, trans. D. Grene (Chicago: University of Chicago Press, 1991), ll. 245–47. I also consulted Hugh Lloyd-Jones's translation in the 1998 Loeb edition, *Sophocles II* (Cambridge, MA: Harvard University Press, 1998).

52. Cavarero, *Stately Bodies*, 14.

53. See especially Butler, *Antigone's Claim*; Luce Irigaray, *Speculum of the Other Woman*, trans. G. C. Gill (Ithaca, NY: Cornell University Press, 1985), 214–26.

54. Cavarero, *Stately Bodies*, 13.

55. Cavarero, *Stately Bodies*, 38

56. Agamben's gloss on biological life at the end of *Homo Sacer*, 188.

57. Cavarero, *Stately Bodies*, 37.

58. Cavarero, *Stately Bodies*, 28; *Stately Bodies*, 30.

59. Cavarero, *Stately Bodies*, 28.

60. Cavarero, *Stately Bodies*, 29–30.

61. Sophocles, *Antigone*, ll. 423–25, as cited in Cavarero, *Stately Bodies*, 37.

62. Cavarero, *Stately Bodies*, 32.

63. Cavarero, *Stately Bodies*, 32.

64. Sophocles, *Antigone*, ll. 460–70, 900–915.

65. Sophocles, *Antigone*, ll. 855–65; on this point, see Mary Beth Mader, "Antigone's Line," in *Feminist Readings of Antigone*, ed. Söderbäck, 155–72.

66. Cavarero, *Stately Bodies*, 36.

67. Cavarero, *Stately Bodies*, 32–3.

68. Cavarero, *In Spite of Plato*, 107–20.

69. Sophocles, *Antigone*, ll. 415–20.

70. Cavarero, *In Spite of Plato*, 116.

71. Cavarero, *Stately Bodies*, 37.

72. Here, I am attempting to think with the second part of Cavarero's suggestion, drawing on a formulation borrowed from Bonnie Honig, that what is at stake in a relational ontology of inclined bodies rooted in birth "is not biological life but both *plus de vie* (more life) and *plus que vie* (more than life)" (Cavarero, "Violent Female Bodies," 140). I am interested in the ways in which the singular-plural lives—or liv*ing*—of the "more than life" might displace the biopolitical echoes in "(more) life." Cavarero's ongoing dialogue with Arendt is crucial here: specifically, Arendt's claim that "there is always more at stake in life than the sustenance and

procreation of individual living organisms." Arendt, "Collective Responsibility," cited in Cavarero, "Violent Female Bodies," 140.

73. Cavarero, *In Spite of Plato*, 114, citing Clarice Lispector, *The Passion According to G.H.*

74. A similar relation of oblique displacement rather than direct opposition emerges between Agamben's and Cavarero's readings of Hobbes. If Agamben shows that the Hobbesian state of nature where "man is a wolf to men" is not a "prejuridical condition" but a constitutive state of exception that remains always present in the city (*Homo Sacer*, 105–107), Cavarero casts her sideways glance on Hobbes's text to retrieve an obscured opening toward maternal generative power. By identifying maternal dominion in the state of nature with the power to determine whether the already born infant lives or dies, Hobbes throws into relief what he refuses: maternal generative power understood as a capacity to birth or not to birth that precedes (temporally and ontologically) the quest for self-preservation that forms the wolfish premise of sovereign power. See Cavarero, *Horrorism*, 22–23; and "Violent Female Bodies," 135–38.

75. Creon's edict results in Antigone's expulsion from the polis, living entombment, and death, depriving her also of the possibility of sharing in maternal generative power (Sophocles, *Antigone*, ll. 910–20).

76. At the end of the play, Creon repeatedly describes himself as already dead; Sophocles, *Antigone*, ll. 1260–330.

77. Cavarero, *In Spite of Plato*, 64 (emphasis added).

78. Cavarero, *In Spite of Plato*, 7.

79. Cavarero, *In Spite of Plato*, 63.

80. Cavarero, *In Spite of Plato*, 82.

81. Cavarero, *In Spite of Plato*, 82, 84. The reference to a beginning already started "inside the mother" contrasts with the emphasis on the gaze (*Relating Narratives*) or the inclined gesture (*Inclinations*) shared between a mother and their already born child and invites reflection on how the gestating body that bears another within (rather than leaning toward an other "outside") might further complicate a relational ontology that displaces the sovereign individual.

82. "The Greek word *physis*, from *phyein*, to be born, connotes the act of generating as a way of manifesting oneself, of growing, and of becoming present." Cavarero, *In Spite of Plato*, 59.

83. Cavarero, "Violent Female Bodies," 134.

84. Cavarero, *In Spite of Plato*, 66; 84–85.

85. Cavarero, *In Spite of Plato*, 82.

86. In its denial of natal and sexuate corporeality, this is the fantasized geometry of no one and no body (Cavarero, *Relating Narratives*, 9; and "Violent Female Bodies," 134–35). Nonetheless, historically, it has privileged the verticality of a paradigmatically male, white, heterosexual, middle-class, and able-bodied figure, as attested to by both Cavarero and Hartman.

87. Cavarero, *Horrorism*, 30.
88. Judith Butler, *Precarious Life* (New York: Verso, 2004).
89. Cavarero, *Horrorism*, 20–22, 30.
90. On the mutual constitution of uniqueness and relationality, see Cavarero, *Relating Narratives*, 43 and 71. Relationality is only possible because of a plurality of unique beings who differ from one another "precisely because" they are "constitutively interwoven" with each other.
91. Cavarero, *Horrorism*, 34, 32, 8.
92. Cavarero, *Horrorism*, 38; Agamben, *Means without End*, 3.
93. Cavarero, *Horrorism*, 42; Cavarero, *In Spite of Plato*, 113.
94. Cavarero, *Horrorism*, 38–39.
95. Cavarero, *Horrorism*, 8, 29.
96. Cavarero, *Inclinations*, 129.
97. Cavarero, *Inclinations*, 105.
98. Cavarero, *Inclinations*, 129, 131.
99. Cavarero, *Inclinations*, 63.
100. Cavarero, *Inclinations*, 10.
101. Ahmed, *Queer Phenomenology: Orientations, Objects, Others* (Durham, NC: Duke University Press, 2006), 65–92.
102. Ahmed, *Queer Phenomenology*, 107.
103. Ahmed, *Queer Phenomenology*, 92, 103, 107.
104. Bianchi, *The Feminine Symptom: Aleatory Matter in the Aristotelian Cosmos* (New York: Fordham University Press, 2014), 241.
105. Cavarero, *Inclinations*, 3; Huffer, *Foucault's Strange Eros* (New York: Columbia University Press, 2020), 8.
106. For extended readings of Cavarero's engagement with the figure of Penelope and her *metis*, see Paula Landerreche Cardillo, "'Taking the Thread for A Walk': Feminist Resistance to the Philosophical Order in Adriana Cavarero and María Lugones" and Rachel Silverbloom, "Stealing and Critical Fabulation: The Counter-Historical Methods of Adriana Cavarero and Saidiya Hartman," both in this volume.
107. Cavarero, *In Spite of Plato*, 12–13, 16, 84.
108. Cavarero, *In Spite of Plato*, 18, 84.
109. Cavarero, *In Spite of Plato*, 22.
110. Cavarero, *In Spite of Plato*, 85.
111. Agamben, *Means without End*, 57.
112. Cavarero, *In Spite of Plato*, 19.
113. Agamben, *Means without End*, 11 (emphasis original).
114. Agamben, *Means without End*, 12; Cavarero, "Politicizing Theory," *Political Theory* 30, no. 4 (2002), 506–32.
115. Cavarero, *In Spite of Plato*, 18–19, 28–30.
116. On withdrawal as a counter to matricidal violation, see *In Spite of Plato*, 79.

117. See Emily Parker's sustained and important examination of this issue in *Elemental Difference and the Climate of the Body* (Oxford: Oxford University Press, 2021).

118. Hartman, *Wayward Lives*, xiv–xv.

119. Hartman, *Wayward Lives*, 347 (emphasis original).

120. Hartman, *Wayward Lives*, 227.

121. Hartman, *Wayward Lives*, 348.

122. Hartman, *Wayward Lives*, xv, 349.

123. Naranch, "Bodies in Relation," in this volume.

124. Hartman, "The Belly of the World," 171.

125. Cavarero, "Violent Female Bodies," 136.

126. Hartman, "The Belly of the World," 168; and *Wayward Lives*, 184–86. See also Hortense Spillers's pathbreaking and now classic essay, "Mama's Baby, Papa's Maybe: An American Grammar Book," *Diacritics* 17, no. 2 (1987).

127. Hartman, *Wayward Lives*, 227.

128. Hartman, *Lose Your Mother*, 6; "The Belly of the World," 171.

129. Hartman, "The Belly of the World," 171. See also Hartman, *Wayward Lives*, xiv–xv.

130. This points to a potential friction between Hartman's and Cavarero's perspectives insofar as Cavarero's recent work foregrounds an Arendtian distinction between insurgency or liberation and the experience of freedom and democracy in their nascent, germinal state. See Cavarero, *Surging Democracy*, trans. M. Gervase (Stanford, CA: Stanford University Press, 2021), 8–14.

131. Hartman, *Wayward Lives*, 348.

132. Cavarero, *In Spite of Plato*, 106; see also "Violent Female Bodies," 133.

133. Françoise Vergès, *The Wombs of Women: Race, Capital, Feminism*, trans. K. L. Glover (Durham, NC: Duke University Press, 2020), 49–62.

134. Patterson, *Slavery and Social Death*, 5–10.

135. Jennifer Morgan, "*Partus sequitur ventrem*: Law, Race, and Reproduction in Colonial Slavery," *Small Axe* 22, no. 1 (55) (2018): 2–17. See also Christina Sharpe's brilliant *In the Wake: On Blackness and Being* (Durham, NC: Duke University Press, 2016).

136. Hartman, *Wayward Lives*, 228.

137. Spillers, "Mama's Baby, Papa's Maybe"; Hazel V. Carby, *Reconstructing Womanhood: The Emergence of the Afro-American Woman Novelist* (Oxford: Oxford University Press, 1987).

138. Hartman, "The Belly of the World," 171.

139. Hartman, *Wayward Lives*, 157, 184.

140. Hartman, "The Belly of the World," 169.

141. Hartman, *Wayward Lives*, 249, 21.

142. Hartman, *Wayward Lives*, 22, 61. My thanks to the editors of this volume for drawing my attention to these liminal spaces. For an analysis of the ways

in which Cavarero's approach displaces the public/private divide, see Elisabetta Bertolino, "One's Body in Political Engagement: Changing the Relation between Public and Private," in this volume.

143. Hartman, *Wayward Lives*, 184. On the ungendering of Black flesh, see Spillers, "Mama's Baby, Papa's Maybe."

144. Hartman, *Wayward Lives*, xv; Cavarero, *In Spite of Plato*, 113. On Penelope's gestures as "a rhythm that produces its own temporality" in ways that also elude the public/private divide, see Paula Landerreche Cardillo, "'Taking the Thread for a Walk,'" in this volume.

145. Hartman, *Wayward Lives*, 74.

146. Hartman, "The Belly of the World," 169, 171, referencing Audre Lorde's poem, "A Litany for Survival."

147. Hartman, *Wayward Lives*, 227, see also 347.

148. M. Detienne and J.-P. Vernant, *Cunning Intelligence in Greek Culture and Society*, trans. J. Lloyd (Chicago: Chicago University Press, 1978), 3.

149. Detienne and Vernant, *Cunning Intelligence*, 4.

150. Detienne and Vernant, *Cunning Intelligence*, 3; Hartman, *Wayward Lives*, 78.

151. Hartman, *Wayward Lives*, 348, 33.

152. Danielle C. Skeehan, *The Fabric of Empire: Material and Literary Cultures of the Global Atlantic 1650–1850* (Baltimore: Johns Hopkins University Press, 2020), 73.

153. Skeehan, *The Fabric of Empire*, 72. See also Douglas Hall, *In Miserable Slavery: Thomas Thistlewood in Jamaica 1750–86* (Kingston, JM: University of the West Indies Press, 1989), 159.

154. Elsewhere, Thistlewood distinguishes "Egypt Coobah" from "Phibbah's daughter"; Hall, *In Miserable Slavery*, 118.

155. See Morgan, "*Partus sequitur ventrem*."

156. Skeehan, *The Fabric of Empire*, 72; see also 82–83.

157. Skeehan, The Fabric of Empire, 83.

158. Hartman, *Wayward Lives*, 227.

159. Hall, *In Miserable Slavery*, 153, 184. This is the "Egypt Coobah" referred to in note 157.

160. Hall, *In Miserable Slavery*, 191–95.

161. Hartman, *Wayward Lives*, 228.

162. Cavarero, "Violent Female Bodies," 140.

163. Hartman, *Wayward Lives*, 6, 234 (emphasis original).

164. Hartman, *Wayward Lives*, 349.

Bibliography

Agamben, Giorgio. *The Coming Community*. Translated by Michael Hardt. Minneapolis: University of Minnesota Press, 1993.

———. *Homo Sacer: Sovereign Power and Bare Life*. Translated by Daniel Heller-Roazen. Stanford, CA: Stanford University Press, 1998.
———. *Means without End: Notes on Politics*. Translated by Vincenzo Binetti and Cesare Casarino. Minneapolis: University of Minnesota Press, 2000.
Ahmed, Sara. *Queer Phenomenology: Orientations, Objects, Others*. Durham, NC: Duke University Press, 2006.
Bianchi, Emanuela. *The Feminine Symptom: Aleatory Matter in the Aristotelian Cosmos*. New York: Fordham University Press, 2014.
Butler, Judith. *Antigone's Claim*. New York: Columbia University Press, 2000.
———. *Precarious Life*. New York: Verso, 2004.
Carby, Hazel V. *Reconstructing Womanhood: The Emergence of the Afro-American Woman Novelist*. Oxford: Oxford University Press, 1987.
Cavarero, Adriana. *For More Than Once Voice*. Translated by Paul A. Kottman. Stanford, CA: Stanford University Press, 2005.
———. *Horrorism: Naming Contemporary Violence*. Translated by William McCuaig. New York: Columbia University Press, 2009.
———. *Inclinations*. Translated by Adam Sitze and Amanda Minervini. Stanford, CA: Stanford University Press, 2016.
———. *In Spite of Plato: A Feminist Rewriting of Ancient Philosophy*. Translated by Serena Anderlini-D'Onofrio and Áine O'Healy. Cambridge: Polity Press, 1995.
———. "Politicizing Theory." *Political Theory* 30, no. 4 (2002): 506–32.
———. *Relating Narratives: Storytelling and Selfhood*. Translated by Paul A. Kottman. New York: Routledge, 2000.
———. *Stately Bodies: Literature, Philosophy, and the Question of Gender*. Translated by Robert de Lucca and Deanna Shemek. Ann Arbor: University of Michigan Press, 2002.
———. *Surging Democracy*. Translated by Matthew Gervase. Stanford, CA: Stanford University Press, 2021.
———. "Violent Female Bodies: Questioning Thanatopolitics." *Graduate Faculty Philosophy Journal* 36, no. 1 (2015): 129–44.
Cavarero, Adriana, and Angelo Scola. *Thou Shalt Not Kill*. Translated by Margaret Adams Groesbeck and Adam Sitze. New York: Fordham University Press, 2015.
Chanter, Tina. *Whose Antigone? The Tragic Marginalization of Slavery*. Albany: State University of New York Press, 2011.
Detienne, Marcel, and Jean-Pierre Vernant. *Cunning Intelligence in Greek Culture and Society*. Translated by Janet Lloyd. Chicago: Chicago University Press, 1978.
Guenther, Lisa. *The Gift of the Other*. Albany: State University of New York Press, 2006.
Hall, Douglas. *In Miserable Slavery: Thomas Thistlewood in Jamaica 1750–86*. Kingston, JM: University of the West Indies Press, 1989.
Hartman, Saidiya. "The Belly of the World: A Note on Black Women's Labors." *Souls* 18, no. 1 (2016): 166–73.

———. *Lose Your Mother: A Journey along the Atlantic Slave Route*. New York: Farrar, Straus, and Giroux, 2007.

———. *Scenes of Subjection*. Oxford: Oxford University Press, 1997.

———. *Wayward Lives, Beautiful Experiments*. New York: Norton, 2019.

Huffer, Lynne. *Foucault's Strange Eros*. New York: Columbia University Press, 2020.

Irigaray, Luce. *Speculum of the Other Woman*. Translated by Gillian C. Gill. Ithaca, NY: Cornell University Press, 1985.

Mbembe, Achille. *Necropolitics*. Translated by Steven Corcoran. Durham, NC: Duke University Press, 2019.

Morgan, Jennifer. "*Partus sequitur ventrem*: Law, Race, and Reproduction in Colonial Slavery." *Small Axe*, 22 no. 1 2018): 1–17.

Parker, Emily. *Elemental Difference and the Climate of the Body*. Oxford: Oxford University Press, 2021.

Patterson, Orlando. *Slavery and Social Death*. Cambridge, MA: Harvard University Press, 1982.

Sharpe, Christina. *In the Wake: On Blackness and Being*. Durham, NC: Duke University Press, 2016.

Skeehan, Danielle C. *The Fabric of Empire: Material and Literary Cultures of the Global Atlantic 1650–1850*. Baltimore: Johns Hopkins University Press, 2020.

Söderbäck, Fanny, ed. *Feminist Readings of Antigone*. Albany: State University of New York Press, 2010.

Sophocles, *Antigone*. In *Sophocles I*. Translated by David Grene. Chicago: University of Chicago Press, 1991.

———. *Sophocles II*. Translated by Hugh Lloyd-Jones. Cambridge, MA: Harvard University Press, 1998.

Spillers, Hortense. "Mama's Baby, Papa's Maybe: An American Grammar Book." *Diacritics*, 17, no. 2 (1987): 64–81.

Vergès, Françoise. *The Wombs of Women: Race, Capital, Feminism*. Translated by Kaiama L. Glover. Durham, NC: Duke University Press, 2020.

Weigel, Sigrid. "Double Focus: On the History of Women's Writing." In *Feminist Aesthetics*, edited by Gisela Ecker, 59–80. Boston: Beacon Press, 1986.

Ziarek, Ewa. "Bare Life." In *Impasses of the Post-Global: Theory in the Era of Climate Change*, vol. 2, edited by Henry Sussman, 194–211. Ann Arbor: Open Humanities Press, 2012.

Eight

Bodies in Relation

Ontology, Ethics, and Politics in
Adriana Cavarero and Giorgio Agamben

Laurie E. Naranch

Political philosophers Adriana Cavarero and Giorgio Agamben are both concerned with the status of life as an ontological and political matter. Through rigorous critiques of modern violence and the dominant individualist subject, both offer alternative views of ethics and politics that refigure how we relate to others in nonviolent ways. Both are also deeply invested in how embodiment offers figures from history, law, philosophy, and Western art a way to cease the persistence of dehumanization and imagine nonviolent futures. However, their views are rarely placed in conversation with each other despite the fact that they are among the most influential contemporary Italian philosophers today.[1] Cavarero is known for her feminist work on the narratable self and a postural ethics of inclination that foregrounds the relationality we have to each other as vulnerable beings from the time of birth. Agamben is known for his work on biopolitics: the paradox of modern sovereignty where, in the name of security, any body is subject to being killed with impunity, the sacrificial logic of the law that manages life. Both philosophers make references to ancient political philosophy, leftist politics, Catholicism, and contemporary horrors from the Holocaust to the war on terror, to the rising crises of authoritarianism, to global pandemics.

Both draw on art to develop key concepts, and both take inspiration from the work of Hannah Arendt.[2] They are also contemporaries: Agamben born in 1942 in Rome and Cavarero in 1947 in Bra, Italy. Both have taught in Italian universities as well as lectured extensively internationally. While there is a great deal of secondary literature on Agamben's work linking him to a variety of thinkers, rarely is Cavarero in these conversations.[3]

I draw out resonances in their work, revealing the power of their ontological investigations as a "kind of look" to shake loose dominant ways of thinking and reconfigure violence to nonviolence.[4] That is, I explore how each rethinks the status of the modern, individualist subject in ways that are distinctly embodied and relational, whether through birth or biopolitics. As a feminist scholar concerned with equal liberty for all gendered and sexed bodies, I am drawn to how each offers resistance to violence by engaging with feminine figures. I evaluate the affirmative vision both philosophers offer by reading how they stage resistant actions through their aesthetic analyses at feminine figures. I suggest that Cavarero and Agamben offer two kinds of outlooks valuable for feminist thinking that put bodies into relation in new ways: ontology is a kind of orientation showing how exposure to violence reveals our fundamental vulnerability to others or to sovereignty, and it is coupled in their affirmative ethics and politics with an aesthetic look to unsettle stereotypical or seemingly familiar female figures for nonviolent purposes. I am drawn to this figurative register of their political philosophy because it reveals that how we think about embodiment through images and figuration matters for how political concepts such as being and life develop. Despite my appreciation of Agamben's critical and reconstructive project, I suggest that Cavarero's ontological look at vulnerable bodies and the ethics of inclination illustrated through her aesthetic analysis of feminine figures is better able to dislodge the idea of the isolated individual and open possibilities for nonviolence than Agamben's view of inoperativity and the glorious body—what I will refer to in this essay as a distinction between ordinary and extraordinary bodies in relation. In this, I follow Bonnie Honig's astute claim that Agamben's concept of inoperativity has a purism that "abandons the city" and "suspends the everyday" in favor of a refusal that is more contemplative than material or engaged in contestation with others, even as she reworks his idea for a feminist theory of refusal.[5] Cavarero's ethical inclination offers more opportunities to expand our gaze of how sexed bodies could be in relation in nonviolent ways. If we expand on her example of the artist Artemisia Gentileschi, we can stage multiple scenes for imagining nonviolence in a more egalitarian, feminist, and materialist direction that instructs us in the different supports needed for feminist freedom.[6] For feminist and democratic thinkers, the ordinary bodies Cavarero presents reveal the conditions in which bodies come into relationship with each other. Feminist materialism can illustrate how nonviolence as an egalitarian political project depends on multiple forms of relationality with people, cultural narratives, economies, and institutions.

How Life and Bodies Matter

How life matters to politics is central to egalitarian visions seeking freedom for all bodies. As Judith Butler suggests, we must ask what makes a "livable life."[7] Diagnosing a livable life has a long tradition in political philosophy, where the maintenance of life was the work of the household, done by women and slaves, which allowed the demos to emerge: its male citizens having time to be active in the ancient Greek polis. How life matters to being human, as a person and a citizen, shapes how we come into relation with others in situations of harm or care. The ontological investigations of Agamben and Cavarero address ancient and modern experiences of the dispossession of life, labor, and bodily autonomy. While some may disagree that thinking ontologically can be fruitful for political interventions to counter violence, both Agamben and Cavarero do so in order to reframe and refigure the defining categories of life, which they suggest could lead to a reconstructed politics of nonviolence. As Christine Battersby writes, "Neglecting ontological dependencies and power inequalities, philosophers and political theorists overprivilege fully autonomous, and ideally equal adult selves."[8] She says this in relation to Cavarero's work, but it can apply to Agamben's corpus as well. For neither Cavarero nor Agamben does ontology necessarily lead to particular political outcomes, but thinking ontologically is ground-level philosophical work that articulates ways to overcome or dismantle the dominant metaphysics of a Western tradition that enshrines violence exercised by state sovereignty (Agamben) and patriarchal power (Cavarero) through the figure of the supposedly autonomous and self-governing individual. By working at the level of ontology, they attempt to shift the terrain of resistance from the "violence that posits the law, central to the revolutionary tradition, to a radical heterogeneity," as German Eduardo Primera says of Agamben's work.[9] As a thinker articulating a feminism of possibilities, Cavarero's feminine figures serve this imaginative function to shift the terrain of resistance to pluralize the bodies who matter.

This means acknowledging sexual difference in multiple ways and tracking how bodies are dispossessed of humanity, personhood, and citizenship. This affirmative vision of Cavarero's ordinary feminine bodies lends itself to a radical materialism that helps us to reimagine our relationships to others and to situations and conditions that are necessary to secure freedom in everyday settings.[10]

Exposures and Figures of the Thinkable

Agamben and Cavarero both utilize what Cornelius Castoriadis calls a "figure of the thinkable," an abstract, generalized figure that unlocks criticism and imagines new futures.[11] For Agamben, the critical figure is the Homo sacer drawn from Roman law, a being who can be killed but not sacrificed. For Agamben, this explains the power of sovereignty to operate at the level of bare life (zoe) to control and contain who lives and who dies through the exercise of law and punishment. Sovereignty operates both as state-repressive violence and also as biopolitics. This vision of biopolitics extends the work of Michel Foucault, who argues that biopower appears in how modern bureaucratic apparatuses "make live and let die" through managing populations in different authoritative settings (like hospitals, schools, and the state).[12] Agamben boldly argues in relation to modern political life, "If the essence of the [concentration] camp consists in the materialization of the state of exception and in the subsequent space in which bare life and the juridical rule enter into a threshold of indistinction, then we must admit that we find ourselves virtually in the presence of a camp every time such a structure is created."[13] That is, the camp becomes the model of modern political life institutionalizing the state of exception exercised by sovereignty as normal. Certainly, this is a claim more provocative than "fully supportable,"[14] as it was meant to spark attention to limitless state violence and the ongoing production of bare life, a life rendered disposable.[15]

The point here is that the motivations for destroying and abusing bodies in these systems of organized political power are built from an ontological view of the body as meant for use. While Agamben has explored many topics, his interest in the use of bodies and their exposure to violence remains a theme over the nine books referred to as the Homo Sacer series: from the first book, *Homo Sacer*, culminating in the last, *The Use of Bodies* (*L'uso dei corpi*).[16] Agamben's work in *The Use of Bodies* starts with Aristotle and moves genealogically through a wide range of sources, ending with analyzing Plato and Christian thought to rethink forms of life that are not modeled on use or ownership.

Cavarero's critical figures are repeatedly the woman and the mother, which she uses to unlock her criticism that the uniqueness of each person—if a woman or mother—has been systematically denied and denigrated in the history of Western political philosophy and patriarchal societies. Her well-known method is one of stealing back from the tradition its feminine figures such as Penelope and Diotima.[17] Cavarero revalues their actions as agentic and instructive for ethics and shared political power.[18] Tracing figurations in her work allows for ambiguity and difficulty to emerge, such as in her recent work on mothers who do not fit simply into the dichotomous categories of good or evil.[19]

Offering figures of the thinkable as ways to see embodied life through destruction or silencing shapes the work of Cavarero and Agamben. Both investigate exposure to violence. Agamben analyzes extreme cases such as life in the Holocaust camps, where the label *Muselmänner* was given to those rendered as walking dead, thus signaling the excessive destructiveness of human life in modernity. Cavarero extends this exposure to violence to think about suicide bombers who are generally assumed to be male and framed through terrorism as an operative category that names that experience of violence as one of utter destructiveness and isolation. Cavarero focuses on cases of female suicide bombers, who particularly confound categories of thought given the stereotypical associations of women with care. Cavarero offers the concept of horrorism to show ontologically how the particular horror of using a woman's body as an explosive device reveals our extreme vulnerability to others.[20]

While both Agamben and Cavarero look at extreme violences in the West to try to undo the logics that allow these to occur, for many, their work reveals a love of death or thanatopolitics at the heart of Western life. Agamben is most associated with this framework of thinking. Cavarero challenges the claims that thanatopolitics or biopolitics are adequate frames through which to think contemporary politics. Observing life through female bodies, Cavarero reminds us that women's bodies have been expelled from political life from the onset of Western politics, which reveals our inability to take account of what is particularly horrific about violence: the body is at stake and at stake in different ways depending on the particularities of gender, sexuality, race, ethnicity, religion, class, and ability. She writes, "Beginning from the model of the ancient [polis], political systems expel the body from their proper realm, or in other words, ensure that body and life are produced and reproduced by women, in a separate, but socially controlled, marginal, but necessary domain."[21] This is why she finds Agamben's categories of bare life, when deployed to explain cases like the horror of female suicide bombers, to be inadequate for making sense of the killer's active position when they are a woman. Instead, she suggests this figure opens up a different horror given the association of women as mothers with life and the importance of valuing life.[22] This relates to her concern that what is needed is not simply attention to bare life but to more life.

What Cavarero explores is an ontology neither of death nor use but of birth, "our original and unilateral exposure to others," which she says surpasses the distinction between bare life and *bios* (form of life) to give rise to an "alternative narrative" of "more life."[23] This allows us to move beyond Agamben's victimized body in the biopolitics he traces.[24] To point to the spaces where we are cared for because we are so exposed to violence, Cavarero's attention shifts to the postures of bodies in *Inclinations*.[25] Arguing that the Western tradition privileges rectitude or erectness of the individual, autonomous, masculine subject or being, Cavarero finds an alternative posture through scenes of inclination to others. Putting her work in *Inclinations* in conversation with Agamben's text *Nudities*[26] further reveals what is at stake in considering embodiment as ontologically relational. As I'm suggesting here, for Cavarero and for Agamben, focusing on ontology allows us to think about the frames through which we think the human body and our exposure to others as fundamental to being. This kind of look leads to other ways of seeing bodies in relation since both philosophers have constructive projects of an ethical and philosophical nature that open up new political horizons.

Bodies in Relation, or Thinking Otherwise through Altruistic Care or Destituent Power

As Fanny Söderbäck[27] suggests, Cavarero offers a normative distinction between wounding and violence, love and care. In *Inclinations*, Cavarero parses the meaning of the term vulnerability to develop this distinction. The term has roots in the Latin *vulnus*, or wound. Cavarero says "*vulnus* is essentially the result of a violent blow, inflicted from the outside by a sharp instrument with blunt force, tearing and gashing the skin."[28] This attention to skin leads Cavarero to mine another valence of the term, that of nudity, which becomes "exposure without defense."[29] Vulnerability relates to the human body in absolute nakedness, an exposure that opens the body to a wound or to a caress, and the scene of birth is illustrative of this exposure. The distinction between wound and caress is what shapes the normative registers of justice and freedom and how exposure is treated. Cavarero's own view of vulnerability as exposure stages a contrast between pathological relationality and altruism, or care: that is, an altruistic ethics of care.

For Cavarero, when nudity "becomes exposure without defense"[30] we have the possibilities of violence or nonviolence in how we relate to others, especially in situations of asymmetrical power. In earlier works, Cavarero explores nonviolence with the idea of the narratable self recognizing the dependency we have on others in the story of ourselves, revealing both an ethical and a nascent democratic politics.[31] With *Inclinations*, she turns to the bodily gesture of leaning toward for a nonviolent relationality. Her signature example is Leonardo da Vinci's painting of the Madonna leaning toward the infant Jesus accompanied by her mother, *The Virgin and Child with St. Anne* (1503–1519). Cavarero writes of the ethical implications of this inclination, saying: "The mother bent over her child: precisely this gesture allows inclination to be deployed strategically as a good point of departure for rethinking the ontology of the vulnerable, together with its constitutive relationality, in terms of postural geometry that, far from limiting itself to the axis of uprightness, arranges the human along multiple coexisting lines, what may be contingent and intermittent, and at times even random."[32] Drawing on Hannah Arendt's work, Cavarero's relational ontology centers natality with the ordinary fact of birth as an embodied experience and ongoing relationship, with mother and child as a figures showcasing our relationality to others. Cavarero is critical of Arendt's neglect of the maternal body. Cavarero reiterates this saying: "As I have argued in *Inclinations*, I accuse Arendt—and I think I am right in this—of having been able to give the value to the category of birth by placing it at the foundation of her political thought without, however, considering, not even as a theme, that necessary figure, always present at birth, that is the mother—and actually, not even the infant is considered."[33] In returning to the example of the mother inclined toward the child,[34] Cavarero reviews her hypothesis, finding "imaginary resources for pacifism residing in the face of the mother inclined over her child—which, not by chance, is often represented in art as elusive and enigmatic."[35] This inclination, Cavarero argues, is hiding in plain sight in the iconography around us. Her Arendtian view about bodies and the ways in which bodies connect through birth, voice, closeness, song, and collective action are deeply complex. And yet, her intense focus on the scene of the mother and child raises a host of issues about inclusion if the exemplary scene for an altruistic ethics is *The Virgin and Child with St. Anne*.[36]

Attention to wounding and care is also something that interests Agamben in texts such as *Nudities* and *The Use of Bodies*. This links to his critique of use in totalitarian and democratic politics alike, which for him are systems of unlimited power without the "reciprocal limit" found between the ancient Roman Senate and populous, the medieval pope and emperor, or the eighteenth-century limits of natural and positive law. Agamben offers suggestive remarks pitting use—that is, the instrumentalization of bodies in law and authoritative systems like the economy—against care. Care, in his view, is care of the self, drawn from Plato and Foucault; "What uses the body and that of which one must take care, Socrates concludes [. . .] is the soul."[37] Rather than Hegel's dialectic of master and slave, which shows the dependency of the master on the slave—or as Foucault's analysis of sadomasochism puts it, where the submissive is in control—Agamben finds that neither can render the dialectical relationship at stake inoperative despite the fact that each shows the foundations of modernity as dependent on exploited others.[38] For this reason, he calls for *destituent* power (a force that would inactivate a government machine) and inoperativity to stop the instrumental nature of use.[39] Agamben explains destituent power this way: "Starting with the French revolution, the political tradition of modernity has conceived of radical changes in the form of a revolutionary process that acts as the *pouvoir constituant*, the 'constituent power' of a new institutional order. I think that we have to abandon this paradigm and try to think something as a *puissance destituante*, a 'purely destituent power,' that cannot be captured in the spiral of security."[40] Agamben's reconstructed view of politics wants to jam the system. This explains why he turns to examples of destitutent power in *Nudities* through figures in Western and Christian art that are still and appear in positions of uselessness. This reveals how inoperativity can be a radical counter power to the constituting power of horror, which is continually created in modern political life.

Agamben offers rich insights from the world of art, addressing the sexed body in his exploration of destituent power and inoperativity through women's bodies, which is unusual in his work on bare life.[41] In the chapter "Nudity" he meditates on the ethical and theological resonances of nakedness and nudity. He starts with a 2005 performance piece staged by artist Vanessa Beecroft featuring one-hundred nude women staring in formation in Berlin's Neue Nationalgalerie. "Clothed men who observe nude bodies: this scene irresistibly evokes the sadomasochistic ritual of power."[42] Until it doesn't. It is not like the scene of Abu Ghraib in Iraq, where American military police stood in front of piles of naked bodies, but something else, he says. It wasn't a scene of torture or capture but "simple nudity."[43] Nudity, Agamben thinks, is related to grace and contrasted to the bodily exposure of nakedness. Through a detailed reading of the Fall and the expulsion of Adam and Eve from Eden, Agamben explores this nudity without shame. The removal of clothes is what he refers to as grace. Grace offers an exposure to the other, or to God, that is nonviolent.[44] In an interpretation of Beecroft's art, Agamben describes the hundred female bodies of various ages, races, and shapes, calling into question the nudity of the body as simply for use.[45] This is an opportunity for Agamben to frame nudity as not for the use of others, which is why Agamben talks about nudity as "the problem of human nature in relation to grace."[46] It is grace, he explains, and the glorious body that can jam the logic of use and open up a new, ethical relationality with others and with God.

Juxtaposed to Cavarero's critique of rectitude in favor in inclinations, Agamben seems to offer an alternative reading of rectitude to counter the dominant tradition of use. For example, in remarks on Helmut Newton's photographic diptych *They Are Coming* (1981), he turns to female bodies to theorize inoperativity. The first photograph shows four women naked except for dress shoes; the second photograph shows the same women in the same walking pose but clothed in business-like attire. For Agamben, the contrast between not clothed and clothed bodies depicts an Edenic fall into knowledge—where, unclothed, the women's bodies appear with neither "shame nor glory," just nude.[47] On some level, we might applaud this reading of women's bodies as not for the use of others, challenging a male gaze or the many ways in which women's bodies are used by patriarchal, capitalist, and colonial systems. Yet despite the female bodies under view, Agamben pays little attention to systemic issues of patriarchal or gendered power. This is despite the fact that he says one might have expected sexist hostility at the Beecroft exhibit: "*Something that could have, and, perhaps should have happened did not take place.*"[48] That is, there could have been a violation of naked female bodies, not the "almost military ranks of the hostile, naked bodies."[49] He assumes a male figure as the viewer and a female body under view for male consumption being challenged. This could be an opportunity for deeper thinking about inegalitarian power, but Agamben is less interested in questions of gendered power than the possibility for overcoming a circuit of consumption in looking, staged in this stereotypical way to shock the system.

There are other extraordinary bodies that Agamben offers for theorizing inoperativity, such as the clothing of Eve depicted in an eighteenth-century silver reliquary. In this relief, Eve is being forced into a tunic by another figure. The woman, he says, "resists this divine violence with all her might."[50] Her resistance to being clothed "is an extraordinary symbol of femininity"; that is, "this woman is the tenacious custodian of paradisiacal nudity."[51] Despite the importance of resistance Agamben sees in this image, he keeps in place traditional feminine and masculine stereotypes even when he tries to think of her bodily exposure as grace and the violence enacted on her body to be clothed. Unlike Cavarero, who wants to leverage the stereotype for more disruptive and potentially ethical ordinary relations, Agamben's Eve is singularly alone in resisting the garment going over her head; she is not in solidarity or even in contestation with others. This is a relation of imposition she resists singularly. While each of Agamben's choice of images shows a militancy of feminine bodies, none are particularly persuasive for reimagining erectness in ways that could refigure relations among women and men. There is also little attention to collective actions or, as Honig would say, agonistic solidarity. Instead, these figures appear quite alone, even if standing with others.[52] These are extraordinary bodies that, while confounding logics of use, seem to have little to say to each other and fail to be lively enough to represent ordinary living bodies in democratic interactions.

To push further the limits of Agamben's extraordinary bodies for feminist ethics and politics, we can look more closely at the glorious body. In a reading of Christian debates about what the function of organs would be in a resurrected body—the liver, the womb, and substances like bile or semen—we learn they would exist but not function.[53] While Agamben acknowledges that resurrected bodies would retain their sexual difference, sexual organs would have no use since these glorious bodies are rendered static at a prime age (said to be around thirty) and remain still in the sense that hair or nails would not grow and bodily organs would not function. Agamben says, "The glorious body is an ostensible body whose functions are not executed but rather displayed. Glory, in this sense, is in solidarity with inoperativity."[54] Anyone concerned with reproductive and sexual rights should pause at this description of a glorious body as a potential resistant figure to our contemporary use of bodies.

On the one hand, in the images and figures Agamben reads, we might see an intriguing reframing of erectness in the female form that, while aesthetically positioned as beautiful, is taken out of the circulation of use, patriarchal or otherwise. However, on the other hand, the beautiful feminine body is a version of a glorious body that is not to be used for arousal or exploitation, or anything at all really. Honig is right to argue that Agamben's glorious body turns into a body without functioning organs and that his body seems to be unbothered by "the body's needs, demands and pleasures."[55] This is surely not an ordinary human body that requires health care, food, and free movement. Agamben's inattention to ordinary bodies is telling in terms of his turn to Paul as an example of a body who, through messianic faith, can "deactivate" law with respect to sin and so render the law "destitute of its power to command."[56] What is law without command? The aesthetic, glorious body in a contemplative state of freedom is remarkably unsticky, unexperienced in tense or loving relations to other bodies. Agamben's utopian horizon dematerializes bodies and democratic politics in exchange for a theological frame as a way to get to a nonviolent space. In this regard, he is not far from a critique of Karl Marx's vision of laboring bodies as unalienated after the ultimate revolutionary moment after class struggle. Despite the brilliance of Marx's critique of capitalism, his political theory does not imagine an ongoing politics of contestation with others to ensure nonviolence.[57]

Cavarero offers us other feminine figures of resistance, who open up more possibilities for feminist critique of existing power structures and new relations of nonviolence. I turn to a chapter from *Inclinations* that hasn't gotten as much attention, "Artemisa: The Allegory of Inclination." Cavarero uses the example of the Italian seventeenth-century female painter Artemesia Gentileschi and her painting the *Allegory of Inclination* (1615), commissioned by Michelangelo's grandnephew. The painting on the ceiling of his house shows a woman's body drawn toward a shining star, her naked bust and head inclining to the right.[58] The woman's inclination to an external force of creativity shows "an act of courage and defiance," Cavarero says, in depicting the young woman, assumed to be Artemisia herself, as naked and exposed. In this depiction, we see a feminine figure embodying courage relating to creativity but also in risking bodily exposure, which is all the more pointed since Artemisia was raped and endured a humiliating public trial, a double violation still common today.[59] Cavarero recognizes how this naked exposure is a resistant gesture of an agentic female body. That this body is unsettling in its exposure and inclination to create work is illustrated by the fact that a few decades later, the grandnephew had her nakedness covered over through painted veils and drapes.

Cavarero argues that Artemisia herself is inclining toward the pull of artistic talent in a situation where, as a woman, she is not authorized to do so. And yet, she does. Cavarero says this image is a rare instance of a positive representation of inclination in Western art and philosophy, and it was painted by a woman. "Philosophers, convinced of the normativity of the straight axis, generally think all inclinations, despite their variety,

Figure 8.1. Artemisia Gentileschi, *Allegoria dell'inclinazione*. Wikimedia Commons, public domain.

are basically malign or dangerous and hence in need of correction."[60] But not in this case. Here is an inclination that is unusual in that it does not relate to a particular other or signal a weakness or disability; rather, it is an act of creative genius making art. I appreciate Cavarero's method of distilling by reading closely, but there is value in adding to her feminine figures. I suggest we look more at Artemisia's[61] work and add to the images under scrutiny, her *Self-Portrait as the Allegory of Painting* (1638–1639) and a different scene of birth, *The Birth of Saint John the Baptist* (1635), to better draw out feminine resistance and the importance of collective life even in the private space of a scene of birth. This makes an altruistic ethics of inclination all the more material and political in how we see labor, collective representation, and possibilities for nonviolence.

In the *Self-Portrait*, painted when she was invited to London by Charles I, Artemisia presents herself as *Painting* itself. That is, Artemisia personifies an allegory typically depicted in female form with the specificity of her body. In the painting, Artemisia leans her left arm on a table with pallet in hand, her brush reaching from her right hand to a canvas out of view of the audience; she is clothed in a green dress. We see in this work the dynamism of her creativity, her clever retaking of the allegorical figure using her embodied self, the fact that this is a commission through which she earns money, and the skill she shows in its execution. This is not the contemporary "leaning in" of the willful self of contemporary culture;[62] this is another inclination. We see a female artist leaning into a creativity that is not yet available to her, creating a new place in the world as a working

Figure 8.2. Artemisia Gentileschi, *Self-Portrait as the Allegory of Painting*. Wikimedia Commons, public domain.

artist, an occupation that was not available to women of her time. That is, the portrait depicts an act of novelty or natality in her skill. This matters materially since after she and her husband separated, she needed to have an income. Not only that, it demonstrates that Artemisia had a drive to create in ways that suggested other postures of inclination.

While distilling inclination to a central image is a valuable method for shaking loose accepted categories of being—as Cavarero says she follows Arendt in this method of bringing some intuitions to the extreme to make "stereotypes speak differently," such as the Madonna and child[63]—it can obscure other ways to be in relation with others and systems of power. Artemisia's *The Birth of Saint John the Baptist* is one of a series of scenes from the life of Saint John commissioned in Naples.[64] In this painting we see the child surrounded by four midwives with the exhausted looking mother, Elizabeth, in the left background with another woman; in the left foreground is her husband, Zechariah, who is writing down the name of the foretold child. In the Biblical story, Zechariah did not believe a child to be truly coming, given he and his wife's advanced age, and this disbelief rendered him mute. When the baby is born and to be named, he writes the name John and, in writing down the name, he gains his voice back. Following Cavarero, we can see multiple inclinations of care signaling a fundamental dependence on many others—Elizabeth looking to another woman in the left background, Zechariah leaning over to write the child's name in the ledger, the women surrounding and leaning in to the child, holding him over a basin, in the foreground. We could say this image might reinforce stereotypical assumptions about feminine labor or women's status as mothers and caregivers. We can also, with Cavarero, shake loose these stereotypes and look more at the cooperation in care: how the midwives look at each other, how the name is registered at birth—recognizing a social and political environment—and the lively scene surrounding the birth. As Battersby suggests in relation to *Inclinations*, "At stake is a broader issue, in that it seems to me that Cavarero's ontology, with its emphasis on asymmetrical relationality, needs a further swerve so as to include arcs of dependence that are appropriate to friendship between individuals, states, and other social groupings."[65] Or, as Rachel Jones nicely argues, when we draw attention to the morphological resonances between other oblique or slanted relations that "epitomize the asymmetries of inclination, and the 'queer' contestations of the moralizing hegemony of 'straightness,'" we offset the risks of Cavarero's exaggerated method.[66] Adding these two other examples from Artemisia allows us to see multiple arcs of relationality in

Figure 8.3. Artemisia Gentileschi, *The Birth of St. John the Baptist*. Wikimedia Commons, public domain.

ethical, political, and productive formations that deepen the materialism of embodiment valuable to all bodies in search of possibilities of nonviolence.

Conclusion

Thinking through exposures to violence in ways that articulate nonviolent alternatives is a contribution both Cavarero and Agamben make to a materialism that pays attention to life and the bodies that are made and unmade in the context of violences by the state, patriarchy, and capitalism. I have suggested that while each philosopher pays attention to sexual difference in the artistic representations they deploy, both for critique and to open up a more utopian political horizon, Agamben tends to dematerialize the body as a glorious body, rendering the lived reality of bodies stranded in an ontology of grace and a politics of destituent power and inoperativity. Cavarero offers a richer view of embodiment, centering sexual difference and birth as examples for thinking about our fundamental dependency on and vulnerability to others. Her feminist viewpoint is important for challenging the ontological, ethical, and political registers of how we might relate to others without violence as unique embodied beings.

In a democratic sense, ordinary bodies are needed when we must act together to create a shared world and to institute our limits as ordinary individuals.[67] Collective action is important for countering the exposures to violence resurging through division and the stoked hatred of others. Cavarero address this in *Surging Democracy*, where bodies act together for inclusive, egalitarian goods, often singing and chanting together against authoritarian threats when taking to the streets, which was a challenge during the coronavirus pandemic lockdowns. These lively bodies are essential to democratic health. But we can still ask of her work, given that she is invested in how bodies come together in wounding and care, How do we desire to care for the other? Or, as Wendy Brown writes, "There is one last contemporary challenge for those who believe in popular rule, perhaps the most serious challenge of all. As we have already said, the presumption of democracy as a good rests on the presumption that human beings want to be self-legislating and that rule by the demos checks the dangers of an unaccountable and concentrated political power."[68] With Cavarero, we can move away from the idea that democracy and nonviolence toward others requires an erectness of purpose or that democratic self-legislation could be done without individuals, institutions, and economies that can support, rather than simply use up, bodies for the profit of a few.

Notes

1. Many thanks to Lori Marso and Rachel Jones for their incredibly helpful comments on this chapter. "Italian philosophy" is a useful but contested category. Timothy Campbell suggests that rather than offering a solid definition of Italian philosophy, we should think of how texts add up to "Italian political thought" in an "interval, a milieu with shifting boundaries, reciprocities, and allegiances." Timothy Campbell, "The Will-To-The-Common in Italian Thought," *Diacritics* 39, no. 4 (Winter 2009): 101–2. Or, as Roberto Esposito puts it, "language was one of Italian philosophy's main pillars, but always in close relation with the constitutive categories of Italian thought: namely, history, politics, and life." "The Return of Italian Philosophy," *Diacritics* 39, no. 33 (Fall 2009): 55–61. While I have been drawn especially to the work of Adriana Cavarero, my ongoing reading of and interest in Giorgio Agamben's work seemed to dovetail with concerns in Cavarero's

work of a material and ethical-political nature. See also the collection *Contemporary Italian Women Philosophers: Stretching the Art of Thinking*, ed. Silvia Benso and Elvira Roncalli (Albany: State University of New York Press, 2021).

2. Agamben, in fact, wrote to Arendt in February 1970 and enclosed an essay he had written, now published in English. "On the Limits of Violence," trans. Lorenzo Fabbri and Elisabeth Fay, *Diacritics* 39, no. 4 (Winter 2009): 103–11. https://www.jstor.org/stable/23256452. Agamben also references Arendt's work many times, such as in *Homo Sacer: Sovereign Power and Bare Life*, trans. Daniel Heller-Roazen (Stanford, CA: Stanford University Press, 1998).

3. For a few exceptions, see Bonnie Honig, "How to Do Things with Inclination: Antigones, with Cavarero," in *Toward a Feminist Ethics of Nonviolence*, ed. Timothy J. Huzar and Clare Woodford (New York: Fordham University Press, 2021), 63–89. See also the first part of Chiara Bottici, "Rethinking the Biopolitical Turn: From the Thanatopolitical to the Geneapolitical Paradigm," *Graduate Faculty Philosophy Journal* 36, no. 1 (2015). In this volume, see Rachel Jones "Inclining toward New Forms of Life: Cavarero, Agamben, and Hartman." Interestingly, there is no entry for "Cavarero" in the *Internet Encyclopedia of Philosophy*, but there is for Agamben, while there are seven references to Cavarero in topical categories of the *Stanford Encyclopedia of Philosophy* and five for Agamben https://plato.stanford.edu/search/searcher.py?query=cavarero; https://plato.stanford.edu/search/search?query=agamben.

4. Thanks to Lori Marso for this phrasing.

5. Bonnie Honig, *A Feminist Theory of Refusal* (Cambridge, MA: Harvard University Press, 2021), in particular chapter 1, "Inoperativity and the Power of Assembly: Agamben with Butler," 14–44.

6. Cavarero addresses collective actions in her recent work. See Adriana Cavarero, *Surging Democracy: Notes on Hannah Arendt's Political Thought*, trans. Matthew Gervase (Stanford, CA: Stanford University Press, 2021). That freedom is central to feminist thought is evident in the work of Simone de Beauvoir, *The Second Sex*, trans. Constance Borde and Sheila Malovany-Chevallier (New York: Vintage Books, 2011); and Angela Davis, *Women, Race and Class* (New York: Knopf, 1983); see also Lori Marso, *Politics with Beauvoir: Freedom in the Encounter* (Durham, NC: Duke University Press, 2017); Linda Zerilli, *Feminism and the Abyss of Freedom* (Chicago: Chicago University Press, 2005); and Patricia Hill Collins, *Black Feminist Thought: Knowledge, Consciousness, and the Politics of Empowerment* (London: Routledge, 1988).

7. Judith Butler, *Bodies That Matter: On the Discursive Limits of Sex* (New York: Routledge, 2011).

8. Christine Battersby, "Cavarero, Kant, and Arcs of Friendship," in *Toward a Feminist Ethics of Nonviolence*, 110. See also Bernardo, et al., who say: "Materialism dethroned the conception of an abstract political subject and the centrality of state institutions in favour of a materialist critique centered on the materiality of

social relations." Bernardo Bianchi, Emilie Filion-Donato, Marlon Miguel, and Ayşe Yuva, "From 'Materialism' towards 'Materialities,'" in *Materialism and Politics*, ed. Bernardo Bianchi, Emilie Filion-Donato, Marlon Miguel, and Ayşe Yuva (Berlin: ICI Berlin Press, 2021): 1–18. https://doi.org/10.37050/ci-20_000.

9. German Eduardo Primera, *The Political Ontology of Giorgio Agamben: Signatures of Life and Power* (London: Bloomsbury, 2019).

10. Cavarero remarked that her work is closer to that of Robert Esposito than to Giorgio Agamben when it comes to biopolitics. Adriana Cavarero, "Elena Ferrante and the Uncanny of Motherhood" (keynote lecture, Society for Italian Philosophy Conference, virtual, June 11, 2022). See also Chiara Bottici, "Rethinking the Biopolitical Turn: From the Thanatopolitical to the Geneapolitical Paradigm," *Graduate Faculty Philosophy Journal* 36, no. 1 (2015): 175–97.

11. Cornelius Castoriadis, *Figures of the Thinkable*, trans. Helen Arnold (Stanford, CA: Stanford University Press, 2007).

12. Michel Foucault, *Society Must Be Defended: Lectures at the College de France 1975–1976*, ed. Alessandro Mauro and Fontana Bertani, trans. David Macey (New York: Picador, 2003).

13. Agamben, *Homo Sacer*, 174.

14. Leland de la Durantaye, "To Be and to Do: The Life and Work of Giorgio Agamben," *Boston Review*, July 26, 2016.

15. See Rachel Jones's essay in this collection, "Inclining toward New Forms of Life: Cavarero, Agamben, and Hartman." This has been a productive lens through which to think about the war on terror led by the United States, the legal framing of torture as "enhanced interrogation techniques," and the treatment of migrants held in refugee camps by democratic states. Many Afropessimists follow this logic of bare life in the context of colonization and enslavement. See, for example, Frank B. Wilderson III, *Afropessimism* (New York: Liveright, 2020); and Saidiya Hartman, *Lose Your Mother: A Journey Along the Atlantic Slave Route, and Scenes of Subjection* (Oxford: Oxford University Press, 1997).

16. Giorgio Agamben, *The Use of Bodies*, trans. Adam Kotsko (Stanford, CA: Stanford University Press, 2016); Giorgio Agamben, *The Omnibus Homo Sacer* (Stanford, CA: Stanford University Press, 2017).

17. Adriana Cavarero, *In Spite of Plato: A Feminist Rewriting of Ancient Philosophy*, trans. S. Anderlini-D'Onofrio and Á. O'Healy (Cambridge: Polity Press, 1995).

18. Cavarero, *In Spite of Plato*.

19. Adriana Cavarero, and Elena Ferrante, "The Uncanny of Motherhood," Keynote talk, Society for Italian Philosophy Conference, June 9–11, 2022, virtual.

20. Adriana Cavarero, *Horrorism: Naming Contemporary Violence*, trans. W. McCuaig (New York: Columbia University Press, 2009).

21. Adriana Cavarero, "Violent Female Bodies: Questioning Thanatopolitics," *Graduate Faculty Philosophy Journal* 36, no. 1 (2015): 134. https://doi.org/10.5840/gfpj20153618.

22. Cavarero, "Violent Female Bodies," 139. Cavarero notes that Agamben's category of bare life is often used in a way that is at odds with how he understands the concept, including who is put outside of law by legal means. Cavarero appreciates how Agamben draws on Arendt's formulation of the public realm and what is outside work and labor to "reset Foucault's vocabulary on biopower" (140).

23. Cavarero, "Violent Female Bodies," 140–41.

24. Thanks to the editors for this point.

25. Adriana Cavarero, *Inclinations: A Critique of Rectitude*, trans. A. Minervini and A. Sitze (Stanford, CA: Stanford University Press, 2016).

26. Agamben, *Nudities*, trans. David Kishik and Stefan Pedatella (Stanford, CA: Stanford University Press, 2011).

27. Fanny Söderbäck, "Natality or Birth? Arendt and Cavarero on the Human Condition of Being Born," *Hypatia* 33, no. 2 (Spring 2018): 283, https://doi.org/10.1111/hypa.12403.

28. Cavarero, *Inclinations*, 158–59.

29. Cavarero, *Inclinations*, 160.

30. This is in relation to a discussion of Emmanuel Levinas in Cavarero, *Inclinations*.

31. Nascent because Cavarero spends little time exploring politics through the lens of collective action, although this always occurs in social and structural relations of power writ large.

32. Cavarero, *Inclinations*, 129.

33. Adriana Cavarero and Nidesh Lawtoo, "Mimetic Inclinations: A Dialogue with Adriana Cavarero," in *Contemporary Italian Women Philosophers: Stretching the Art of Thinking*, ed. Silvia Benso and Elvira Roncalli (Albany: State University of New York Press, 2021), 193.

34. This view has been criticized by Bonnie Honig as needing more pluralization in different scenes of inclination (A Feminist Theory of Refusal, 53).

35. Cavarero and Lawtoo, "Mimetic Inclinations," 173.

36. It's telling that the majority of the chapters in *Toward a Feminist Ethics of Nonviolence* raise a series of important concerns with this iconography. See Judith Butler, "Leaning Out, Caught in the Fall: Interdependency and Ethics in Cavarero"; Bonnie Honig, "How to Do Things with Inclinations: Antigones, with Cavarero"; Christine Battersby, "Canavero, Kant, and the Arcs of Friendship"; Lorenzo Bernini, "Bad Inclinations: Cavarero, Queer Theories, and the Drive"; Mark Devenny, "Queering Cavarero's Rectitude"; and Clare Woodford, "Queer Madonnas: In Love and Friendship."

37. Agamben, *Use of Bodies*, 31.

38. Agamben, *Use of Bodies*, 36–37.

39. While she only references Agamben's work in footnotes, Sara Ahmed rightly says that Agamben's view of use is "overly narrow." She writes that while Agamben offers a "close and careful reading of Aristotle," Agamben shows how use

does not differentiate an object from a subject that can be distinguished from an instrument that creates an external good (the use of a chair for sitting is understood as different from the use of a loom to create wool). The problem is the implication that "today use has lost meaning other than the instrumental creation of an external good." For Ahmed, use is a broader, livelier, and stranger category. She concludes the note saying, "The narrowness of Agamben's archive has consequences, in my view, for the scope of his argument." See Sara Ahmed, *What's the Use? On the Uses of Use* (Durham, NC: Duke University Press, 2019) 2n7, 32.

40. Giorgio Agamben, "For a Theory of Destituent Power," *Critical Legal Thinking* 5 (February 2014), https://criticallegalthinking.com/2014/02/05/theory-destituent-power/

41. See Anna Marie Smith, "Neo-Eugenics: A Feminist Critique of Agamben," *Occasion: Interdisciplinary Studies in the Humanities* 2 (December 20, 2010), http://occasion.stanford.edu/node/59; and Stephen Thomson, "Whatever: Giorgio Agamben's Gender Trouble," *Textual Practice* 35, no. 5 (2021):787–807, https://doi.org/10.1080/0950236X.2020.1731585.

42. Agamben, *Nudities*, 55.

43. Agamben, *Nudities*, 56–57.

44. Agamben also notes: "Fashion is the profane heir of a theology of clothing, the mercantile secularization of a prelapsarian Eden" (*Nudities*, 80).

45. Agamben, *Nudities*, 57. Also, Vanessa Beecroft is a complicated artist when it comes to bodies and histories of radicalized colonialism. Her *White Madonna with Twins* (2006) is a photograph of her with two Sudanese twin infants breastfeeding, taken when she travelled to Sudan while still breastfeeding one of her children. The subsequent controversy over the image raised concerns about colonialism, racism, and artistic exploitation, revealing a deep complexity about the figuration of maternal care through the iconic image of the Madonna and implications of a prominent Italian-American artist visiting a still war-torn Sudan, let alone questions of the use of Blackness throughout much of her work. See Michael Anthony Farley and Corinna Kirsch, "Vanessa Beecroft Continues to Prove She Doesn't Deserve Comparison with Rachel Dolezal," *ArtFCity*, August 9, 2016, http://artfcity.com/2016/08/09/vanessa-beecroft-continues-to-prove-she-doesnt-deserve-comparison-with-rachel-dolezal/.

46. Agamben, *Nudities*, 60.

47. Agamben, *Nudities*, 80.

48. Agamben, *Nudities*, 55 (emphasis original).

49. Agamben, *Nudities*.

50. Agamben, *Nudities*, 61.

51. Agamben, *Nudities*, 62.

52. Honig, *A Feminist Theory of Refusal*. Honig turns to the feminine figures of Antigone and the women of the *Bacchae* for feminist refusals.

53. Agamben, *Nudities*, 91–103.

54. Agamben, *Nudities*, 98.

55. Bonnie Honig, "How to Do Things with Inclination," 65–66. See also Bonnie Honig, *A Feminist Theory of Refusal*, especially chapter 1, "Inoperativity and the Power of Assembly: Agamben with Butler."

56. Agamben, *Nudities*, 273.

57. Agamben writes, "It is a destituent power of this sort that Benjamin has in mind in his essay *On the critique of violence* when he tries to define a pure violence which could 'break the false dialectics of lawmaking violence and law-preserving violence,' an example of which is Sorel's proletarian general strike. 'On the breaking of this cycle' he writes in the end of the essay 'maintained by mythic forms of law, on the destitution of law with all the forces on which it depends, finally therefore on the abolition of State power, a new historical epoch is founded.' While a constituent power destroys law only to recreate it in a new form, destituent power, in so far as it deposes once and for all the law, can open a really new historical epoch." Agamben, "For a Theory of Destituent Power." See also Miguel Vatter, "In Odradek's World: Bare Life and Historical Materialism in Agamben and Benjamin," *Diacritics* 38, no. 3 (Fall 2008): 45–57, 59–70.

58. Cavarero, *Inclinations*, 89.

59. Cavarero, *Inclinations*, 90.

60. Cavarero, *Inclinations*, 92.

61. As Rebecca Mead points out, it is conventional to refer to Artemisia by her first name to distinguish her from her artist father, Orazio Gentileschi. "A Fuller Picture of Artemisia Gentileschi," *New Yorker*, September 28, 2020, https://www.newyorker.com/magazine/2020/10/05/a-fuller-picture-of-artemisia-gentileschi.

62. See Lori Jo Marso for an argument against the leaning in of uprightness popularized by Facebook executive Sheryl Sandberg's 2010 Ted Talk and 2013 book by the same title, *Lean In*, encouraging women to just "lean in" to be successful in their careers. "Freedom's Poses," *Political Research Quarterly* 70, no. 4 (2017): 720–27.

63. Cavarero and Lawtoo, "Mimetic Inclinations," 191.

64. Artemisia Gentileschi, "The Birth of Saint John the Baptist," Museo del Prado, https://www.museodelprado.es/en/the-collection/art-work/the-birth-of-saint-john-the-baptist/65572d18-d9a1-42b8-bddd-f931c4b88da6.

65. Battersby, "Arcs," 110–11.

66. Jones, "Inclining toward New Forms of Life," in this volume.

67. I am referencing a definition of democracy Castoriadis gives as the regime of self-limitation; he notes that in a democratic form of government, we can do anything but we ought not to, hence the democratic paradox to give ourselves limits. See "The Greek Polis and the Creation of Democracy," in *The Castoriadis Reader*, trans. David Ames Curtis (London: Wiley-Blackwell, 1997).

68. Wendy Brown, "We Are All Democrats Now," in *Democracy In What State?* ed. Giorgio Agamben, Alain Badiou, Daniel Bensaid, Wendy Brown, Jean-Luc Nancy, Jacques Rancière, Kristin Ross, and Slavoj Žižek, trans. William McCuaig (New York: Columbia University Press, 2011), 54.

Bibliography

Agamben, Giorgio. "For a Theory of Destituent Power." *Critical Legal Thinking*, February 5, 2014. https://criticallegalthinking.com/2014/02/05/theory-destituent-power/.

———. *Homo Sacer: Sovereign Power and Bare Life*. Translated by Daniel Heller-Roazen. Stanford, CA: Stanford University Press, 1998.

———. *Nudities*. Translated by David Kishik and Stefan Pedatella. Stanford, CA: Stanford University Press, 2011.

———. *The Use of Bodies*. Translated by Adam Kotsko. Stanford, CA: Stanford University Press, 2016.

Agamben, Giorgio, Lorenzo Fabbri, and Elisabeth Fay. "On the Limits of Violence." *Diacritics* 39, no. 4 (2009): 103–11.

Battersby, Christine. "Cavarero, Kant, and Arcs of Friendship." In *Toward a Feminist Ethics of Nonviolence: Adriana Cavarero with Judith Butler, Bonnie Honig and Other Voices*, edited by Timothy J. Huzar and Clare Woodford, 109–20. New York: Fordham University Press, 2021.

Benso, Silvia, and Elvira Roncalli, eds. *Contemporary Italian Women Philosophers: Stretching the Art of Thinking*. Albany: State University of New York Press, 2022.

Bottici, Chiara. "Rethinking the Biopolitical Turn: From the Thanatopolitical to the Geneapolitical Paradigm." *Graduate Faculty Philosophy Journal* 36, no. 1 (2015): 175–97.

Brown, Wendy. "We Are All Democrats Now." In *Democracy In What State?* edited by Giorgio Agamben, Alain Badiou, Daniel Bensaid, Wendy Brown, Jean-Luc Nancy, Jacques Rancière, Kristin Ross, and Slavoj Žižek, translated by William McCuaig, 44–57. New York: Columbia University Press, 2011.

Butler, Judith. *Bodies That Matter: On the Discursive Limits of Sex*. New York: Routledge, 2011.

Campbell, Timothy. "Introduction: The Will-to-the-Common in Italian Thought." *Diacritics* 39, no. 4 (2009): 101–2.

Castoriadis, Cornelius. *The Castoriadis Reader*. Translated by David Ames Curtis. London: Wiley-Blackwell, 1997.

———. *Figures of the Thinkable*. Translated by Helen Arnold. Stanford, CA: Stanford University Press, 2007.

Cavarero, Adriana. *Horrorism: Naming Contemporary Violence*. Translated by William McCuaig. New York: Columbia University Press, 2009.

———. *Inclinations: A Critique of Rectitude*. Translated by A. Minervini and A. Sitze. Stanford, CA: Stanford University Press, 2016.

———. *In Spite of Plato: Feminist Rewriting of Ancient Philosophy*. Translated by Serena Anderlini-D'Onofrio and Áine O'Healy. Cambridge: Polity Press, 1995.

———. *Relating Narratives: Storytelling and Selfhood*. Translated by Paul A. Kottman. New York: Routledge, 2000.

———. *Stately Bodies: Literature, Philosophy, and the Question of Gender*. Translated by Robert DeLuca. Ann Arbor: University of Michigan Press, 2002.

———. *Surging Democracy: Notes on Hannah Arendt's Political Thought*. Translated by Matthew Gervase. Stanford, CA: Stanford University Press, 2021.

———. "Violent Female Bodies: Questioning Thanatopolitics." *Graduate Faculty Philosophy Journal* 36, no. 1 (2015): 129–44. https://doi.org/10.5840/gfpj20153618.

Cavarero, Adriana, and Nidesh Lawtoo. "Mimetic Inclinations: A Dialogue with Adriana Cavarero." In *Contemporary Italian Women Philosophers: Stretching the Art of Thinking*, edited by Silvia Benso and Elvira Roncalli, 183–99. Albany: State University of New York Press, 2021.

de la Durantaye, Leland. "To Be and to Do: The Life and Work of Giorgio Agamben." *Boston Review*, July 26, 2016.

Esposito, Roberto, and Zakiya Hanafi. "The Return of Italian Philosophy." *Diacritics* 39, no. 3 (2009): 55–61.

Ferguson, Kathy. "Politics That Matter: Thinking about Power and Justice with the New Materialists." *Contemporary Political Theory* 14, no. 1 (August 2014): 63–89.

Honig, Bonnie. *A Feminist Theory of Refusal*. Cambridge, MA: Harvard University Press, 2021.

Huzar, Timothy J., and Clare Woodford, eds. *Toward a Feminist Ethics of Nonviolence*. New York: Fordham University Press, 2021.

Jones, Rachel. "Inclining toward New Forms of Life: Cavarero, Agamben, and Hartman." In *Political Bodies: Writings on Adriana Cavarero's Political Thought*, edited by Paula Landerreche Cardillo and Rachel Silverbloom, 155–184. Albany: State University of New York Press, 2024.

Marso, Lori Jo. "Freedom's Poses." *Political Research. Quarterly* 70, no. 4 (2017): 720–27.

Primera, German Eduardo. *The Political Ontology of Giorgio Agamben: Signatures of Life and Power*. London: Bloomsbury, 2019.

Söderbäck, Fanny. "Natality or Birth? Arendt and Cavarero on the Human Condition of Being Born." *Hypatia* 33, no. 2 (Spring 2018): 273–88. https://doi.org/10.1111/hypa.12403.

Wingrove, Elizabeth. "Materialisms." In *The Oxford Handbook of Feminist Theory*, edited by Lisa Disch and Mary Hawkesworth, 454–71. Oxford: Oxford University Press, 2016.

Part Four

Political Violence, Voice, and Relational Selves

Nine

Sexual Violence as Ontological Violence
Narration, Selfhood, and the Destruction of Singularity

Fanny Söderbäck[1]

Three decades ago, the American philosopher Susan Brison found herself "face down in a muddy creek bed at the bottom of a dark ravine, struggling to stay alive."[2] It was a gorgeous summer day and she had set out to take a walk on a country road outside of Grenoble, France. Attacked by a stranger, she was "grabbed from behind, pulled into the bushes, beaten, and sexually assaulted."[3] He then repeatedly strangled her, beat her with a rock, and left her for dead in the ravine, a victim of what she herself calls "attempted sexual murder."[4]

It took her ten years to write a book about her experience, published as *Aftermath: Violence and the Remaking of the Self*. Early on in that autobiographical account, Brison defends the notion of a fundamentally relational self: "capable of being undone by violence, but also of being remade in connection with others."[5] In this chapter, I want to examine both sides of this claim—that we can be *undone* by others, and that we need others to *remake* a broken self. Moreover, and again following Brison, I argue that narration has an important role to play in the "remaking of a self shattered by trauma," potentially enabling the survivor to process and heal.[6]

My analysis of Brison's testimony will be framed in relation to Adriana Cavarero's work. I will take as my point of departure Cavarero's claim that certain forms of violence are of an ontological kind, insofar as their aim is the destruction of the human condition of relationality as such, more so than the homicidal aim to end a particular human life. I will, furthermore, examine Cavarero's work on narration so as to lay bare some of the philosophical presuppositions that underpin Brison's account but also to raise questions about the relationship between biographical and autobiographical forms of narration in the context of trauma testimonies and attempts at "narrating the unspeakable" or making a self reemerge "from the ruins of a self."[7]

Relational and Vulnerable Selfhood: On Being Made and Unmade by Others

In the preface of her book, Brison reflects on her initial attempt to write something, only months after the attack, when all she could come up with was, as she puts it, "a list of paradoxes."[8] Despite her philosophical propensity for sense-making, all of a sudden nothing made sense, recovery seemed impossible, and the trauma was all-encompassing. And yet, at the time, she could not yet anticipate that "the worst—the unimaginably painful aftermath of violence—was yet to come."[9] The brutal attack had forced her to venture "outside the human community," and she was struggling to figure out "how to get back."[10]

Indeed, she recalls that the most difficult aspect of recovering from the assault had to do precisely with the inability of those around her to respond to her experience in a manner that would do it justice: their lack of empathy, their tendency to repeatedly forget the gravity of the event, their insistence that she had been lucky to survive, and their fear in the face of her terrifying fate, which ultimately reminded them of their own lack of control, of vulnerability and woundability as constitutive features of human life. As trauma theorist Cathy Caruth notes in an interview: "I tend to think of the word 'trauma' as saying: 'You don't get me, I am not yet, I am out of context.' Or: 'Wake up! Don't you see I'm burning?' Then you wake up and it is already too late; you have missed the burning."[11] To have lost one's sense of self and one's belonging in the world and to not be seen, heard, validated in that very experience. That is the aftermath. The haunting aftermath. And it is what must be narrated if something like selfhood is to be resurrected from its ashes.

Throughout her work, Cavarero, alongside thinkers like Judith Butler, embraces vulnerability and relationality as constitutive dimensions of the ontology of the self—dimensions that ought to be celebrated rather than overcome. It is as vulnerable beings that we can experience love, intimacy, and the joys of sharing, caring, and being cared for. Relational ontologies of uniqueness, thus, situate thinkers like Cavarero and Butler in radical contrast with traditional notions of selfhood couched in terms of autonomy understood as independence, self-determination, or sovereignty. They seek to challenge the hegemonic ideology of individualism. Time and again, Cavarero invites us to reflect on what has been lost in a world where the individual—understood as independent and self-sufficient—has become the indisputable normative ideal, insisting that such individual is a masculine fantasy made possible by oblivion, erasure, and oppression.

But if we are constitutively relational; if, as Butler has put it, we are "undone, in the face of the other, by the touch, by the scent, by the feel, by the prospect of the touch, by the memory of the feel,"[12] then it is clearly also the case, as Jean Améry reminds us in his account of the torture he suffered at the hands of SS soldiers during the Holocaust, that "if I am to have trust, I must feel on [my skin] only what I *want* to feel."[13] If indeed we are committed to relational ontology, and even if we ultimately believe that acknowledging our shared exposure might serve as an important starting point for an ethics that veers away from the standard morality of autonomy à la Kant, it is nevertheless clear that we can be taken advantage of in our vulnerability, that it exposes us not only to intimacy and love but also to wounding and harm. The kind of violence Brison endured is a case in point. As we engage the problem of sexual violence (and here, the focus will be on the lived experience of its aftermath more so than on the traumatic event itself or the legal discourse surrounding sexual violence in general), we must, therefore, couple our commitment to relational ontology with a robust account of bodily integrity.[14] As Brison herself puts it in her autobiographical narrative, if "the self is created and sustained by others," then it can also "be destroyed by them."[15]

Interestingly, Brison goes on to explain that "the right sort of interactions with others" are "essential to autonomy" and that "the autonomous self and the relational self are [. . .] interdependent, even constitutive of one another."[16] Instead of rejecting autonomy altogether, then, Brison seems to suggest that we ought to rethink autonomy in relational terms, such that selfhood is always understood as located between exposure-vulnerability-relationality and a kind of bodily integrity that is not premised on the denial of those former features but rather intertwined with them.

As much as Cavarero is often read as someone who rejects autonomy altogether, it is in fact possible to trace a kinship between her ontology of relational uniqueness and Brison's claim—in the wake of her sexual assault—that autonomy and relationality can be seen as interdependent and co-constitutive. Indeed, while Cavarero consistently defines selfhood in terms of corporeal exposure and constitutive relationality—the self, on her account, "is of a totally expositive and relational character" for whom "*being* and *appearing*" coincide in that we are "totally *external*," always already constituted by and given over to others, fragile and unmasterable, altruistic by constitution rather than by choice—she nevertheless maintains that the unique and unrepeatable self is *one*: this and not another.[17]

While the essentially external self for Cavarero is antithetical to the infamous interiority of autonomous subjectivity, it is nevertheless a self that is defined by figural unity. Sharply critical of post-structuralism's demonization of unity and its privileging of a fragmented multiplicitous self, Cavarero draws attention to the etymologically intimate relation between *uniqueness* (*unicità* in Italian) and *unity* (*unità* in Italian). In Arendtian fashion, she contends that our being distinct from others and our being in relation with them are flipsides of the same coin: each life "is different from all others precisely because it is constitutively interwoven with many others."[18] Her relational self is "a *unique unity*, about whom multiplicity, or fragmentation or discontinuity, cannot yet be predicted."[19] The *who* that inhabits her philosophy of relational uniqueness is "the unrepeatable existence of a *single* insubstitutable being."[20]

The paradigmatic figure of this unity appears in the introduction to *Relating Narratives*, where Cavarero reads Karen Blixen's short story about a man who stumbles out into the night to fix a leak in his garden only to find the following morning that his footprints, to his great surprise, "had traced the figure of a stork on the ground."[21] Does, Cavarero asks, "the course of every life allow itself to be looked upon in the end like a design that has a meaning?"[22] For Cavarero, the dignity and integrity of the unique self ultimately depend on this figural unity: to feel on our skin only what we want to feel but also to be able to discern in our life stories a meaningful pattern, a figure, a stork. We all desire to have our life be told, we all desire a stork: "From the beginning," Cavarero explains, "*uniqueness* announces and promises to identity a *unity* that the self is not likely to renounce."[23] The disfiguration, dehumanization, and dismembering that occurs in scenes of violence—when the wounding inscribed in the *vulnus* of our shared vulnerability dominates rather than the care that is inscribed as its possible other pole—is a threat to uniqueness as such, tearing at the self in its corporeal singularity, undermining the possibility for a stork to be traced.

Before I move into an analysis of Brison's and Cavarero's engagements with these matters, let me flag that as much as I am acutely aware of the need to be able to think bodily integrity such that we can claim the right to feel on our skin only what we want to feel, I am also a bit suspicious of this call for unity—perhaps especially in the context of thinking selfhood in the aftermath of trauma. Both Cavarero and Brison seem to ultimately suggest that healing requires a kind of recuperation of oneness and wholeness, even in the face of an event that might render such terms impossible or even undesirable. To be sure, we are ultimately constituted not only by relations of care but also by those of wounding in ways that remain unpredictable and sometimes irreversible. In what follows, my goal is, therefore, not to subordinate the aftermath of trauma (and aftermath *as* trauma) to linear-progressive narratives of healing as sense-making or becoming whole again. But I do want to trace the conceptual parameters for thinking selfhood as singularity-relationality in the wake of experiences that serve to annihilate those very features of human experience.[24]

Horrorism as Ontological Violence: From Vulnerability to Helplessness

In *Horrorism*, Cavarero examines the destruction and disfiguring of human uniqueness in the context of extreme horror in Auschwitz, Abu Ghraib, and the scenes of suicide bombings. Arguing that we need a new vocabulary to bespeak the specific forms of violence that plague our own present—violence that "strikes mainly, though not exclusively, the defenseless"—Cavarero coins the term *horrorism* and stresses that if we "observe the scene of massacre from the point of view of the helpless victims rather than that of the warriors [. . .] the rhetorical façade of 'collateral damage' melts away, and the carnage turns substantial."[25] She defines *horrorism* as an ontological crime, which, "not content merely to kill because killing would be too little, aims to destroy the uniqueness of the body, tearing at its constitutive vulnerability."[26] Put differently, horror is ontological because "at stake is not the end of a human life but the human condition itself, as incarnated in the singularity of vulnerable bodies."[27] The ontological crime of horrorism consists in undoing our incarnate uniqueness, which is to say that it is an assault on the dignity and integrity of the human form that renders the human body unrecognizable.[28]

If terror has its etymological as well as experiential roots in bodily movements such as trembling and flight, horror is instead defined by a state of paralysis, and more than fear, it has to do with repugnance.[29] Cavarero makes a conceptual distinction between vulnerability and helplessness.[30] Her discussion of the camps takes an unexpected turn when she introduces the idea that what was ultimately destroyed there was nothing less than the human condition of vulnerability itself: "Not only is horror confirmed as a peculiar form of violence that exceeds simple homicide; it reveals itself, in the case of the Lagers, as a violence deliberately intended to produce helpless beings paradoxically no longer vulnerable [. . .] Invulnerability does not occur in nature; it has to be produced artificially [. . .] Totally engaged in its own destructive passion, violence ends, in the horrorist laboratory of the Lager, by producing victims who can no longer suffer from it."[31] In contrast to the phenomenon of helplessness, Cavarero reminds us that "the human condition of vulnerability entails a constitutive relation to the other: an exposure to wounding but also to the care that the other can supply."[32]

We must, thus, distinguish vulnerability, which she views as the ontological condition for ethics in that it consists of the two poles of wounding and caring,[33] from an artificially fabricated helplessness of a degenerated kind, which she views as the result of an ontological crime in that it represents the destruction of the human condition of uniqueness as such.[34] By severing the very ties that make up the web of human relations, a perverted form of independence is produced, one where we have lost our ability both for intimacy and suffering and that is embodied, in her reading, by the Musulman: the living corpse or bundle of flesh that was produced in the Lager. Helplessness thus marks the annihilation of our human condition of being-with-others, turning death into an all-encompassing and totalizing horizon without hope for new beginnings. If vulnerability and relationality are conditions of possibility for human uniqueness, helplessness and loneliness mark the destruction of human uniqueness and the rendering of singular individuals into superfluous victims.

That none of the chapters in Cavarero's *Horrorism*—chapters that often depict women as perpetrators of horrorist violence, such as female suicide bombers in Palestine or female torturers grinning at the camera in Abu Ghraib—are devoted to sexual violence as a form of horrorist violence is a curious fact. Yet, while Cavarero's own silence on matters of sexual violence is perhaps symptomatic, I want to suggest in what follows that her analysis of horrorist violence, as well as her insistence on reclaiming singularity where it has been violated, can be powerful resources as we try to make sense of the kind of harm that results from sexual violence. Her insistence that we examine violence from the point of view of its victims can serve as a cue as we approach the topic of sexual violence and try to listen to what survivors have said about their own lived experiences. In the spirit of Cavarero's work, then, I want to suggest that if we want to truly understand sexual violence and its aftermath, we need to tune in to the voices of its defenseless victims. Survivor-centered accounts of rape are bound to tell a story different than the ones that transpire in legal discourse.

Sexual Violence as Ontological Violence: Rape and the Destruction of the Self

In her book *Rape and Resistance*, Linda Martín Alcoff argues that the complexity of sexual assault requires that we critically examine not only instances of physical coercion or forcible rape (what she labels sexual violence) but also the manifold ways in which sexual transgression comes to shape our agency, subjectivity, and will (what she instead calls sexual violation).[35] While Brison's case ultimately is an example of what the court defined as rape, I am less concerned with the legal category of rape and the physical coercion it involves and more interested in examining how Brison's story might illuminate the manner in which sexual assault—and its aftermath—inflicts harm on one's sense of selfhood, where Cavarero defines selfhood as singular yet constitutively relational. Alcoff warns against the use of the term *violence* to describe the broad range of events that might result in the violation of our will and sexual agency. She thinks the term is "misleading" and too narrow to be able to fully capture the complexities of sexual violation.[36]

In what follows, I will nevertheless use the language of violence. In fact, following Cavarero, I will use the even narrower term *ontological violence*—or *horrorism*—to try to show that one way of complexifying our understanding of sexual violence is to examine the specific ways in which it is aimed at destroying the singularity of its victim.[37] I am aware, however, that by maintaining the language of violence—even ontological violence—my discussion remains all-too-narrow and cannot be applied to any and all cases of what Alcoff calls sexual violation. The scope of my argument is limited, but I nevertheless think it has the potential to address important issues, both in terms of better understanding Cavarero's analysis of violence and narration and in terms of our ability to make sense of the specific harm that certain forms of sexual assault and its aftermath can inflict.

For Brison, there was what some might call "justice." Her assailant served time in prison. She was not blamed for what happened to her on that summer day. And yet, the task of narrating the events fell on her as she struggled to venture back into the human community that she lost through the attack and as she tried to regain trust in the world and rebuild her broken self in the aftermath of an attempted sexual murder that had left her to lead "a spectral existence" as though she had "somehow outlived" herself.[38] Her descriptions of what happened to her that day resonate with what Cavarero says about horrorism in that she, too, reflects on violence in ontological terms. The attempted murder was no simple homicide. It reached beyond the act of killing.[39] The harm that was done to her served to sever the very ties that defined her as a human person. Her "being undone" at the hands of her perpetrator was fundamentally different from the "being undone" that Butler celebrates in her work as the condition of possibility for intimacy and community. If vulnerability and exposure are conditions of possibility for existence as being-with-others, what Brison experienced on that summer day was the destruction of vulnerability to the point of helplessness. Left to die at the bottom of a ravine, the task ahead was not merely to crawl up to the road and seek medical help and legal counsel but also, and at far greater difficulty, to find a way back to the human community from which she had been expelled on that day. Subsequently, in the aftermath of the attack, her "sense of unreality was fed by the massive denial of those around [her]—a reaction [she] had learned is an almost universal response to rape."[40]

In the aftermath of her assault, she was faced with being a different person than she had been before it happened, including having a different relationship to her body.[41] Borrowing Cathy Winkler's concept of *social murder*, Brison ascribes to the idea that "during a rape, the victim is defined out of existence by the attitudes and actions of the rapist, which incapacitate the victim's self."[42] Following Améry, she confirms the feeling of having lost "trust in the world," of no longer feeling physically and epistemologically "at home in the world," and, citing Levi, she speaks of the "demolition" of her humanity.[43] Reflecting on her own experience, she notes that "the survivor's bodily sense of self is permanently altered by an encounter with death that leaves one feeling 'marked' for life."[44] Her language echoes Cavarero's in *Horrorism* in that she consistently indexes her assault as having had the effect of destroying her very self, undermining her belonging in the world and with others, tearing at the bonds that up until that day had allowed her to feel at one with herself and at home with her surroundings. The questions, then, become the following: "How does one remake a self from the scattered shards of disrupted memory?"[45] What would "piecing together a dismembered self" entail?[46] Can this be done? Are recovery and healing possible?

Before we try to address (more so than answer) these questions, it is worth recalling that Cavarero repeatedly emphasizes the fact that horrorist violence aims at something more than just killing or wounding. It aims at the human condition of vulnerability as such; and, therefore, it is ultimately related to the philosophical tendency to annihilate singularity in the name of autonomous subjectivity, abstract universality, or disembodied reason. As Cavarero herself puts it: "The attack on the ontological dignity of the singular being [. . .] in fact pertains to the speculative method of philosophy as a discipline" insofar as it has concerned itself with fictitious entities such as *anthropos*, the individual, and the subject, rather than singular human beings.[47] That the philosophical concept of Man is "a universal that applies to everyone precisely because it is no one" foreshadows the reduction of humans "in flesh and blood—necessarily unique, particular, and finite" to superfluous victims.[48]

In the aftermath of her assault, Brison "turned to philosophy for meaning and consolation and could find neither."[49] But it was not just that philosophy lacked the resources to make her "feel at home in the world": to some extent, philosophy itself seemed to do harm by way of intellectual scrutiny.[50] On her account, René Descartes comes to embody the philosophical-violent gesture that turns everything—including the self—into an object of study subjectable to rational abstraction. In his own "autobiographical narrative," the meditations in which he grounds the subject of thought—the *cogito*, the "I think"—as the first principle of philosophy proper, Descartes set out to "raze everything to the ground and begin again from the original foundations."[51] Meanwhile, as a victim of violence, Brison's own task was to *recover* a world that had been demolished for her.[52] Both found themselves alone, withdrawn from the world and human relations, but while for Descartes this was a voluntary act to allow for the complete demolishment of his beliefs (although, as Cavarero would argue, an illusory one, since there is no such thing as a self outside of human relations), Brison found herself on a "year-long disability leave from teaching" so that she could rebuild the beliefs that had been shattered by her assailant.[53] Similarly, she experienced her assault as "an incomprehensible random event, surely a nightmare," and she describes her situation as "a reversal of the epistemological crisis provoked by Descartes' question, 'What if I'm dreaming?' Instead, I asked myself in desperation, 'What if I'm awake?' "[54]

As we try to approach horrorism understood as ontological violence, philosophical discourse not only fails to offer the vocabulary needed for sense-making but, what is worse, it might perpetuate the very violence we set out to analyze. Because of this, Cavarero and Brison alike identify a need to venture beyond philosophical discourse, or to redefine what we mean by philosophy, such that we can articulate our analysis "from the point of view of the helpless victims rather than that of the warriors," as Cavarero puts it in the introduction to *Horrorism*.[55] While "a philosophical examination of violence and its aftermath" might offer some helpful tools if developed with care, Brison insists that it must be interwoven with "a first-person narrative" for "facilitating our understanding of trauma and victimization."[56] The task of understanding (or what Brison calls "living to tell") and recovering from (what she calls "telling to live") ontological violence requires narration rather than philosophy.[57]

Brison's language here echoes Cavarero's description of Scheherazade in one of the final chapters of *Relating Narratives*: "In addition to finding herself in a situation that requires her to tell stories in order to stay alive, Scheherazade lives in order to tell stories—and in order that other women live."[58] Clearly, Brison's narrating her experience of having been raped not only serves to save herself from the abyss of trauma but also mirrors Scheherazad's narration in the sense that she tells her story "in order that other women live." The sharing of such narratives—like the sharing implied in the narrative gesture of the #MeToo movement—can be a powerful tool for survivors of sexual violence, especially for those whose own experiences remain buried in silence. In what follows, I want to thematize this question of narration, think about how it differs from philosophical discourse, and reflect on its potential to speak the unspeakable while setting into motion a process of healing.

The Redemptive Power of Narration: Living to Tell and Telling to Live

If philosophy has been concerned with naming the *what* of universal abstract Man, Cavarero turns to narration as a kind of discourse that holds the promise of teasing out the *who* of singular, embodied individuals. As Laurie E. Naranch puts it: "Whereas traditional philosophy traffics in abstraction, narrative is about the unique."[59] Whether Cavarero turns to Sophocles or Shakespeare, to Gertrude Stein or Scheherazade, to Homer or Karen Blixen, she views literature and narratives as capable of giving voice to the singular experience that philosophical discourse has been careful to mute.[60]

If much feminist theory has relied on the notion of a *narrative* self—the idea that the self comes into existence through the very practice of self-narration—Cavarero instead insists on a *narratable* self. Following Arendt, she suggests that the telling of our life stories depends entirely on others, the spectators and onlookers who bear witness to our lives as they unfold, in large part unbeknownst to us, retrospectively and from the outside: "Exposed, relational and contextual, the Arendtian self leaves behind a life story that is constitutively interwoven with many other stories."[61] In *Relating Narratives*, she recounts the story of Emilia and Amalia, two close friends, the former trying and failing repeatedly to coherently narrate her life and the latter finally writing it for her such that she can carry it in her handbag, reading it "again and again, overcome by emotion."[62] Emilia weeps as her story is told to her, confirming her desire to achieve unity through narration, to have her life take shape or form a pattern.[63]

With Arendt, Cavarero believes in the "redemptive power of narration" since it "saves and hands down to posterity" both our singular life stories and history more broadly construed.[64] Narration, in other words, is the most powerful remedy for our finitude and the fragility of human life; through narration, we are made immortal as our life is put into a story to be retold and remembered. It is worth noting, however, that Emilia and Amalia are the best of friends. And Gertrude Stein and Alice Toklas—another pair that comes to exemplify the necessary other on the scene of narration for Cavarero—are lovers. As others have pointed out before me, these are pairs marked by mutual respect and a desire to get the story right, to tell it truthfully if you will, to celebrate the uniqueness of the narratable other in the life story they are trying to narrate. But on the scene of violence, where one finds oneself mutilated and helpless, destroyed at the hands of another and without trust in the world, how would one trust another—even a benevolent other—to tell one's story?[65] To be sure, these might be the very moments when it is especially important that we are able to tell our own story, and doing so might allow us to process and even heal. Yet, what modes of representation are available to us as we try to recount violent (and at times repressed) events—events that might well have eroded our very capacity for articulation and meaning-making in the first place?[66]

As we have seen, Cavarero (in the wake of Arendt) makes a distinction between philosophy and narration where the latter, she insists, "does not explain, does not organize nor understand the events from within a conceptual framework" but rather "reveals the meaning without the error of defining it."[67] What is more, it "saves this meaning from oblivion, a forgetfulness that [. . .] is not the consequence of the simple passing of time, but the intentional outcome of violent erasure."[68] Narration, in other words, is a restorative response to violence: it not only serves as a remedy to our finitude (after the fact, once we are no longer), but it is also a form of resistance and remedy against the destruction that we might experience in the course of our lives. Narration can bring us back from the dead not only because a life put into a story can be remembered into posterity but also because the very act of telling can serve to animate a self whose selfhood has been under attack to the point of erasure and silence—the almost-complete isolation that Brison gives witness to in the aftermath of the crime committed against her.

The temporality of narrating trauma—and of bringing a self back to life from the brink of death—is hardly linear, and it is full of paradoxes. As María del Rosario Acosta López eloquently puts it: "How to represent that which, in the strict sense, has not yet made itself present?"[69] Indeed, the wound of trauma—that which has not yet made itself present but which can only be experienced (and thus represented) retrospectively—is, on Caruth's reading of Sigmund Freud, a "breach in the mind's experience of time, self, and the world."[70] It is not a "simple and healable event" but an event that "is experienced too soon, too unexpectedly, to be fully known and is therefore not available to consciousness until it imposes itself again, repeatedly, in the nightmares and repetitive actions of the survivor."[71] Therefore, "trauma is not locatable in the simple violent or original event in an individual's past, but rather in the way that its very unassimilated nature—the way it was precisely *not known* in the first instance—returns to haunt the survivor later on."[72] The trauma *is* its aftermath. Yet, the aftermath is also the very site where narration as healing can take place. There is, thus, a sense in which the doing and the undoing of the traumatic experience are simultaneous: violence and the remaking of selfhood are both part of the aftermath of traumatic wounding. Indeed this, it seems to me, is how we should understand the title of Brison's book.

Narrative Against Destruction: Restoring Relational Selfhood

In her essay "Narrative Against Destruction," Cavarero examines the circumstances under which a self can "emerge from the ruins of a self" through narration.[73] More specifically, her focus is on the totalitarian dismantling of the human being during the Shoah, and she attempts to resurrect singular human beings out of oblivion. Citing first Arendt and then Levi, she stresses as before that "human nature as such," more so than human suffering or human lives, was at stake in a totalitarian machine aimed at the "demolition of man."[74] Her claim, then, is that the saving power of life stories has the capacity to restore the human status of uniqueness to victims of ontological violence. Narrative is a form of rehumanization, a "redemption of the meaning of the human from the ruins of the inhuman."[75] But this work of narration does, again, have a complex relation to the work of philosophy. It is less a matter of understanding the horror, of offering an analysis that would capture correctly its undoing powers. Rather, and here again Cavarero follows Arendt, it "belongs to the sphere of *poiesis*: of making, constructing, creating."[76] Biographical writing, on Cavarero's account, "is not merely a 'reconstructing' the thread of a life story; it is above all opposing the work of destruction that has devoured life itself. It is ultimately a making against destroying, a creating against demolishing, a doing against undoing."[77]

Note that here, as elsewhere, Cavarero focuses on biographical narration, of telling the life story of an *other*.[78] Contrary to Cavarero, Brison is, as one might expect, a proponent of autobiographical narratives, especially in the context of trauma. She insists on the "necessity of first-person narratives" both for the "remaking of a self shattered by trauma" and for "facilitating our understanding of trauma and victimization."[79] She argues that those who have survived acts of violence need to "tell of their experiences in their own words."[80] And yet, consistent with her commitment to relational ontology, she, too, acknowledges that such autobiographical narration depends on those who are present to listen. As Alcoff puts it in *Rape and Resistance*: "Brison argues that her very ability to make sense of the event, and to bring it within the existing narrative of her life, *required* a dialogic context of supportive and emphatic understanding in which she could regain the voice that had been nearly destroyed."[81] In Brison's own words: "In order to construct self-narratives we need not only the words with which to tell our stories, but also an audience able and willing to hear us and to understand our words as we intend them."[82] Her lack of an audience—and this lack is all too common—had traumatizing effects on her as she navigated the aftermath of her own experience: "Each time someone failed to respond I felt as though I were alone again in the ravine, dying, screaming."[83] So, while there is a clear difference between Cavarero's privileging of biography and Brison's insistence on the power of autobiography, both depend heavily on a *relational* understanding of narration as ultimately taking place *between* teller and listener, and both believe in narration's capacity to restore and heal a broken self and the relational ties that constitute it.

Cavarero, again, does not discuss narration in the aftermath of sexual violence. Instead, she offers a reading of W. G. Sebald, who attempted in his work to narrate the stories of "ordinary individuals" who had survived the Holocaust, stories that might otherwise have been lost and silenced.[84] In *The Emigrants*, for example, Sebald draws from interviews and archival research to narrate the lives of four survivors (two of whom, like Améry, ended up committing suicide). These were life stories that "would have never seen the light of day" had they not been put into a narrative by the author.[85] The work of narration, in this context, constitutes an aporia of sorts; as Cavarero herself puts it, it entails the task of "narrating the unspeakable."[86] To be sure, Sebald's narration cannot bring lost ones back to life, but he "restores the damage and destruction wrought on these lives, a damage and destruction that would too often remain silent (if not invisible)."[87] At stake, again, is the possibility of rendering audible and visible each of their uniqueness—put into the form of a narrative—by assembling "the fragments of a life experience that disclose the meaning of the uniqueness of that very life" here and now and for posterity.[88] Cavarero notes that there is an ethical dilemma in soliciting traumatic memories to put them into a story. Sebald himself spoke of the "collateral damage" that such intrusion can cause, and Cavarero alludes to a "reluctant narratable self" that is made to "emerge from the ruins of a self that the totalitarian machine has intentionally tried to destroy."[89] If Emilia wept as she read her own story as Amalia had written it down, then "what tears must the victims of the totalitarian catastrophe shed," Cavarero asks, "when forced to tell their stories to the narrator who may be able to retell them?"[90]

But, as Timothy J. Huzar has pointed out before me, "the status of the narratable self whose conditions of narratability have been radically undermined" nevertheless remains "under-specified" in Cavarero's work.[91] She does not explicitly address the consequences of the paradoxical fact that the self "is both totally expositive and yet not absolutely nullified in isolation."[92] If helplessness and loneliness were produced in Auschwitz (as we saw in the discussion of the Musulman previously), then it is hard to understand how those lives could nevertheless be put into a narrative. Huzar articulates this paradox succinctly: "The life exposed to Auschwitz retains 'narrative unity' but has lost its 'narratability.' How can uniqueness be both annulled in the *Lager* and yet somehow be present in the biographical accounts offered by Sebald or others?"[93] He adds that "narrative plays an important role in negotiating this paradoxical status of an imperiled uniqueness that both is and is not destroyed."[94] This has to do with the fact that the destruction of uniqueness entails isolation—the loneliness felt by Brison—yet narration requires that we appear. How does one square the destruction of the self with the narratability of that same self? How can there even be a story to be told about those whose ties to the web of human relations have been severed? Is it the case that it is not the self that is actually destroyed but one's intelligibility as a certain kind of self (a unified self)? These are questions that Cavarero's own work ultimately leaves unanswered, so we would need to extend beyond it to make sense of the paradoxes of what Huzar has called "a fugitive uniqueness that escapes its capture and evades its solitary confinement."[95]

Huzar turns to a fascinating example recounted by Miklós Nyiszli: a young woman survived an Auschwitz gas chamber, only to subsequently be killed since she had witnessed the unwittnessable and could not be allowed to live to tell of it. The Sonderkommando were so perplexed by the woman emerging alive from a space of certain death that they fed her, warmed her, and cared for her. Levi, too, reflects on the story: "These slaves, debased by alcohol and the daily slaughter, are transformed; they no longer have before them the anonymous mass, the flood of frightened, stunned people coming off boxcars: they have a person."[96] The story illustrates what Huzar describes as an excess of singularity.[97] The woman has been exposed to the most extreme form of dehumanization and terror, yet her singularity persists, even if just barely. She is utterly disoriented and at a loss as to what has just happened, but she nevertheless appears to those around her and is able to share her story: "her singularity punctuates the deadened, deadening rationality that permeates the camp," and thus, "the woman becomes a paradox, the presence of a person in a place where she could not have been: there is no hope in Auschwitz, and *she*, in all of the singular particularity that is carried with the pronoun, was there."[98]

Nyiszli, however, is unable to tease out the *who* of this paradoxically singular individual. Instead of telling *her* biography—instead of allowing her voice and story to appear in their irreducible uniqueness—he tells his own story, as an author, in his voice. As he speculates about her experience and life story, his narration robs her of her agency, and she becomes a character in his story rather than the person who appeared before him in her naked singularity. Nyiszli, who ultimately becomes both narrator and protagonist, is guilty of a "narrative failure," whereas Levi proves to be better equipped at reinscribing her singularity on the scene of narration.[99] The example is a reminder of how fragile an enterprise it is to try to narrate someone else's life story—especially if it involves traumatic experiences that threaten their status as a singular unique individual. In this case, self-narration would have not been possible (the woman did not live to tell her own story), but one can see why Brison (who did live to tell) would want to be the author of her own story and why the very telling of that story also made living in the aftermath possible.

Nyiszli's narrative failure serves as a reminder, then, of the fragility of narration and the risks involved when we try to tell the stories of victims of horrorist violence. Elsewhere, Cavarero describes "the physics of horror" as having to do with the fact that "it constitutively withdraws from the sphere of language."[100] She concludes that horror is "inconceivable and unspeakable," that it "blocks not only bodies, but also speech."[101] This is why the only real witnesses to the horrors of the Holocaust—Levi's "drowned" who had touched the depths of suffering—either did not return to tell about their experiences at all or "returned mute."[102] And tellingly, Brison speaks of the aftermath of her being raped in terms of an "ontology of silence."[103] Recall her attempt to tell her story, only to arrive at "a list of paradoxes."[104]

In the face of such silence and paradoxes, Cavarero and Brison nevertheless believe in the power of narration. As we have seen, the former insists that we need others to tell our story, whereas the latter maintains that she alone could have told her story and that telling it was essential to the remaking of a self shattered by violence. It does seem to me that on the scene of horrorist violence—and in the aftermath of such violence—the wounded might need to tell their own stories, however incomplete and tentative they might be. Sometimes they must tell to live, or their telling allows others to live. Their telling—but also their attending to the silence and lists of paradoxes—allows them to reinsert themselves into the web of human relations while also reconfiguring that web such that stories may be born and heard that challenge hegemonic identities and normative frameworks that have served to reproduce forms of violence in the name of narrowly defined autonomous selfhood.

Folks who are disproportionally exposed as vulnerable—those whose lives have been rendered unliveable and ungrievable through the appropriation and dehumanization enacted against them—might need to give voice to their own story or attend to their silences and paradoxes on their own terms. This may well involve severing ties with those whose appropriating and dehumanizing tendencies have threatened their singularity. But while such a mode of telling to live might demand that certain ties be severed, it also makes other ties and, in turn, alternative webs of relation and coalition possible. Writing in the aftermath—writing the aftermath—thus has the capacity to piece together the shards of a broken self, to reinsert that self into a community, as well as to make community itself survive in the face of division and separation. Narrating in the aftermath—narrating the aftermath—makes linkages and reconstitutes a narratable self such that new stories and relations can be born.

Notes

1. I am immensely grateful for the gift of learning from my students. The idea of reading Cavarero's *Horrorism* alongside Brison's *Aftermath* was born already in 2016, when I co-taught The Symposium on Living Philosophers on the work of Cavarero with Laurie Naranch at Siena College. In that class, one of our students, Courtney Tomeny, was interested in thinking about sexual violence as a form of horrorism. This prompted a dialogue about Brison's autobiographical account. Courtney's sophisticated analysis inspired me to pursue this project, and for that I am thankful. My gratitude also goes to the students who took my capstone seminar on Cavarero's thinking and to those who took my graduate seminar on her philosophy of singularity, both at DePaul University in 2018, in which we read Cavarero and Brison together to explore what it might mean to think of sexual violence as ontological violence.

I am, of course, deeply grateful for Paula Landerreche Cardillo and Rachel Silverbloom, who emerged out of my graduate seminar hungry to put this important volume together and who generously invited me to contribute this chapter. I cannot think of a more rewarding outcome of a class than seeing your students pursue and attain their own scholarly goals with great success, and in this case, by bringing together a community of scholars, many of whom participated as guests in our seminar. Olivia Guaraldo, Laurie Naranch, and Adriana Cavarero herself spent a whirlwind of a week with us, and María del Rosario Acosta López was our companion for the duration of the quarter. My work is profoundly indebted to these amazing women, and each in their own way has supported me, nourished me, and challenged me. María was particularly helpful in pointing me to resources on trauma, and we read an early version of her contribution to this volume in class—an essay that clearly has shaped my thinking on matters of trauma, sexual violence, and narration.

Much of the work writing this chapter took place during my time as a visiting scholar at Södertörn University in Stockholm, Sweden, where I also had the privilege to teach a seminar on Cavarero's work in 2019. Thanks to my colleagues at Södertörn and to the wonderful students who took my seminar there. My gratitude also goes out to the folks in the Department of Comparative Literature at Södertörn, where I presented an earlier version of this chapter and received helpful questions and feedback. I would like to especially thank Amelie Björck for inviting me. I also had the opportunity to present this work in the Northwestern University Graduate Student Political Theory Workshop in 2022. Thanks to Sam McChesney and Usdin Martínez for organizing that event, to Tim Charlebois for his commentary, and to the students who participated. Final revisions to this paper were made after I presented a late draft at the Stockholm University Department of Gender Studies in 2023. Thanks to Anna Nyström and Malena Gustavsson for inviting me, and to the wonderful group of participants who provided invaluable feedback. Finally, generous funding for this project was provided by the DePaul University Research Council through a paid leave.

 2. Susan J. Brison, *Aftermath: Violence and the Remaking of a Self* (Princeton, NJ: Princeton University Press, 2002), 2.

 3. Brison, *Aftermath*, 2.

 4. Brison, *Aftermath*, 91.

 5. Brison, *Aftermath*, xi. Brison revisits this claim later in the book (41, 61).

 6. Brison, *Aftermath*, xii.

 7. Adriana Cavarero, "Narrative Against Destruction," trans. Elvira Roncalli, *New Literary History* 46 (2015): 7–8.

 8. Brison, *Aftermath*, ix.

 9. Brison, *Aftermath*, x.

 10. Brison, *Aftermath*, ix, x.

 11. Cathy Caruth, Romain Pasquer Brochard, and Ben Tam, "'Who Speaks from the Site of Trauma?' An Interview with Cathy Caruth," *Diacritics* 47, no. 2 (2019): 64.

 12. Judith Butler, *Precarious Life: The Powers of Mourning and Violence* (New York: Verso Press, 2004), 24.

 13. Jean Améry, *At the Mind's Limits: Contemplations by a Survivor on Auschwitz and Its Realities*, trans. Sidney Rosenfeld and Stella P. Rosenfeld (Bloomington: Indiana University Press, 1980), 28.

 14. Cavarero consistently points out that the word vulnerability derives from the Latin term *vulnus*, to wound. Griselda Pollock elaborates: "To be vulnerable is to be at risk of being wounded. In Greek the word for the *piercing* wound is *trauma*.

Thus trauma might be understood metaphorically as the wounding of the utterly vulnerable, the unarmed, the defenseless." See Griselda Pollock, "From Horrorism to Compassion: Re-Facing Medusan Otherness in Dialogue with Adriana Cavarero and Bracha Ettinger," in *Visual Politics of Psychoanalysis*, ed. Griselda Pollock (London: I. B. Tauris, 2013), 162.

15. Brison, *Aftermath*, 62.
16. Brison, *Aftermath*, 61.
17. Adriana Cavarero, *Relating Narratives: Storytelling and Selfhood*, trans. Paul A. Kottman (New York: Routledge, 2000), 20, 23, 83.
18. Cavarero, *Relating Narratives*, 71.
19. Cavarero, *Relating Narratives*, 72.
20. Cavarero, *Relating Narratives*, 73.
21. Cavarero, *Relating Narratives*, 1.
22. Cavarero, *Relating Narratives*, 1.
23. Cavarero, *Relating Narratives*, 37.
24. Thanks to Rachel Silverbloom, as well as my interlocutors at a workshop I gave at Northwestern University in May 2022, for pushing me on these issues. Thanks also to Sarah Lee, with whom I have had multiple conversations about the non-linear temporality of trauma in the context of an independent study she did with me at DePaul University in spring 2022.
25. Adriana Cavarero, *Horrorism: Naming Contemporary Violence*, trans. William McCuaig (New York: Columbia University Press, 2011), 2–3. As Pollock has pointed out, the translation of the title of this book misses the mark in terms of the attention given in the original to the defenseless victim on the scene of violence. The Italian title is *Orrorismo: Ovvero della violenza sull'inerme*, where *l'inerme* "is literally the unarmed, the vulnerable par excellence." See Pollock, "From Horrorism to Compassion," 162.
26. Cavarero, *Horrorism*, 8.
27. Cavarero, *Horrorism*, 8.
28. See Ann V. Murphy, "Corporeal Vulnerability and the New Humanism," special issue, *Hypatia* 26, no. 3 (2011): 585. Thomas Gregory has extended Cavarero's analysis of ontological violence to examine the violence inflicted by US troops on the corpse of an unarmed murdered boy in an Afghan village in 2010. Gregory seeks to discern "the political significance of a violent act that exceeds what is necessary to kill the victim and focuses instead on the destruction of their body." See Thomas Gregory, "Dismembering the Dead: Violence, Vulnerability and the Body in War," *European Journal of International Relations* 22, no. 4 (2015): 2. He is particularly interested in the uneven distribution of vulnerability—"that certain bodies are much more woundable than others"—in the context of structural racism (3).
29. Cavarero, *Horrorism*, 4, 7.
30. This distinction can be said to echo the one Butler makes between precariousness and precarity, although in Cavarero it lacks a robust analysis of power dynamics. See Judith Butler, *Frames of War: When Is Life Grievable?* (New York:

Verso Press, 2009). I have previously discussed this distinction in my essay "Natality or Birth? Arendt and Cavarero on the Human Condition of Being Born," *Hypatia* 33, no. 2 (2018): 273–88.

31. Cavarero, *Horrorism*, 34–35.

32. Cavarero, *Horrorism*, 38.

33. Anne Murphy, *Violence and the Philosophical Imaginary* (Albany: State University of New York Press, 2012), 98.

34. Cavarero, *Horrorism*, 30.

35. Linda Martín Alcoff, *Rape and Resistance: Understanding the Complexities of Sexual Violation* (Cambridge: Polity Press, 2018), 12.

36. Alcoff, *Rape and Resistance*, 12.

37. It should be noted, though, that the kind of rape I am speaking of here—an unpredictable attack by a total stranger—is but one kind of sexual violence, and it is probably the least common kind. As is well known, sexual violence is far more likely to happen in intimate relations, and it is typically ongoing and habitual rather than a sudden and isolated event. While I think it makes sense to speak of different kinds of sexual violence in terms of ontological violence, intimate and habitual violence would nevertheless have to be treated in its own terms, and such a task falls outside of the scope of this chapter. Thanks to Lisa Käll for bringing this issue to my attention.

38. Brison, *Aftermath*, 9.

39. As Gregory puts it: "This level of violence is no longer concerned with questions of life and death, but seeks to destroy the body as body." See Gregory, "Dismembering the Dead," 1.

40. Brison explains: "Even those who are able to acknowledge the existence of violence try to protect themselves from the realization that the world in which it occurs is their world and so they find it hard to identify with the victim. They cannot allow themselves to imagine the victim's shattered life, or else their illusions about their own safety and control over their own lives might begin to crumble" (*Aftermath*, 9).

41. Cavarero, *Horrorism*, 44; see also 47.

42. Cavarero, *Horrorism*, 45.

43. Cavarero, *Horrorism*, 46, 50.

44. Cavarero, *Horrorism*, 49.

45. Cavarero, *Horrorism*, 49.

46. Cavarero, *Horrorism*, 56.

47. Cavarero, *Horrorism*, 44.

48. Cavarero, *Relating Narratives*, 9; Cavarero, *Horrorism*, 44.

49. Brison, *Aftermath*, ix. Caruth consistently confirms this notion that trauma "fundamentally puts every act of theorization into question," in part because of its "rupturing of all previous frameworks of knowledge" (Caruth, Brochard, and Tam, "'Who Speaks from the Site of Trauma?'" 49). If trauma ultimately questions "the

condition of the possibility of speaking," then we must indeed ask "what strategies of testimony we are left with" (49). María del Rosario Acosta López's ongoing work on grammars of listening powerfully engages this issue of navigating a situation where all previous frameworks of knowledge have been ruptured.

50. Brison, *Aftermath*, x.

51. René Descartes, *Meditations on First Philosophy*, trans. Donald A. Cress (Indianapolis: Hackett Publishing, 1993), 13.

52. Brison, *Aftermath*, 25.

53. Brison, *Aftermath*, 26.

54. Brison, *Aftermath*, 31–32.

55. Cavarero, *Horrorism*, 1.

56. Brison, *Aftermath*, xii.

57. Brison, *Aftermath*, xii.

58. Cavarero, *Relating Narratives*, 123.

59. Laurie E. Naranch, "The Narratable Self: Adriana Cavarero with Sojourner Truth," *Hypatia* 34, no. 3 (2019): 427.

60. Of course, any and all such rigid distinctions are ultimately bound to be limited and limiting. Rather than saying that there is an absolute difference between narration and philosophy, it might make more sense to highlight how and why it is that philosophers depend on narration without recognizing and acknowledging that this is so. To be sure, the very philosophers we tend to point to as the ultimate examples of the privileging of universal abstractions—I am thinking here of Plato and Descartes among others—depend completely on narrative tropes such as fiction, mythology, and autobiography for constructing their arguments. Plato might insist that art must be banned from the city, yet his own dialogues depend on artistic imagery and stories throughout. Descartes might claim that experience is antithetical to philosophical clarity, yet he draws from his own experience, even if just rhetorically, at every step of his philosophical work. Rather than being separate and distinct genres, philosophy and narration are thus co-constitutive and codependent in ways that philosophers have tended to deny. It is, therefore, also not really the case that philosophy merely deals with abstract-rational truth while narration deals with singular-lived experience. As much as philosophers would like to uphold such distinctions, they are bound to collapse and undo themselves, such that singularity always rears its head even in the most abstract-philosophical accounts, albeit quietly and from the margins of the text. Cavarero is a master of seeking it out and rendering it audible and visible where we least expect it.

61. Cavarero, *Relating Narratives*, 124.

62. Cavarero, *Relating Narratives*, 55.

63. Cavarero elaborates: "The *who* of Emilia shows itself here with clarity in the perception of a narratable self that desires the tale of her own life-story. However, it is the other—the friend who recognizes the ontological roots of this desire—who is the only one who can realize such a narration" (*Relating Narratives*, 56).

64. Cavarero, "Narrative Against Destruction," 4.

65. For a rich discussion of these matters in relation to Cavarero and Sojourner Truth, see Laurie E. Naranch, "The Narratable Self."

66. Of course, there is a huge body of literature that deals with this question as it pertains to both individual and collective trauma. See, for example, Cathy Caruth, *Unclaimed Experience: Trauma, Narrative, and History* (Baltimore: Johns Hopkins University Press, 1996); Cathy Caruth, *Literature in the Ashes of History* (Baltimore: Johns Hopkins University Press, 2013); Nelly Richard, *Eruptions of Memory: The Critique of Memory in Chile, 1990–2015*, trans. Andrew Ascherl (Cambridge: Polity Press, 2019); and Cristina Rivera Garza, *Grieving: Dispatches from a Wounded Country*, trans. Sarah Booker (New York: The Feminist Press, 2020). Due to word limit constraints, I will not be able to engage this body of work in any detail here. I am primarily interested in thinking about how, specifically, Cavarero's conception of narration might offer tools for understanding how a self can be reborn in the aftermath of ontological violence. I will simply note here that much of the existing literature on these matters seeks to address the fact that bearing witness to trauma—and being on the receiving end of such testimonies—ultimately requires new forms of representation. More often than not, trauma theorists locate such efforts in poetic and artistic modes of expression rather than in theoretical reflection. Cavarero's privileging of narration over philosophy in the context of recovering a singular self from the ruins of ontological violence is similar in this regard. Acosta López formulates the task at hand succinctly in a recent essay on the work of Cathy Caruth: "The task [. . .] is not to re-signify what has been ripped out of language, but instead to seek new forms of representation that can bear witness to such catastrophic disruption of meaning. Thus, the task seems to be the search for new languages or modes of signification, new frameworks of meaning that can testify *to* trauma without remaining trapped within its unknowability" (María del Rosario Acosta López, "Grammars of Addressing: On Memory and History in Cathy Caruth's Work," *Diacritics* 49, no. 2 [2021]: 151). For Acosta López, the task is to develop new grammars for listening to trauma—a claim that echoes both Brison's and Cavarero's insistence that the narration of trauma is fundamentally relational, requiring empathetic witnessing (which, arguably, also requires listening). For an extended discussion of these matters and how they relate to Cavarero's work, see Acosta López's essay in this volume, "Being Robbed of One's Voice: On Listening and Political Violence in Adriana Cavarero."

67. Cavarero, "Narrative Against Destruction," 9.

68. Cavarero, "Narrative Against Destruction," 9.

69. Acosta López, "Grammars of Addressing," 150.

70. Caruth, *Unclaimed Experience*, 4.

71. Caruth, *Unclaimed Experience*, 4.

72. Caruth, *Unclaimed Experience*, 4.

73. Cavarero, "Narrative Against Destruction," 7.

74. Cavarero, "Narrative Against Destruction," 6.
75. Cavarero, "Narrative Against Destruction," 10.
76. Cavarero, "Narrative Against Destruction," 14.
77. Cavarero, "Narrative Against Destruction," 14.
78. "Autobiography does not properly respond to the question 'who am I?' Rather, it is the biographical take of my story, told by another, which responds to this question" (Cavarero, *Relating Narratives*, 45).
79. Brison, *Aftermath*, xii.
80. Brison, *Aftermath*, 6.
81. Alcoff, *Rape and Resistance*, 210.
82. Brison, *Aftermath*, 51.
83. Brison, *Aftermath*, 16. María del Rosario Acosta López's essay in this volume is a powerful attempt to examine the registers of audibility and silence through a reading of Ariel Dorfman's *Death and the Maiden*. Her engagement with Paulina's experience of being raped by her torturer in that play is, as she herself puts it, not intended as "an explanation or a definition of the kind of violence implicated in the destruction and colonization of the voice," but it serves, rather, "as an attempt to tune our ears to the voice that resonates out of the site of that destruction." See María del Rosario Acosta López, "Being Robbed of One's Voice: On Listening and Political Violence in Adriana Cavarero," in this volume.
84. Cavarero, "Narrative Against Destruction," 7.
85. Cavarero, "Narrative Against Destruction," 7.
86. Cavarero, "Narrative Against Destruction," 8.
87. Timothy J. Huzar, "Destruction, Narrative and the Excess of Uniqueness: Reading Cavarero on Violence and Narration," *Critical Horizons* 19, no. 2 (2018): 159.
88. Cavarero, "Narrative Against Destruction," 9.
89. Cavarero, "Narrative Against Destruction," 7.
90. Cavarero, "Narrative Against Destruction," 7.
91. Huzar, "Destruction, Narrative and the Excess of Uniqueness," 168.
92. Huzar, "Destruction, Narrative and the Excess of Uniqueness," 160.
93. Huzar, "Destruction, Narrative and the Excess of Uniqueness," 160.
94. Huzar, "Destruction, Narrative and the Excess of Uniqueness," 160.
95. Huzar, "Destruction, Narrative and the Excess of Uniqueness," 160.
96. Primo Levi, *The Drowned and the Saved*, trans. Raymond Rosenthal (London: Abacus, 1989), 39.
97. Huzar, "Destruction, Narrative and the Excess of Uniqueness," 166–69.
98. Huzar, "Destruction, Narrative and the Excess of Uniqueness," 161.
99. Huzar, "Destruction, Narrative and the Excess of Uniqueness," 163.
100. Adriana Cavarero, "'Destroy Your Sight with a New Gorgon': Mass Atrocity and the Phenomenology of Horror," in *Emotions and Mass Atrocity: Philosophical and Theoretical Explorations*, ed. Thomas Brudholm and Johannes Lang (Cambridge: Cambridge University Press), 127.

101. Cavarero, "'Destroy Your Sight with a New Gorgon,'" 127.
102. Levi, *The Drowned and the Saved*, 84.
103. Brison, *Aftermath*, 117.
104. Brison, *Aftermath*, ix.

Bibliography

Acosta López, María del Rosario. "Being Robbed of One's Voice: On Listening and Political Violence in Adriana Cavarero." In *Political Bodies: Writings on Adriana Cavarero's Political Thought*, edited by Paula Landerreche Cardillo and Rachel Silverbloom, 237–264. Albany: State University of New York Press, 2024.

———. "Grammars of Addressing: On Memory and History in Cathy Caruth's Work." *Diacritics* 49, no. 2 (2021): 147–57.

Alcoff, Linda Martín. *Rape and Resistance: Understanding the Complexities of Sexual Violation*. Cambridge: Polity Press, 2018.

Améry, Jean. *At the Mind's Limits: Contemplations by a Survivor on Auschwitz and Its Realities*. Translated by Sidney Rosenfeld and Stella P. Rosenfeld. Bloomington: Indiana University Press, 1980.

Brison, Susan J. *Aftermath: Violence and the Remaking of a Self*. Princeton, NJ: Princeton University Press, 2002.

Butler, Judith. *Frames of War: When Is Life Grievable?* New York: Verso Press, 2009.

———. *Precarious Life: The Powers of Mourning and Violence*. New York: Verso Press, 2004.

Caruth, Cathy. *Literature in the Ashes of History*. Baltimore: Johns Hopkins University Press, 2013.

———. *Unclaimed Experience: Trauma, Narrative, and History*. Baltimore: Johns Hopkins University Press, 1996.

Caruth, Cathy, Romain Pasquer Brochard, and Ben Tam. "'Who Speaks from the Site of Trauma?' An Interview with Cathy Caruth." *Diacritics* 47, no. 2 (2019): 48–71.

Cavarero, Adriana. "'Destroy Your Sight with a New Gorgon': Mass Atrocity and the Phenomenology of Horror." In *Emotions and Mass Atrocity: Philosophical and Theoretical Explorations*, edited by Thomas Brudholm and Johannes Lang, 123–41. Cambridge: Cambridge University Press, 2018.

———. *Horrorism: Naming Contemporary Violence*. Translated by William McCuaig. New York: Columbia University Press, 2011.

———. "Narrative Against Destruction." Translated by Elvira Roncalli. *New Literary History* 46 (2015): 1–16.

———. *Relating Narratives: Storytelling and Selfhood*. Translated by Paul A. Kottman. New York: Routledge, 2000.

Descartes, René. *Meditations on First Philosophy*. Translated by Donald A. Cress. Indianapolis: Hackett Publishing, 1993.
Gregory, Thomas. "Dismembering the Dead: Violence, Vulnerability and the Body in War." *European Journal of International Relations* 22, no. 4 (2015): 1–22.
Huzar, Timothy J. "Destruction, Narrative and the Excess of Uniqueness: Reading Cavarero on Violence and Narration." *Critical Horizons* 19, no. 2 (2018): 157–72.
Levi, Primo. *The Drowned and the Saved*. Translated by Raymond Rosenthal. London: Abacus, 1989.
Murphy, Ann V. "Corporeal Vulnerability and the New Humanism." Special issue, *Hypatia* 26, no. 3 (2011): 575–90.
———. *Violence and the Philosophical Imaginary*. Albany: State University of New York Press, 2012.
Naranch, Laurie E. "The Narratable Self: Adriana Cavarero with Sojourner Truth." *Hypatia* 34, no. 3 (2019): 424–40.
Pollock, Griselda. "From Horrorism to Compassion: Re-Facing Medusan Otherness in Dialogue with Adriana Cavarero and Bracha Ettinger." In *Visual Politics of Psychoanalysis*, edited by Griselda Pollock, 159–89. London: I. B. Tauris, 2013.
Richard, Nelly. *Eruptions of Memory: The Critique of Memory in Chile, 1990–2015*. Translated by Andrew Ascherl. Cambridge: Polity Press, 2019.
Rivera Garza, Cristina. *Grieving: Dispatches from a Wounded Country*. Translated by Sarah Booker. New York: The Feminist Press, 2020.
Söderbäck, Fanny. "Natality or Birth? Arendt and Cavarero on the Human Condition of Being Born." *Hypatia* 33, no. 2 (2018): 273–88.

Ten

Being Robbed of One's Voice

On Listening and Political Violence in Adriana Cavarero[1]

María del Rosario Acosta López

This chapter addresses Adriana Cavarero's treatment of the voice as the locus of singularity in ethical and political life. By questioning how one is seen through someone else's telling of one's life story in *Relating Narratives*, and thus, questioning listening to one's story in the voice of another, Cavarero has moved more explicitly in her work, in projects like *For More than One Voice*, to question what it means to have a voice, to make oneself not only visible but also audible to another. Even though these questions were already present, somewhat, in *Relating Narratives*, I want to stress the importance of Cavarero's more explicit turn toward audibility in her later work in order to inquire about the implications of this move for her conception of the political.

However, I also question the limits of this turn in Cavarero's work and point to what I'll describe as an attachment to the regime of visuality that impedes her capacity to entirely move to a regime of audibility in her philosophical analyses. In order to get there, I concentrate on the moments in Cavarero's work where, beyond a phenomenology of voice, she also attends to a phenomenology of violence. Following her turn toward the voice and the audible, such a phenomenology needs to attend to questions concerned with epistemic and hermeneutical forms of violence—more specifically, forms of violence that have to do with stripping one's voice and replacing it with someone else's.[2] Thus, from the question of listening, I move with Cavarero to question how we listen to the kinds of silences that are left by a violent deprivation of one's voice and, even further, examine how the complicated combination of deprivation and colonization impacts one's voice. My concerns here are twofold. On the one hand, there is the question of how one speaks where there is no longer a voice that speaks for oneself, and that allows one to appear, and to be audible, even to oneself. On the other hand, there is also the question about the conditions of possibility for the kind of listening that this loss of voice requires. How can we listen to voices that have been erased, smothered, replaced, and taken away?

In order to address this set of issues, I attend to a literary work that has allowed me to better understand the nuances involved in these questions. To speak about singularity and the embodied experience of having one's voice stripped away—and, moreover, having it replaced (colonized) by someone else's—I follow the character of Paulina in Ariel Dorfman's *The Death and the Maiden*. Paulina is a torture survivor in the aftermath of a dictatorship.[3] The play starts when Paulina recognizes, without having ever seen him, her torturer by his voice. As the play develops and as we hear, but never really get to listen to, Paulina's version of the events, we realize how torture has not only robbed her of her voice but also of her capacity to listen, even to herself. Both, her voice and her listening, have been colonized by her torturer. I explore the ways in which the play seems to simultaneously reflect on and perform the experience of this colonizing and how Paulina's experience complements, but perhaps also challenges, Cavarero's reflections on the voice as the site of political appearance.

Ultimately, in light of the kind of questions that are opened by Dorfman's play, I ask to what extent Cavarero's philosophical approach helps us think of political violence as the erasure and colonization of the voice. This question is connected not only to the kind of listening that is required by, and much too often denied to, survivors of traumatic forms of political violence, but it also inquires about traumatic forms of violence *as* colonizing, suggesting that these violences cannot be understood only as assaults on life but must also be understood as assaults on the conditions for the production of sense that make life legible as such. In my work, I emphasize how traumatic and colonizing forms of violence operate at the *aesthetic* level, even before, or at least parallel to, epistemic and political levels, rendering the very forms of life that are produced through their violence inaudible, imperceptible, illegible, and unbelievable.[4] In what follows,

I point to the insufficiency of attending to these effects through a grammar oriented exclusively or primarily by visuality. A grammar of listening, or a grammar of the aural, may take us to the (in)audible and not only the (in)visible effects of violence. In introducing audibility as another perspective on the question of political violence, my intention is not to propose audibility as the leading organizing principle of our perception but rather to call for a disorganization of the hierarchies that usually frame the aesthetics of violence as well as the aesthetics at play in our philosophical critiques.

From Seeing to Listening in Adriana Cavarero's Work

The original title of Relating Narratives in Italian (*Tu che mi guardi, tu che mi racconti*) pays particular attention to the idea of visibility and to the look or gaze as the space of ethical and political appearance. Following Hannah Arendt, Cavarero approaches the question of the political as a "plural network of gazes,"[5] where, in our appearing to each other, we come to know who we are and reveal this who to others and to ourselves through the gazes of others. This is also connected to Cavarero's idea of a "narratable self."[6] When we appear in the public realm, Cavarero insists, we appear in our uniqueness precisely because of the story of our life: a story that is told by others and that becomes constitutive of who we are. Cavarero writes, "Correcting Arendt we will therefore say not only that who appears to us is shown to be unique in corporeal form and sound of voice, but that this who also already comes to us perceptibly as a narratable self with a unique story."[7]

But unlike a more traditional emphasis on a narratable self by the self (autobiography), Cavarero explains that this constitutive narratability, which she wants to add to Arendt's "radical phenomenology" (where being and appearing coincide), is ultimately relational. Taking Arendt's idea of the privileged standpoint of the storyteller to interpret and give meaning to action, Cavarero insists that the "story" of our lives is to be told by others. Thus, we ontologically long and desire, Cavarero argues, to *hear* one's story in the words of another.[8] This is the central idea of Cavarero's *Relating Narratives*, which concerns relational identity and proposes an ethics of care as and through narration.

One could argue that even though the idea of a gaze situates this reflection in the realm of visibility—and visibility certainly plays a central role in the language Cavarero employs throughout the book—a desire to listen is already emphasized at the very center of Cavarero's project.

After all, it is only in the experience of listening to another tell my story that I can truly understand the uniqueness of my own life and truly be recognized by another. Even further, if the political realm is the space of coappearance, of mutual exposure to one another, listening is an essential part of the openness of the political scene since it is through my ears and not through my eyes that I hear the other telling my story. It is as much a community of listeners, therefore, as it is a plurality of gazes that opens up the realm of the ethical and the political for Cavarero. And it is precisely in "paying careful attention" to others,[9] in listening to and caring for them that "the creation of a relational space of reciprocal exhibition"[10] and reciprocal care takes place. As Cavarero herself clarifies further into the book, "visibility" is just a metaphor for all the different senses: "The self once again finds her familiar *taste* [*sapore*] in the active relation with the one who grants her wish to *hear* herself narrated [. . .] just as blindness is a metaphor for the absence of relation, seeing here is a symbol for all five senses. It indicates simply that the relation is perceived, empirical, present."[11] One can understand and present Cavarero's trajectory in these terms even more so if one considers her next book, *For More than One Voice*, where her Arendtian emphasis on uniqueness is tied corporeally to the tone and specific resonance of the human voice. Thus, the kind of relationality that Cavarero described before in terms of narratability becomes located in a much more bodily—and according to her, more primordial (as in, *prior to meaning*)—experience of the self. As she puts it in a 2007 essay, where she does a beautiful job recounting her reflections on the voice and the corporeal:

> In the emission of sound that comes from the depths of the body and escapes to the outside in order to penetrate the ear of another, thus evoking another voice in response, the reciprocity of communicating is a revelation, a relation, and an (inter)dependence. Tone and emotional expressivity, as well as musicality and even speech, are always contained in this primary relationality of the human voice. No coincidence, then, that the voice is thought of as traditionally feminine; the voice alludes to a body, singular but not sealed off in its individual self-sufficiency, which opens and welcomes another, tuning the body's music to the rhythms of life.[12]

The emphasis on the voice is thus Cavarero's way of distancing herself from the disjunction still present in Arendt between a material ontological horizon of plurality, a kind of sheer relationality between embodied uniqueness, and the realm of action and meaning where—and only where, according to Arendt—our political existence takes place. For Cavarero, it is important that we go back to the corporeality of the voice—the body that is the voice and the voice that is the body—to understand what she calls in the quoted passage the "primary relationality of the human voice."[13]

The voice, Cavarero writes, "puts hearing in play even before listening."[14] We "recognize" others by the sound of their voice; we appear to one another even before we speak and act. Who we are is somehow already contained in, carried by, and communicated in the singularity of our voice, and it is in the experience of hearing, for Cavarero, that a primary phenomenal relationality of the voice is sustained: "Though predisposed to the perception of sound in general, the human ear is, above all, tuned to this vocal emission that reveals singular bodies to one another."[15]

The project, as it was first undertaken in *For More than One Voice*, confronts a tradition that has deprived the voice of its voice, reducing it to a mere instrument of speech and robbing its "sonorous physicality" to turn it into the most incorporeal of all "voices" (if it can be considered a voice at all): the voice of reason.[16] "In this binary," Cavarero continues, "one typical of logocentrism, the corporeality of the voice has a depreciating effect, rendering it a secondary and merely instrumental component of language when compared to language's semantic-rational component."[17] To think the voice anew, to disrupt the reduction of voice to speech and language to a "rational system of signification," means to think the bodily dimension of the voice: its physicality and corporeal manifestation. It means to even put the question of listening to a halt since it is perhaps always already tied to a logocentric reduction of sound to language. She writes, "The pleasure of giving a personal form to sound waves [. . .] is ultimately tied to sound emission and not only to auditory reception—to the personal voice and not only to the other's ear, as the fable of the Sirens would have it."[18]

Not only must the idea of the voice be untied from the concept of "being listened to." To even ask what it means to be listened to, what it means to be understood and be rendered audible, one should first consider that meaning is not what defines but rather what responds and results from the experience of the radical singularity of the corporeal voice. Such as it happens in "societies without writing," Cavarero suggests, where "the voice not only plays an essential role but influences the very structure of the word itself and, therefore, of language, which now bends to the rhythmic and sonorous demands of vocality."[19]

Thus, Cavarero moves in her work, first, from relationality to narratability and, second, from narratability to the voice. One would expect, given this trajectory, that the emphasis on visibility in her previous works would give way to an emphasis on audibility in her more recent writings. Not only has Cavarero's work insisted, since *Stately Bodies*, on questioning and displacing the reduction of the body to an incorporeal political metaphor that, paradoxically, guarantees only the actual erasure of the body from and by politics,[20] she has also called for retuning the political to the essential role that listening and the voice play in what has traditionally been conceived mostly as the realm of political visibility and invisibility. I believe this turn is essential both to Cavarero's conception of the political and, in her more recent work, to her conception of violence and her reflections on political and collective agency. A turn toward the audible, an acute attention to the bodily dimensions of the voice, and an emphasis on the relational experience of listening and being listened to are all central elements of Cavarero's invitation to both rethink conceptions of self and world that orient our political experiences and to question the very frameworks that define what we perceive and, thus, experience and recognize as political.

However, there is still something about the privilege of sight in Cavarero's thought that seems to impede, at least to a certain extent, her shift in implementing a regime of audibility as an essential perspective for rethinking the grammars that define the political realm. As if following her own warning, "the problem of an acoustic sphere" would risk "remaining trapped in the visual."[21] The clearest way for me to show this is to go to those places where Cavarero more directly confronts herself with the problem of political violence because it is precisely there where one can see that, even if the political has been introduced in her work following and doing justice to the acoustics of the voice, Cavarero still defines violence predominantly through a language of the visual, even when she herself is attentive to the prevalence of this metaphor and has tried to complicate the story.

The Gorgon's Soundless Howl: On Voice and Political Violence

Cavarero develops her reflections on political violence more clearly in her book *Horrorism*, which was written right after *For More than One Voice*.

According to Cavarero, the character of political violence today is best described using the concept of horror (rather than the idea of terror). Thus, she coins the word *horrorism* to emphasize the radical challenge that violence poses to our established categories. Horrorism, she argues, attempts to respond to the need for an appropriate vocabulary that conveys the specific character of political violence today and acknowledges that a "certain model of horror," beyond and different from terror, "is indispensable for understanding our present."[22]

One of the traditional images for depicting horror, Cavarero tells us, is the figure of the Medusa. For Cavarero, one of the essential differences between horror and terror is that the latter makes us want to flee, whereas the former has a totally paralyzing effect. The Medusa is an image of horror, then, because it represents a form of violence that both paralyzes and produces repugnance. The chapter on the figure of the Medusa in *Horrorism* is important for my argument for at least two reasons. On the one hand, it is important because of what Cavarero does not say about the Medusa, which is symptomatic of the form of violence she attends to; Cavarero completely ignores that the mythological character, besides representing a kind of terror that paralyzes, is herself the survivor of trauma. At least in the version of the myth recounted by Ovid in the *Metamorphoses*, Medusa has been raped by Poseidon in Athena's temple, and as punishment (unfortunately, like today, she is punished and silenced for being raped), the goddess turns her hair into snakes.[23]

On the other hand, what Cavarero says about the Gorgon and its particular form of silence is telling for Cavarero's own perspective. It is through her attention to the image of the Gorgon's decapitation by Perseus and Medusa's howling sound that Cavarero addresses the difference between the regimes of visibility and audibility and their significance for the question of violence:

> The depiction of Medusa with her mouth wide open is not a simple accident, or a secondary adjunct, of her fundamental belonging to the realm of the eye. In fact, eye and voice here encounter each other. The unwatchable, as dismembered body, outraged in its singularity, also occurs as a howl [. . .] But since we are still dealing with a visual image, this howl is soundless. There is no acoustic vibration, only a wide-open mouth. The extreme cry remains mute. And yet something in this inaudible, frozen, breathless cry is more disturbing to the viewer than

Medusa's eyes are. As though, through the characteristic game of mirrors, we, the ones doing the looking, were the ones emitting a soundless howl. Or as though the experience of horror had strangled the cry in (her, our) throat.[24]

There is a paradox here in the entanglement between the regimes of visibility and audibility in the case of Medusa's incorporeality: The eyes "meet" the howl rather than her gaze; it is the cry in its muteness rather than Medusa's eyes, Cavarero suggests, that paralyzes us. Medusa's violence—or the kind of violence that her image represents in the way Cavarero takes up her story—is one mostly related to the eye, to the regime of the visible; it is a viewer that confronts Medusa's gaze, even when it is the soundless, mute, and silenced violence that seems to be at center stage here. The smothering of Medusa's story, which Cavarero adds unintentionally in her recount, is another layer at play in more generally reducing the acoustic to a grammar governed by the visible. In Cavarero's account, we are not dealing here, at least not primarily, with a violence that silences but with one that is mostly depicted and perceived as silent. The silent character of violence has the effect of being "more disturbing" to the viewer, Cavarero remarks, and of mirroring itself in the spectator as a soundless reaction. But again, all this happens only from the perspective of a regime of visibility, as Cavarero herself clarifies, "since we are still dealing with a visual image."

However, we can also ask: How should we address violence when it is not only seen but also heard? When it is not only meant to be rendered visible but also audible? When it is not only understood as silent but also as silencing? Even though these are not the explicit questions Cavarero asks, they are still present in the language she uses to describe the relation between the eye and the voice. The experience of horror, she says, "strangles the cry in (her, our) throat."[25] How, then, are we to give voice to this mute cry? How are we to lend an ear to its soundless howl? Or, better, how are we to render it audible beyond the grammars of visibility at play in Cavarero's account?

The "acoustic dimension" is, Cavarero writes, part of Medusa's essence.[26] As one of the Gorgons, the etymology of her name points not only to the idea of a paralyzing, repugnant form of visibility—"to being unable to be seen (*me idosan*)"[27]—but also to a guttural murmur, a sound that has not yet reached words. "Horror," Cavarero continues, "is revealed without words, without sounds, turning toward *an ear frozen in expectation* of a howl it will be unable to bear."[28] It is this howl that is "unable to bear" that seems to be the key here. Is the howl unable to bear only by our sight? What happens to whoever is willing to listen? And is a disposition to listen enough to break through the unbearable soundless cry? The central question here could also relate to how we should think about this acoustic dimension of violence that Cavarero seems to put at center stage, only to then leave unheard. And how do we think acoustically when confronted with the specific inaudibility of horror—an inaudibility that has to do, on the one hand, with the strangling of the cry but also, on the other, with our incapacity to bear its sound? Violence needs to be understood, therefore, both in connection to silencing and in connection to the difficulties of lending an ear to the unheard, what Cavarero herself has described as the "sonic untranslatability of the outrage" of violence.[29]

I've examined elsewhere the two sides of violence's inaudibility by connecting them to the two meanings the word *inaudito* bears in Spanish: that which (1) remains unheard, inaudible, and untouched by words precisely because it also (2) confronts us with its indigestible, unprecedented, and ethically unacceptable character.[30] Cavarero does attend to the "unheard and unheard-of" nature of certain forms of violence. She mostly connects violence to its unspeakable character and the way it paralyzes our capacity to respond and do justice to the kind of muteness it leaves behind as a sign of the radical, ontological damage it produces in those who manage to survive. She goes back, once again, to the Gorgon to signal this unspeakability of violence, following Primo Levi's famous passage: "Those who saw the Gorgon have not returned to tell about it or have returned mute."[31] Once again, however, she stays with a visual interpretation of the metaphor, relating muteness to a challenge for visibility—the "drowned" become "unwatchable" in Cavarero's interpretation of Levi[32]—and as a consequence of the unbearable experience of looking to violence, confronting it face to face. What would it mean to stay with the aural metaphor, letting it resonate in its specifically sonorous, acoustic nature? What would it mean, ultimately, to let ourselves be undone by the look of the Gorgon in order to hear her cry, to hear the violence her silence tells us about?

In spite of her attention to the voice in her previous work, Cavarero seems to operate almost exclusively through a regime of visibility in *Horrorism* that, as I have mentioned throughout this chapter, is sometimes complicated and problematized but nonetheless permeates most of her approaches to the kind of violence 'horrorism' seeks to name. She writes, "The violence that dismembers it [the body] ends the ontological dignity that the human figure possesses and renders it unwatchable. More repugnant than any other body part is the head, the most markedly human of the remains, on which the singular face can still be seen."³³ And later, "Horror always concerns the face. Or at any rate concerns it first and foremost, given that the uniqueness displayed in physiognomic features is immediately visible and that it discloses itself [si affaccia] by exposing itself to the other's eyes as the windows of the soul."³⁴

I understand Cavarero's need to emphasize the horrific *scene* of violence, but I would also like to push her ideas further to think of the horrific *audibility* in the acoustic effects of the violence that Cavarero connects to and seeks to name through the notion of horrorism. Indeed, even though Cavarero does not discuss it, violence needs to be understood also in connection to its silencing power, not only at the level of eliminating the voice—and the muteness that comes with the Gorgon's howl—but also in its attempt to entirely break the survivor's capacity for sense making and the tools and frameworks we have at our disposal, as "viewers" and listeners, to interpret it, recognize it, and make it audible. Violence's capacity is, ultimately, not only to destroy but also to colonize, or to destroy by colonizing; thus, violence uses its aesthetic mechanisms to render itself imperceptible, erase its traces, and leave behind only silences to speak of its annihilating power.

In thinking the same kind of violence Cavarero works with in *Horrorism*, "a violence that, tearing furiously at the body, works not simply to take away its life but to undo its figural unity,"³⁵ I aim to push Cavarero's thinking further by thinking of the body, as she herself has done it elsewhere, also as voice. I consider the voice, like Cavarero, as "the quintessence of an incarnated uniqueness that, in expressing itself, exposes itself" and, therefore, also as that "which extreme violence has chosen for its object."³⁶

There are forms of violence that, as Cavarero puts it, are not just related to the threat of death. *Horrorism* seeks to name an "excessive form of violence"³⁷ that, "not content merely to kill because killing would be too little, aims to destroy the uniqueness of the body, tearing at its constitutive vulnerability. What is at stake is not the end of a human life but the human condition itself, as incarnated in the singularity of vulnerable bodies."³⁸ Torture is precisely one example of this particular kind of violence. Cavarero writes that, in torture,

> Several peculiar aspects of horrorism are thereby fully disclosed. [. . .] Death may come at the end, but it is not the end in view. The dead body, no matter how mutilated, is only a residue of the scene of torture. The special form of horrorism of which the

torturer is the featured protagonist actually prefers to consummate itself on the living body [. . .] As every torturer knows, the vulnerable is not the same as the killable.³⁹

In this sense, it is particularly relevant to speak of Dorfman's play, which can be read as a reflection on the potential and limitations of Cavarero's thought on political violence, her silence on sexual violence, and the ways in which audibility and inaudibility aren't entirely centered in her critique of violence. And, perhaps, the latter is one cause for the former; that is, perhaps Cavarero's inattention to the (in)audible (and the radical silencing power of certain forms of violence) has caused her to not be able to hear and address the theme of sexual violence precisely where its howl, even though muted, is explicit and eloquent.⁴⁰ In listening to Paulina's experience of being unheard in Dorfman's play, I push this reflection further by proposing that in torture (and in Paulina's case, being tortured and raped, with rape as a form of torture), it is not only the voice that gets stripped away but also the experience of listening and being listened to—being heard and hearing oneself as believable and truthful. Thus, it is only through their (in)audibility that certain sides of these phenomena can be brought to our attention.⁴¹

"And Do Not Touch Me": Having One's Voice and Listening Colonized

The Maiden:
Pass me by! Oh, pass me by!
Go, fierce man of bones!
I am still young! Go, rather,
And do not touch me.
And do not touch me.
Death:
Give me your hand, you beautiful and tender form!
I am a friend, and come not to punish.
Be of good cheer! I am not fierce,
Softly shall you sleep in my arms!⁴²

Ariel Dorfman's play *Death and the Maiden*, originally written in Spanish and translated by Dorfman himself into English, takes its title from Franz

Schubert's "Der Tod und das Mädchen," a song written in 1817 based on a poem by Mathias Claudius and then turned into a string quartet (no. 14 in D minor), which Schubert composed in 1824 after he suffered a serious illness and realized he was dying. The string quartet is, in a way, Schubert's testament to death, and the lyrics of the original song bear witness to the uncanny experience of death's closeness, made evident by the last two verses of the first stanza, in which the Maiden begs Death "not to touch her."

The issue of touch plays an important role in Dorfman's play, particularly if one considers that the verb *to touch* in Spanish (*tocar*) does not only refer to haptic experiences but also to auditory ones: it is used in the context of *playing* a recorded song aloud, *playing* a musical instrument, and *performing* a musical piece to an audience. As I demonstrate, these connections are central to Paulina's experiences. The historical context of the play is in the aftermath of the dictatorship, and Gerardo, Paulina's husband, has just been appointed by the transitioning government to serve as president of the National Commission for Memory and Reconciliation. Paulina's experiences, and particularly the memories she carries from her torture, are entirely wrapped in the tacit connection between the different meanings of the verb tocar, as she was raped by her torturer, and thus *touched* in the worst imaginable ways, while Schubert's lied *played* in the background. Her recollection of the events is permeated by the perverse combination of the music—repeated over and over from a cassette player—with her torture, rape, and the penetrating voice of her rapist whispered "in her ear."[43]

Dorfman clearly plays with the multiple meanings of the word throughout the script, though this is almost completely lost in the English translation of the play. Thus, in a passage where Paulina has just started to confront her torturer, Dr. Miranda, tying him to a chair to interrogate him, we don't know yet what has happened to her, but the allusions to touch in the passage make it clear right away for a Spanish-speaking audience. She says:

> ¿Sabía que Schubert era homosexual? Pero claro que lo sabe, si fue usted el que me lo repitió una y otra vez, acá en el oído, mientras *me tocaba* justamente "La Muerte y la Doncella." Esta casete que le encontré, ¿es la misma que usted *me tocó*, doctor Miranda, o la va renovando todos los años para que el sonido esté siempre . . . prístino?[44]

> Did you know that Schubert was homosexual? But of course you do, you're the one who kept repeating it over and over again

[into my ear] while you played "Death and the Maiden." Is this the very cassette [you played for me], Doctor, or do you buy a new one every year to keep the sound pure?⁴⁵

This is just the first time we hear about Paulina's rape, though it is not explicit. Her descriptions of her torture throughout the play are always tied to these audible experiences as well as to various forms of silence and silencing.

This is all reinforced by the connection between the play's title and Schubert's Lied, which right away establishes the context for what the play attempts to perform. The play confronts us with that twofold experience regarding Cavarero's attention—and lack of attention—to the (in)audible side of violence: to hear, on the one hand, the voice of death, its presence, its threatening closeness—in this case, presented as a perverse combination of whispered voices, beautiful music turned into the site of horror, and a muted, smothered cry—and to listen, on the other hand, to the voice that comes out of death's encounter, represented in the play most evidently by Paulina, who, we learn quickly, has not yet been and will not get to be heard. The title, therefore, invites the audience before the performance has even started to relate to the play as an acoustic, and not only visual, performance. Further, it asks us to shift our attention from what we see to what we hear.

The script also points right away to the limits of a regime of visibility for approaching the kind of political violence Paulina's character represents. From the first conversation between Paulina and Gerardo, we are told that the National Commission can only attend to the cases of those who have disappeared. Having survived is, therefore, literally an inaudible act, like having one's voice taken away from the site of the trial:

> PAULINA: Tell me who's supposed to listen to my accusations against this doctor, who, Gerardo? [. . .] the members of the Commission only deal with the dead, with those who can't speak. And I can speak [. . .] I'm not dead, I thought I was but I'm not and I can speak, damn it.⁴⁶

The Commission's justice, therefore, is a form of justice that is not willing to listen and does not allow listening to take place. It deals only with those who can no longer speak. The possibilities for recognizing the crime, being listened to, and sharing one's story are denied in the face of a form of justice that is only concerned with political (in)visibility (disappearance), not with political voice and its silencing. For the same reasons, Paulina has "no case," and no "real proof" against her torturer. Since she never got to see him, the only proof she has against him—which is far from "incontrovertible," as her husband immediately points out to her—is the sound of his voice:

> [Gerardo enters the scene, Paulina has Dr. Miranda tied to a chair and is pointing a gun at him.]
>
> GERARDO: Paulina! What is this? What in the name of . . . Roberto . . . Doctor Miranda! *He moves toward Roberto.*
>
> PAULINA: Don't touch him.
>
> GERARDO: What?
>
> PAULINA (*Threatening him with the gun*): Don't touch him.
>
> GERARDO: What the hell is going on here, what kind of madness is—
>
> PAULINA: It's him.
>
> GERARDO: Put . . . put the gun down.
>
> PAULINA: It's him.
>
> GERARDO: Who?
>
> PAULINA: It's the doctor.
>
> GERARDO: What doctor?
>
> PAULINA: The doctor who played Schubert.
>
> GERARDO: The doctor who played Schubert.
>
> PAULINA: That doctor.
>
> GERARDO: How do you know?

PAULINA: The voice.

GERARDO: But weren't you—you told me—what you told me was all through those weeks . . .

PAULINA: Blindfolded, yes. But I could still hear.

GERARDO: You're sick.

PAULINA: I'm not sick.

GERARDO: You're sick.

PAULINA: All right then, I'm sick. But I can be sick and recognize a voice. Besides, when we lose one of our faculties, the others compensate, they get sharper. Right, Doctor Miranda?

GERARDO: A vague memory of someone's voice is not proof of anything, Paulina, it is not incontrovertible—

PAULINA: It's his voice. I recognized it as soon as he came in here last night. The way he laughs. Certain phrases he uses.

GERARDO: But that's not . . .

PAULINA: It may be a teensy-weensy thing, but it's enough for me. During all these years not an hour has passed that I haven't heard it, that same voice, next to me, next to my ear, that voice mixed with saliva, you think I'd forget a voice like his? (*Imitating the voice of Roberto, then of a man.*) "Give her a bit more. This bitch can take a bit more. Give it to her." "You sure, Doctor? What if the cunt dies on us?" "She's not even near fainting. Give it to her, up another notch."[47]

For Paulina, it is almost as if after her torture there was no sound but that voice. Not an hour passes when she does not hear it resonating once and again in her ear. Torture has completely occupied her sensory, and particularly her auditory, experience of the world, and it is described throughout the play not only as the experience of having lost her own voice but also of having lost the ability to "listen to herself speak": "It's been years since I murmured even a word, I haven't opened my mouth to even whisper a breath of what I'm thinking, years living in the terror of my own."[48] This is paradoxically so; even though listening became Paulina's leading sense—it became sharper after being blindfolded for so long—it is also the sense that has been most invaded, colonized, and taken away by her torturer. She is trapped there in that room, blindfolded, her ears filled with the sound of Dr. Miranda's voice, with the music he plays while he rapes her:

> PAULINA: Do you know doctor how long it has been since I listened to this quartet? If it's on the radio, I turn it off, I even try not to go out much, though Gerardo has all these social events he's got to attend [. . .] but I always pray they won't put Schubert. One night we were dining with—they were extremely important people, and our hostess happened to put Schubert on, a piano sonata, and I thought, do I switch it off or do I leave, but my body decided for me, I felt extremely ill right then and there and Gerardo had to take me home, so we left them listening to Schubert and nobody had knew what had made me ill, so I pray they won't play that anywhere I go, any Schubert at all, strange isn't it, when he used to be, and I would say, yes I really would say, he's still my favorite composer, such a sad, noble sense of life.[49]

As is the case with colonizing forms of violence, Paulina is not only silenced but, even further, her voice and her capacity to listen, even to herself, is substituted. As Franz Fanon explains in the context of our psyches being colonized, any attempt to utter one's voice is experienced only as the sound of another's echo.[50] The ventriloquism implicated here is, thus, a very specific form of silencing because the voice is somehow always already too late to find audibility as anything other than the repetition of what silences it. There is no voice and no listening of one's own.

In the play, this goes hand in hand with the emphasis some characters put on the importance, and absence, of memories of the country's past. The trials are meant to bring to light (once again, a justice conceived of in terms of visibility) the "truth" about what happened: "to find truth once and for all" and "to close an exceptionally painful chapter in our history."[51] This is paralleled with Paulina's own execution of a trial, which, rather than seeking to making the truth visible, seeks to produce an *audible recording*—an indexing or historical engraving, as the Spanish word for recorder is the same as the word for engraver—of the story of her torture in the voice of her torturer.

> PAULINA: And you know what conclusion I came to, the only thing I really want? (*Brief pause.*) I want him to confess. I want him to sit in front of that cassette recorder and tell me what he did—not just to me, everything to everybody [. . .] I would keep a copy forever—with all the information, the names and data, and all the details. That's what I want.
>
> GERARDO: He confesses and you let him go.
>
> PAULINA: I let him go.
>
> GERARDO: And you need nothing more from him?
>
> PAULINA: Not a thing.[52]

The confession, Paulina demands, needs to be recorded, and it is in listening to this recording, she says, to the "whole truth" in his own words, that she'll be able to let him go. The recording will be a substitute for the absence of any other record or memory of her story. Through his use of the Spanish word *recordar*, meaning both to remember and to remind, Dorfman seems to be aware of this play on words, which serves to signal an auditory form of memory vis a vis a more traditional conception of memory as visual. In the absence of any other form of remembrance, memory is available to Paulina only as an acoustic experience in which, instead of listening to herself or having others listen to her story, she will have to listen to her story in the voice of her torturer. In the absence of a trial where she can tell her story in her own words, the recording of her torturer's version will be the only available account of her truth. Not only is her listening colonized by her torturer but even her voice is replaced by her torturer's voice in the telling of her story.

In this scene, the play skillfully performs the repetition of Paulina's silencing, replacing her voice with the voices of others and reducing her "narratable self"—going back to Cavarero—to a version told by her perpetrator. Paulina never really gets to speak her truth. Every time she is about to share her testimony, she either interrupts herself or gets interrupted by

Gerardo, who also constantly asks her to "listen" and to "not interrupt."⁵³
The only time we learn about her being raped is in the words of Gerardo:

> PAULINA: Tell me, tell me.
>
> GERARDO: They—tortured you. [. . .]
>
> PAULINA: And what else? What else did they do to me, Gerardo?
>
> GERARDO: They raped you.
>
> PAULINA: How many times?
>
> GERARDO: More than once.
>
> PAULINA: How many times?
>
> GERARDO: You never said. I didn't count, you said.
>
> PAULINA: It's not true.
>
> GERARDO: What's not true?
>
> PAULINA: That I didn't count. I always kept count. I know how many times. (*Brief pause.*) And that night, Gerardo, when I came to you, [. . .] when I started to tell you, what did you swear you'd do to them when you found them? "Someday, my love, we're going to put these bastards on trial. Your eyes will be able to rove"—I remember the exact phrase, because it seemed, poetic—"your eyes will be able to rove over each one of their faces while they listen to your story. We'll do it, you'll see that we will."⁵⁴

We learn then, at that moment, that she has never really told her story, not even to Gerardo, and the only time Paulina is about to tell it to the audience, her voice is replaced by Dr. Miranda's:

> PAULINA: At first, I thought he would save me. He was so soft, so—nice, after what the others had done to me. And then, all

of a sudden, I heard a Schubert quartet. There is no way of describing what it means to hear that wonderful music in the darkness, when you haven't eaten in three days, when your body is falling apart, when . . . (*In the darkness, we hear Roberto's voice overlapping with Paulina's and the second movement of Death and the Maiden.*)

ROBERTO'S VOICE: I would put on the music because it helped me in my role, the role of a good guy, as they call it, I would put on Schubert because it was a way of gaining the prisoners' trust. But I also knew it was a way of alleviating their suffering. You've got to believe it was a way of alleviating the prisoners' suffering. Not only the music, but everything else I did. That's how they approached me, at first. (*The lights go up as if the moon were coming out. It is nighttime. Roberto is in front of the cassette recorder, confessing. The Schubert fades.*)[55]

Paulina, in a way, does get to hear her story told by another. It is a perverse version of the form of relationality Cavarero speaks about in *Relating Narratives*, of course, but its perversity is telling. Paulina's desire to listen to her story can only be satisfied by reproducing the kind of violence that torture has inflicted on her. It is only in the voice of her torturer, the voice that has substituted her own, that she gets to listen to a truth she herself was unwilling to speak up—as we now know—mostly because of a lack of a true listener. However, to hear the truth told by her torturer is also, for Paulina, a way of rendering her experience, her trauma, believable to herself. Roberto's confession is proof, against her husband's constant gaslighting, that Paulina is right: "PAULINA: Gerardo was right in his way. Proof, hard proof—well, I could have been mistaken. But I knew that if you confessed—and when I heard you, my last doubts vanished."[56]

It is at this point in the play that we also realize the version Paulina told in the darkness to Gerardo, that the audience never gets to hear, is not the truth. She has tailored her own testimony, introducing inaccuracies here and there in order to prove that Dr. Miranda is her torturer, trusting that by the time he tells the story—a story that, allegedly, Dr. Miranda is just repeating from Gerardo's recount of Paulina's testimony to him—the doctor will betray himself and tell the story as it is. Only he, then, and not she, gets to tell their story. Furthermore, he does not tell Paulina's story, he tells his own, and that is all that we, the audience as well as Paulina, get to hear. His voice, once again, is the only one resounding—in her ears as much as in ours. To render herself believable, Paulina has to silence her own voice and renounce the possibility of telling her own story. She does get to listen to her story "from the mouth of another," but the experience of listening is the experience of her voice being taken away from her and colonized by her torturer once again.

∽

"They freeze in their positions as the lights begin to go down slowly. We begin to hear music from the last movement of Mozart's Dissonance Quartet."[57] The third act is almost over, and we no longer listen to Schubert but to Mozart—a quartet again. We are left to wonder if perhaps the fourth voice in the play, the one that we never get to hear, is Paulina's. A mirror descends, taking her and the doctor out of sight and putting the audience instead face to face with themselves. The mirror, like a visual metaphor for resonance,[58] does the opposite of opening a site for listening: it bounces the audience's reflection back at them, disconnecting them once again from the chance to listen to Paulina. Like Perseus's mirror, we are deviated from Paulina's look, her dismembered voice, and the unsustainable pain she carries with her. Once again, Paulina has been smothered. Her voice, like Medusa's, has been severed from her body and her listening, once again, has been taken away from her.

Afterword

In "Narrative against Destruction" Cavarero speaks of Arendt's emphasis on storytelling in the context of listening to the testimonies coming out of the concentration camps as an awareness of "the necessity of a new literary genre to narrate the lives lost in the horror of extermination."[59] This new genre would have to be a kind of narrative able to preserve and communicate the reluctance of the witness to speak: a "narrative style" able to convey what resists coming to words *as* resistance or, in Cavarero's words, to "account for this resistance effectively."[60] The narrative, therefore, should be able to fulfill a twofold task: "on the one hand, to preserve the unspeakable horror of the perpetrated destruction that, precisely because of its excess, risks escaping the tangles of history as the storybook of mankind. On the other hand, [. . .] to recover individual stories from silence, stories that otherwise would risk remaining meaningless."[61] What I have tried to do thus far is to take Cavarero's reflections further, asking about the conditions of possibility for such a narrative. More precisely, I ask about the kind of listening that would be able to approach this "unspeakable horror" not only in terms of visibility—its unbearable sight, as Cavarero often describes it—but also by hearing the sound of its multiple silences. This means understanding the depths of the destruction brought about by traumatic forms of violence and the loss that pervades the surviving body in its audible/inaudible character. It also means understanding violence as the destruction and silencing of the voice and of the very possibility of listening that challenges us from the site of trauma.

How, then, are we to offer a form of listening able to preserve the unspeakability of violence while providing a space where it can become audible? It seems that only if we insist on truly shifting our attention to a regime of the audible and, thus, to producing grammars that allow the unheard and unheard-of to resound and be listened to can the voice be "stolen from silence," even though the horror and its inexplicability, "its laceration and excess," will always remain. But "rather than being forgotten, and therefore erased," Cavarero writes, "the inexplicability of the horror, its excesses compared to the limits of language, remains consequently there; that is, it does not get resolved in a frame that articulates it or explains it. Actually, it is preserved in the life stories that hold its trace. Rather than being forgotten, and therefore erased, inexplicability thereby assumes a different intensity that interrogates us even more categorically."[62] It is precisely by intensifying listening that I have tried to bring Dorfman's play to the fore in tension and in dialogue with Cavarero's work, not as an explication or definition of the kind of violence implicated in the destruction and colonization of the voice but rather as an attempt to tune our ears to the voices that resonate out of sites of destruction.

Now, one further clarification is required before ending this chapter. As I mentioned at the beginning of this essay, the emphasis of my contribution is to inquire about the importance and limitations of Cavarero's turn toward the audible. My intention has been to bring to our attention the aesthetics at play in Cavarero's conception of the political and the relevance of this approach for the kinds of critique of violence she proposes to develop in her work. This means I have mostly focused on the destructive and colonizing aspects of the kinds of violence Cavarero refers to with her notion of hororism. I have also added to her questions the question of sexual violence as one particularly worthy of attention because of the consequences it has on that ontological uniqueness that Cavarero relates to the human voice: the voice that is the body and the body that is the voice.

There is, however, a whole other side of these questions that has to do with the power of resistance and the subversive, decolonizing strategies that can be—and are, in fact—given shape to in the face of violence's attempts to silence, smother, and erase every trace of its effects. As I've argued, violence has colonizing effects on not only the body and the voice but also on the aesthetic and epistemic conditions of possibility that allow the body to be voiced and the inaudible to be listened to. Rosaura Martínez describes the upheaval effects, namely in the context of the healing possibilities opened up by listening, as "the inauguration of the unexpected as resistance to destiny."[63] Thus, while in my reading of Dorfman the character of Paulina is represented mostly as a victim, as a colonized voice and self, she represents another very important aspect. Her silence is not only a disempowering effect of trauma, but it is also her power: power to exercise resistance in the face of terror; to defy torture and never give up the name of her lover; to survive, remember, and reclaim a space for herself, even if only in the form of an echo, in a world where everyone around her denies her the chance to be heard.[64]

Paulina's voice may resound to us only as an echo, but as Cavarero has pointed out regarding the mythological character that bears this very same name, Echo may have been entirely robbed of her own voice, but she became, on the other hand, the very site of resonance, reclaiming her voice through the same repetition that had stolen it from her.[65] Through a process that liberates voice from speech and communicability from communication, Echo is a figure for the kind of relationality that the uniqueness of the voice ultimately inaugurates: a relationality in which what counts is not what is said but the fact that every voice, as Cavarero puts it, is always already summoning another's. "This rhythm (of repetition, as in the case of Echo) confirms that each voice, as it is *for* the ear, demands at the same time an ear that is *for* the voice."[66] Cavarero concludes, "Echo comes to appear as the divinity who teaches an acoustic relationality [. . .] in which uniqueness makes itself be heard as voice."[67]

The last scene of Dorfman's play may also attempt to turn a stolen voice into a site of resonance and, thus, into a radical demand for the acoustic relationality that Echo, interpreted according to Cavarero, teaches us about. The mirror is still down, still facing the audience, and Paulina sits next to Gerardo in a concert hall. The lights come down, and "Death and the Maiden" starts playing in the background. Through the mirror, we see Paulina listening to the music while she meets the gaze of Dr. Miranda, who is sitting elsewhere on the stage. The script specifies it is unclear whether he is actually there or being imagined by Paulina. "*After a few instants, she turns slowly and looks at Roberto. Their eyes interlock for a moment, then she turns her head and faces the stage and the mirror. The lights go down while the music plays and plays and plays.*" Paulina may not have recovered her voice, but she has reclaimed her listening, and the resonance of this reclaiming is made visible to us through her repeated (echoed) image in the mirror. This image, which we are meant not only to see but also to let resonate in its repetitive echoes, is therefore not just a visual metaphor but also the grammar of a listening that can happen only in and as repetition: one that, as such, subverts the silence imposed on it by having been turned into a mere echo of someone else's voice.

Notes

1. This chapter is based on a lecture I first gave at the fourth Workshop on Violence and Literature, *Violence Incorporated*, hosted by Eric Santner and myself at the Franke Institute of the Humanities at the University of Chicago and co-organized with Ilit Ferber, Adam Lipszyc, and Nassima Sahraoui on March 23 and 24, 2018. I presented it again in the context of Fanny Söderbäck's graduate seminar on Cavarero at DePaul University during the fall of 2018. I thank all the participants of both the workshop and the seminar for their insightful comments and various follow-up engagements with my work. The essay was published in a previous and somewhat different version in Spanish: "Perder la voz propia: De una fenomenología feminista de la voz a una aproximación a la violencia política desde la escucha," in *Fuera de sí mismas: Motivos para dislocarse*, trans. Juan Diego Pérez, ed. Luciana Cadahia and Ana Carrasco, 121–56 (Madrid: Herder, 2020).

2. For the purposes of this paper, I will presuppose rather than explicitly address the body of literature that has been produced more recently around what Miranda Fricker originally coined as "testimonial and hermeneutic injustices" in *Epistemic Injustice: Power and the Ethics of Knowing* (Oxford: Oxford University Press, 2007). I am particularly interested in the development of these notions in connection to what Kristi Dotson calls epistemic violence, and more specifically, epistemic silencing and smothering ("Tracking Epistemic Violence, Tracking Practices of Silencing," *Hypatia* 26, no. 2 [2011]: 236–57) and what José Medina has worked out as the political and social aspects of hermeneutical injustice ("Hermeneutical Injustice and Polyphonic Contextualism: Social Silences and Shared Hermeneutical Responsibilities," *Social Epistemology* 26, no. 2 [2012]: 201–20). I am, however, interested in adding to this body of literature questions about what kind of listening is required in cases of traumatic violence, the specific forms of epistemic and aesthetic silencing that need to be brought to light and confronted in such cases,

as well as the specific forms of responsibility and "hermeneutical virtues" that are demanded by them. In the context of this paper, I also want to stage a dialogue between this set of questions and Cavarero's work.

    3. It could be Pinochet's dictatorship in Chile, but the play explicitly omits the specificities to let the play speak about experiences beyond geographies.

    4. On the conceptual connections between what I am calling traumatic forms of violence and their colonizing effects, see María del Rosario Acosta López, "Gramáticas de la escucha como gramáticas descoloniales: Apuntes para una descolonización de la memoria," *Eidos* 34 (2020): 14–40; and "From Aesthetics as Critique to Grammars of Listening: On Reconfiguring Sensibility as a Political Project," *Journal of World Philosophies* 6 (2021): 139–56.

    5. Adriana Cavarero, *Relating Narratives: Storytelling and Selfhood* (New York: Routledge, 2000), 23.

    6. Cavarero, *Relating Narratives*, 34.

    7. Cavarero, *Relating Narratives*, 34.

    8. Cavarero, *Relating Narratives*, 85.

    9. In Spanish the expression for listening to someone attentively is literally a form of care: "poner *cuidado*."

    10. Cavarero, *Relating Narratives*, 60.

    11. Cavarero, *Relating Narratives*, 100 (emphasis added).

    12. Adriana Cavarero, "The Vocal Body," *Qui parle* 21, no. 1 (2012): 81.

    13. Cavarero, "The Vocal Body," 81.

    14. Cavarero, "The Vocal Body," 71.

    15. Cavarero, "The Vocal Body," 71.

    16. Cavarero, "The Vocal Body," 72.

    17. Cavarero, "The Vocal Body," 75.

    18. Cavarero, "The Vocal Body," 81.

    19. Cavarero, "The Vocal Body," 78.

    20. Adriana Cavarero, *Stately Bodies: Literature, Philosophy, and the Question of Gender* (Ann Arbor: University of Michigan Press, 2002).

    21. Cavarero, "The Vocal Body," 79.

    22. Adriana Cavarero, *Horrorism: Naming Contemporary Violence* (New York: Columbia University Press, 2009), 29.

    23. I owe this insightful realization about Cavarero's silence regarding this issue to Aurora Laybourn-Candlish's "Cavarero's Repugnance: Naming Sexual Violence," shared in the context of Fanny Söderbäck's seminar on Cavarero at DePaul University in 2018. For other ways of addressing the question of sexual violence in Cavarero's work, see Söderbäck's contribution in this volume: "Sexual Violence as Ontological Violence: Narration, Selfhood, and the Destruction of Singularity."

    24. Cavarero, *Horrorism*, 17.

    25. Cavarero, *Horrorism*, 17.

    26. Cavarero, *Horrorism*, 17.

27. Cavarero, *Horrorism*, 16.
28. Cavarero, *Horrorism*, 18 (emphasis added).
29. Cavarero, *Horrorism*, 18.
30. Cf. Acosta López, "From Aesthetics as Critique to Grammars of Listening," 145. Also, on the indigestible in Cavarero, the importance it plays for her assessment of the violence against the body, and political violence as the reduction of the body to the political, see Paula Landerreche Cardillo, "'Her Organs Were a Question of the State': Reading Adriana Cavarero in the Latin American Postcolony" (PhD diss., DePaul University, 2023).
31. Primo Levi, *The Drowned and the Saved* (London: Abacus, 1989), 84. Quoted in Cavarero, *Horrorism*, 34. Cavarero goes back to this quote again to develop a somewhat similar interpretation in a more recent essay: "'Destroy Your Sight with a New Gorgon': Mass Atrocity and the Phenomenology of Horror," in *Emotions and Mass Atrocity: Philosophical and Theoretical Explorations*, ed. Thomas Brudholm and Johannes Lang (Cambridge: Cambridge University Press, 2018), 123–41.
32. Cavarero, "Destroy Your Sight with a New Gorgon," 135.
33. Cavarero, *Horrorism*, 8.
34. Cavarero, *Horrorism*, 15.
35. Cavarero, *Horrorism*, 15.
36. Cavarero, *Horrorism*, 16.
37. Cavarero, *Horrorism*, 11.
38. Cavarero, *Horrorism*, 8.
39. Cavarero, *Horrorism*, 31.
40. I take Söderbäck to also suggest something of this sort in her essay "Sexual Violence as Ontological Violence." It might be precisely because Cavarero is not radically questioning—but rather being complicit in—certain forms of silencing in the aftermath of sexual violence that the subject does not come up in *Horrorism*, even though it would seem that sexual violence is precisely one of those forms of violence that embodies everything Cavarero is attempting to think through this concept.
41. I only refer to Dorfman's play to develop this point. However, I truly understand the depth of this issue; I was able to hear it in Dorfman's text and later also in my own experience with trauma and sexual violence working with survivors of police torture in the South Side of Chicago and at the Chicago Torture Justice Center. It was in listening to their experiences about losing both their voices and the possibility for communicating about their voicelessness—deprived of the possibility to hear themselves narrate the events in their own voices and being heard and believed as truthful—that I have come to better understand this "acoustic" side of torture and, thus, the acoustic side of this kind of violence. I am particularly thankful to Gregory Banks, Darrell Canon, Ollie Hammonds, and Anthony Holmes for opening up, being willing to share their stories, and bravely fighting for the right to be listened to on their own terms.

42. Franz Schubert, based on a poem by Mathias Claudius. The original in German: *Das Mädchen*: Vorüber! Ach, vorüber! / Geh, wilder Knochenmann! / Ich bin noch jung! Geh, lieber, / Und rühre mich nicht an. / Und rühre mich nicht an. *Der Tod*: Gib deine Hand, du schön und zart Gebild! / Bin Freund, und komme nicht, zu strafen. / Sei gutes Muts! ich bin nicht wild, / Sollst sanft in meinen Armen schlafen!

43. Ariel Dorfman, *La muerte y la doncella* (New York: Siete Cuentos, 1992), 35.
44. Dorfman, *La muerte y la doncella*, 35 (emphasis added).
45. Ariel Dorfman, *Death and the Maiden* (New York: Penguin, 1992), 22. The additions in square brackets are retranslations of the Spanish, lost in English, which reinforce the allusions to the touching that took place while Schubert's music played in the background.
46. Dorfman, *Death and the Maiden*, 37.
47. Dorfman, *Death and the Maiden*, 22–23.
48. Dorfman, *Death and the Maiden*, 37.
49. Dorfman, *Death and the Maiden*, 21.
50. See, particularly, David Marriott's interpretation of Fanon in "Blackness: N'est Pas," *Propter Nos* 4 (2020): 27. I have also shown elsewhere how the ways in which trauma colonizes its survivors are connected to the ways in which coloniality has historically perpetrated an epistemic and aesthetic form of violence on the colonized. I do not have the space to develop this here. Cf. María del Rosario Acosta López, "Gramáticas de lo inaudito as Decolonial Grammars: Notes for a Decolonization of Memory," *Research in Phenomenology* 52, no. 2 (2022): 203–22; and my forthcoming book, *Gramáticas de la escucha* (Barcelona: Herder, 2024).
51. Dorfman, *Death and the Maiden*, 14–15.
52. Dorfman, *Death and the Maiden*, 41.
53. See, for instance, Dorfman, *Death and the Maiden*, 30–31.
54. Dorfman, *Death and the Maiden*, 30–31.
55. Dorfman, *Death and the Maiden*, 58.
56. Dorfman, *Death and the Maiden*, 63.
57. Dorfman, *Death and the Maiden*, 66.
58. I owe this insight to Elena Cardona.
59. Adriana Cavarero, "Narrative against Destruction," *New Literary History* 46 (2015): 5.
60. Cavarero, "Narrative against Destruction," 7.
61. Cavarero, "Narrative against Destruction," 7.
62. Cavarero, "Narrative against Destruction," 7.
63. Rosaura Martínez, "Justicia social y psicoanálisis: Escucharme a través de la voz del otro," in *Fuera de sí mismas: Motivos para dislocarse*, ed. Luciana Cadahia and Ana Carrasco (Madrid: Herder, 2020), 159. Martínez's text is a commentary on the Spanish version of this paper—I thank her for more explicitly bringing out the connections between my reading of Cavarero and a political approach to trauma studies.

64. I thank Adelaida Barrera for pointing this out to me in her very insightful reading of a previous version of this paper presented at the Universidad de los Andes in the fall of 2018.
65. Cavarero, *For More than One Voice*, 165–72.
66. Cavarero, *For More than One Voice*, 170.
67. Cavarero, *For More than One Voice*, 172.

Bibliography

Acosta López, María del Rosario. "From Aesthetics as Critique to Grammars of Listening: On Reconfiguring Sensibility as a Political Project." *Journal of World Philosophies* 6 (2021): 139–156.

———. *Gramáticas de la escucha*. Madrid: Herder, Forthcoming 2024.

———. "Gramáticas de la escucha como gramáticas descoloniales: Apuntes para una descolonización de la memoria." *Eidos* 34 (2020): 14–40.

———. "Gramáticas de lo inaudito as Decolonial Grammars: Notes for a Decolonization of Memory," *Research in Phenomenology* 52, no. 2 (2022): 203–22.

———. "Perder la voz propia: De una fenomenología feminista de la voz a una aproximación a la violencia política desde la escucha." In *Fuera de sí mismas: Motivos para dislocarse*, edited by Luciana Cadahia and Ana Carrasco, 121–56. Madrid: Herder, 2020.

Cavarero, Adriana. "'Destroy Your Sight with a New Gorgon': Mass Atrocity and the Phenomenology of Horror." In *Emotions and Mass Atrocity: Philosophical and Theoretical Explorations*, edited by Thomas Brudholm and Johannes Lang, 123–41. Cambridge: Cambridge University Press, 2018.

———. *For More than One Voice: Towards a Philosophy of Vocal Expression*. Stanford, CA: Stanford University Press, 2005.

———. "Narrative Against Destruction," *New Literary History*, vol. 46 (2015): 1–16.

———. *Relating Narratives: Storytelling and Selfhood*. New York: Routledge, 2000.

———. *Stately Bodies: Literature, Philosophy, and the Question of Gender*. Ann Arbor: University of Michigan Press, 2002.

———. "The Vocal Body." *Qui parle* 21, no. 1 (2012): 71–83.

Dorfman, Ariel. *Death and the Maiden*. New York: Penguin, 1992.

———. *La muerte y la doncella*. New York: Siete Cuentos, 1992.

Dotson, Kristi. "Tracking Epistemic Violence, Tracking Practices of Silencing." *Hypatia* 26, no. 2 (2011): 236–57.

Landerreche Cardillo, Paula. "'Her Organs Were a Question of the State': Reading Adriana Cavarero in the Latin American Postcolony." PhD diss., DePaul University, 2023.

Laybourn-Candlish, Aurora. "Cavarero's Repugnance: Naming Sexual Violence." Unpublished paper shared with Fanny Söderbäck's seminar, DePaul University, 2018.

Levi, Primo. *The Drowned and the Saved*. London: Abacus, 1989.
Marriott, David. "Blackness: N'est Pas." *Propter Nos* 4 (2020), 27–51.
Martínez, Rosaura. "Justicia social y psicoanálisis: Escucharme a través de la voz del otro." In *Fuera de sí mismas: Motivos para dislocarse*, edited by Luciana Cadahia and Ana Carrasco, 156–61. Madrid: Herder, 2020.
Medina, José. "Hermeneutical Injustice and Polyphonic Contextualism: Social Silences and Shared Hermeneutical Responsibilities." *Social Epistemology* 26, no. 2 (2012): 201–20.
Söderbäck, Fanny. "Sexual Violence as Ontological Violence: Narration, Selfhood, and the Destruction of Singularity." In *Political Bodies: Writings on Adriana Cavarero's Political Thought*, edited by Paula Landerreche Cardillo and Rachel Silverbloom, 211–235. Albany: State University of New York Press, 2024.

Part Five

Uncanny Bodies

Eleven

Elena Ferrante and the Uncanny of Motherhood

Adriana Cavarero

The extraordinary success of Elena Ferrante's novels—in Italy and beyond—has by now given rise to a vast range of studies, both literary and philosophical, on her works. This is testified, throughout several articles and essays, by the insightful monographs recently published by Tiziana De Rogatis, Isabella Pinto, Stiliana Milkova, and Alessia Ricciardi—texts that include a vast critical bibliography confirming the "Ferrante-fever" among the international intellectual community.[1] Of particular interest, according to many interpreters, is the way in which Ferrante treats the question of motherhood, not only because, as Jacqueline Rose has pointed out, "her lack of inhibition on the subject of mothers plays a decisive part in her extraordinary success" but also because "motherhood is the irreducible core of her fiction."[2] Ferrante herself observes in *Frantumaglia* that "the literary truth of motherhood is yet to be explored"; "the task of a woman writer today is not to stop at the pleasure of the pregnant body, of birth, of bringing up children, but to delve truthfully into the darkest depth."[3] More precisely, she claims, "it's also essential to describe the dark side of the pregnant body, which is omitted in order to bring out the luminous side, the Mother of God."[4] Here, Ferrante lays out the juxtaposition between obscurity and light—that is, between the darkness of that which is yet to be explored and the light emitted by the banality of stereotypes—in very clear terms. The side of motherhood her writing engages with is obscure, according to Ferrante, because it touches on the generative process of the living matter that pulses within the maternal body in the depths of both flesh and psyche. But obscure—or better still, obscured—is this field of exploration because the image of the Mother of God, of Mary and baby Jesus as a representation of a happy, self-sacrificing mother possesses a blinding luminosity, one which drags all idyllic representations of motherhood into its cone of light and pushes the female experiences of the pregnant body, giving birth and—not least—the mother-daughter relation, into the shadows. The image of Mary and baby Jesus—an icon that great artists have made familiar to the whole world, far beyond the Christian universe—is notoriously one of the most symbolically powerful cultural images celebrating the relation between mother and son, relegating the relation between mother and daughter to the shadows. It is not by accident that Ferrante, in emphasizing that her writing attempts to tell the literary truth of motherhood, claims that "the mother-daughter relationship is a central issue in my books"; "I think I haven't written about anything else."[5] There is an essential connection in Ferrante's texts—first and foremost in *Troubling Love* and in *The Lost Daughter*—between the tasks of rendering in words the literary truth of the obscure side of motherhood and recounting the relation between mother and daughter. What unites these tasks—and indeed makes them inseparable—is first of all the presence of that which Ferrante herself calls the *tremendo*, a term rendered in the English translations of her books as "formidable," "tremendous," or "awesome" but which is probably much closer to the semantic field of the "uncanny." Although hers is a pen name and we ignore who she is, we know from her essays that Ferrante has a background in classics and declares her love for Sophocles. The uncanniness of which she speaks cannot but evoke the Greek word *deinon* (δεινόν), a term that is almost impossible to translate; the concept refers to something scary and disorientating, at the very limit of the utterable. The broad philosophical reflection on the *deinon* that lies at the heart of the famous chorus of Sophocles's *Antigone* is well-known. In the twentieth century, philosophers starting with Heidegger used the German word *unheimlich* in an effort to name what, although congenial to the human, upsets and questions precisely the most familiar features of the human itself. As Ferrante suggests, exploring the darkest side of motherhood and the mother-daughter relationship means investigating precisely that uncanny knot in which this side and this relationship make contact, latching onto each other. Or, to put it in a seemingly more philosophical way: if birth as a coming into the world is the origin, there too the mother-daughter relationship finds its origin; if birth from the body of woman is the worldly appearance of the singular being as incarnated uniqueness, then it is there too, immersed within the infinite chain of generating mothers, that the relational singularity of the daughter, rather than that of the son, finds its own source. This means—and this is the crucial aspect, philosophically speaking—that the subjectivity which emerges from Ferrante's pages on motherhood is, *ab origine*, characterized by an imbalanced, complex, and constitutive relationality, an *uncanny* one that stands in direct contrast to the celebrated paradigm of the autopoietic and self-sufficient subject of individualist ontology.

In *The Days of Abandonment*, Ferrante claims that to write "is to speak from the depth of the maternal womb."[6] We might say that all of her writing, including the expressive style of her storytelling, bears witness to the fact that "speaking from the womb" is not, for her, to be understood merely as a metaphor. "In literary fiction," she claims, "you have to be sincere to the point where it's unbearable."[7] Filling words with truth so that the narrative becomes true in itself rather than banally imbued with verisimilitude (and thus, habitual, comfortable) means, for her, becoming aware that the maternal womb is the place of origin for our embodied singularity, a place that takes the form of the division *from* the female other and *within* the female other: "that sort of original fragmentation that is bringing into the world—coming into the world. I mean feeling oneself a mother at the price of getting rid of a living fragment of one's body," "I mean feeling oneself a daughter as a fragment of a whole and incomparable body."[8] A son is also, clearly, such a fragment. Every human being, as somebody born from a mother, is such a fragment. But the male body does not inscribe itself into the genealogy of the singular living organism: that infinite chain of mothers that experiences origin as a division and displays how the relational form is indispensable. To steal an expression from Hannah Arendt, we might for expediency's sake describe this relation as "two-in-one" without forgetting, however—as Arendt tended to—that this is a primary relation made from splitting the living organism, pulsating flesh, mind, and body of a singular being in order to put another singular being into the world, thus breaking itself apart.

The *truth* is always a suspicious term in philosophy, and to get philosophically closer to Ferrante's literary truth about maternity is no easy undertaking. On the other hand, there is little difficulty—in light of the decades-long, vast feminist critique of the patriarchal symbolic order—in accepting her initial invitation "to see ourselves outside the tradition through which men have viewed, represented, valued, and cataloged us—for millennia."[9] Yet, smoothing out the narrative knots that Ferrante uses to tie the concept of the uncanny to motherhood presents a far greater challenge. At the center of the narrative plot, we find her belief that the experience of the pregnant body brings us not only very close to our animal nature—to the animality of the human being as such—but beyond, to our being organisms of a larger and more general living matter, which, precisely in the acts of pregnancy, birth, and childcare, manifests some of its own processes. Ferrante stresses that typical "female attraction-repulsion toward the animal world and hence toward the animal nature of our bodies" that puts us in touch "with the living material, to where language becomes reticent and leaves a space, enclosed between obscenity and scientific terminology, where everything can happen."[10] Symptomatically, language pulls back, and the mediation of words proves weak when faced with this feminine, bodily experience of living matter pulsing through one's veins: the perception of the pregnant woman—or the woman in labor—of the "instability of the forms assumed by life" within the dark scenery of the original fragmentation.[11] Motherhood is tremendo, first of all, because it brings an embodied uniqueness, a stable form of life that is a singular organism—in other words, an individual self—to face the impersonal process of infinite life that its body is carrying out. Tremendo, repulsive but at the same time attractive, is being two-in-one in the original process of splitting and generating. Tried and tested for describing motherhood according to the traditional canon, language does not have words for this dark, uncanny side; it struggles to express "that tangle of veins, blood, liquids, flesh that is our body" when the pregnant woman feels inside her that living matter's rhythm—which, generating, regenerates itself.[12] This also explains why, for Ferrante, the task of the writing woman today is, above all, to speak about the darkest side of motherhood: to write from the maternal womb. But this also explains why the story, the fiction novel, might be more suitable to this task than traditional philosophical work. In fact, the gymnasium of the philosophical tradition in which the work of the concept has been trained is too abstract and, anyhow, totally ignorant of female bodily experience. Philosophy is too engaged in modulating the problem of origin by asking questions about "being" rather than "nothingness" than to turn its attention to the maternal body—an incarnated singularity which, by fragmenting itself, generates another incarnated singularity—where the origin of someone, of everyone, takes place. Where the origin of everyone, far from being a speculative category, is a distinct beginning.[13] Ferrante, thus, justly counts the power of "a story that tends toward truth by pushing stylizations to their limit."[14] In other words, as we read in *Frantumaglia*, she decides to engage in "telling the truth as only literary fiction allows one to."[15]

Crucially, Ferrante revealed in an interview that she has been greatly assisted in her writing by *The Passion According to G. H.* by Clarice Lispector—a book she defines as "extraordinary."[16] Lispector's text recounts a day in the life of a woman from the Brazilian bourgeoisie who, without leaving her comfortable apartment, nevertheless exits from the stable form of her "organized" ego by melting into the cosmic, primal dimension of "an infinite piece of meat," the "forbidden fabric of life," "the hell of living matter": "raw life."[17] The protagonist of the book—which truly is extraordinary and challenging—undergoes an itinerary of passions, at times very mystical and religious, that brings her to understand the transformation of organic material in the female body as illimitable and ineffable life, allowing her to feel the workings of a metamorphic cycle in which "matter vibrates with attention, vibrates with process, vibrates with inherent present time."[18] The landing point of this itinerary of passion, which passes symptomatically through a communion with animality—symbolized in the text by a repulsive cockroach—is the vision of the immense, vibrating matter of which everything that individually lives is only a temporary expression—an "unstable form," Ferrante might say—within a darker, swarming reality of raw, unlimited life. Lispector writes: "I saw, and I was frightened by the brute truth of a world whose greatest horror is that it is so alive that, in admitting I am as alive as it is—and my worst discovery is that I am as alive as it is—I shall have to heighten my consciousness of exterior life until it becomes a crime against my personal life."[19] It is because of the "terror of remaining undelimited," Lispector insists, that G. H. "succumbs to the need for form."[20] As an organized system, the delimited personal life—the self—fears contact with the limitlessness of the immense and impersonal living matter of which it is a temporary expression. It fears the threshold between the singularity of the self and the swarming sea of infinite life, "the terrible general nature."[21] This threshold can obviously be identified with the moment of death, the dissolution of the self into undelimited living matter, but in Lispector, significantly, this threshold instead evokes birth. For her, the female body experiences such a threshold as an animal body "of great moist depths," in which life itself procreates through the "fifteen million daughters" that the great chain of mothers has put into the world.[22] The maternal body—site of moist depths, generative flesh—understands the tremendo through the original fragmentation that allows organic matter to regenerate in singular forms of life. In other words, motherhood goes to the very roots, the generative core "of matter that is the indifferent explosion of itself"; the "matter of the body precedes the body" because is it, above all, the pregnant body in its own generative flesh that experiences the uncanny—Lispector says the horror—of the threshold between living singularity and infinite life.[23] In this sense, motherhood is the site of relation in which the "vibrating" female body reveals how the human being, precisely in the phase of gestation and in the moment of birth, is inserted into an infinite and non-human cycle of regeneration. There is a non-human—if not inhumane—character to this contact with "an existence satisfied with its own process, deeply occupied with no more than its own process, and the process vibrates entirely."[24]

Tellingly, G. H.'s decisive step in her journey toward the horror of raw, undelimited matter is her meeting with a cockroach, whose body she crushes with a cupboard door, forcing forth a thick and disgusting fluid from the insect's body. Here, we are confronted with the disgust and repulsion that the self, as a singular and delimited form of life, feels in front of that unlimited and undifferentiated living matter that Lispector also calls "neutral" and "inexpressive." For human beings, repugnance arises from the site where the borders containing a single form disintegrate, where living matter exposes its impersonal, indifferent process, exhibited in the thick plasma that issues from the cockroach's body—the very same plasma we are made of. Language that attempts to describe the experience of the tremendo must, above all, deal with this repugnance and disgust for the disintegration of borders and margins that ensure a stable form of life for the self, even though this form, as Lispector writes, this bounded ego is nothing other than an "accretion" of the impersonal plasma of life.[25] It is no accident that Lispector insists on using the word *horror*, underlining that the uncanny nature of this horror exceeds the word as such; in describing this form of horror she ought "to translate the unknown into a language I don't speak."[26] As I argued in my own book *Horrorism*, one of the characteristics of the phenomenology of horror—and of the feelings of disgust that horror provokes—is precisely disfigurement: the dismembering of the singular body as a delimited, bounded form.[27] In this sense, horror and the tremendo are two attempts at naming the same ineffable feeling of repulsion.

As I have noted, there are pronounced mystical and religious tones in Lispector's *The Passion According to G. H.*, which Ferrante symptomatically does not reprise. Clearly, that which interests her is recounting the literary truth of the tremendo, recounting the darkest side of motherhood and the relation of mother and daughter that tradition has either ignored or covered up with edifying imagery. In Ferrante's descriptions of motherhood there is, in truth, very little of the edifying luminosity of the Mother of God or the good mother. Her texts "challenge the socially and religiously constructed stereotypes of the nurturing, self-abnegating, and asexual mother."[28] It is worth reiterating that her portrayals of maternity are dominated by repulsion as the essential experience of the uncanny. We find this in her novel *The Lost Daughter*, whose protagonist Leda, a wrongdoing mother who once abandoned her daughters, thus describes her second pregnancy: The creature I was carrying in my womb "attacked my body, forcing it to turn on itself, out of control [. . .] My body became a bloody liquid: suspended in it was a mushy sediment inside which grew a violent polyp, so far from anything human that it reduced me, even though it fed and grew, to rotting matter without life."[29] The theater of origins, the site of beginning, "that sort of original fragmentation that is bringing into the world—coming into the world"—summons "the blind cruelty of living matter as it expands."[30] At stake is not simply suffering, or a difficult pregnancy, or the pain of giving birth but an encounter with the knot of the tremendo, in which singular forms of life and living matter are entangled. Here, the limitlessness of which Lispector writes becomes darker and more terrifying because it definitively concerns the internal threshold: the womb. Ferrante often uses the term *smarginatura* (the dissolution of margins) to describe a phenomenon that—in the specific instance of motherhood—represents breaking apart one organism's boundaries into another's and, at the same time, into the blind matter that shudders within the vital drive toward regeneration.

I must stress that there are no mystical accents in Ferrante's writing on motherhood as an experience of the dissolution of margins internal to the singular body touching the impersonal swarm of life, nor are there vitalist tones. Indeed, far from being vitalistic, her vision is one which we have good reason for describing as materialistic. Rather than focusing on the vital process as effervescence or creative energy, Ferrante's attention falls on the attractive/repulsive core of the tremendo that characterizes motherhood as a material and fleshly site of origins where individual organisms come into the world: a single form of existence at the beginning, the very beginning, of everybody's life. If death is the dissolution of the singular form into general, pulsing life matter, birth is instead the splitting *of* and *within* the maternal body, where the labor of organic life generates another living, singular—indeed, unique—being. The darkest side of motherhood does not relate to scientific knowledge of the biological process of generation; today's science has no more mysteries to motherhood, for technology has rendered it fully visible. It relates instead to the maternal experience—the intimate, visceral experience—of the two-in-one, splitting apart the singular flesh, and germination within a singular form of life, which canonical representations of motherhood (as evidenced by the blinding luminosity of the Mother of God) leave in the shadows and condemn to invisibility and ineffability. To speak of origin—a task that philosophy has always assumed but to which it has mostly replied with abstractions—means precisely to speak of the uncanny of motherhood: that which in Ferrante's feminine writing, as in Lispector's, is eventually put into words. It is not only that everybody is born from a mother and thus is born from within this relation, but it is also that a constitutive relation with an other of the feminine sex lies at the origin of everybody who comes into the world. This relation is rooted in the bowels of the maternal body and, summoning the organic process of living matter, is as originary as the germination of the singular form of life. Ferrante not only engages in telling the literary truth that pertains to this theater of the uncanny, to this site of beginning, but she also pushes her narration to speak of pregnant women who—as in the case of Lila in the Neapolitan Quartet—put up resistance, more or less spontaneously aborting their pregnancies. It is again interesting to cite Lispector here; in *The Passion* she tells us how the protagonist had chosen to have an abortion in the past because during her pregnancy, "the pores of a child were devouring like the mouth of a waiting fish."[31] "Pregnancy: I had been flung into the happy horror of the neutral life that lives and moves," she writes.[32] There are no moralistic tones here, no regret or repentance in relation to the choice of an abortion. Like Ferrante after her, Lispector instead stresses an experience of the uncanny that can even seem intolerable due to its disgusting, repugnant nature, up to the point that the body itself—the singular flesh that touches the very workings of the infinite flesh—sometimes spontaneously refuses it. Put another way: the dark side of motherhood addresses the truth of that experience of procreation in which a human being—fragmenting its singular flesh into another singular flesh—is forced into knowing the impersonal nature of the living matter that constitutes both its substance and origin; it is forced to taste the disgusting, bodily, and psychic depths of the dissolution of margins. An exclusively female phenomenon, pregnancy allows women to understand an essential "truth" of the human condition that the other sex's integral body is not permitted to experience. Furthermore, it is precisely this specifically female experience that displays the essential bond between mother and daughter, even if the daughter will never herself be pregnant and may never herself give birth. In fact, while the son is excluded from the bodily experience of the uncanny, in terms of origin and beginning, the female body is always a potentially generative one. It is the body in which human life takes its millions of unique, irreplaceable singular forms through the "fifteen million daughters" to which the great chain of mothers has given birth.

Mother and daughter share a generating body, we might even say a potential to face the uncanny of origins within the vibrations of vital matter that works within their womb. As Ferrante does not fail to remind us, menstrual blood is part and parcel of these workings. For women, the dark side of motherhood is already there in adolescence. In other words, the female body—precisely in its incarnate singularity—is connected to origin and beginning long before the act of procreation, even if a woman decides not to procreate. This ought to facilitate the daughter's identification with the mother: a relation of similitude and complicity. In Ferrante's texts, however, such a relation, in fidelity to real experience, is mostly described as very tormented and conflictual. Her novels recount maternal figures subjugated to the patriarchal order, wretched women who cower beneath domestic violence, exemplars whose imitations their daughters reject. Indeed, daughters actively fear reincarnating their mothers. It is not by chance that the plot occasionally presents daughters who exhibit a deep sense of disgust toward the maternal body and role. In accordance with dynamics of the uncanny, such disgust is symptomatically caught between repulsion and attraction. One might even speak of a tension between hatred and love if it were not the case that here hatred is suffocated by a primary, extraordinary love. Highlighting "the feminine need to learn to love one's mother" in *Frantumaglia*, Ferrante pauses on "the exclusive love for the mother, the single great tremendous original love, the matrix of all loves, which cannot be abolished."[33] For women, she adds, every relation of love is based "on the reactivation of the primitive bond with the mother" and manifests as the "troubling love for the maternal image, the *only* love-conflict that in every case lasts forever."[34] Even if, in Ferrante's words, the maternal body as a pregnant body is repellent, like "everything that refers to our animal nature," it also emits an "erotic vapor" that will always be for the daughter both a cause for regret and a goal.[35] The claim is very intriguing and has rightly attracted the attention of many interpreters; the eros that emanates from the maternal body in Ferrante's texts coexists with the disgust for the repellent fluids and mushy sediments that it contains and expels. This is exemplified by the case of a doll in *The Lost Daughter* that vomits putridity and a worm from its mouth, undoubtedly the most disgusting of the many dolls that populate Ferrante's narrative with multifaceted symbolic value.[36] Yet, it is worth noting we are well beyond banal pop-psychology here and even beyond the wealth of psychoanalytic speculation around female childhood and the girl's attachment to the mother, which Ferrante—citing Melanie Klein—claims to know and appreciate but which she requests we do not overestimate when interpreting her novels.[37] In my opinion, it is not so much a psychoanalytic filter but a materialist one related to feminist tradition that renders Ferrante's narrative texts particularly insightful.[38] In her writing, the primitive bond between mother and daughter is rooted in their sharing of a generating body that experiences the tremendo—a body that carries within itself that inner, visceral core around which the singular form of life and the process of vital matter coils. Ferrante claims that "writing is also a kind of reproduction of life, one marked by contradictory and overwhelming emotions," at the same time asserting that, throughout her books, she has not written about anything other than the roles of mothers and daughters and the tremendo within them.[39] On the one hand, it is obvious, almost commonplace, that repulsion is accompanied by fascination, if not by erotic pleasure. Less obvious, however, is that Ferrante pushes toward the literary truth of the daughter's repulsion for the mother in terms of hatred, matricide, and matrophobia without, nevertheless, falling into patriarchal stereotypes. On the other hand, she does not hesitate to criticize the artificial and false reciprocal fascination between mother and daughter that is so often presented as idyllic love.[40] Far from recycling trite stereotypes, in Ferrante's works the dynamic of repulsion and attraction within the mother-daughter bond is always brought back to the knot of the tremendo and thus to the female experience of origin as embedding, fragmenting, and generating the singular form of life within the regeneration of living matter. Indeed, it is the origin itself—as generating female flesh—that evokes repulsion and attraction according to the sentiments of hatred, love, similitude, adoration, and refusal between mother and daughter, whose stories Ferrante assumes the task of narrating, "telling the truth as only literary fiction allows one to."[41]

In Ferrante's texts there is even a role reversal that makes the daughter into her own mother's mother. This is not in the usual sense, where the daughter must take care of an aging, sick mother with a maternal inclination, but rather in the much more disturbing sense of the image, where the daughter carries her mother within her. In the Neapolitan Quartet, Lenù's dying mother reveals to her that the most beautiful moment of her life was when her daughter had exited from her belly. Lenù notes to herself that "when she embraced me before I left, it was as if she meant to slip inside me and stay there, as once I had been inside her."[42] The psychoanalytic paradigm of the dying human being returning to the maternal uterus is here clearly—and paradoxically—remodulated as the mother slipping into the womb of the daughter, a regeneration of the mother within the daughter. The image is, in fact, that of birth winning out over death: the rebirth of the dying mother through the daughter, who regenerates the mother within her womb. The power granted to the female body to touch living matter through the experience of its generative fragmentation is here imagined as a healing power that makes birth out of death, overturning the coordination of genealogical time that sets mother before daughter and not vice versa. Restoring the workings of origins to the mother that had originated her, turning dying into beginning, here the daughter reverses the arrow of time and forces temporality itself into a bodily circularity in which life becomes a perennial regeneration, with death torn away: a reversed cycle from which the son is clearly excluded.

We find a not dissimilar scene in a theatrical text entitled *Antigone's Tomb* by the Spanish philosopher María Zambrano. The author suggests that, walled up alive within an underground cave by the tyrant Creon, Antigone did not commit suicide (as Sophocles would have us believe) but instead experienced a rebirth "penetrating within her own interior."[43] Zambrano has the young heroine meet the shades of her past loved ones. Among these is the shade of her mother, who slips into Antigone's womb, rendering her pregnant: "The shadow of my mother has entered into me," the young woman says, "and I, a virgin, have felt the burden of being a Mother."[44] This powerful inversion of the generative cycle is emphasized in Zambrano's image by identifying uterus with tomb through the dark cave, "the most suitable site for germination."[45] Again, the female body is exalted for its generative potential: the germinating flesh of an "inextinguishable life" in whose nascent status daughter and mother meet and interpenetrate each other—even if, paradoxically, according to an overturned genealogical temporality. We might consider this overturning part of a fabulation connected to a vision of the human condition experienced within the fleshly conjuncture of its origins. Or, on the other hand, we might speak of materialism (in Zambrano's case with strong mystical accents) if not of bio-ontology as such. With Ferrante and Lispector's texts, however, we are very far from the varied constellation of styles of thought that have been collected in recent decades under the rubric of biopolitics. Rather than raising questions of having power over life or reducing human beings to bare life, these narrative texts explore the darkest side of motherhood, focusing instead on the issue of origin as the fragmentation of a singular form of life that, through generating a new singular form of life, experiences the generation of living matter within its own flesh. In other words, the issue here is one of the human condition of natality and how it is investigated within the visceral depths of the becoming body. It relates to origin in terms of coming to life, beginning. Therefore, the issue is essentially ontological and, to draw again on Ferrante's words, pushes the narrative to describe the pregnant body's uncanny contact "with the living material, [. . .] where language becomes reticent and leaves a space, enclosed between obscenity and scientific terminology, where everything can happen."[46] In this sense, the literary truth of motherhood about which Ferrante writes proves to be not only narratively but also philosophically important. It invites our ontological perspectives to bring the issue of origin back to the material, fleshly horizon of *bios* or, better, of *zoe* without sentimentalism or technologism challenging the reticence of a language that, for millennia, when it speaks of the origin, and even when it speaks of life, speaks of anything but.

Ferrante is not a philosopher but a storyteller; we know it. But there is perhaps more truth about the human condition in her stories than in that which the speculative eye of the philosopher contemplates.

Notes

1. See Tiziana De Rogatis, *Elena Ferrante: Parole Chiave* (Rome: Edizioni e/o, 2018); Isabella Pinto and Elena Ferrante, *Poetiche e politiche della soggettività* (Milan: Mimesis, 2020); Stiliana Milkova, *Elena Ferrante as World Literature* (New York: Bloomsbury, 2021); and Alessai Ricciardi, *Finding Ferrante: Authorship and the Politics of World Literature* (New York: Columbia University Press, 2021).

2. Jacqueline Rose, *Mothers: An Essay on Love and Cruelty* (London: Faber and Faber, 2018), 179, 115.

3. Elena Ferrante, *Frantumaglia: A Writer's Journey* (New York: Europa, 2016), 347, 350.

4. Ferrante, *Frantumaglia*, 221.

5. Ferrante, *Frantumaglia*, 251.

6. Elena Ferrante, *The Days of Abandonment* (New York: Europa, 2005), 127.

7. Ferrante, *Frantumaglia*, 80.

8. Ferrante, *Frantumaglia*, 224.

9. Ferrante, *Frantumaglia*, 361.
10. Ferrante, *Frantumaglia*, 222.
11. Ferrante, *Frantumaglia*, 222.
12. Ferrante, *Frantumaglia*, 121.
13. On the issue of origin and beginning, see Luce Irigaray, *Speculum of the Other Woman* (Ithaca, NY: Cornell University Press, 1985), 41, together with the important reflections of Fanny Söderbäck, *Revolutionary Time: On Time and Difference in Kristeva and Irigaray* (Albany: State University of New York Press, 2019), 244–61.
14. Ferrante, *Frantumaglia*, 331.
15. Cited and translated from the Italian edition; the essay in question ("Tredici lettere: Risposte alle domande di Mauricio Meireles," i.e., "Thirteen Letters: Replies to Mauricio Miereles's Questions") was not included in the English edition. See: Elena Ferrante, *La Frantumaglia: Nuova edizione ampliata* (Rome: Edizione e/o, 2016), 290.
16. Ferrante, *Frantumaglia* (English edition), 373.
17. Clarice Lispector, *The Passion According to G. H.*, trans. Idra Novey (London: Penguin Books, [1964] 2014), 6, 7, 53, 34.
18. Lispector, *The Passion According to G. H.*, 144.
19. Lispector, *The Passion According to G. H.*, 14.
20. Lispector, *The Passion According to G. H.*, 7.
21. Lispector, *The Passion According to G. H.*, 28.
22. Lispector, *The Passion According to G. H.*, 117, 60.
23. Lispector, *The Passion According to G. H.*, 132, 185.
24. Lispector, *The Passion According to G. H.*, 144.
25. Lispector, *The Passion According to G. H.*, 183.
26. Lispector, *The Passion According to G. H.*, 13.
27. See Adriana Cavarero, *Horrorism: Naming Contemporary Violence* (New York: Columbia University Press, 2009), 7–9.
28. Katrin Wehling-Giorgi, "Playing with the Maternal Body: Violence, Mutilation, and the Emergence of the Female Subject in Ferrante's Novel," *California Italian Studies* 7 (2017): 1.
29. Elena Ferrante, *The Lost Daughter* (New York: Europa, 2007), 110.
30. Ferrante, *Frantumaglia*, 224, 122.
31. Lispector, *The Passion According to G. H*, 90.
32. Lispector, *The Passion According to G. H.*, 91.
33. Ferrante, *Frantumaglia*, 21, 123.
34. Ferrante, *Frantumaglia*, 140.
35. Ferrante, *Frantumaglia*, 220–21.
36. See Siliana Milkova, "Mothers, Daughters, Dolls: On Disgust in Elena Ferrante's La figlia oscura," *Italian Culture* 31, no. 2 (2013): 91–109; and Siliana Milkova, *Elena Ferrante as World Literature*, 74–86.
37. Ferrante, *Frantumaglia*, 122.

38. On the feminist materialist tradition see Söderbäck, *Revolutionary Time*, 190, 338n22.
39. Ferrante, *Frantumaglia*, 251.
40. See Tiziana De Rogatis, *Elena Ferrante: Parole chiave*, 91–121.
41. Ferrante, *Frantumaglia*, 290.
42. Elena Ferrante, *The Story of the Lost Child* (New York: Europa, 2015), 208.
43. María Zambrano, *La tomba di Antigone* (Milan: SE, 2014), 25.
44. Zambrano, *La tomba di Antigone*, 56.
45. Zambrano, *La tomba di Antigone*, 27.
46. Ferrante, *Frantumaglia*, 222.

Bibliography

Cavarero, Adriana. *Horrorism: Naming Contemporary Violence*. New York: Columbia University Press, 2009.
De Rogatis, Tiziana. *Elena Ferrante: Parole Chiave*. Rome: Edizioni e/o, 2018.
Ferrante, Elena. *The Days of Abandonment*. New York: Europa, 2005.
———. *Frantumaglia: A Writer's Journey*. New York: Europa, 2016.
———. *The Lost Daughter*. New York: Europa, 2007.
———. *The Story of the Lost Child*. New York: Europa, 2015.
Irigaray, Luce. *Speculum of the Other Woman*. Ithaca, NY: Cornell University Press, 1985.
Lispector, Clarice. *The Passion According to G. H.* Translated by Idra Novey. London: Penguin Books, 2014.
Milkova, Stiliana. *Elena Ferrante as World Literature*. New York: Bloomsbury, 2021.
———. "Mothers, Daughters, Dolls: On Disgust in Elena Ferrante's *La figlia oscura*." In *Italian Culture* 31, no. 2 (2013): 91–109.
Pinto, Isabella, and Elena Ferrante. *Poetiche e politiche della soggettività*. Milan: Mimesis, 2020.
Ricciardi, Alessai. *Finding Ferrante: Authorship and the Politics of World Literature*. New York: Columbia University Press, 2021.
Rose, Jacqueline. *Mothers: An Essay on Love and Cruelty*. London: Faber and Faber, 2018.
Söderbäck, Fanny. *Revolutionary Time: On Time and Difference in Kristeva and Irigaray*. Albany: State University of New York Press, 2019.
Wehling-Giorgi, Katrin. "Playing with the Maternal Body: Violence, Mutilation, and the Emergence of the Female Subject in Ferrante's Novel." *California Italian Studies* 7 (2017): 1–15.
Zambrano, María. *La tomba di Antigone*. Milan: SE, 2014.

Appendices

Appendix 1: Works by Cavarero in English

Books

In Spite of Plato: Feminist Rewriting of Ancient Philosophy. Translated by Serena Anderlini-D'Onofrio and Áine O'Healy. New York: Polity Press, 1995.
Relating Narratives: Storytelling and Selfhood. Translated by Paul A. Kottman. New York: Routledge, 2000.
Stately Bodies: Literature, Philosophy, and the Question of Gender. Translated by Robert de Lucca and Deanna Shemek. Ann Arbor: University of Michigan Press, 2002.
For More than One Voice: Toward a Philosophy of Vocal Expression. Translated by Paul A. Kottman. Stanford, CA: Stanford University Press, 2005.
Horrorism: Naming Contemporary Violence. Translated by William McCuaig. New York: Columbia University Press, 2011.
Cavarero, Adriana, and Angelo Scola. *Thou Shalt Not Kill: A Political and Theological Dialogue.* Translated by Margaret Adams Groesbeck and Adam Sitze. New York: Fordham University Press, 2015.
Inclinations: A Critique of Rectitude. Translated by Adam Sitze and Amanda Minervini. Stanford, CA: Stanford University Press, 2016.
Surging Democracy: Notes on Hannah Arendt's Political Thought. Stanford, CA: Stanford University Press, 2021.

Journal Articles

"Regarding the Cave." Translated by Paul Kottman. *Qui Parle* 10, no. 1 (1996): 1–20.
"Politicizing Theory." *Political Theory* 30, no. 4 (2002): 506–32.
"Judith Butler and the Belligerent Subject." Translated by Anne Tordi. *Annali d'Italianistica* 29 (2011): 163–70.
"The Vocal Body: Extract from A Philosophical Encyclopedia of the Body." Translated by Matt Langione. *Qui Parle* 21, no. 1 (2012): 71–83.

"Rectitude: Reflections on Postural Ontology." *Journal of Speculative Philosophy* 27, no. 3 (2013): 220–35.
"'A Child Has Been Born unto Us': Arendt on Birth." Translated by Silvia Guslandi and Cosette Bruhns. *philoSOPHIA* 4, no. 1 (2014): 12–30.
"Narrative Against Destruction." Translated by Elvira Roncalli. *New Literary History* 46, no. 1 (2015): 1–16.
"Violent Female Bodies: Questioning Thanatopolitics." *Graduate Faculty Philosophy Journal* 36, no. 1 (July 1, 2015): 129–44.
"The Soundscape of Darkness." *Conradiana* 48, no. 2/3 (2016): 117–28.
"Human Condition of Plurality." *Arendt Studies* 2 (2018): 37–44.
"Feminist Thought. A Theoretical Approach." Translated by Daniele Fulvi. *Journal of Continental Philosophy* 2, no. 1 (December 2, 2021): 159–201.

Book Chapters

"The Need for a Sexed Thought." In *Italian Feminist Thought*, edited by Paola Bono and Sandra Kemp, 181–85. Oxford: Blackwell, 1991.
"Equality and Sexual Difference: Amnesia in Political Thought." In *Beyond Equality and Difference: Citizenship, Feminist Politics and Female Subjectivity*, edited by Gisela Bock and Susan James, 32–47. London: Routledge, 1992.
"Towards a Theory of Sexual Difference." In *The Lonely Mirror: Italian Perspectives on Feminist Theory*, edited by Paola Bono and Sandra Kemp, 189–221. New York: Routledge, 1993.
"The Envied Muse: Plato versus Homer." In *Cultivating the Muse: Struggles for Power and Inspiration in Classical Literature*, edited by Efrossini Spentzou and Don Fowler, 47–67. Oxford: Oxford University Press, 2002.
"Doppelganger Temptations." In *Ethics and Law in Biological Research*, edited by Cosimo Marco Mazzoni, 195–202. Leiden: Brill, 2002.
"*Who* Engenders Politics?" In *Italian Feminist Theory and Practice: Equality and Sexual Difference*, edited by Graziella Parati and Rebecca West, 88–103. Translated by Carmen di Cinque. London: Associated University Presses, 2002.
"On the Body of Antigone." In *Feminist Readings of Antigone*, edited by Fanny Söderbäck, 45–63. Albany: State University of New York Press, 2010.
"Inclining the Subject: Natality, Alterity, Ethics." In *Theory after Theory*, edited by Jane Elliott and Derek Attridge, 194–204. New York: Routledge, 2011.
"Feminism and Ancient Greek Philosophy." In *The Routledge Companion to Feminist Philosophy*, edited by Ann Garry, Serene J. Khader, and Alison Stone, 23–34. New York: Routledge, 2017.
"'Destroy Your Sight with a New Gorgon': Mass Atrocity and the Phenomenology of Horror." In *Emotions and Mass Atrocity: Philosophical and Theoretical Explorations*, edited by Johannes Lang and Thomas Brudholm, 123–41. Cambridge: Cambridge University Press, 2018.

"Scenes of Inclination." In *Toward a Feminist Ethics of Nonviolence*, edited by Timothy J. Huzar and Clare Woodford, 33–45. New York: Fordham University Press, 2021.

"Vocalising Honey." In *The Female Voice in the Twentieth Century*, edited by Serena Facci and Michela Garda. London: Routledge, 2021.

"Rethinking Radical Democracy with Judith Butler: The Voice of Plurality." In *Bodies That Still Matter*, edited by Annemie Halsema, Katja Kwastek, and Roel van den Oever, 141–54. Amsterdam: Amsterdam University Press, 2021.

INTERVIEWS/CONVERSATIONS

Cavarero, Adriana, and Elisabetta Bertolino. "Beyond Ontology and Sexual Difference: An Interview with the Italian Feminist Philosopher Adriana Cavarero." *Differences* 19, no. 1 (2008): 128–67.

Cavarero, Adriana, Konstantinos Thomaidis, and Ilaria Pinna. "Towards a Hopeful Plurality of Democracy: An Interview on Vocal Ontology with Adriana Cavarero." *Journal of Interdisciplinary Voice Studies* 3, no. 1 (2018): 81–93.

Cavarero, Adriana, Isabella Pinto, and Stiliana Milkova. "Storytelling Philosophy and Self Writing—Preliminary Notes on Elena Ferrante: An Interview with Adriana Cavarero." *Narrative* 28, no. 2 (2020): 236–49.

Cavarero, Adriana, and Lawtoo Nidesh. "Mimetic Inclinations: A Dialogue with Adriana Cavarero." In *Contemporary Italian Women Philosophers: Stretching the Art of Thinking*, edited by Silvia Benso and Elvira Roncalli. Albany: State University of New York Press, 2021.

Cavarero, Adriana, and Elvira Roncalli. "An Imaginary of Hope." In *The Future of the World is Open: Encounters with Lea Melandri, Luisa Muraro, Adriana Cavarero, and Rossana Rossanda*, edited by Elvira Roncalli. Albany: State University of New York Press, 2022.

Appendix 2: Secondary Bibliography on Cavarero

Adami, Rebecca. "Human Rights for More than One Voice: Rethinking Political Space beyond the Global/Local Divide." *Ethics and Global Politics* 7, no. 4 (January 1, 2014): 163–80.

Ajana, Btihaj. "Recombinant Identities: Biometrics and Narrative Bioethics." *Journal of Bioethical Inquiry* 7, no. 2 (June 1, 2010): 237–58.

Battersby, Christine. "Introduction: Fleshy Metaphysics." In *The Phenomenal Woman: Metaphysics and the Patterns of Identity*, 1–14. New York: Routledge, 1998.

Benjamin, Lucy. "Ethical Inclinations: Relational Ontologies in Cavarero, Benjamin, and Arendt." *Philosophy Today* 64, no. 3 (October 30, 2020): 671–89.

Bertolino, Elisabetta R. *Adriana Cavarero: Resistance and the Voice of Law*. New York: Routledge, 2019.
Bhattacharjee, Tuhin. "Antigone/Mother: Second Death and the Maternal in Lacan and Cavarero." *philoSOPHIA* 10, no. 2 (2021): 190–206.
Butler, Judith. "Transformative Encounters." *Counterpoints* 242 (2001): 81–98.
Cahill, Ann J. "Vocal Politics." *philoSOPHIA* 10, no. 1 (2020): 71–94.
Dohoney, Ryan. "An Antidote to Metaphysics: Adriana Cavarero's Vocal Philosophy." *Women and Music: A Journal of Gender and Culture* 15, no. 1 (November 16, 2011): 70–85.
———. "Echo's Echo: Subjectivity in Vibrational Ontology." *Women and Music: A Journal of Gender and Culture* 19, no. 1 (September 10, 2015): 142–50.
Dominijanni, Ida. "Wounds of the Common." *Diacritics* 39, no. 4 (2009): 135–45.
Evans, Fred. "Adriana Cavarero and the Primacy of Voice." *Journal of Speculative Philosophy* 32, no. 3 (2018): 475–87.
Forrest, Michelle. "Sonorous Voice and Feminist Teaching: Lessons from Cavarero." *Studies in Philosophy and Education* 34, no. 6 (November 2015): 587–602.
Freitas, Elizabeth De. "(Dis)Locating Gender Within the Universal: Teaching Philosophy Through Narrative." *Journal of the Canadian Association for Curriculum Studies* 2, no. 2 (2004): 61–72.
Gregory, Thomas. "Dismembering the Dead: Violence, Vulnerability and the Body in War." *European Journal of International Relations* 22, no. 4 (December 1, 2016): 944–65.
———. "Drones, Targeted Killings, and the Limitations of International Law." *International Political Sociology* 9, no. 3 (September 1, 2015): 197–212.
Guaraldo, Olivia. "The Lungs that We All Are: Rethinking Life in Times of the Pandemic." In *Rethinking Life: Italian Philosophy in Precarious Times*, edited by Silvia Benso, 91–106. Albany: State University of New York Press, 2022.
———. "Thinkers That Matter: On the Thought of Judith Butler and Adriana Cavarero." *AG-Aboutgender* 1, no. 1 (2012): 92–117.
———. "To the Narrative Turn and Back: The Political Impact of Storytelling in Feminism." In *Travelling Concepts of Narrative*, edited by Mari Hatavara, Lars-Christer Hydén, and Matti Hyvärinen. Amsterdam: John Benjamins Publishing Company, 2013.
Guenther, Lisa. "Being-from-Others: Reading Heidegger after Cavarero." *Hypatia* 23, no. 1 (2008): 99–118.
———. "The Body Politic: Arendt on Time, Natality and Reproduction." In *The Gift of the Other: Levinas and the Politics of Reproduction*, 29–47. Albany: State University of New York Press, 2006.
Hanafin, Patrick. *Conceiving Life: Reproductive Politics and the Law in Contemporary Italy*. Abingdon, OX: Routledge, 2007.
Honig, Bonnie. *A Feminist Theory of Refusal*. Cambridge, MA: Harvard University Press, 2021.

Huzar, Timothy J. "A Politics of Indifference: Reading Cavarero, Rancière and Arendt." *Paragraph* 42, no. 2 (2019): 205–22.

———. "Destruction, Narrative and the Excess of Uniqueness: Reading Cavarero on Violence and Narration." *Critical Horizons* 19, no. 2 (2018): 157–72.

———. "Horrorism in the Scene of Torture: Reading Scarry with Cavarero." *Journal of Interdisciplinary Voice Studies* 2, no. 1 (2017): 25–43.

Huzar, Timothy J., and Clare Woodford, eds. *Toward a Feminist Ethics of Nonviolence*. New York: Fordham University Press, 2021.

Hyland, Drew A. "Cavarero's Plato." In *Questioning Platonism: Continental Interpretations of Plato*, 155–64. Albany: State University of New York Press, 2004.

Jones, Rachel. "'Nocheinmal zurückkommen': Reading Köhler with Irigaray and Cavarero." In *An Odyssey for Our Time: Barbara Köhler's Niemands Frau*, edited by Georgina Paul, 89–116. Amsterdam: Brill, 2013.

———. "The Relational Ontologies of Cavarero and Battersby: Natality, Time and the Self." In *The Other: Feminist Reflections in Ethics*, edited by Helen Fielding, Gabrielle Hiltmann, Dorothea Olkowski, and Anne Reichold, 105–37. London: Palgrave Macmillan UK, 2007.

Lawtoo, Nidesh. "Adriana Cavarero: Introduction." *Joseph Conrad Today* 42, no. 2 (2017): 11–12.

Leon, Maria. "Relationality of Self and Other: Reciprocity of Life Stories." Paper presented at the European Society for Research on the Education of Adults, Life History and Biography Network Conference, Volos, Greece, March 2–5 2006.

Moreno, Jairo. "On the Ethics of the Unspeakable." In *Speaking of Music: Addressing the Sonorous*, edited by Keith Chapin and Andrew H. Clark, 212–41. New York: Fordham University Press, 2013.

Murphy, Ann V. "Corporeal Vulnerability and the New Humanism." Special issue, *Hypatia* 26, no. 3 (2011): 575–90.

Naranch, Laurie E. "The Narratable Self: Adriana Cavarero with Sojourner Truth." *Hypatia* 34, no. 3 (2019): 424–40.

Perpich, Diane. "Subjectivity and Sexual Difference: New Figures of the Feminine in Irigaray and Cavarero." *Continental Philosophy Review* 36, no. 4 (December 1, 2003): 391–413.

Pollock, Griselda. "From Horrorism to Compassion: Re-Facing Medusean Otherness in Dialogue with Adriana Cavarero and Bracha Ettinger." In *Visual Politics of Psychoanalysis: Art and the Image in Post-Traumatic Cultures*, edited by Griselda Pollock, 159–89. London: I. B. Tauris, 2013.

Powell, Michelle. "Doing 'Voice' Differently: Adriana Cavarero on Narrative as Ethical Encounter." *Philosophical Studies in Education* 51 (2020): 71–79.

Pulkkinen, Tuija. "Vulnerability and the Human in Judith Butler's and Adriana Cavarero's Feminist Thought: A Politics of Philosophy Point of View." *Redescriptions: Political Thought, Conceptual History and Feminist Theory* 23, no. 2 (December 15, 2020): 151–64.

Richardson, Janice. "Beyond Equality and Difference: Sexual Difference in the Work of Adriana Cavarero." *Feminist Legal Studies* 6, no. 1 (March 1, 1998): 105–20.

———. "Elizabethan 'Spinning' and Penelope's Weaving: The Political, the Common Law and Stately Bodies." *Law and Critique* 17, no. 2 (July 1, 2006): 135–51.

———. "Unique, Sexed Selves, and Radical Democracy: An Interview with Adriana Cavarero." *Women's Philosophy Review* 21 (1999): 7–25.

———. "Untimely Voices." *Angelaki* 16, no. 2 (June 1, 2011): 143–57.

Rimell, Victoria. "Philosophy's Folds: Seneca, Cavarero, and the History of Rectitude." *Hypatia* 32, no. 4 (2017): 768–83.

Ryan, Kevin. "Thinking Sexual Difference with (and against) Adriana Cavarero: On the Ethics and Politics of Care." *Hypatia* 34, no. 2 (May 1, 2019): 222–41.

Ryther, Cathrine. "The Other Argument, the Other Existent: A Complicated Conversational Method." *Otherness: Essays and Studies* 4, no. 1 (2013): 1–23.

Sambuco, Patrizia. "Psychoanalytic Accounts of Sexual Difference: Luce Irigaray and Italian Feminism." In *Corporeal Bonds: The Daughter-Mother Relationship in Twentieth-Century Italian Women's Writing.* Toronto: University of Toronto Press, 2012.

Smart, Mary Ann. "Theorizing Gender, Culture, and Music." *Women and Music: A Journal of Gender and Culture* 9, no. 1 (November 28, 2005): 106–10.

Söderbäck, Fanny. "Natality or Birth? Arendt and Cavarero on the Human Condition of Being Born." *Hypatia* 33, no. 2 (2018): 273–88.

———. "Singularity in the Wake of Slavery: Adriana Cavarero's Ontology of Uniqueness and Alex Haley's Roots." *Philosophy Compass* 15, no. 7 (2020).

Stone, Alison. *Being Born: Birth and Philosophy.* Studies in Feminist Philosophy. Oxford: Oxford University Press, 2019.

———. "Natality and Mortality: Rethinking Death with Cavarero." *Continental Philosophy Review* 43, no. 3 (August 1, 2010): 353–72.

Thomaidis, Konstantinos. "The Revocalization of Logos? Thinking, Doing and Disseminating Voice." *Studies in Musical Theatre* 8, no. 1 (March 1, 2014): 77–87. https://doi.org/10.1386/smt.8.1.77_1.

Thomaidis, Konstantinos, and Ilaria Pinna. "Towards a Hopeful Plurality of Democracy: An Interview on Vocal Ontology with Adriana Cavarero." *Journal of Interdisciplinary Voice Studies* 3, no. 1 (January 1, 2018): 81–94.

Todd, Sharon. "Educating beyond Cultural Diversity: Redrawing the Boundaries of a Democratic Plurality." *Studies in Philosophy and Education* 30, no. 2 (March 1, 2011): 101–11.

Urquiza-Haas, Nayeli. "Mistranslating Vulnerability: A Defense for Hearing." *Tilburg Law Review* 22, no. 1/2 (October 5, 2017): 5–30.

Weber, Cynthia. "Encountering Violence: Terrorism and Horrorism in War and Citizenship." *International Political Sociology* 8, no. 3 (September 1, 2014): 237–55.

Whitaker, Emilie. "Social Media—Narrating and Othering Our Selves." *Social Epistemology Review and Reply Collective* (blog), June 30, 2014.

Contributors

María del Rosario Acosta López is professor of Latin American studies in the Department of Hispanic Studies at the University of California, Riverside. She teaches and conducts research on aesthetics, critical theory, political philosophy, and decolonial studies, with an emphasis on questions of memory and trauma in the Americas. Her most recent publications are devoted to an aesthetics of resistance in Latin American art, decolonial perspectives on memory and history, epistemic injustice and epistemic violence, and women philosophers in Colombia. She is currently working on the manuscript of her next book, *Grammars of Listening: Philosophical Approaches to Memory after Trauma*, and on the final editions of two forthcoming books: one in Spanish on community in Hegel, Nancy, Esposito, and Agamben (*Narrativas de la comunidad: De Hegel a los pensadores impolíticos*) and one in English (*The Unstoppable Murmur of Being-Together*) co-authored with Jean-Luc Nancy and the Group on Law and Violence.

Elisabetta Bertolino is an interdisciplinary scholar who holds a PhD from the School of Law at BBK College, University of London and has also completed other postgraduate studies. She currently teaches legal English at the University of Palermo in Italy as well as critical analysis of literature and history. She has long been interested in the work of Adriana Cavarero, especially her concept of the voice, and has published, among other things, an interview with Cavarero in *differences* in 2008 and a recent monograph titled *Adriana Cavarero: Resistance and the Voice of Law*.

Adriana Cavarero is professor of political philosophy at the University of Verona. Cavarero received her doctoral degree in Philosophy at University of Padua in 1971. She has been a visiting professor at Harvard University, University of California at Berkeley, University of California at Santa

Barbara, New York University, and University of Warwick. She has published numerous books, of which the following have been translated into English: *In Spite of Plato* (1995), *Relating Narratives* (2000), *Stately Bodies* (2002), *For More than One Voice* (2005), *Inclinations* (2016), and *Surging Democracy* (2021). Cavarero is respected as one of the most prominent feminist scholars on ancient thought and philosophy and is known for her groundbreaking work on Plato.

Olivia Guaraldo is professor of political philosophy at the University of Verona, where she also directs the Hannah Arendt Center for Political Studies. Her field of research comprises modern and contemporary political thought. She has worked extensively on the thought of Hannah Arendt, having published two monographs on her work in 2001 and 2014 and an Italian edition of Arendt's essay *Lying in Politics*. She also works in contemporary feminist political theory, investigating the theoretical and political relationships between Italian feminist philosophy and Anglo-American gender theory. Guaraldo has edited and published introductions to the Italian translations of Judith Butler's works *Precarious Life* (Rome 2004, Milan 2013) and *Undoing Gender* (Rome 2006, Milan 2014). Among her most recent publications are "Thinking Materialistically with Locke, Lonzi, and Cavarero" (in Clare Woodford and Timothy J. Huzar, eds., *Toward a Feminist Ethics of Nonviolence*, 2021); "'The Political Sphere of Life, Where Speech Rules Supreme': Hannah Arendt's Imaginative Reception of Athenian Democracy" (in Giovanni Giorgini and Dino Piovan, eds., *Brill's Companion to the Reception of Athenian Democracy*, 2020); and "Public Happiness: Revisiting an Arendtian Hypothesis" (*Philosophy Today*, 2018).

Julian Honkasalo is an Academy of Finland postdoctoral research scholar in gender studies at the University of Helsinki. Honkasalo obtained their PhD in gender studies at the University of Helsinki in 2016, with a dissertation on feminist interpretations of Hannah Arendt. They obtained a second PhD in political science at the New School for Social Research in 2018, with a dissertation on Hannah Arendt and biopolitics; the dissertation was awarded the New School's Hannah Arendt Award in Politics. Honkasalo's forthcoming book is titled *From the Absence of Gender to Feminist Solidarity: Hannah Arendt's Political Philosophy*. During their postdoctoral research, Honkasalo has published about contemporary offshoots of twentieth-century eugenic discourse with a particular focus on the politics of transgender sterilization legislation. Their current research focuses on anti-gender mobilization and biopolitical violence.

Timothy J. Huzar is an interdisciplinary scholar whose work explores philosophical issues around politics, violence, narration, and care. His work has been published in numerous academic journals, and he is a co-editor of *Toward a Feminist Ethics of Nonviolence*, a collected volume on the thought of Cavarero. Tim is a lecturer in cultural competency at King's College London and a research associate at the Centre for Rights and Anti-Colonial Justice, University of Sussex.

Rachel Jones is associate professor of philosophy and program faculty in women and gender studies at George Mason University. She is the author of *Irigaray: Towards a Sexuate Philosophy* (2011) and has published articles and book chapters putting Irigaray into critical dialogue with Kant, Hegel, and Lyotard as well as Jane Bennett and Daniel Maximin on topics including the sublime, materiality, critical pedagogies, and the decolonization of difference. She works on Kant and post-Kantian European philosophy as read through feminist, queer, decolonial, and critical race perspectives; her current project involves rethinking Irigaray's and Cavarero's philosophies of sexual difference in the context of race and colonialism. She is interested in contested subjects, resistant objects, and relational ontologies that attend to bodily differences, plural singularity, birth and natality, and human and more-than-human materialities.

Paula Landerreche Cardillo is assistant professor of philosophy at Lewis University. She received her PhD in philosophy from DePaul University and her MA in philosophy with a minor in psychoanalytic theory, as well as a graduate certificate in gender and sexuality studies, from the New School for Social Research. Her work concentrates on feminist philosophy and decolonial theory, particularly on the ways in which the notions of sexual difference and colonial difference might inform each other. She has presented at numerous conferences on feminist philosophy, aesthetics, philosophy of art, and decolonial thought. Her review of Adriana Cavarero's *Surging Democracy* is published in *Philosophy Today* (2022).

Laurie E. Naranch is professor of political science and director of the Women's, Gender, and Sexuality Studies Program at Siena College. She researches in the areas of political philosophy, democratic theory, feminist theory, critical theory, craft, narrative, and aesthetics. She recently published "'The Narratable Self': Adriana Cavarero and Sojourner Truth" in the journal *Hypatia*. Her current projects are centered around the demonization of mothers in the carceral state, materialisms in Italian philosophy, and the philosophy and politics of craft and textiles; her current book project analyzes the aging body and political theory.

Rachel Silverbloom is a Mellon Postdoctoral Fellow in Feminist Philosophy at Vassar College. She holds a PhD in philosophy from DePaul University, with certifications in women's and gender studies and biomedical ethics. Her research examines questions of temporality, history, and political imagination at the intersections of feminist theory, queer theory, and Black studies. Her work also engages with art as a site of political refusal and imagination. Her essay "The Critical Power of Ugliness" was published in *On the Ugly: Aesthetic Exchanges* (2019).

Fanny Söderbäck is associate professor of philosophy at Södertörn University. She holds a PhD in philosophy from the New School for Social Research, and has held positions at Siena College and DePaul University. She is the co-founder and co-director of the Kristeva Circle. The author of *Revolutionary Time: On Time and Difference in Kristeva and Irigaray* (SUNY Press, 2019), Fanny has also edited *Feminist Readings of Antigone* (SUNY Press, 2010) and is a co-editor of the volume *Undutiful Daughters: New Directions in Feminist Thought and Practice* (2012). Her work has appeared in scholarly journals such as *Diacritics, Hypatia, Journal of French and Francophone Philosophy, Journal of Speculative Philosophy, Signs*, and *Theory and Event*. She is currently working on a monograph on Adriana Cavarero (forthcoming with SUNY Press), in which she puts Cavarero's work into conversation with queer and trans theories as well as Latinx, Black, and decolonial feminisms to reenvision selfhood and human relations through the framework of singularity.

Index

#MeToo movement, 220

9/11, 27–30

abandonment, 158, 161–62, 166
ability, 189
abortion, 100, 274
abstract, 3–4, 75, 77, 144, 175n3, 188, 231n60, 270; ideas, 4, 97; individual, 146; individuality, 139; Man, 75, 200; origin of life, 12; philosophical discourse, 8; space, 146; subject, 40, 61–62, 64, 66, 142, 147, 151, 201n8; universal, 67, 75; universality, 155, 219
abstraction, 67, 69, 71, 76, 93, 116, 121, 219, 221, 231n60, 274
Abu Ghraib, 193, 215, 216
acoustic, 232–46, 261n41; dimension, 244–45; experience, 253; performance, 249; relationality, 258; sphere, 242; vibration, 243; of violence, 245, 261n41
action, 3, 22–23, 31–33, 38–40, 45–46, 49, 74, 93, 140, 142–44, 146, 149, 168, 239, 241; as beginning, 40, 51n7, 51n9; collective, 60–61, 77, 171, 191, 194, 200, 201n6, 203n31; common, 144; ethical, 148; glorious, 74; of inclining, 148; linear-progressive, 113–14, 116; masculine, 116; participatory, 22; political, 31, 33, 39, 77, 103, 113, 143, 148; resistant, 186; theory of, 7; time of, 114; womanly, 91
active resistance, 93, 94, 97
active subjectivity, 8, 88, 94, 96, 98, 100–3
Acuña, Claudia, 107n52
Adamson, Glenn, 87
adoration, 276
aesthetics, 186, 195, 239, 257, 259n2, 262n50
affection, 48, 162
African American studies, 9
Afropessismists, 202n15
aftermath, 212–13, 217–20, 226–27; of trauma, 215, 222; of sexual violence, 224, 261n40; of violence, 212, 217, 226
Agamben, Giorgio, 10, 156–61, 169, 177n41, 179n74, 185–90, 192–95, 199, 200n1, 201n2, 202n10, 203n22, 203n39

agency, 8–9, 47, 98, 174, 217, 226; collective, 242; female, 86; feminist, 94; political, 242; sexual, 217
agent: historical, 9, 109; political, 103, 109; rational, 4; resistant, 96
agora, 90, 139, 144, 147
Ahmed, Sara, 34n38, 94–95, 104n18, 168, 203n39
Albers, Anni, 103n1
Alcoff, Linda Martín, 217, 223
alienation, 8, 11, 172, 195
Allegory of Inclination, 195–96
alternative, 63, 68, 166, 168–69; maternal, 45; meaning systems, 98; narrative, 123, 190; nonviolent, 199; ontology, 62; perspective, 160, 162; political ontology, 10, 157
altruistic, 28–29, 214; ethics, 28, 191–92, 197; subject, 28
ambiguity, 162, 166, 189
ambivalence, 9, 75, 138–39
American: feminists, 3, 38; military police, 193; philosopher, 211; Revolution, 32
Améry, Jean, 213, 218, 224
Ancient Greek, 160, 176n49; art, 173; myths, 111; polis, 187; political philosophy, 38
anguish, 162. See also mourning
animal, 71–73, 156, 163; body, 271; lives, 166; nature, 270, 275; political, 24 (see also *zoon politicon*)
animality, 138, 270–71
anonymity, 116, 124
anthropocentrism, 72, 74–75
anthropology, 50, 140
anthropomorphism, 163
anti-Blackness, 10, 79n8, 156, 171
antibodies, 140–41, 145

Antigone (character) 138, 161–65, 177n50, 179n75, 204n52, 277
Antigone (text), 138, 161, 166, 268
Antigone's Tomb, 277
anxiety, 43, 168
Anzaldúa, Gloria, 96–99, 101
appearance, 24, 64, 89, 114, 150, 269; political, 87, 238–39; space of, 21–22, 32, 87, 239
apprehension, 62, 66
appropriation, 129, 164, 176n22
Arab Spring, 31
archaeology, 7, 21
Archaeology of Post-Truth, An, 20
archive 9, 109–11, 116–23, 130n44, 224; limits of, 110, 122; of slavery, 110–11, 116–17, 125; violent, 109, 111, 120
Arendt, Hannah, 2–3, 5, 7–9, 21–26, 30–32, 39–43, 45–50, 50n1, 51n7, 51n9, 52n28, 60–61, 63, 71, 72, 74–76, 78, 92–93, 115, 121, 139, 141–45, 147–48, 150, 169, 175n3, 178n72, 186, 191, 198, 201n2, 203n22, 221–23, 239–41, 256, 269; body politics, 144; political philosophy, 7, 115; politics, 142–43; theory of action, 7; thought 21, 23. See also Arendtian; Arendtian philosophy; Arendtian plurality
Arendtian, 22–27, 31, 181n130, 214, 240; Cavarero as, 3–4, 21, 25–27, 32, 34n20, 37–41, 43, 47, 60; feminist, 36–38, 50; natality, 149; ontology, 24; politics, 60, 143, 149; self, 221; spirit, 32; studies, 25; technique, 43. See also Arendtian philosophy; Arendtian plurality

Arendtian philosophy, 2–3, 21, 23, 25, 27, 32, 37, 45, 50, 34n20, 38, 47, 191
Arendtian plurality, 25, 27, 70, 78, 149. See also plurality
Aristotelian binary, 70
Aristotle, 21, 24, 26, 168, 188, 203n39
arousal, 194
art, 86–87, 185, 191–93, 195–96, 231n60
Artaud, Antonin, 73
articulation, 222
assembling, 31, 123, 224
asymmetry, 28, 113, 148, 155, 157, 166, 191, 198
attachment, 163, 172, 174, 276
attention, 87, 115, 120, 240
attraction, 270, 275–76
audibility, 11, 233n83, 237, 239, 242–47, 252
Augustine, 40
Auschwitz, 215, 225
authoritarianism, 24, 185
authority, 9, 77, 110, 112, 118, 126–27
autobiography, 224, 231, 239
autohistoria/teoría, 99, 105n40
autonomy, 103, 166, 187, 213–14
Aymara, 86

bacteria, 140
Bal, Mieke, 118
banality, 50, 72, 75, 78, 81n43, 267
bare life, 10, 75, 156–58, 160, 162, 166–68, 176n27, 176n34, 188, 189, 192, 202n15, 203n22. See also *zoe*
Bataille, Georges, 72
Battersby, Christine, 188, 198
beauty, 117, 122, 130n43
Beecroft, Vanessa, 192–93, 204n45

beginnings, 39–40, 42, 159, 165, 216. See also origin
being, 25, 40, 44, 64, 69–70, 113, 147–48, 158, 186, 188, 190, 214, 239, 270; autonomous, 190; categories of, 198; existing, 63; individual, 190; insubstitutable, 214; living, 273; masculine, 190; sexuate, 176n34; unique, 64, 144, 273; unrepeatable, 63; ways of, 73, 157, 170. See also human being
beings, 4, 148; bodily, 10, 157, 163, 166; corporeal, 143–44, 148; embodied, 200; existing, 66; finite, 41; helpless, 167, 216; inclined, 10, 157; living, 158; material, 143; natal, 165, 167; non-human, 163; relational, 10, 23; singular, 155, 159–60, 176n34, 219; singular-relational, 163; vulnerable, 176n34, 185, 213, 216; un-political, 176n34; unique, 23, 26, 46, 143, 161, 180n90, 200. See also human beings
being-from-birth, 41
being-toward-death, 41
being-with-others, 216, 218
belonging, 31, 114, 140, 158, 212, 218, 243
Berlin, Germany, 192
Bertolino, Elisabetta, 4, 9
Bianchi, Emanuela, 168
binary, 47, 61, 63, 65, 241; Aristotelian, 70; what/who, 65
bio-ontology, 277
biographical, 6; knowledge, 67; narration, 11, 212, 223; narrative, 5, 213; writing, 121, 223
biography, 25, 125, 177, 224, 226
biology, 50

biopolitical, 178n72; contexts, 138–39, 140; discourse, 9; lens, 75; turn, 75
biopolitics, 75, 139–42, 185, 188–90, 278
biopower, 188, 203n22
bios, 139, 141, 145, 158–61, 163–64, 168, 174, 177n34, 190, 278
bios politikos, 21
birth, 2, 3, 10, 13, 23, 25–26, 39–43, 45–48, 49, 92–93, 143, 155–56, 159, 161–65, 167–69, 171–72, 174, 176n22, 178n72, 179n74, 185–86, 190–91, 197–98, 200, 267–73, 275, 277
Birth of Saint John the Baptist, The, 196, 198–99
Black, 204n45; Atlantic, 171, 175n10; community, 173; feminism, 115; feminists, 158; feminist scholarship, 76, 172; flesh, 171; girls 10, 115–16, 122–25, 130n43, 132n92, 156, 170–72; life, 79n8, 122–23, 132n92, 172; maternity, 171; radicalism, 171; Venus, 117
Black Power movement, 74
Black women, 10, 115–16, 122–25, 130n43, 132n92, 156, 170–73; captive, 173; care, 129n30, 171, 173; enslaved, 172; labor 129n30, 171, 173; flesh, 172; reproduction, 171
Blixen, Karen, 5, 214, 221
BLM, 32
bodies, 2, 4–5, 12, 13n12, 94–95, 101, 103, 106, 140–42, 144–51, 177, 186–95, 199–200, 204n45, 226, 270; clothed, 193; concrete, 149; dematerialized, 195; dependent, 148; dismembered, 2; divine, 10; extraordinary, 186, 193–94; female, 159, 189, 193; feminine, 188, 194; gestating, 100, 106n45; glorious, 194; inclined, 178n72; laboring, 195; lively, 200; living, 10, 194; naked, 10, 193; nude, 192; ordinary, 186–87, 194–95, 200; political, 5; pregnant, 2; private, 144; protesting, 2; relational, 151; resurrected, 194; sexed, 2, 10, 91, 186; singular, 241; singularity of, 2, 215; unalienated, 195; unique, 5, 144, 145, 149; vocal, 2; vulnerable, 2, 5, 10, 146–47, 149, 215, 246; women's, 100, 189, 190, 192–93; woundable, 229n28
bodily, 241–42, 274; autonomy, 187; awareness, 87; beings, 10, 157, 163, 166; circularity, 277; experience, 240, 270, 275; exposure, 193–95; functions, 86, 143; integrity, 213, 215; knowledge, 8, 86, 88–89, 99, 102; life, 4, 92, 162; metaphors, 138; movements, 215; organs, 194; realm, 169; sense of self, 218; separation, 141
body-self, 146–47, 149–50; relational, 147, 149; unique, 137, 147; vulnerable, 147
Bono, Paola, 3
borders, 12, 97, 106n48, 272; bodily, 12; of the home, 92; national, 141; page, 6
breath, 140–41, 252
breathing, 145
Brison, Susan, 11, 211–15, 217–20, 222–26, 227n1
Brown, Wendy, 38, 41, 200
Butler, Judith, 1, 26–31, 60, 76, 78, 166, 187, 212–13, 218, 229n30

INDEX

camps, 167, 216, 255; concentration, 158, 188, 256; extermination, 32; death, 156, 166, 167, 175; Holocaust, 189; refugee, 202
Campbell, Timothy, 200n1
canon, 99, 274; philosophical, 1–2, 6, 44, 100, 110; traditional, 270
capitalism, 199; critique of, 195; racial 171, 176n20
capture, 125, 161, 164–65, 171–72, 192–93, 225
care, 2, 5–6, 9, 29–30, 111, 117–18, 120, 123, 126–27, 260n9, 276; Black women, 129n30, 171, 173; ethics of, 191, 239; fugitive, 173; gesture of, 126; inclination of, 198; insurgent, 173–74; maternal, 204n45; narratives of, 118; politics of, 9; reciprocal, 240; resistant, 113, 157; work, 115
Carby, Hazel V., 172
caress, 191
caring, 29–30, 149–50, 213, 216, 240
Caruth, Cathy, 212, 222, 232n66
Castoriadis, Cornelius, 188, 205n67
Catholicism, 184
Cavarero, Adriana, 1–12, 13n12; as Arendtian, 3–4, 21, 25–27, 32, 34n20, 37–41, 43, 47, 60; critique of Kristeva, 39; dialogue with Butler, 26, 28–31; feminist framework, 2; feminist reading, 94; feminist theft, 126; intellectual trajectory, 18, 32; methodology, 7, 37, 49, 90, 113–14, 125, 128n14, 129n41, 196, 198; oeuvre, 28, 62; ontology, 78, 148, 190–91, 198, 213; philosophy, 4, 50n1; philosophy of voice, 47–49; and Plato, 6, 19–25, 27–28, 127n2; political philosophy, 151; political thought, 7, 63, 139; political writings, 6–7, 8–9; project, 37–39, 50, 155, 171; reading of Penelope, 88–94, 96–103, 105n25, 115–16, 123, 131n75; scholarship, 63; tactic of stealing, 110–14; thought, 64; turn toward the audible, 237; work, 59–61, 62, 75–76, 131n68, 155–57, 161, 163–64, 169, 185
Char, René, 32
Charles I, 197
chi'ixi, 85–86
childcare, 270
childhood, 276
children, 149, 172, 204n45, 267. *See also* infant; newborn
Chile, 260n3
chora, 48–49
chorus, 125, 170, 268
citizenship, 3, 21, 126, 142–43, 160–61, 187–88
City of God, 51n7, 51n9
clarity, 86, 106n42
class, 115, 172, 179n86, 189; dynamics, 131n75; hierarchies, 126; struggle, 195
classics, 268
Claudius, Mathias, 248
close narration, 117, 119, 123. *See also* critical fabulation
closeness, 191, 248–49
coappearance, 5, 115, 240
collective, 7, 31, 61, 168; action, 60–61, 171, 191, 194, 200, 201n6, 203n31; activity, 116; agency, 242; body, 78; dimension, 22, 27, 30; identities, 66; injury, 30; life, 197; representation, 197; political action,

collective *(continued)*
　77; power, 31, 78; subject, 61; trauma, 231n66
Collins, Patricia Hill, 71
colonialism, 79n8, 81, 86, 156, 171, 178, 204n45
coloniality, 1, 86
colonization, 202n15, 238; of psyche, 252; of voice, 233n83, 238, 257
colonized, 262n50; listening, 238, 252–53; self, 258; voice, 11, 238, 256, 258
commonness, 30
communicability, 258. *See also* speech
communication, 48, 81n58; human, 49; public, 150
community, 30, 60, 65, 72, 115–16, 140–41, 143, 145, 150–52, 157, 159, 168, 218, 227; Black, 173; coming, 159; human, 161, 212, 218; intellectual, 267; of listeners, 11, 240; political, 31, 68–69, 146; polyphonic, 150; women's, 116
company, 24, 91–92, 101–2, 122
complicity, 121, 146, 169, 275
Conceiving Life, 100
confession, 253, 255
Connolly, Brian, 110, 119
consciousness, 25, 126, 222, 271
consumption, 193
contact, 65, 95, 268, 271–72, 278
contagion, 140–41
contamination, 141
contestation, 76, 194–95
control, 140–41, 146, 188, 192, 212, 230n40
coronavirus, 140–41, 200. *See also* Covid-19
corporeal, 138–39, 143, 161–62, 239–40; beings, 143–44, 148; body, 146;

difference, 50; exposure, 214; form, 239; fragility, 149; geometry, 155; given, 50; labor, 161; materiality, 162; morphology, 50; processes, 169; relationality, 175n3; requests, 140; self, 146, 151; singularity, 214; uniqueness, 144, 159, 175n3; voice, 145, 240–41; vulnerability, 29, 149, 177n41
corporeality, 38, 42, 99, 156, 169; natal, 179; sexuate, 179; of voice, 241
corpse, 161, 216, 229n28
counter-history, 109–10, 125–26
counter-narrative, 123
courage, 195
Covid-19, 9, 138, 140, 142, 145, 150. *See also* coronavirus
craft, 86–87, 114. See also *metis*
creativity, 195, 197
critical fabulation, 9, 105n25, 111, 117–19, 121, 123, 126
criticism, 27, 188–89
critique, 73, 199; Anglophone, 41; of capitalism, 195; of democracy, 20–21; feminist, 30, 49–50, 176, 195, 269; of Marx, 195; materialist, 201n8; philosophical, 239; Platonic, 20; radical, 28; of rectitude, 193; self, 6; of violence, 185, 205, 247, 257

darkness, 255, 257
Das Frauenproblem in der Gegenwart, 37
daughter, 12, 162–63, 165, 174, 268–69, 275–77
da Vinci, Leonardo, 191
Days of Abandonment, The, 269
death, 3, 6, 12, 25, 41, 43–44, 47, 92–93, 110, 163–64, 167–69, 171, 179n75, 189, 216, 218, 222, 225,

248–49, 271, 273, 277; ontology of, 190; social, 122, 160, 172; threat of, 247
Death and the Maiden, The, 11, 233n83, 238, 247–56, 258–59
de Beauvoir, Simone, 40
decolonial: feminisms, 115; thought, 8
deconstruction, 30, 44, 62
dehumanization, 185, 214, 225, 227
delay, 89, 91–92
demagogy, 19–22, 27
Demeter, 164–66
democracy, 7, 19–22, 27, 31–32, 76, 78, 98, 181n130, 200, 205n76; ancient, 21; Athenian, 19; body of, 21; critique of, 20–21; Greek, 21; surging, 31, 70, 76, 98
democratic, 19–21, 32, 200; assembly, 21; government, 205n67; health, 200; interactions, 194; paradox, 205n67; participation, 3; politics, 21–22, 33, 65, 191–92, 195; possibilities, 7; potential, 7; regime, 20; resurgence, 30; self-legislation, 200; states, 202n15; thinkers, 187; traditions, 70
demos, 19, 187, 200
dependence, 31, 148, 198
depoliticization, 5–6
deprivation, 238
De Rogatis, Tiziana, 267
Derrida, Jacques, 50n1
"Der Tod und das Mädchen," 248
Descartes, René, 219–20, 231n60
destruction, 11, 120–21, 129n36, 189, 212, 222–25, 229n28, 256–57; of philosophy, 68; of uniqueness, 215–16, 225; unspeakable, 121; of voice, 233n83, 257; of vulnerability, 218

determination, 61, 96
dialectical thinking, 20
Dialettica e politica in Platone, 19
Di Cesare, Donatella, 141
dictatorship, 238, 248, 260n3
difference, 3, 71, 75, 100, 112, 231n60; corporeal, 50; individual, 23; ontology of, 4; sexuate, 112, 114. *See also* sexual difference
Diotima (character), 45, 110, 127, 189
Diotima (group), 1, 3
disability, 138, 196, 219
disclosure, 46–47, 60
discourse, 24–26, 37, 117–19, 126, 127n4, 129n31, 141, 220; biopolitical, 9; feminist, 30; hierarchy of, 118; historical, 109; immunitary, 9; legal, 213, 217; of Man, 129n31; philosophical, 4, 7–9, 67, 220–221
discrimination, 141, 149
disease, 138, 141
disfiguration, 214
disfigurement, 163, 272
disgust, 12, 272, 275. *See also* repugnance
displacement, 76–77, 113, 161, 179n74
dispossession, 173, 187–88
disruption, 94, 115, 138, 232n66
dissolution, 120; of margins, 273–74; of self, 12, 271
distinctness, 23, 29, 45–46, 48–49. *See also* uniqueness
division, 9–10, 90, 139, 144–45, 147, 149, 200, 227, 269
domestic, 4, 115, 131n68, 172–73; activity, 116; labor, 113, 168; order, 164; sphere, 3, 123, 172; violence, 275; work, 86
domination, 3, 5, 41, 98, 102, 155

Dorfman, Ariel, 11, 233n83, 247–48, 253, 257–58, 261n41
Dotson, Kristi, 259n2
duality, 27
dying, 44, 122–23, 164, 167, 224, 248, 277. *See also* death

ears, 233n83, 240, 252, 256–57
earth, 31, 163, 165–66
echo, 252, 258–59
Echo (mythical figure), 11, 258
economy, 87, 192
Eden, 193
ego, 12, 271–72
egocentricity, 149
Eichmann, Adolf, 50n1
Emancipated Spectator, The, 73
emancipation, 69, 78, 143
embodiment, 1–2, 9, 38, 47, 114, 185–86, 190, 199; individual, 41; maternal, 44; relational, 10
Emigrants, The, 224
emotions, 20, 35, 50, 142, 276
empathy, 212
enclosure, 71, 101, 170, 173
encounter, 64, 88, 94–96, 98, 101, 109, 111, 120, 168, 273; dyadic, 60–61; ethical, 10, 155; philosophical, 99; political, 10, 155
the enslaved, 73, 119, 121, 172–74
epic: drama, 47; hero, 92–93, 101; Homeric, 92; tale, 92
epistemic: error, 60; silencing, 259n2; smothering, 259n2; violence, 238, 259n2, 260n50
epistemology, 71, 81n48
equality, 68, 70, 76–78
equivalence, 68
erasure, 43–45, 112, 116, 120–21, 123–24, 126, 213, 222, 238; of the body, 242; of the feminine, 38; historical, 121; intentional, 120; of verticality, 115; violent, 120, 222; of the voice, 238; of women, 110
erectness, 190, 194, 200
eros, 168, 275
essence, 24, 69, 114, 159, 244
essentialism, 3
Esposito, Robert, 9, 138–41, 200n1, 202n10
eternity, 3, 45, 92
ethical, 4, 200, 240; action, 148; appearance, 239; conviviality, 170; dilemma, 224; doctrines, 27; encounter, 10, 155; inclination, 186; life, 237; necessity, 121; politics, 191; posture, 28; relationality, 148–49, 193; relations, 194; reorientation, 155; responsibility, 120
ethics, 27–28, 159, 177n40, 185, 189, 213, 216; affirmative, 186; altruistic, 28, 191–92, 197; of care, 191, 239; feminist, 168, 194, 168; of inclination, 10, 185–86, 197; postural, 10, 28, 185; queer, 168; of responsibility, 32
Ethics of Sexual Difference, An, 37, 40
ethnicity, 189. *See also* race
etymology, 39, 45, 52n28, 170, 244
Eve, 193–94
evil, 21, 50, 89, 189
excess, 117, 120, 225, 256–57
exclusion, 6, 60, 76, 88, 101, 103, 164; of the body, 146–47; of women, 87, 110. *See also* inclusive exclusion
experience: acoustic, 253; bodily, 240, 270, 275; female, 268, 270, 274, 276; feminine, 270; of listening, 247; maternal, 274; modern, 187; singular, 221; of time, 222

exploitation, 129n30, 194; artistic, 204n45; sexual, 174
exposure, 30–31, 46, 147–48, 155, 159, 161, 175n3, 189–91; bodily, 193–95; corporeal, 214; mutual, 240; to others, 166, 190; naked, 195; nonviolent, 193; reciprocal, 147; shared, 213; to violence, 186, 188–89, 199–200
expropriation, 172
extermination, 32, 256
eyes, 240, 243–44, 246, 254, 259

fabrication, 22
Facebook, 205n62
facts, 118–19, 159
familiarity, 95
Fanon, Franz, 252
fascination, 276
fascism, 21
fate, 94, 117, 120, 124, 212
fear, 48, 141, 212, 216, 271, 275. *See also* horror; terror
female, 41–42, 46, 138; agency, 86; artist, 197; Black, 172; bodies, 159, 189, 193; body, 138, 160, 193, 195, 271–72, 275, 277; experience, 268, 270, 274, 276; figures, 186; flesh, 172, 276; form, 194, 197; genealogy, 45; generative potency, 161; intellectual worker, 44; other, 269; philosopher, 49; realm, 160; subjectivity, 25, 44, 112, 126, 138, 164; temporality, 86
feminine, 26, 38, 45–47, 49–50, 156, 177n39; bodies, 188, 194; body, 2, 194; craft as, 86–87; erasure of, 38; experience, 270; figure, 112, 114, 186–87, 189, 195–96, 204n52; imaginary, 8, 88; labor, 198; narrative, 47; perspective, 38, 41; philosophy, 45, 47; representations, 44; resistance, 197; sex, 274; sexual difference, 50n1; speaking, 50; stereotypes, 194; subjectivity, 110; symbolic order, 42, 164; textual style, 38, 49; thinking, 41–42, 50; voice, 39, 240; welcome, 177n40; work, 99; writing, 274
femininity, 47, 50, 194
feminism, 46–47, 63, 143; Black, 115; decolonial, 115; Italian, 3; of possibilities, 187; of sexual difference, 4, 100; of sisterhood, 27
feminist: agency, 94; Arendtian, 36–38, 50; critique, 25, 30, 49–50, 176, 195, 269; debates, 25–26, 28, 65; deconstruction, 44; discourse, 30; ethics, 168, 194; fights, 85; figure, 113; framework, 8; freedom, 187; future, 94; identity, 26; lens, 3, 7; materialism, 187; methodology, 7; movements, 63; narrative, 115; perspective, 38; philosopher, 2, 47, 50n1; philosophy, 1; politics, 35, 38, 115, 138, 194; projects, 9, 37, 38–39, 49, 88, 100; reading, 7, 94, 115; refusal, 94, 204n52; scholars, 60, 185; task, 42; theft, 126; thinking, 41, 186; theorizing, 38, 50n1; theory, 1, 25–26, 47, 62–64, 186, 221; thought, 1, 9, 201n6; tradition, 276; work, 131n60, 185
feminists, 138, 143; American, 3, 38; Black, 158; British, 3; French, 50; Italian, 50, 66, 77, 131n68; second-wave, 38
Ferrante, Elena, 12, 267–78
fiction, 98, 118, 121, 123–24, 231n60, 267, 269–71, 276

figuration, 45, 69, 186, 204n45
figure of the thinkable, 188–89
finitude, 3, 44, 47, 93, 221–22
fixity, 95
flesh, 65, 70, 75, 79, 116, 138, 143–44, 151, 163, 216, 219, 269–74, 276–78; Black, 171–72; female, 172, 276; generative, 271–72; infinite, 274; living, 12, 114; singular, 274
Floyd, George, 32
foreclosure, 3, 161, 164, 171
forgetting, 40, 44, 171, 269
form-of-life, 158–59, 169, 177n34, 273–74, 276, 278
For More than One Voice, 48, 240–41, 242
Foucault, Michel, 50n1, 139, 188, 192
fragility, 113, 146, 148–50, 22, 226
fragmentation, 101, 214, 269, 272–73, 277–78
Frantumaglia, 267, 271, 275
freedom, 23, 29, 31–33, 40, 139, 142–45, 147–48, 150, 181n30, 187–88, 191, 195, 201n6
French, 81n43; feminist critique, 50; philosophy, 68; revolution, 192
Freud, Sigmund, 222
Fricker, Miranda, 259n2
friendship, 130n43, 174, 198
Fuentes, Marisa, 110, 119
fugitive, 10, 94, 157–58, 171, 173, 225
fugitivity, 76, 78
fungibility, 68, 176
future, 60, 111, 113, 117–19, 125–26, 130n44, 157–58, 188; feminist, 94; nonviolent, 185; radical, 72

gaze, 43, 64, 72, 77, 115, 124, 179, 186, 239, 244; male, 193; reciprocal, 165; shared, 166

gender, 52n31, 178, 189; dichotomized, 151; neutral, 26, 52n31; nonconformity, 173; political philosophy of, 49; studies, 1; theorization of, 37–38
genealogy, 269; female, 45; of Man, 10, 156; of matricide, 39; political, 10, 156; of sovereignty, 156
genocide, 120
Gentileschi, Artemisia, 186, 195–99, 205n61
germination, 98, 274, 277
germinative stasis, 98, 102
germs, 141. *See also* virus
gestation, 272
gesture, 67, 87, 97, 115, 122, 157–58, 161, 163–64, 169, 171, 177n40; bodily, 191; of care, 126; epistemological, 125; founding, 4, 158, 163, 164; inclined, 161, 179n81; narrative, 220; philosophical, 219; political, 160; resistant, 195; sovereign, 157; violent, 219
Gezi Park, 31
gift-giving, 140
Giving an Account of Oneself, 26, 29
Glissant, Édouard, 71
Gorgon, 242–46. *See also* Medusa
grace, 177, 193–94, 199
grammar, 232n66, 239, 242, 244, 257; of the after, 73; of the aural, 239; of listening, 230n49, 239, 259; of visibility, 244; of the what, 72; of the who, 98, 60–61, 66, 68, 77
Grattan, Sean, 63, 71, 73–75
Great Mother, 43–45
Greek, 39, 43, 45, 74, 170, 179, 228n14, 268; democracy, 21–22; demonstrations, 31; world, 93, 171

Guaraldo, Olivia, 6, 7, 60, 227n1

Haley, Alex, 129n36
Haines, Christian, 63, 71, 73–75
Hanafin, Patrick, 100, 106n45
happiness, 22, 140, 147–48, 152; political, 148; public, 3, 31–32, 62, 70, 76, 78, 147
harm, 117, 177, 187, 213, 216–19
Harney, Stefano, 79
Hartman, Saidiya, 9–10, 105n25, 110–11, 116–27, 127n4, 127n11, 130n43, 130n44, 131n75, 132n92, 156, 158, 170–74, 176n20, 179n86
hatred, 200, 275–76
Hatred of Democracy, 70
healing, 11, 215, 219–20, 222, 258, 277
hearing, 122, 223, 239–41, 245, 247, 249, 251, 255–57, 261n41
Hegel, Georg Wilhelm Friedrich, 161, 192
Heidegger, Martin, 24, 40, 41, 44–45, 52n28, 69, 268
helplessness, 215–16, 218, 225
hereness, 72
heroism, 47
hierarchy, 103; of discourse, 118; sexual, 50; of values, 98
historical, 120; agent, 9, 109; context, 248; discourse, 109; erasure, 121; event, 40; instantiation, 66; meanings, 118; narrative, 109–10; practices, 42; realm, 110; remnants, 123; rules of, 120, 122, 125; subjectivity, 9; trajectories, 105n40; transformation, 33; "Truth," 110; usage, 51; violence, 119; writing, 126
history, 9, 38–40, 42, 47, 68, 95–96, 100–1, 109–10, 112, 115–23, 125, 127n4, 185, 220n1, 221, 252, 256; discourse of, 126; dominant 118; limits of 121; living 115; of philosophy, 87, 127n4; of the present, 110; violence of, 123; Western, 110
Hitler, Adolf, 24
Hobbes, Thomas, 28, 179n74
Holocaust, 120, 185, 189, 213, 224, 226
home, 27, 90–95, 97, 102, 144, 147, 169, 172, 218–19
Homer, 90–91, 93–94, 98, 104n18, 110, 112, 126, 221
homo erectus, 151
homophobia, 149
Homo sacer (concept) 156, 160–61, 188. *See also* bare life
Homo Sacer (text), 189, 201n2
Honig, Bonnie, 1, 60, 94, 105n25, 130, 178n72, 186, 194, 203n34, 204n52
Honkasalo, Julian, 7
hope, 33, 34n38, 119, 123, 216, 225
horror, 28–29, 120, 185, 189–90, 215–16, 223, 226, 243–45, 249, 271–72, 274; phenomenology of, 272; power of, 192; unspeakable, 256–57
horrorism (concept), 29, 75, 189, 215, 217–18, 220, 227, 243, 245–47
Horrorism (text), 5, 11, 28–29, 155, 163, 166, 215, 216, 218, 220, 227n1, 242–43, 245–46, 261n40, 272
hospitality, 148
howl, 243–45, 246, 247
Huffer, Lynne, 168
human: activities, 142–43; communication, 49; community, 161, 212, 218; condition, 11, 39,

human (continued)
148, 155–56, 166–67, 212, 215–16, 219, 246, 274, 277–78; existence, 41, 43, 47, 143; life, 74, 159, 189, 212, 221, 246, 275; nature, 112, 193, 223; plurality, 23, 26, 46; relations, 216, 219, 225–26; uniqueness, 215–16; voice, 48, 240–41, 257; vulnerability, 29
human being, 4–5, 23–25, 64, 144, 166, 223, 269, 270, 272, 274
human beings, 24, 39, 46, 52, 129, 143, 156, 159, 163, 166–67, 200, 219, 233, 272, 278
Human Condition, The, 30–31, 38–39, 45, 51n9, 142–43
humanity, 117, 158, 188, 218
Huzar, Timothy J., 8, 94, 96–97, 100, 224–25

iconography, 191
identification, 44, 68, 70, 123, 160, 275
identity, 25–26, 29–30, 63–65, 69, 71, 74, 97, 141, 148, 151, 157, 214; common, 30; feminist, 26; generalizable, 159; physical, 46; relational, 239; unrepeatable, 67
immigrants, 141
immortality, 44, 92–93, 168
immunitary, 141; discourse, 138; paradigm, 140
immunity, 140–42, 145–46, 150
immunization, 142, 150
inaudibility, 245, 247
inclination, 6, 28, 60–62, 166–68, 190–91, 193, 195–98; of care, 198; ethical, 186; ethics of, 10, 185–86, 197; ethos of, 170, 174; maternal, 28, 168, 276; postural, 31; postures of, 198 relational, 149; scenes of, 190, 203n34
Inclinations, 10, 28–29, 155, 190–91, 195, 198
inclined: beings, 10, 157; bodies, 178n72; gesture, 161, 179n81; posture, 113, 147, 157; subject, 28–29
inclusive exclusion, 156, 158, 160–61, 164
incorporeality, 244
independence, 213, 216
indifference, 8, 59, 78, 94, 97
individual: abstract 146; difference 23; embodiment 41; isolated, 186; liberal, 142; of liberalism; self 12, 141, 270; self-centered, 141–42; self-sufficient, 30, 213; sovereign 142, 179n81; subject, 28–29, 190
individualism, 27–28, 30; ideology of, 213; liberal, 72
individuality, 2–3, 98, 139
ineffability, 274
inexplicability, 121, 257
infant, 28, 39, 48–49, 179n74, 191, 204n45. *See also* newborn
infection, 140
injustice, 259n2
inoperativity, 10, 186, 192–94, 199
In Spite of Plato, 6–8, 20, 23, 25, 26, 44, 86, 97, 100, 157, 168
instability, 12, 270
instrumentalization, 199, 126, 192
insurgency, 171, 181n130
intellectuality, 169
intelligibility, 101–2, 225
interaction, 39, 78, 115, 140, 144, 148, 194

interdependence, 31, 240
interiority, 137, 214
interrelationality, 31
intersex, 50n1
intimacy, 38, 79, 122, 159, 168, 171–74, 213, 216, 218
inventiveness, 171, 173
invisibility, 117, 126, 242, 274
invulnerability, 29, 149, 216
Iraq, 193
Irigaray, Luce, 3–4, 7, 37, 39–42, 44, 46, 47, 49, 50n1, 90, 100, 128n14
irreverence, 97
isolation, 189, 222, 225. *See also* loneliness
isonomia, 22
Italian, 214, 229n25; Feminism, 3; feminists, 50, 66, 77, 131n68; feminist thought, 1; philosophers, 185; philosophy, 200n1; political thought, 200n1; thinkers, 9; universities, 186
ivory tower, 73

Jaspers, Karl, 23–24, 26
Jesus, 12, 191, 268
Jones, Rachel, 10, 105n25, 113, 198, 200n1
joy, 31. *See also* happiness
justice, 8, 22, 29, 39, 60, 191, 218, 249, 252

kallipolis, 19
Kant, Immanuel, 69, 149
Kemp, Sandra, 3
killing, 167, 215, 218–19, 246
kinlessness, 172, 174
kinship, 161–62, 164, 173–74, 177n50
Klee, Paul, 103n1

Klein, Melanie, 276
knowledge, 26, 67, 71–73, 86–89, 137, 173, 193, 230n49; biographical, 67; bodily, 8, 86, 88–89, 99, 102; disembodied, 103; embodied, 9, 86, 97; legitimate, 102; localized, 102; production, 9; scientific, 274
Kristeva, Julia, 38–39, 47–49

labor (act of giving birth), 270
labor (as in work), 38, 73–74, 79n7, 126–27, 142–44, 171–74, 187, 197, 203n22, 273; affective, 161; Black women's, 156–57, 171; of care, 131n75, 171; division of, 9; domestic, 113, 168; feminine, 198; intellectual, 87; manual, 173; of philosophy, 87; reproductive, 161; of weaving, 87; of women of color, 129n30
Lacou-Labarthe, Philippe, 68
Lager, 216, 225
Landerreche Cardillo, Paula, 8, 227n1
language, 4, 12–13, 42, 48–50, 66, 112, 145–47, 200n1, 226, 232n66, 241–42, 270, 272, 278; Arendtian, 2; limits of, 257; systemic, 146; of truth, 12; of violence, 217; of vulnerability, 166
law, 159, 160–65, 168–69, 171, 174, 177, 185, 187–88, 192, 195, 203n22, 205n27; and order, 169; of the gods, 160, 162, 165, 177n49; natural, 164–65; of nature, 160, 163; of the polis, 160; suspension of, 158; of Western science, 177n49; withdrawal of, 160
leaning, 167, 179n81, 191, 198. *See also* inclination; inclined

"leaning in," 197, 205n62
Levi, Primo, 218, 223, 225–26, 245
liberal: ideology, 147; individual, 142; individualism, 72; personhood, 71; philosophy, 141, 147; political philosophy, 147; politics, 65, 141
liberalism, 139, 141–42, 144, 152n25
liberation, 32, 98 181n130; women's, 37, 115
liberty, 32, 186
life: bodily, 4, 92, 162; collective, 197; ethical, 237; impersonal, 163, 167, 273–74; infinite, 270–72; livable, 187; management of, 74, 185; material, 156; political, 160–61, 188–89, 192, 237; public, 37, 142; reproductive, 160; resistant, 71; singular, 65; story, 25, 64, 221, 223, 237; unformed, 160, 164; wild, 160, 162; work for, 161, 171
Life of the Mind, The, 45
limits, 43, 106n48, 200, 205n67; of archive, 110, 122; of the body, 148; of ego, 12; of history, 121; of language, 257; of narration, 121; political, 150; of the political, 76; of the possible, 97; of possibility, 101; of the private, 76; of the public, 76; of the social, 76
linearity, 113
linear-progressive: action, 113–14, 116; narrative, 215; order, 113; temporality, 110, 114, 128n14
Lispector, Clarice, 12, 271–74, 277
listening, 11, 19, 122, 232n66, 239–42, 252–53, 256–59; experience of, 247; grammar of, 230n49, 239, 259
literary: elements, 122; examples, 99; experiment, 99; fiction, 269, 271,
276; genre, 256; truth, 267–69, 272–74, 276, 278
literature, 1, 47, 68, 105n40, 125, 221
living: bodies, 10, 194; flesh, 12; material, 270, 278; matter, 268, 270–71, 276–78; singularity, 129n31, 159
logic, 20, 87, 90, 91, 92, 94, 97, 112–13, 151, 159; of autonomy, 103; of bare life, 202; heteronormative, 168; of individuality, 98; of the law, 185; masculine, 113; of oppression, 97–98; oppressive, 113; of patriarchy, 94; of relationality, 98; of sovereign power, 160–61, 167; of sovereignty, 159; subject-predicate, 159; of use, 193
logocentrism, 138, 163, 241
logos, 138
loneliness, 216, 225. *See also* isolation
loss, 29–31, 163, 164, 174, 238, 257
Lost Daughter, The, 268, 273, 276
love, 162, 174, 189, 190, 213, 275–76
Lugones, María, 8, 88, 94, 96–103
luminosity, 268, 273, 274
Luxemburg, Rosa, 32

the Madonna, 191, 198, 204n45. *See also* Mary; Mother of God
male, 40–41, 126, 189; authors, 45; bias, 38; body, 269; citizens, 187; consumption, 193; domination, 41; figure, 47, 156, 179n86, 193; gaze, 193; imaginary, 94; philosopher, 92–93; reason, 138; subject, 40, 44; subjectivity, 138
Man, 3–5, 24–26, 28, 40, 44, 67, 62, 75, 129n31, 155, 163, 166, 168, 219; abstract, 75, 200; forms of,

113, 157; genealogy of, 10, 156; universal, 125
"the many," 7, 21, 25, 27, 30
margins, 12, 100, 231n60, 272–74
Martínez, Rosaura, 258
Marx, Karl, 195
Mary, 12, 268. *See also* Madonna, Mother of God
masculine, 44, 47, 50, 112–13, 129n31; action, 116; being, 190; body, 5, 138; economy, 87; fantasy, 45, 213; frameworks, 10; imaginary, 97–98; narrative, 112; obsession, 3, 44; order, 8, 88, 113–14; sex, 90; space, 90; stereotypes, 194; subject, 5, 190; subjectivity, 111–12, 116; temporality, 113, 128n14
masculinity, 44, 47, 50
master/slave dialectic, 192
material, 47, 49, 111, 143–44, 186, 197, 273, 278; body, 147; life, 156; living, 270, 278; ontology, 240–41; organic, 271; space, 144; uniqueness, 144
materialism, 201n8, 277; of embodiment, 199; feminist, 187; radical, 199
materiality, 4, 12, 42, 45, 47, 95, 144, 149, 162, 169, 201n8
materialization, 95, 188
maternal, 38, 41, 44–45, 47–50, 156; blood, 162; body, 12, 48, 191, 268, 271, 273–75; care, 204n45; dispossession, 173; dominion, 179n74; embodiment, 44; experience, 274; figure, 45, 49, 275; genealogies, 174; generation, 162; generative power, 159, 163–65, 167, 171, 174, 179n74, 179n75 image, 275; inclination, 28, 168, 276; natality, 49; philosophy, 47; relation, 167, 174; role, 275; uterus, 277; voice, 49; womb, 269–70

maternity, 45, 269; Black, 171; dispossessed, 174; portrayals of, 273
matricide, 7, 37–39, 43–44, 47–48, 276
matrophobia, 276
matter, 40, 72, 96, 166, 270–78; living, 268, 270–71, 276–78; non-sentient, 75; spiritual, 65, 66, 76; vital, 275, 276
meaning-making, 87, 222
Medina, José, 259n2
Medusa, 11, 243–45, 256
memory, 26, 86, 96, 102, 114, 213, 219, 253
menstrual blood, 275
Metamorphoses, 243
metaphysics, 4, 43, 49, 50; of European modernity, 60; Western, 20, 40, 44, 75, 187
methodology, 88, 105n25, 110–13, 117, 121, 127n4, 132n82, 132n92; Cavarero's, 7, 90, 113–14, 125, 128n14, 129n41; feminist, 7; of stealing, 110, 113–14, 129n41
metis, 87, 114–15, 169, 173–74. *See also* craft
Michelangelo, 195
Middle Passage, 172. *See also* transatlantic slave trade
midwives, 158, 198
migrants, 202n15. *See also* immigrants
Milkova, Stiliana, 267
modern, 143, 158, 171; age, 32; experience, 187; political life, 188, 192; political thought, 73; political

modern (continued)
  violence, 175n10; sovereignty, 185; subject, 14n21, 186; tradition, 28, 161; universe, 98; violence, 185; West, 61
modernity, 29, 189, 192; European, 60–61, 79, 79n7, 81n48; political, 156; scientific, 177n49; Western, 156, 177n49
Molloy, Sylvia, 105n40
mortality, 23
Mortari, Luigina, 148
Moten, Fred, 79
mother, 45–49, 106n42, 149, 155, 162–67, 174, 176n22, 179n81, 189, 191, 268–69, 273–75; body, 41, 172; figure of, 156, 167
motherhood, 10, 12, 38, 46, 50–51, 267–70, 272–75, 278; dark side of, 267–68, 273–75, 278; representation of, 268, 274; uncanny, 12, 268–75
Mother of God, 267, 273. *See also* Madonna; Mary
mourning, 30–31, 162
Mozart, Wolfgang Amadeus, 256
Muselmänner, 189
music, 48–49, 122, 240, 248–49, 252, 255–56
musicality, 48–49, 240
musicology, 1
muteness, 244–46. *See also* silence
myth, 20, 111, 116, 126, 164–66, 243
mythology, 44, 231n60

nakedness, 191, 193, 195. *See also* nudity
name, 41, 49, 61, 63, 64, 68–70, 111, 116–17, 124, 129n36, 198, 244

Nancy, Jean-Luc, 8, 62–63, 65–69, 71–75, 79, 81n48, 175n3
Naranch, Laurie E., 10, 157, 171, 177n41, 227n1
narratability, 11, 224–25, 239–40, 242
narration, 5, 11, 38, 39, 42, 46, 67, 118–23, 125–27, 211–12, 217, 220–26, 228, 231n60, 231n63, 232n66, 239, 274; autobiographical, 11, 212, 223; biographical, 11, 212, 223; close, 117, 119, 123; failure of, 120; limits of, 121; of trauma, 232n66; work of, 224
narrative 13n12, 47, 67, 70, 109–12, 117–19, 121–23, 125, 130n44, 171, 219–21, 223–26, 256–57, 270, 276; alternative, 123, 190; archival, 111; of art, 86; autobiographical, 213, 219, 223; biographical, 5, 213; cultural, 187; failure, 226; feminine, 47; feminist, 115; first-person, 220, 223; historical, 109–10; linear-progressive, 215; masculine, 112; perspective, 25; practice, 26; singular, 5; world-making, 164
"Narrative Against Destruction," 120–21, 223, 256
natality, 3, 7, 23, 24, 25, 31, 32, 37, 38, 39–41, 47–50, 51n9, 52n28, 143, 149, 169, 191, 198, 278; Arendtian, 149; maternal, 49; sexed, 49
national: body, 141; borders, 141
nationality, 160
nature, 45, 50, 50n1, 74, 159, 160, 177n49, 179n74, 216, 271, 274; animal, 270, 275; human, 112, 193, 223; law of, 160, 163; physical, 43
Neapolitan Quartet, 274, 276–77

necessity, 24–26, 28–29, 121, 138–39, 141–46, 148, 150
neutrality, 2–4
newborn, 26, 46, 147, 149, 165–66, 176n34. *See also* infant
Newton, Helmut, 193
Nietzsche, Friedrich, 24
nomos, 158, 160–61
non-human, 75, 163, 272
nonviolence, 10, 186–87, 191, 195, 197, 199, 200
normality, 140
normativity, 65, 195–96
nothingness, 44, 270
novelty, 114, 198
Nudities, 190, 192
nudity, 176n34, 177n41, 190–94
Nyiszli, Miklós, 225–26

object, 73, 116, 118, 203n39
objectification, 119, 139–40, 147
O'Brien, Mary, 38, 41
obscenity, 270, 278
obscurity, 71, 267
Occupy movements, 31
Odysseus, 88–89, 91–93, 97
Odyssey, The, 42, 52, 87–89, 98–99, 127n4
Oedipus, 44, 67, 162
On Revolution, 31–32
ontological: crime, 5–6, 155–56, 166–67, 215–16; damage, 245; dignity, 245; indeterminacy, 166; investigations, 186–87; orientations, 176n34; paradigm, 28–29; perspectives, 278; uniqueness, 257; violence, 5–6, 11, 212, 217, 220 223, 227n1, 229n28, 230n37, 232n66 (*see also* violence); weakness, 149
ontology, 47, 50, 148, 186, 187, 190–91, 277; alternative, 62; Arendtian, 23; Cavarero's, 78, 148, 190–91, 198, 213; of death, 190; of difference, 4; of grace, 199; individualist, 269; material, 240–41; political, 10, 157; relational, 10, 26, 155–56, 159, 166, 170, 178n72, 179n81, 191, 213, 223; of the self, 213; of sexual difference, 4, 47; of silence, 226; of use, 190; of vulnerability, 59–60, 78, 191
opacity, 71
openness, 4, 240
oppression, 38, 97–100, 128n11, 174, 213
order: domestic, 164; linear-progressive, 113; masculine, 8, 88, 113–14; patriarchal, 92, 112, 114, 123, 168, 275; patriarchic, 47; political, 19, 138, 156; symbolic, 4, 41–42, 44, 50, 94, 113, 151, 165, 269; temporal, 118
origin, 12, 44, 45, 269–70, 274–76, 278. *See also* beginnings
Origins of Totalitarianism, The, 40
otherness, 23, 30, 45, 161
Ovid, 243
ownership, 189. *See also* use

painting, 87, 191, 195–98
Palestine, 216
pandemic, 9, 32, 138, 140–41, 148, 150, 200
paradox, 170, 173, 185, 205n67, 225, 244

Parmenides, 43–44
particularity, 62, 68, 71, 75–76, 225
passion, 216, 271
Passion According to G. H., The, 271–72
passivity, 60, 94, 96
pathos, 20
patriarchal: logic, 97, 115; order, 92, 112, 114, 123, 168, 275; power, 113, 115–16, 131, 187, 193; societies, 189; stereotypes, 276; structures, 100; symbolic order, 113, 269; systems, 193; theoretical thinking, 100; tradition, 41; use, 194
patriarchy, 41, 94, 105n25, 199
Penelope, 8, 42, 59, 86–103, 104n18, 112–16, 127n4, 131n68, 168–70, 172–74, 189; bodily knowledge, 86; Cavarero's, 87–94, 103, 105n25, 123, 126; gestures, 155, 169–70; Homer's, 110; stealing, 91, 105n25, 112, 116, 126, 173; story of, 8, 42, 46, 114–15, 131n75; theft of, 98, 115; work, 88–91, 93–94, 103, 113
performativity, 144
personhood, 71, 188
perversity, 248–49, 255
Phaedo, 87–88, 89–90
phallus, 50n1
phenomenology, 237, 239, 272
photograph, 69, 124, 193, 204n45
physicality, 99, 241
physis, 45, 160–62, 164–65, 179n82
pilgrimage, 101
Pinochet, Augusto, 260n3
Pinto, Isabella, 267
Pitkin, Hanna, 38, 41
Pitts, Andrea J., 105n40
Plato, 3–4, 6–8, 14, 19–27, 32, 87, 89–91, 93, 97, 99–100, 110, 116, 126, 127n4, 176, 189, 192, 231n60

"Platone e la democrazia," 19–20
Platonic: critique, 20; dialogues, 87, 111; distrust, 22, 25; framework, 91, 98; inheritance, 6; mode, 88; model, 19; political philosophy, 28; system, 97; texts, 8, 88; view, 93, 102; violence, 7
plurality, 3, 5, 7, 21–27, 30, 32–33, 39, 42, 61, 74–75, 21–27, 139, 142–44, 147, 150, 151, 155, 159, 169, 175n3, 180n90, 240–41; human, 23, 26, 46; interacting, 21, 32; interactive, 70; paradoxical, 26, 46; participatory, 149; space of, 142
poetics, 8, 59
policing, 72, 172
polis, 3, 6, 19, 21–22, 25, 138, 144, 156, 159–66, 168–71, 179n80, 187, 189
political philosophy, 1, 3, 8–9, 19, 25, 70, 186, 187; ancient, 185; Ancient Greek, 38; Arendt's, 7, 115; canon of, 1; Cavarero's, 151; of gender, 49; liberal, 147; Platonic, 28; traditional, 147; Western, 20, 189
Politics, 24
populism, 22
possibility, 4, 28–29, 31, 96–97, 101, 121, 130n43, 144, 148–49, 159, 164, 167–70, 173, 177, 179, 216, 218, 238, 257–58, 261
post-structuralism, 50, 241
post-truth, 20–22, 32
postural: ethics, 10, 28, 185; geometry, 155, 167, 191; inclination, 31
posture: inclined, 113, 147, 157; vertical, 146
power, 28, 31, 37, 77–78, 97, 109, 113–17, 137–38, 144, 278; archival, 119; asymmetrical, 191; collective,

31, 78; diffuse, 31; discursive, 20; executive, 141; formative, 162; healing, 277; life-forming, 159, 161, 164, 167; maternal generative, 159, 163, 164–67; patriarchal, 113, 115–16, 131, 187, 193; of the polis, 165; political, 141–42, 144, 158, 162; relational, 31; sense-making, 164, 167; sovereign, 10, 156, 158, 160–61, 164, 167, 169–70, 173; of the state, 150; structures of, 126; system of, 20; tyrannical, 162–63; will, 142
Precarious Life, 29
precariousness, 29, 31
pregnancy, 4, 12, 270, 273–74
pregnant: bodies, 2; body, 267–68, 270, 272, 275, 278; women, 106n45, 270, 274
Primera, German Eduardo, 187
private, 3–4, 10, 38, 74, 76, 94, 101–3, 123, 137–39, 141–45, 147, 149–51; bodies, 144; body, 138, 144, 149; home, 144, 147; interiority, 137; limits of, 76; realm, 92; space, 93, 139, 144, 172, 197; sphere, 3, 9, 103, 115, 137, 139, 142, 150; uniqueness, 144
privilege, 28–29, 115, 140, 239, 242
procreation, 178n72, 274–75
Prometheus, 44
protest, 3, 31–32
psyche, 252, 268
public, 3–4, 9–10, 31–33, 38, 60, 74, 76, 90, 92–93, 101–3, 123–24, 137–39, 142–51, 181n142; business, 32; communication, 150; freedom, 32, 139, 147; happiness, 3, 31–32, 62, 70, 76, 78, 147; life, 142; limits of, 76; realm, 46, 74, 90, 143, 203n22, 239; property, 124; space, 22, 25, 31, 33, 90, 93, 101, 137, 139, 144, 148, 150, 172; sphere, 3, 9, 22, 74, 87, 115, 137–38, 147, 150
punishment, 174, 188, 243
purity, 106n42

queer, 168, 198; body, 168; domesticity, 173; ethics, 168; politics, 34n38; theory, 1

race, 1, 10, 156, 171, 189
racial: capitalism, 171; violence, 109, 171, 176n20
racialization, 156, 171–72, 175n10, 177n50
racism, 149, 171, 204n45, 229n8
radical, 70, 144, 164, 247, 258; changes, 192; commitment, 9; counter power, 192; critique, 28; damage, 245; futures, 72; heterogeneity, 187; imagination, 123; materialism, 188; modes of living, 122; otherness, 161; perspective, 147; phenomenology, 239; possibilities, 122, 131n68; potential, 114, 118; singularity, 241; space, 137, 151; tradition, 70; work, 131n68
Rancière, Jacques, 8, 61, 63, 68–71, 73, 76–78
rape, 195, 217–18, 220, 226, 230n27, 233n83, 243, 247–49, 252, 254
rationality, 139, 225
reason, 8, 50, 60, 89, 117, 138, 149; disembodied, 219; male, 138; philosophical, 44; of speech, 70; voice of, 241
rebirth, 277
reciprocal, 25, 28, 276; apprehension, 66; care, 240; exhibition, 240;

reciprocal *(continued)*
 exposure, 147; gaze, 165; interaction, 148; limit, 192; relationality, 28
reciprocity, 140, 166
recognition, 95, 110, 125
rectitude, 168, 190, 193
refuge, 104, 172
refusal, 60–63, 72, 76–79, 103, 113, 121, 139, 171, 183, 186, 276; feminist, 94; politics of, 60, 78
regeneration, 272–73, 276–77
regret, 274–75
rehumanization, 223
Relating Narratives, 5, 25–28, 46, 63, 106n41, 115, 116, 126, 129n31, 131n68, 179n81, 214, 220–21, 237, 239, 255
relational, 13n12, 25–29, 140, 186, 213–14, 217, 224, 232n66, 239; beings, 10, 23; bodies, 151; body-self, 147, 149; embodiment, 10; experience, 242; form, 269; identity, 239; inclination, 149; interactions, 144; ontology, 10, 26, 155–56, 159, 166, 170, 178n72, 179n81, 191, 213, 223; power, 31; practice, 25; self, 2, 211, 214, 221; singularity, 269; space, 102–3, 104n18, 115, 143, 240; subjectivity, 146; uniqueness, 214
relationality, 1, 11–12, 13n12, 30, 42, 92, 94, 131n75, 137, 145–51, 155, 160, 166–67, 175n3, 185, 187, 191, 198, 212, 214–16, 240–42, 255, 258; acoustic, 258; amorous, 47; asymmetrical, 198; complex, 269; constitutive, 3, 5–6, 11, 26, 28, 111, 126, 141, 191, 214, 269; disorienting, 12; dispossessive,

72; ecstatic, 72; embodied, 12; erotic, 47; ethical, 148–49, 193; imbalanced, 269; logic of, 98; nonviolent, 191; pathological, 181; precarious, 166; primary, 240–41; reciprocal, 28; uncanny, 12
relations, 155, 161–64, 167, 22; asymmetrical, 166; blood, 161; of care, 162, 174, 215; community, 146; egalitarian, 70; ethical, 194; generational, 163; gestational, 166; human, 216, 219, 225–26; intimate, 230n37; loving, 195; of nonviolence, 195; oblique, 198; ordinary, 194; with others, 101; of power, 97, 203n31; slanted, 198; social, 140; of wounding, 174
remembrance, 253. *See also* memory
Renaissance, 87
reparation, 29. *See also* care
repentance, 274
repetition, 112–15, 128n14, 169, 252–53, 258–59
representation, 26, 61, 65, 67, 69–70, 77, 112, 195, 221, 232n66; artistic, 199; collective, 197; feminine, 44; of motherhood, 268, 274
reproductive: capacities, 171; function, 165; labor, 161; life, 160; possibilities, 100; rights, 194
repugnance, 12, 216, 243, 272
repulsion, 270, 272–73, 275–76
Republic, 3, 19, 21, 22
resistance, 5, 10, 11, 34n38, 91, 96–101, 106n42, 114, 118, 121, 140, 169, 171, 174, 186, 187, 194–95, 222, 256, 258, 274; feminine, 197; fugitive, 10, 157; political, 100, 103, 115; power of, 258; space of, 34n38,

35, 98, 116, 137; to violence, 186; women's, 172. *See also* active resistance
resistant, 97; actions, 186; actor, 97; agent, 96; care, 113, 157; figure, 194; gesture, 195; knowing, 173; life, 71; subjectivity, 74
resonance, 32, 49, 168, 198, 240, 256, 258–59
responsibility, 29, 69, 150, 259n2; ethical, 120; ethics of, 32
retaliation, 29
revolt, 112–13
revolution, 32, 41, 192
reweaving, 59, 90–91. *See also* weaving; unweaving
rhythm 48–49, 89, 90, 92–93, 115, 165, 167, 170, 173, 240–41, 258, 270. *See also* tempo
Ricciardi, Alessia, 267
Rich, Adrienne, 38, 41
rights, 8, 27, 31, 60, 146; fundamental, 144; political, 38; reproductive, 194; sexual, 194; women's, 37
"right to appear," 31
Rivera Cusicanqui, Silvia, 85–86, 102
Roman, 39, 74; law, 188; senate, 192
romanticization, 119, 126
Rose, Jacqueline, 267
Rühle-Gerstel, Alice, 37

sacrifice, 185, 188
sadomasochism, 192
safety, 102, 230n40
Sandberg, Sheryl, 205n62
Scheherazade, 220–21
schielende Blick, 157, 160, 164
Schubert, Franz, 248–50, 252, 255–56
Sebald, W. G., 121, 224–25

Second Sex, The, 40
security, 139, 141–42, 145–46, 185, 192
self, 11–12, 23, 28, 30, 48–49, 96–98, 137–38, 142, 145–49, 152, 192, 197, 211–14, 218–19, 221–27, 238–40, 258, 269–72; Arendtian, 221; autonomous, 28, 213; broken, 211, 218, 227; corporeal, 146, 151; critique, 6; dismembered, 219; dissolution of, 12, 271; embodied, 197; erect, 28; individual, 12, 141, 270; narratable, 177n34, 185, 191, 224, 227, 231n63, 239, 253; narrative, 221; political, 145; relational, 2, 211, 214, 221; singular, 232n66; unique, 3, 23
self-belonging, 113–15
self-determination, 100, 213
self-exposure, 46
self-generation, 45
selfhood, 12, 65, 212–15, 217, 222, 227
self-limitation, 205
self-narration, 46, 221, 226
self-narratives, 223
Self-Portrait as the Allegory of Painting, 196–98
self-preservation, 179
self-sufficiency, 29, 155, 240
sense-making, 97–98, 102, 164, 169–70, 212, 215, 220
sentimentalism, 278
sex, 26; feminine, 274; masculine, 90; worker, 102
sexed, 26–27, 40, 46; bodies, 2, 10, 91, 186; body, 192; dimorphism, 50; event, 45; human existence, 47; imaginary, 6; natality, 49;

sexed *(continued)*
 philosophy, 91; thought, 6;
 uniqueness, 27
sexism, 171
sexual: agency, 217; assault, 11, 214, 217–19; exploitation, 174; hierarchy, 50; organs, 194; rights, 194; transgression, 217; violation, 217
sexual difference, 7, 9–10, 25, 34n20, 38, 40–41, 44, 46, 48, 50n1, 155–57, 164, 171, 173n34, 188, 194, 199; feminine, 50n1; feminism of, 4, 100; forgetting of, 40; philosophy of, 3–4, 7, 90
sexuality, 49, 168, 189
sexual violence, 11, 172, 213, 216–17, 230n37, 247, 257, 261n41; aftermath of, 224, 261n40; as horrorism, 227n1; survivors of, 220
sexuation, 26
Shakespeare, William, 221
shame, 193
Sharpe, Christina, 110, 122, 132n82
Shoah, 223. *See also* Holocaust
sight, 242, 245, 257. *See also* visuality
signification, 114, 147, 232n66, 241
silence, 60, 120, 220, 222, 243–49 passim, 256–59; ontology of, 226
silencing, 110, 189, 245–47, 249–50, 252–53, 257, 259n2, 261
Silverbloom, Rachel, 9, 105n25, 227n1, 229n24
sin, 195
singular, 24, 77–78, 217, 240; acts, 70; being, 159, 166–67, 176n34, 219, 269, 273; beings, 155, 159–60, 176n34, 219; bodies, 241; entities, 73; existent, 60–61, 63, 67, 75–78; experience, 221; face, 246; flesh, 274; forms of life, 272–76, 278; individuals, 216, 221, 226; life, 65; life stories, 221; lives, 66, 75, 121, 167; narrative, 5; organism, 269–70; particularity, 68, 75–76, 225; self, 232; uniqueness, 63; *who*, 61, 63, 175n34
singularity, 1–2, 25, 46, 60, 62, 64, 66–68, 70–71, 76, 111, 114, 116–17, 129n36, 155, 157, 162, 167, 175n3, 214–17, 219, 225–27, 231n60, 237–38, 243, 246, 270–71; of the body, 26; concrete, 164; corporeal, 214; embodied, 4, 269; excess of, 225; incarnate, 275; incarnated, 270; irreducible, 71; living, 129n31, 159; naked, 226; ontology of, 169; philosophy of, 129n36, 227n1; political, 70; radical, 241; relational, 269; unique, 60; of voice, 241
Skeehan, Danielle, 173–74
skill, 87, 114, 197–98
skin, 96–96, 190, 213–15
slavery, 129, 176n20, 177n50; afterlife of, 171–72; archives of, 110–11, 116–17, 125; time of, 118
Smallwood, Stephanie, 109, 125
smarginatura, 273
social, 34n38, 38, 48, 71, 76, 174; activity, 140; bonds, 30; confinement, 172; death, 122, 160, 172; distancing, 140, 145, 150; environment, 198; existence, 172; fabrics, 127n11; futures, 111; groupings, 198; interactions, 140; life, 158; limits of, 76; meanings, 111; murder, 218; negotiation, 74; oppression, 38; relations, 140, 201n8, 203n31; role, 165

sociality, 168, 173
sociology, 140
Socrates, 21, 87, 89–91, 176n22, 192
Söderbäck, Fanny, 11, 127n4, 129n36, 190, 259n1, 260n23, 261n40
solidarity, 164, 194
solitude, 24
Sommer, Doris, 105n40
Sonderkommando, 225
song, 48–49, 86, 149, 191, 248. See also music
sonority, 70
Sophists, 19–21, 32
Sophocles, 161, 162, 164, 177n50, 221, 268, 277
soul, 44, 89–92, 138, 143, 145, 192, 246
sound, 122, 239–41, 243–45, 250–52, 257
sovereign, 28, 31; eyes, 170; figure, 164; gesture, 157; individual, 142, 179n81; mode, 72; power, 10, 156, 158, 160–61, 164, 167, 169–70, 173; subject, 26, 115
sovereignty, 29–30, 157–58, 185–86, 188, 213; autarchic, 60; genealogy of, 156; lack of, 148; logic of, 157; masculinist, 60; modern, 185; state, 187; violence of, 157
space, 40, 59, 62, 86–87, 94–98, 100–4, 106n48, 113–16, 131n68, 147–48, 166, 168–73, 257–58, 270, 278; abstract, 146; anomalous, 168–69; of appearance, 21–22, 32, 87, 239; confined, 101; counter-hegemonic, 86; enclosed, 102; fugitive, 94; inner, 148; liberatory, 144, 151; masculine, 90; material, 144; movable, 102; nonviolent, 195;
open, 101; of the philosopher, 90; of plurality, 142; political, 113, 116, 131n68, 143, 145, 151; of politics, 87, 98, 100, 103, 137; private, 93, 139, 144, 172, 197; public, 22, 25, 31, 33, 90, 93, 101, 137, 139, 144, 148, 150, 172; radical, 137; relational, 102–3, 104n18, 115, 143, 240; of resistance, 34n38, 98, 116, 137; rhythmic, 92; shared, 143, 147; and time, 40, 92, 94–95; of violence, 102; of visibility, 147
speaking, 11, 50, 61, 122, 143, 145–46, 150, 231, 269. See also speech; voice
speech, 3, 39, 45–46, 48–49, 70, 118, 120, 147, 226, 240–41, 258. See also speaking; voice
Sphinx, 67–68
Spillers, Hortense, 172
spontaneity, 39, 114
state, 67, 140, 187–88, 198–99; archives, 122; democratic, 202n15; institutions, 201n8; power of, 150; sovereignty, 187; violence, 188
state of exception, 158, 179n74, 188
Stately Bodies, 4, 138, 242
stealing, 7, 9, 49, 91, 100, 105n25, 110–14, 116, 126, 129n31, 189
Stein, Gertrude, 221
stereotypes, 116, 194, 198, 267, 273, 276
stories, 5, 110–12, 114, 116–23, 125–26, 214, 220–21, 223–24, 226–27, 231n60, 256–57, 261n41, 276, 278; war, 47; of women, 9, 110
story, 5, 11, 25–26, 42, 63–64, 67, 99–100, 112, 115–20, 122–25, 126, 127n4, 173, 176n34, 191, 217,

story (continued)
  220–27, 237, 239–40, 242, 244, 249, 253–56, 270–71
storytelling, 25, 42, 256, 269
strategist, 102. See also tactical thinker
streetwalker, 101–3
subject, 14n21, 26, 28–30, 34n20, 40, 62, 64–72, 76–77, 81n48, 138–39, 142, 146–49, 155, 203n39, 219, 261; abstract, 40, 61–62, 64, 66, 142, 147, 151, 201n8; active, 98, 102–3; altruistic, 28; anthropocentric, 72; atomistic, 2; austere, 149; autonomous, 5, 28, 40, 167, 190; autopoietic, 269; balanced, 149; divided, 151; equal, 65; equivalent, 65; erect, 5; essential, 64; formation, 47; fragmented, 61; free, 65; fungible, 65; generic, 151; inclined, 28–29; individual, 28–29, 190; individualist, 185–86; isolated, 146; of liberalism, 152n25; male, 40, 44; masculine, 5, 190; metaphysical, 64; modern, 14n21, 86; non-sovereign, 148; philosophical, 12; political, 5, 10, 70, 76, 115, 139, 146, 148–49, 201n8; predetermined, 146; postmodernist, 64; public, 149; rational, 5, 149; self-referential, 147, 149, 151; self-sufficient, 2, 151, 269; sovereign, 26, 115; substitutable, 65; thinking, 4; unique, 26; unrepeatable, 26; upright, 149; vertical, 14n21, 149; vulnerable, 29
subjecthood, 69, 72; anthropocentric, 72; autonomous, 10; fragmented, 63
subjectivity, 62, 71–74, 217, 269; autonomous, 214, 219; colonial, 86; constructed, 152; contemporary, 73; female, 25, 44, 112, 126, 138, 164; feminine, 110; historical, 9; male, 138; masculine, 111–12, 116; oppressed, 96; political, 5, 8–10, 114; postcolonial, 86; relational, 146; resistant, 74; resisting, 96; split, 152. See also active subjectivity
subordination, 96, 110
Sudan, 204n45
suffering, 216, 223, 226, 255, 273
suicide, 224, 277
Surging Democracy, 3, 7, 30, 60, 63, 98, 101, 200
surplus, 70, 75
survival, 11, 167, 170, 173–74, 249
survivor, 11, 211, 217–18, 220, 222, 238, 243, 246, 261n41, 262n50
sustenance, 171, 177n72
symbolic, 47–48; constellation, 88; event, 43; figure, 45; framework, 91; order, 4, 41–42, 44, 50, 94, 113, 151, 165, 269; structure, 8, 48, 88, 100; twist, 112; universe, 100; value, 276
Symposium, 104n11

tactical thinker, 102–3
tantear, 101–2, 103, 106n48
technologism, 278
technology, 274
tempo, 113–14. See also rhythm
temporal, 157; force, 72; logic, 93; order, 118; sequence, 118; structure, 111, 113
temporality, 40, 44, 68, 92, 113–14, 128n14, 165, 222, 277; female, 86; genealogical, 277; linear-progressive, 110, 114, 128n14; masculine, 113, 128n14; of mimesis, 128n14

tenderness, 171
terror, 28, 215, 225, 243, 252, 258, 271. *See also* horror
terrorism, 189
testimony, 11, 211, 241, 253, 255. *See also* story
text, 88, 95–99
thanatopolitics, 189
theater of cruelty, 77
theft, 98, 112, 115, 126
theoria, 46, 169
theory, 40, 73–75, 77, 87, 169; fabric of, 100; feminist, 1, 25–26, 47, 63–64, 186, 221; political, 75, 87, 195; queer, 1
theory of action, 7
They Are Coming, 193
time, 31–33, 40, 72, 91–95, 100, 113–14, 118, 122–23, 158, 169; cyclical, 113; experience of, 222; genealogical, 277; impenetrable, 92, 113; passing of, 222; of the philosopher, 92; of politics, 103; present, 271; of slavery, 118; and space, 40, 92, 94–95
togetherness, 22, 24. *See also* company
Toklas, Alice B., 221
torture, 193, 202, 216, 239, 246–56, 258, 261n41
totalitarian: annihilation, 40, 51; catastrophe, 224; drive, 26; governments, 24; machine, 223–24; masses, 3, 7, 22; regime, 7; politics, 192; specter, 24
totalitarianism, 23–24, 30, 144
touch, 62, 79, 97, 213, 247–48, 262n45, 273–74, 277
tradition, 77, 92, 112, 138, 241, 270, 273; Continental, 38; democratic,

70; of European modernity, 61, 79, 79n7; far-right, 21; feminist, 276; materialist, 9–10; patriarchal, 41; patriarchic, 45; philosophical, 64, 67, 110; philosophical work, 270; of philosophy, 40, 43, 50, 72; political, 160, 192; possessive, 79n7; radical, 70; revolutionary, 187; of thinking, 41; of thought, 61–62; Western, 22, 24, 41, 60–61, 99, 100, 110, 156, 159–61, 187, 190
transatlantic slave trade, 10, 79, 110, 116, 156, 171–72
trauma, 11, 29–31, 211–13, 220, 222–24, 228–29, 230n49, 232n66, 255, 261n41; aftermath of, 215, 222; collective, 232n66; as colonizing, 262n50; narrating, 222; political, 30; social, 30; studies, 262n63; survivor, 11, 232n66, 238, 243; testimonies, 212
tremendo, 268, 270, 272–73, 276
Trouillot, Michel-Rolph, 109
truth, 8, 20–22, 24, 26, 29, 60, 89, 121, 127n4, 146, 252–53, 255, 271, 274, 278; eternal, 90; historical, 110; language of, 12; literary, 267–69, 272–74, 276, 278; philosophical, 24; rational, 21, 231n60
Turkey, 31
two-in-one, 269–70, 274
tyranny, 32, 163

uncanny, 115, 162, 248; contact, 278; motherhood, 12, 268–75; relationality, 12
undercommons, 94, 97
undoing, 113, 169, 215, 222–23
ungendering, 172

unheimlich, 268
uniformity, 26
unique, 219, 221, 239; actions, 39; being, 64, 144, 273; beings, 23, 26, 46, 143, 161, 180n90, 200; bodies, 5, 144, 145, 149; body, 144–46, 163; body-self, 137, 147; deeds, 39; distinctness, 23, 39, 45–46, 49; existence, 163; existent, 60, 67, 74, 76–78; forms, 275; individual, 226; infant, 39; self, 3, 23, 147, 214; singularity, 60; story, 25, 239; subject, 26; unity, 214
uniqueness, 3–5, 7, 11–12, 21, 23–27, 46, 48–49, 60–63, 65–66, 70, 74–77, 79, 115–16, 141, 143–48, 150–51, 157, 159, 166–67, 175n3, 176n34, 189, 213–16, 221, 223–26, 239–40, 246; bodily, 4; of the body, 144, 150, 246; corporeal, 144, 159, 175n3; destruction of, 215–16, 225; disclosure of, 46, 60, 155; embodied, 12, 26–27, 241, 270; fugitive, 225; fragile, 127; human, 215–16; imperiled, 225; incarnate, 215; incarnated, 246, 269; individual, 71; irreducible, 226; material, 144; ontological, 257; ontologies of, 213; private, 144; relational, 214; sexed, 27; singular, 63; space of, 115; unrepeatable, 115; unsubstitutable, 166; of the voice, 258
unity, 5, 25, 46, 116, 176n34, 214–15
universality, 2, 64, 67, 111; abstract, 155, 219; monstrous, 129
unweaving, 59, 86, 89–94, 98, 100, 104n18, 113–14, 116, 118, 123. *See also* reweaving; weaving
use, 189–90, 192–94, 203n39

usefulness, 91–92
uselessness, 192
Use of Bodies, The, 188–89, 192
uterus, 48, 277

vaccine, 140, 145
vagina, 50n1
ventriloquism, 252
Venus, 116–19, 122–25
"Venus in Two Acts," 116, 118, 121, 123, 130n43
verisimilitude, 269
vertical, 28, 151; approach, 137; politics, 146; posture, 146; subject, 14n21, 149
verticality, 115, 146, 149, 151, 179n86
victim, 211, 217–19, 229n25, 229n28, 230n40, 258
violation, 156, 159–60, 163–64, 167, 171, 193; double, 195; sexual, 217
violence, 11, 28–29, 31, 47, 102, 109, 111, 117, 119, 121, 150, 155–58, 166–67, 172, 174, 185–91, 194, 205n57, 211–13, 216, 255–57; acoustic of, 245, 261n41; aesthetic, 262n50; aftermath of, 212, 217, 226; bodily, 141; critique of, 185, 205, 247, 257; divine, 194; domestic, 275; effects of, 239, 246, 258; epistemic, 238, 259n2, 262n50; exposure to, 186, 188–89, 199–200; gendered, 109; global, 28; historical, 119; of history, 123; horrorist, 5, 216, 219, 226; inaudibility of, 245; of instrumentalization, 126; language of, 217; modern, 185; ontological, 5–6, 11, 212, 217, 220 223, 227n1, 229n28, 230n37, 232n66; phenomenology

of, 237; Platonic, 7; political, 9, 11, 175n10, 238–29, 243, 247, 249, 261n30; racial 109, 171–72, 176n20; repressive, 188; resistance to, 186; of romanticization, 126; rupturing, 174; scene of, 214, 221, 229, 246; as silencing, 247; of sovereignty, 157; space of, 102; state, 188; teleological, 119; of torture, 246–47, 255; traumatic, 11, 259n2; unspeakability of, 257. *See also* sexual violence

violent: archives, 109, 111, 120; erasure, 120, 222; gesture, 219

Virgin and Child with St. Anne, The, 191–92

virus, 140–41

visibility, 147, 163, 239–40, 242–45, 249, 252, 257; political, 249; regime of, 11, 243–45, 249

visuality, 237, 239

vitalism, 70

vocality, 11, 241

voice, 4, 11, 13, 47–49, 70, 140–41, 145–46, 162, 191, 223, 226–27, 237–59; acoustics of, 242; colonized, 233n83, 258; corporeal, 145, 240–41; destruction of, 233n83, 257; dismembered, 256; feminine, 39, 240; human, 48, 240–41, 257; loss of, 238; maternal, 49; personal, 241; phenomenology of, 237; political, 250; of reason, 241; singularity of, 241; stolen, 258; uniqueness of, 258

voicelessness, 261n41. *See also* silence; silencing

void, 30, 47

vulnerability, 9, 29–31, 138, 145–51, 160, 166–67, 169–70, 190–91, 200, 212–16, 218–19, 228n14, 229n28; of the body, 146, 148–49; constitutive, 6, 215, 246; common, 29; corporeal, 29, 149, 177n41; destruction of, 218; diverse, 150; extreme, 189; fundamental, 186; human, 29; language of, 166; ontology of, 59–60, 78, 191; shared, 30–31, 214; theories of, 62; undeniable, 29

vulnerable, 5–6, 126, 145–47, 166, 191, 227, 228n14, 229n25, 247; beings, 176n34, 185, 213, 216; bodies 2, 5, 10, 146–47, 149, 215, 246; body, 137, 142, 146, 149; body-self, 147; life events, 151; lives, 121; relation, 159; selves, 149; subject, 29

vulnus, 166, 190, 214, 228n14. *See also* wound

wake work, 122–23

war on terror, 185, 202n15

Wayward Lives, Beautiful Experiments, 122, 130n43

waywardness, 76, 170–72

weakness, 138, 148–49, 196

weaving 42, 71, 86–99, 113–16, 118; labor of, 87; as metaphor, 42, 127n11; room, 91–94, 101, 103, 104n18, 115–16, 131n75; task of 89; work of, 86–87, 90, 94. *See also* reweaving; unweaving

Weigel, Sigrid, 157

welcome, 171–72, 177n40, 240

Western: art, 185, 192, 195; canon, 99–100; culture, 13n15, 87, 116; life, 189; metaphysics, 20, 40, 44, 75, 187; modernity, 156, 177n49; philosophy, 24, 40, 43, 50, 72, 116, 160; political philosophy, 20, 189;

Western *(continued)*
  political thinking, 97; politics, 189; thinking, 100; thought, 38–40, 45, 88; tradition, 22, 24, 41, 60–61, 99, 100, 110, 156, 159–61, 187, 190
the what, 61, 63–65, 70, 71–75, 220. *See also* the *who*
whatness, 70, 72–75
White Madonna with Twins, 204n45
the *who*, 5, 8, 60–72, 79n7214, 221, 226, 231n63; grammar of, 98, 60–61, 66, 68, 77; politics of, 8, 60, 62–63, 66, 77–78
"*Who* Engenders Politics?," 62–63, 77
wholeness, 93, 215
will, 142, 217
Winkler, Cathy, 218
wisdom, 21, 63, 173
withdrawal, 160, 168–70
witness, 5, 117, 221–22, 225–26, 232n66, 248, 256
womanhood, 50, 63
womb, 194, 273, 275, 277; of the daughter, 277; maternal, 269–70; mother's, 41, 45–46
women: bodies, 100, 189, 190, 192–93; of color, 115, 129; communality, 131n75; erasure of, 110; exclusion of, 87, 110; liberation of, 37, 115; movement, 38; mythical, 110; objectification of, 119; and philosophy, 6; political party, 38; resistance, 172; rights, 37; social role, 165; stories of, 9, 110; white, 115, 129, 172. *See also* Black women
wonder, 34n38
work, 70, 74, 142–44, 187, 195, 203n22; of destruction, 223; domestic, 86; feminine, 99; feminist, 131n60, 185; liberatory, 101; for life, 161, 171; meaningless, 94; of narration, 224; Penelope's, 88–91, 93–94, 103, 113; of the philosopher, 89–90; philosophical, 187, 231n60, 270; of philosophy, 87, 223; political, 87, 131n68; of repetition, 114; rhythmic 93, 113; of weaving, 86–87, 90, 94; of unweaving, 91, 100, 114. *See also* labor
workers' movement, 38
World War II, 32
wound, 30, 190–91, 222, 228
wounding, 5, 111, 113, 126, 157, 159, 161, 166–69, 172, 174, 190, 192, 200, 213–16, 219, 222, 228n14
writing, 40, 42, 47, 96, 99, 105n40, 122, 125–26, 198, 221, 227, 241, 270, 276; biographical, 121, 223; bodily, 105n40; feminine, 274; "impossible," 119

Xanthippe, 87

Zambrano, María, 277
Ziarek, Ewa, 158
zoe, 158–64, 168, 174, 176, 188, 278. *See also* bare life
zoon politikon, 24–26

www.ingramcontent.com/pod-product-compliance
Lightning Source LLC
Chambersburg PA
CBHW030522230426
43665CB00010B/726

A Critical Collection on Alejandro Morales

University of New Mexico Press / Albuquerque

Edited by Marc García-Martínez
and Francisco A. Lomelí

A Critical Collection on Alejandro Morales Forging an Alternative Chicano Fiction

© 2021 by the University of New Mexico Press
All rights reserved. Published 2021
Printed in the United States of America

First paperback printing 2025 | ISBN 978-0-8263-6808-9

Library of Congress Cataloging-in-Publication Data
Names: García-Martínez, Marc, editor. | Lomelí, Francisco A., editor.
Title: A critical collection on Alejandro Morales: forging an alternative Chicano fiction / edited by Marc García-Martínez and Francisco A. Lomelí.
Description: Albuquerque: University of New Mexico Press, [2021] | Includes bibliographical references and index.
Identifiers: LCCN 2021032884 (print) | LCCN 2021032885 (e-book) | ISBN 9780826363091 (cloth) | ISBN 9780826363107 (e-book)
Subjects: LCSH: Morales, Alejandro, 1944– Criticism and interpretation. | LCGFT: Literary criticism. | Essays.
Classification: LCC PS3563.O759 Z64 2021 (print) | LCC PS3563.O759 (e-book) | DDC 813/.54—dc23
LC record available at https://lccn.loc.gov/2021032884
LC e-book record available at https://lccn.loc.gov/2021032885

Founded in 1889, the University of New Mexico sits on the traditional homelands of the Pueblo of Sandia. The original peoples of New Mexico—Pueblo, Navajo, and Apache—since time immemorial have deep connections to the land and have made significant contributions to the broader community statewide. We honor the land itself and those who remain stewards of this land throughout the generations and also acknowledge our committed relationship to Indigenous peoples. We gratefully recognize our history.

Cover photograph courtesy of Alejandro Morales.
Designed by Mindy Basinger Hill

CONTENTS

1   **INTRODUCTION** / Alejandro Morales / An Errant Maverick Faces the Literary Canon and History / *Marc García-Martínez and Francisco A. Lomelí*

13   **ONE** / Submersion, Suffocation, and Entombment of the Mexican and Immigrant Body in *River of Angels*—Probing Figurations of Violence and Isolation / *Marc García-Martínez*

35   **TWO** / The Analogous Correspondence of an Extreme Poetics between Stanley Kubrick's *A Clockwork Orange* and Alejandro Morales' *Barrio on the Edge* / *Francisco A. Lomelí*

53   **THREE** / Alejandro Morales' *The Captain of All These Men of Death* and Philip Roth's *Nemesis*: Parallels and Contrasts / *Stephen Miller*

71   **FOUR** / Tropes of Ecothinking and the Spatial Imaginary in Alejandro Morales' *River of Angels* / *Sophia Emmanouilidou*

89   **FIVE** / History, Spatial Justice, and the *Esperpento* in Alejandro Morales' *Pequeña nación* / *Jesús Rosales*

109   **SIX** / Heterotopia and the Emergence of the Modern *Ilusa* in *Waiting to Happen* / *Margarita López López*

127   **SEVEN** / City History and Space Politics: Los Angeles in Morales' *River of Angels* / *Baojie Li*

143   **EIGHT** / *Pequeña nación* / Big (Feminist) Revolution / *Amaia Ibarraran-Bigalondo*

161	**NINE** /	Bodies in Motion in *The Place of the White Heron*, Volume Two of the Heterotopian Trilogy / *A Glance through the Panopticon* / Adam Spires
179	**TEN** /	Race, Space, and Magical Realism in *The Brick People* and *River of Angels* / Adina Ciugureanu
197	**ELEVEN** /	Mestizaje, Cultural Identity, and Environmental Degradation in Alejandro Morales' *The Rag Doll Plagues* / Manuel M. Martín-Rodríguez
213	**TWELVE** /	Translation as Rewriting and Resituating / The Two English Versions of *Caras viejas y vino nuevo* by Alejandro Morales / Elena Errico
227	**THIRTEEN** /	History and Fiction in Alejandro Morales' Narratives / Luis Leal
247	**FOURTEEN** /	Epidemics, Epistemophilia, and Racism: Ecological Literary Criticism and *The Rag Doll Plagues* / María Herrera-Sobek
263	**FIFTEEN** /	A Dialogue with the Writer Alejandro Morales / Francisco Lomelí, Marc García-Martínez, and Daniel Olivas
285		Bibliography / Donaldo W. Urioste
307		Contributors
311		Index

A Critical Collection on Alejandro Morales

INTRODUCTION / Alejandro Morales /
An Errant Maverick Faces the Literary
Canon and History / MARC GARCÍA-MARTÍNEZ
AND FRANCISCO A. LOMELÍ

Literature is not merely language; it is also the will to figuration, the motive for metaphor that Nietzsche once defined as the desire to be different, the desire to be elsewhere . . . to be different from oneself . . . to be different from the metaphors and images of the contingent works that are one's heritage: the desire to write greatly is the desire to be elsewhere, in a time and place of one's own, in an originality that must compound with inheritance, with the anxiety of influence. —Harold Bloom, *The Western Canon*, 1994

Alejandro Morales has been a steady presence in the thematic diversification of the Chicano/a novel that followed the first wave of fiction writers sparked by the Chicano Movement, referred to as the Quinto Sol Generation (between 1967–1974) and known for its openly cultural nationalist aesthetic agenda. Novels from this first wave included Tomás Rivera's . . . *Y no se lo tragó la tierra* (. . . And the Earth Did Not Part [1971]), Rudolfo A. Anaya's *Bless Me, Ultima* (1972), Oscar Zeta Acosta's *The Autobiography of a Brown Buffalo* (1972), Rolando Hinojosa's *Estampas del Valle y otras obras* (Sketches of the Valley and Other Works) (1973) and Miguel Méndez M.'s *Peregrinos de Aztlán* (1974), among others. In a watershed moment in 1975, however, Alejandro Morales composed *Caras viejas y vino nuevo*, a work that marked a definite shift away from epic and cultural nationalist representations in favor of depicting an unforgiving, hard-core barrio.

Rather than offering burnished or romanticized views of a relegated cultural history or environment, Morales focused on discerning the inner—and occasionally ambiguous—qualities of characters steeped in the contradictions of a raw and even savage reality. Along with a small group of other writers such as Ron Arias (*The Road to Tamazunchale* [1975]), Isabella Ríos (*Victuum* [1976]), Phil Sánchez (*Don Phil-O-Meno sí la mancha* [1977]), John Rechy (*The Sexual Outlaw* [1977]), and Aristeo Brito (*El diablo en Texas* [1976]), Morales emphasized craft and far-reaching novelistic experimentations through largely unconventional means. Chicano/a culture no longer had to be mirrored, or even reinvented, because what mattered most was zeroing in on the capabilities of the genre in order to further probe or capture Chicanos/as in their multiple and widespread sociocultural manifestations.

The work of Alejandro Morales constitutes a bold alternative, both to the Quinto Sol Generation and to the newer group of authors with whom he had an affinity. His literary representation of the mentioned sociocultural manifestations is so persistently unconventional that it challenges and at times even effaces the much-affirmed panoply that is Mexican American and Chicano/a letters. Morales stands out for his audacious and dauntless incursions into explorations of subject matters that others either outright avoid or shy away from in this literature, in great part because they require not only meticulous research into their respective backdrops and sociohistorical contexts but also a willingness to face the wholesale rawness of human existence. His breadth and range are remarkable, as he does not restrict himself to what is fashionable for the sake of popularity or marketability. Indeed, his works present a wide spectrum of thematic and metaphoric representations, extending from an almost monomaniacal dedication to recovering and revisioning history to exploring the disturbing role of epidemic diseases. Morales not only looks at what might have happened within the annals of history and its corresponding backdrop—oftentimes understood as the views and experiences of Chicanos/as below Anglo-America's radar—but also focuses on purported documents that authenticate a social history that has otherwise remained unknown, or "invisible." This Chicano author wants us to contemplate that a significant group of Mexican descendants were not only subjugated but were virtually erased by the majority society after the Mexican-American War of 1848. His works evince a predilection for the intrahistorical and the fanciful, as he seeks to extricate meaning and validation on behalf of a full-fledged, culturally informed subset that has struggled to survive within a hegemonic system. In his writing Morales ruminates on both the past and the future, offering incisive reflections to help the reader better understand how a conquered people may constitute a reality of new possibilities. Still, he sometimes writes as if he and his readers have an old score to settle, challenging their complacency through the unusual plot twists he hurls at them. In some cases, we are overwhelmed with bizarre characters of noir narratives and speculative imaginations, visceral figurations, overlapping symbologies, somatic encodings, and other elements that produce a shock that is hard to ignore.

There is something undeniably challenging and alternative about Morales' literary methods, which have been characterized by Antonio C. Márquez as "interlaced with surrealism, dream-narrative, magic realism, ample touches of the grotesque, and elements of the fantastical" (1995, 79). Others, like José Antonio Gurpegui, fittingly stress "la riqueza imaginativa de Alejandro Morales"—the richness of his creative vision and the wealth of imagination found in his work (1996, 43). While his writings never fail to produce verbally and visually rich incantations, they nonetheless always manage to form an intense assemblage of plot, voice, motif, complex metaphor, and stirring diegesis, arousing a genuine unease in the reader. The presence of these elements exerts considerable leverage on the way in which we come to understand both the author and the man. No doubt due to the aforesaid shock and unease, publishers initially rejected Morales' manuscripts—literary testimonials deemed painfully crude, disturbingly exotic, and just a bit too surreal. Even so, to this day his works firmly and unapologetically comprise a veritable library of crude counterhistories, exotic metanarratives, and surreal "flesh-and-blood" aesthetic experimentation.[1]

In doing so, Alejandro Morales' inimitable works contest and confront the present-day literary canon, both Chicano/a and international. Through innovative iterations of power struggles and strange, unvarnished apocalyptic renderings, and atmospheres and interrelations of considerable strife, his fictional works represent an ongoing experimentation with form, time, characterization, and geography. There arises from his novels a distinctive narrative voice that articulates a fascination with both the omnipresent trope of the metonymic barrio around East Los Angeles and the ever-changing geo-demographic developments in Los Angeles as a zone of intense hybridities and cultural admixtures, which he positions within a factual and fictionalized region that extends all the way to Mexico City. In engaging with his prolific library of work, the reader must contend with dynamics of realism versus the magical real, infrarealism versus "mystic realism," ethnohistory versus official history, intrahistory versus antihistory, chronicle versus testimonial, biography versus autobiography, myth versus legend, science versus popular medicine, surrealism versus hyperrealism, contemporaneity versus futurism, ambiguity versus speculative allusions, colonialism versus postcolonialism, dystopia versus heterotopia, race versus eugenics, "extreme poetics" versus sanitized portrayals, and natural diseases versus apocalyptic epidemics.[2] Because he freely and creatively indulges in the construction of metanovels that breach the gap between Chicano/a lived experience and how Anglo-America has attempted to define and ensnare Chicanos/asas a recycled, ahistorical living stereotype, Morales' work breaks the canonical shackles of space, history, unilingualism, character normativities, narrative modalities, and conventional approaches. He often refers to his characters' migratory patterns but does not necessarily limit himself to coming-of-age immigrant tales or to the sociopolitical polemics of the border. He prefers to unearth through aesthetic means troubling and problematic systemic constructions that have built barriers tending to hinder and encircle not only Chicano/a but *human* existence.

Thus, Morales does not fit neatly into a single classification in literary terms, due to his unprecedented eclecticism, worldview, and cutting-edge imaginary of emerging vanguard creations. Though he is a harsh, confrontational iconoclast who creates works that some readers and critics avoid, Morales nonetheless won UC Santa Barbara's prestigious Luis Leal Award for Distinction in the Arts in 2007. Moreover, 2020 marked the forty-fifth anniversary of the publishing of *Caras viejas y vino nuevo*, his first and most pivotal novel that made a major splash in Chicano/a letters. Nine novels and a collection of three novellas later, his work has been published worldwide and translated into Spanish, Italian, Dutch, and German. He is indeed an ethnic writer, but this should not be understood in reductionist terms situating him within one specific trend or category, for there is always something intranational and extranational about him.

And yet despite all this, it must be affirmed that Morales' literary art is cognate to literary art that came before; indeed, he admits a connection to and respect for past writers that inform his work. He possesses a vast knowledge of Chicano/a literature, of course, and yet is also influenced by the Latin American Boom writers (Carlos Fuentes, Gabriel García Márquez, José Donoso, Julio Cortázar, Mario Vargas Llosa), by the Mexican La Onda group (José Agustín, Gustavo Sáenz), by key North American voices (John Dos Passos, William Faulkner, Ernest Hemingway), and by prominent European writers (James Joyce, Alain Robbe-Grillet, Camilo José Cela). Chicano/a literary historians—namely, Luis Leal, Genaro Padilla, María Herrera-Sobek, Ramón Gutiérrez, and Francisco Lomelí—have sensed and often noted this knowledge and influence operating in his works. Nonetheless, Morales offers much beyond this influence, synthesis, or rematerialization, because he actively engages in creating new representations in order to visualize all literary possibilities, particularly when applied to his concepts of the future and what it might hold. Simply put, he has a persistent penchant for innovation.

This includes not repeating literary formulas, instead favoring trailblazing tales on unusual topics as well as multifarious experimentations, ranging from obscure or noir fictional worlds, backward plots, totalizing novelistic ventures of crisscrossing stories, the novel within a novel framework, echoes of resurrected protagonists or monster characters, and expansive personifications of geographies (i.e., the Los Angeles River, Irvine, Texan towns, the Simons Brickyard Factory, and a realm that he refers to as "Lamex") to the role of plagues as an atavistic reminder of past human struggles that somehow reemerge in modern and future times. We are convinced that attending to these histories, distressing ventures, character constructs, personifications, and innovative representations best permits us to isolate and measure the force that propels his literature. It would be a fallacy to deem this force as purely residing in Morales' natural talent or coming from a deep craving to express himself, or to claim that it is solely sourced in the author's personal history as son of Mexican immigrants growing up in a relatively stable working-class environment yet witnessing the harsher and poorer realm of the surrounding East L.A. barrios. It cannot be necessarily found in any of these reasonably predictable sources, but rather stems from what he himself calls "not being in one particular place at one specific time . . . where I see myself traveling through the past, present and future. I refuse to be limited to space, time or topic. Writing should always be a site of complete and unconditional freedom. I have always been a maverick, nonconformist writer who prefers to work independently unencumbered by outside expectations. . . . I can be anywhere in the expanding sphere of knowledge and, most importantly, of the imagination and creativity."[3] Morales speaks here of a will to create otherworldly temporal chronicles and to fashion original work mirroring unlimited and universal experiences. Asserting the existence of a resolve to regard but differentiate himself from his predecessors and contemporaries, exploring head-on uncharted dimensions of time, place, content, and form, his words send a clear signal that one of the most reliable ways to isolate and measure the power propelling Moralesian literature is to chart his determination to be "nonconformist" and "unencumbered"—that is, to probe his craving to be free in aesthetic imagination and unencumbered by reader expectations or canonical categories.

Morales' unrepentant individualism invites an explicit affirmation that he may arguably be in a category all his own, though paradoxically within and somehow beyond the genus of Chicano/a letters. The latter is characterized by Ramón Saldívar (1990, 5) as not only provocative, demanding, and strategic but also as one of the most striking, ambiguous, and demanding literature forms produced in the United States (10). Such a characterization, we believe, accurately pertains to Morales' vast and varied writings. Yet there is another compelling categorization of Chicano/a literature pertinent to Morales' work, namely, Luis Leal's claim that such texts ought to readily connect with Mexico, Mexican culture, or various content- and aesthetic-based works related to that country (Rosales 2014, 115). This is more or less true. Leal highlights the "many connections" that organically exist between Chicano/a and Mexican literary production, contending that "Chicano literature's roots are in Mexican literature" (116). His interconnection premise might be categorical, perhaps even controversial, but it is apropos to Alejandro Morales—fulfilled and well substantiated by much of the latter's literary output. If Mexico is not always in the foreground of Morales' tales, it is indeed a significant part of the background, or a subtle reminder, and/or a combination thereof.

Case in point, he has actively sought validation and support from Mexican publishing houses for his literature. His first two works were both written in Spanish and published in Mexico City by Joaquín Mortiz—*Caras viejas y vino nuevo* in 1975 (translated a few years later by Max Martínez as *Old Faces and New Wine* and two decades later by Francisco Lomelí as *Barrio on the Edge*), and *La verdad sin voz* in 1979 (translated nearly a decade later by Judith Ginsberg as *Death of an Anglo*). For the latter, Morales chose the novel's title from a quote by twentieth-century Mexican writer, essayist, and political activist José Revueltas. In addition, *La verdad sin voz* makes direct and indirect references to contemporary Mexican history, specifically, to the Mexico City Tlatelolco student massacre in 1968, the various guerrilla actions of the 1970s, and the myriad institutional and political violence perpetrated by the Mexican government. Morales' third work was the novel *Reto en el paraíso*, a bilingual and complex book centering on the social, historical, cultural, geopolitical, and (especially) emotive dynamics of Mexicans who lost their land in old California. *Reto en el paraíso* focuses on the progeny of these Mexicans, and all the sociocultural and psychosexual dynamics at work in their much-fragmented Mexican American identities. *The Brick People*, his subsequent effort from 1988, tells a story of Mexican migration and immigration, highlighting Mexican small-town realties via the example of

Quiseo de Abasolo in the central Mexico state of Guanajuato. In the novel, this Mexican town serves as the origin of most of the immigrant workers who appear in its overarching narrative.

The publication of *The Rag Doll Plagues* (in 1992) significantly altered the narrative landscape of Morales' writings. It is a novel composed of three interdependent cross-temporal and cross-geographic books that range from (past) colonial Mexico to (present-day) Southern California, and then to a (future) Mexico City-Los Angeles monolithic geopolitical corridor. His subsequent and exceedingly intricate work *Waiting to Happen* (2001) depicts the conditions and dynamics of Mexico and its often-warped sociopolitical relationship with the United States, while his novella compilation *Pequeña nación* (translated from the 2005 Spanish version as *Little Nation and Other Stories* by Adam Spires in 2014) presents a minichronicle entitled "Quetzali" about an Aztec mother encountering the brutal effects of the conquest of Tenochtitlán.

His next novel, *The Captain of All These Men of Death* (2008), takes us back from this relationship to the Mexican homeland and into a Southern California cosmos, distinguishing itself for its unusual and unexpected exploration of the effects of tuberculosis as a disease that impacts the Mexican American community. And his most recent novel, *River of Angels* (2014), weaves an epic narrative of immigrant and then first- and second-generation Mexican American families who interact within the immediate space of the Los Angeles River. It is a novel that masterfully unveils the tapestry of cultures and histories that interface throughout time.

Finally, in his aforementioned novella collection (*Pequeña nación*) Morales presents new experimentations that push the limits of some of his narrative imagination: a moving narration (in "Pequeña nación") about a group of L.A. barrio women who find the social agency to safeguard their neighborhood; a story ("Los jardines de Versalles") about a French emigrant couple who become marginalized within their community; and a tale ("La penca") told from the point of view of *esperpento* or gross exaggeration, in which an artist imposes his sordid desires onto a painting of the venerated Virgin de Guadalupe. Though many other Chicano/a and Mexican American writers do, in fact, proficiently reference Mexico, Mexican culture, and various content- and aesthetic-based works of that country in their prose and poetry, Morales appears most consistent in doing so, indisputably fulfilling Leal's aforesaid criterion of an undeniable Mexican connection.

There is no doubt that Morales' exception within Chicano/a literature is steadily becoming recognized, as his multihued works continue to receive attention by the general reader and critical scrutiny by various scholars. To read and grasp the aesthetic ingredients as well as the experimental strategies of his tales can be a rewarding exercise for the reader. For the scholar, however, demonstrating the full force of Morales' inimitable oeuvre by analyzing its persistent willful figurations, tense narrations, mysterious characterizations and imagery, and allusive coded sociocultural ironies may seem a nearly unworkable task. Even so, it has been attempted in ways that have achieved a nicely critical and textual equilibrium up to this point. There are, for example, Marc García-Martínez's and Jesús Rosales' full-length critical tomes, *The Flesh-and-Blood Aesthetics of Alejandro Morales: Disease, Sex and Figuration* (2014) and *La narrativa de Alejandro Morales: Encuentro, historia y compromiso social* (1999), respectively. There is Max Martínez's aforementioned translation of *Caras viejas y vino nuevo*, Judith Ginsberg's rendering of *La verdad sin voz* into *Death of an Anglo*, and Francisco Lomelí's and Adam Spires' cited translations of *Caras viejas y vino nuevo* and *Pequeña nación*. There is moreover José Antonio Gurpegui's mini-Festschrift from 1996, peculiarly titled *Alejandro Morales: Fiction Past, Present, Future Perfect*, which also contains poetry and an essay by Morales. The new, comprehensive bibliography by Donaldo W. Urioste presented in this compendium is also an authentication of Morales' prolific five-decade long production in terms of assorted novels, a collection of novellas, sporadic short stories, and a book of poetry; it also includes interviews and numerous scholarly essays on Morales' work. Accolades from an ever-expanding academy of contemporary critical circles have accumulated notably, placing Morales at the zenith of Chicano/a novelists in recognition of his relentless aspiration to tell stories that others have not been so able or prepared to do. As evidence of such notoriety, Stanford University formally acquired his personal papers and manuscripts in 2008, establishing an Alejandro Morales archive. Far from retiring, as of this writing Morales finds himself working on three works at initial stages of development. One is a biographical novel tentatively entitled *Rainbow of Colors*, which takes place in Japan from the 1920s to the beginnings of World War II. A second one, tentatively entitled *The Place of the White Heron*, deals with Mexico City, as well as Los Angeles and related sites in the near future, while the third is an ambitious speculative work that challenges widespread scientific beliefs. He is also working on a collection of short stories, tentatively called *The Integrals*, as well as *Zapote Tree*, a volume of poetry. The full force of his production, and the production of scholarly criticism, is therefore steadily swelling; indeed, it is intensifying, and there seems no end in sight.

Regarding the scholarly criticism, all endeavors to unearth important insights related to this author's historical, rhetorical, narratological, and experimental innovations open up new thematic understandings and consideration of his work—work that, once again, must be addressed for its stylistic nonconformity, as Daniel Schreiner underscores, "the socio-critical prose and the literary techniques of the Californian writer and scholar Alejandro Morales are unique within the canon of Mexican American literature of the last decades. Morales's style and variety of themes differs significantly from other contemporary Chicana/o authors, influenced as it is by his education in Latin and world literatures at US universities. . . . Being positioned more or less outside the mystic-Marxist-Chicano nationalist discourse, Morales hence must be considered as an important international author of contemporary world literature who masters various techniques of style and narration" (2017, 171).

Morales' aesthetic more often than not frees itself from such discourse, especially from such predictable ideological or political binds. As Schreiner observes, Morales exemplifies a global artistic vantage point, producing narrative exegeses and enigmas that challenge international readers and scholars to decipher all of his stylistic codes of meaning and systemic patterns of word phrasings. In order to fully appreciate the nuances of the narrative intricacies in his work, it is necessary for readers and (particularly) scholars to keep in mind that Morales' literature—to apply Roland Barthes' phrase—is "coded to a very high degree" (Barthes and Duisit 1975, 265). Even then, it remains in certain ways mysterious, convoluted, and difficult to apprehend, sometimes so intensely metaphorical as to almost thwart any attempt to reliably judge or adequately explicate it. And yet, the respective chapters constituting this compendium seek to do just that.

Keeping the above in mind, we have attempted to capture and suggest the expansiveness, richness, intricacy, and far-reaching nature of Morales' literary imagination in this volume, which offers the most recent crop of scholarly perspectives on the subject. By "intricate," we mean how each chapter explores Morales' pages by focusing on a singular explicative phenomenon and then broadening the lens to a more panoptic perspective. We mean "far-reaching" both literary and figuratively, as we included in this collection not only critical articles that more or less cover Morales' novels and short stories but also critical articles from around the globe—produced by scholars from China, Spain, Canada, Romania, Italy and Greece, as well as by various specialists on the author's writings working in the United States. This assemblage of intra- and international critical articles comprises a nonchronological effort to probe the temperament and singular complexities of Alejandro Morales' literature. It is a scholarly and approachable presentation of diverse methodologies that elucidate and demystify his unrelenting literary labor. Though distinct, these perspectives intersect as they confront the content of his novels and short stories both as acute renderings of Mexican, Mexican American, and Chicano/a experiences and as ideological works that forge definitive statements about history, ethnicity, race, and our aberrant yet enduring human condition.

All in all, the thought-provoking chapters that follow ultimately form a united heuristic voice, with which we argue that *listening to* is how one best measures the full force, impact, and promise that have driven this unyielding author throughout his long lifetime of writing.

NOTES

1. For further explanation, see García-Martínez (2014).
2. See Francisco Lomelí's article in this compendium, "The Analogous Correspondence of an Extreme Poetics between Stanley Kubrick's *A Clockwork Orange* and Alejandro Morales' *Barrio on the Edge*."
3. See the chapter "A Dialogue with the Writer Alejandro Morales" in this compendium.

WORKS CITED

Acosta, Oscar Zeta. 1972. *The Autobiography of a Brown Buffalo*. San Francisco: Straight Arrow Books.
Anaya, Rudolfo A. 1972. *Bless Me, Ultima*. Berkeley, CA: TQS.
Arias, Ron. 1975. *The Road to Tamazunchale*. Reno, NV: West Coast Poetry Review.
Barthes, Roland, and Lionel Duisit. 1975. "An Introduction to the Structural Analysis of Narrative." *New Literary History* 6, no. 2 (Winter): 237–72.
Bloom, Harold. 1994. *The Western Canon: The Books and School of the Ages*. New York: Harcourt Brace.
Brito, Aristeo. 1976. *El diablo en Texas*. Tucson: Editorial Peregrinos.
García-Martínez, Marc. 2014. *The Flesh-and-Blood Aesthetics of Alejandro Morales: Disease, Sex, and Figuration*. San Diego: San Diego University Press.
Gurpegui, José Antonio. 1996. *Alejandro Morales: Fiction Past, Present, Future Perfect*. Tempe, AZ: Bilingual Press / Editorial Bilingüe.
Hinojosa, Rolando. 1973. *Estampas del valle y otras obras / Sketches of the Valley and Other Works*. Berkeley, CA: Editorial Justa Publications.

Márquez, Antonio C. 1995. "The Use and Abuse of History in Alejandro Morales's *The Brick People* and *The Rag Doll Plagues*." In *Alejandro Morales: Fiction Past, Present, Future Perfect*, edited by José Antonio Gurpegui, special issue, *Bilingual Review / Revista Bilingüe* 20, no. 3 (September–December 1995): 76–85.

Morales, Alejandro. 1981. *Old Faces and New Wine*. Translated by Max Martínez. San Diego: Maize Press.

———. 1988. *Death of an Anglo*. Translated by Judith Ginsberg. Tempe, AZ: Bilingual Press/ Editorial Bilingüe.

———. 1998. *Barrio on the Edge / Caras viejas y vino nuevo*. Translated by Francisco A. Lomelí. Tempe: Bilingual Press / Editorial Bilingüe.

———. 2014. *Little Nation and Other Stories*. Translated by Adam Spires. Houston: Arte Público Press.

Méndez, Miguel M. 1974. *Peregrinos de Aztlán*. Tucson: Editorial Peregrinos.

Rechy, John. 1977. *The Sexual Outlaw: A Documentary: A Nonfiction Account, with Commentaries, of Three Days and Nights in the Sexual Underground*. New York: Grove Press, 1977.

Ríos, Isabella. 1976. *Victuum*. Ventura, CA: Diana-Etna.

Rivera, Tomás. 1971. *. . . Y no se lo tragó la tierra* (. . . And the Earth Did Not Part). Berkeley, CA: Quinto Sol Publications.

Rosales, Jesús. 1999. *La narrativa de Alejandro Morales: Encuentro, historia y compromiso social*. New York: Peter Lang.

———. 2014. *Thinking En Español: Interviews with Critics of Chicana/o Literature*. Tucson: University of Arizona Press.

Saldívar, Ramón. 1990. *Chicano Narrative: The Dialects of Difference*. Madison: University of Wisconsin Press.

Sánchez, Phil. 1977. *Don Phil-O-Meno sí la mancha*. San Luis, CO: Sánchez.

Schreiner, Daniel. 2017. "The Once and Future Chicano—World Literatures between Intra-History and Utopian Vision: An Interview with Alejandro Morales." In *Symbolism 17: Latina/o Literature: The Trans-Atlantic and the Trans-American in Dialogue*, edited by Rüdiger Ahrens, Florian Kläger, and Klaus Stierstorfer, 171–84. Boston: Walter de Gruyter.

ONE / Submersion, Suffocation, and Entombment of the Mexican and Immigrant Body in *River of Angels*— Probing Figurations of Violence and Isolation / MARC GARCÍA-MARTÍNEZ

> Water is nebulous, it has no shape, you can pass your hand right through it; yet it can kill you. The force of such a thing is its momentum, its trajectory. What it collides with, and how fast.... —Margaret Atwood, *The Blind Assassin,* 2001

> ... it was discovered, when they attempted to remove him, that the water which had dripped upon him for ages from the crag above, had coursed down his back and deposited a limestone sediment under him which had glued him to the bed rock upon which he sat, as with a cement of adamant.... —Mark Twain, "Petrified Man," 1862

In Alejandro Morales' saga *River of Angels* (2014), the early twentieth-century conurbation of Los Angeles is at a precarious crossroads with its ethnic populace. The novel charts the winding, generations-long course of the Mexican American Rivers family in the growing and often volatile City of Angels. Encroaching tides and shifting currents of people from diverse cultural backgrounds and castes are transforming the restless city's milieu, spawning social anxieties, Aryan ideologies, and eugenics schemes, as well as economic competition and worker exploitation. Morales renders this transformation by constructing gripping metaphorical exemplars and connotative moments to reveal the ever-cruel toil of the subordinate working class, the assorted ruptures of overwhelming racism, and the heartrending dispossession of human dignity and life. *River of Angels* is hermeneutically structured by a series of harsh and evocative instances involving bodies that are submerged, entombed, lacerated, and liquified. These episodes involve dramatis personae who become encased in asphyxiating tombs. There are those who drown in the savage flow of river water or lose their mobility in paralyzing mud. Some end up collapsed and submerged in their own bodily fluids and waste, while others lie beaten, castrated, and fractured by forces outside their control. There are also characters who become engulfed both in indelible love and in savage odium. The aesthetic power of the novel—its remarkable capacity to secrete unexpected degrees of figuration and far-reaching emotional complexion into the overall reading experience—lies in this progression of metaphorical exemplars and connotative moments.[1]

One of the more emotive, horrific moments in this progression involves the entombment of a "mongrel," "retarded," "docile," and "stupid" unnamed Mexican worker, buried alive in a pit of smothering concrete (86). Preparing foundations for an immense water tank facility for the wealthy railroad entrepreneur Samuel P. Huntington's personal cattle herd on the edge of Los Angeles' renowned Griffith Park, Mexican workers are measuring and pouring copious amounts of fast-drying concrete into massive forms. As they measure and pour, the workers cautiously position themselves in and around the ponderous machinery. Suddenly, calamity strikes, the aesthetic overtone of which exposes the tragic futility of monolingualism alongside the disposability and disappearance of helpless immigrants:

> Ernest, the foreman and several young Mexican workers watched as two men squatted under the huge scoop shovel to check the locks. Ernest could see only one of the men, while the other man checked the lock on the other side of the scoop. The man whom Ernest could see signaled that his side was secure. Ernest immediately ordered the foreman to carry on the pour. While the crane slowly lifted the scoop, shouting broke out from the far side. Ernest did not understand Spanish. He ignored the workers' screams and motioned to the crane operator to position the fully loaded scoop over the pit. . . . At that instant Ernest saw a worker hanging by his arm, trapped in the latch release lock that was almost fully opened. The cement started to pour, the worker's arm freed as he screamed, falling to the bottom of the foundation. Five hundred pounds of fast-drying Portland cement entombed the Mexican worker. The crane shut down. Silence fell on the site. (86–87)

Ernest makes a hasty choice "between deadline and life," an impulsive decision that causes the luckless Mexican worker to be horrifically buried alive. The reader's reaction certainly must run the range from quiet surprise that this could happen to outright shock that it did and in this particular manner. Yet with this incident Alejandro Morales pushes the reader further past their surprise or shock, forcing them to grasp its savage irony. As the poor laborer's entombed body becomes one with the molten mineral grave, it fatefully becomes one with the edifice to be completed within the affluent landscape. The man is no doubt also buried evermore in the minds and memories of his fellow laborers, and any individual or collective taphephobia they already suffer as a result of their jobs must be amplified by this atrocious incident.

Such an incident is rife with Moralesian overtones of near-homicidal injustice, reverberating with a mournful emotional dimension. Resisting some reductive example of racial discrimination or clichéd antipathy (such as a landlord wrongfully evicting their ethnic tenant or some inflamed gang street brawl), Morales creates a more sophisticated episodic connotative device that resonates deep inside the reader. This device undercuts Ernest the foreman's apparent matter-of-fact indifference toward his drowned, crushed laborer. From this we perceive not just the author's intimation of our woeful mortality but his verification of how wealth entitlement and business economics converge to create hardships for the cross-racial classes in his intensifying literary setting of Los Angeles:

> Everyday at the lumber yard and at the construction sites a parade of mixed-race workers, mostly Mexicans, reported to work. Ernest had to consider the budget, had to deal with the reality of business economics. The only way he could make a substantial profit was to employ Mexicans eager to work for him in dangerous working conditions and for substandard wages. . . . He saw his worker at the last second. There was nothing he could have done; it was over in seconds. Ernest's thoughts came fast. He looked up to see the crane operator still staring at him, now surrounded by the Mexicans who had shut down the crane. Ernest looked down into the pit. He took his hat off and ran his hand through his hair, walked off the scaffolding, got to his car thinking that the job was simply too difficult for some men. (Morales 2014, 86–87)[2]

The death of this Mexican laborer is not just a denoted case in point of occupational hazard. It is a transfixing metaphorical death associated with inferior human worth, with the impossibility of shared sensibilities between overseer and drudge, with affluence that figuratively and literally builds on the corpses of an ethnic stratum. Through this metaphorical lens we witness the sacrifice of "mongrel," "retarded," "docile," "stupid," and "foolish" souls for a greater purpose that in turn parallels the virtual death of the indigenous Los Angeles River by the ensuing erection of its concrete tomb. Morales writes in the novel of powerful interests striving "to bury, disfigure, and control the Los Angeles River . . . to smother, oppress the natural waterways" (xi), and those same interests sadly do the same to mortal lives. The disfiguring entombment of the hard-working Mexican worker connotes cultural humiliation and exploitation to the extent that he is permanently prevented from ever openly speaking his name in the story and from ever overcoming the tenacious caste boundaries imposed on him by industrialist forces building all around the venerable Southern California city.

The tragedy is also brilliantly allusive, for this harrowing moment in the narrative evokes a powerful echo of a bygone era, namely that of gruesome superstition and subjugation in the ancient legendary Japanese ritual of *hitobashira*. Known as the "human pillar" (Frédéric 2005, 337), "person-post" (Mitchelhill 2003, 8), "human foundation" (Blake 1902, 586), or "man-pillar" (Munro 1908, 640), hitobashira was by all accounts a ritual that necessitated a human being buried alive directly within or right underneath solid complex edifices such as large-scale dams, castles, fortresses, and especially bridges. William Aston's *Shinto: The Way of the Gods* (2013) explains that "there are several indications of the existence of this practice in still older times. Human sacrifices to river-Gods have already been mentioned. We have seen that when a Mikado died a number of his attendants were buried alive round his tomb, from which it may be inferred that considerations of humanity would not have prevented similar sacrifices to the Gods. Cases are also recorded of men being buried alive in the foundations of a bridge, a castle, or an artificial island. These were called *hitobashira*, or human pillars" (29).

Noritake Tsuda's 1918 exploration of human sacrifices in Japan corroborates Aston's report:

> The tradition of human sacrifices is also concerned with the building of large bridges. For example, in the *Yasiitomi-ki*, a diary of the fifteenth century, a famous tradition is contained, called Nagara-no Hito-bashira (*hitobashira*, "human pillar"). According to the tradition, a woman who was carrying a boy on her back was caught while she was passing along the

river Nagara, and was buried at the place where a large bridge was then to be built (763). . . . The Hito-bashira or "human pillar" traditions are always connected with some important enterprise and mostly with water. In large enterprises human lives are often lost in the work itself, therefore in some cases such loss of human life would have been looked upon as a human sacrifice. (763–67)

It is generally accepted that these sacrificial beings included debased servants, sick or indigent women, and as one might expect, actual hapless laborers constructing those very edifices. According to Munro, "under the name of *Hitobashira* (man-pillar) the practice of human sacrifice by burying alive at the foundations of buildings and especially bridges to ensure their stability by placating the soil or river god, was prevalent in Japan" (641). Aston emphasizes that the hitobashira practice was a bold offering of souls for a greater purpose—not so much outwardly commercial or economic as strictly religious. This ritual practice disturbingly operated as an appeasing "prayer" to supernatural deities to protect against physical disaster or attack on the newly constructed works (Tsuda 1918, 763–64). Running counterpoint to construction or creation, hitobashira is paradoxical in all respects. Given its dependence on death, this so-called human foundation is contrastive to creation, and with regards to the Mexican worker's sacrificial entombment it connotes a pure irony as Keller's construction site undeniably becomes a destruction site.[3]

In crafting his fictional twentieth-century version of the savage rite of hitobashira, Morales launches this irony squarely at the reader. Remarkably, there is a nonfictional twentieth-century version providing a measure of alarming realism to the episode in the novel. In 1944 a dangerous conflagration ignited in a number of subterranean passageways of the Miike Plant Coal Mine in Japan. Many of the miners at the plant were actually Chinese conscript laborers. In order to shield unmined coal in adjoining tunnels, the mine company directors ordered the erection of a huge cement wall to plug the path of the fire and prevent a detrimental financial loss. The Chinese laborers—dispensable lives in contrast to valuable ore—were entombed and buried alive. Referred to as the "Miike Coal Mine Hitobashira" (Kozaki 1973), it was a death sentence imposed on those ill-fated workers by the dictatorial industrialist forces leading the Miike Plant Coal Mine.[4]

For our purposes, both the poor Mexican worker's body and the draftee Chinese workers' bodies are interred in a dialectical space entrapped by industrial labor and corporate plantation values. This dialectic can never resolve itself, for within the cement and unforgiving earth the fictional worker and nonfictional coal miners become immobile statues incapable of ever thinking or speaking again. As statues they posses no agency, effectively metamorphosed from a once-dynamic animal state into a static mineral one. They bear out Ollivier Dyens' claim that the body is at all times tenuous and susceptible to natural and unnatural forces beyond its control. In *Metal and Flesh—The Evolution of Man* (2001), Dyens stresses how the body can be readily transformed into any figure or shape due to "its materiality and its essence, hav[ing] no absolute integrity, being nothing more than malleable and flexible material" (58). This reinforces a poignant theme in *River of Angels*, namely that Mexicans are a malleable and dispensable utensil used in certain settings toward certain entrepreneurial ends. Whatever justifications exist for the gruesome hitobashira, whatever its cultural-corporeal abstractions, it registers the existence and effect of a powerful form of caste schism that Morales develops throughout his novel. As such, the *River of Angels* becomes a compelling social critique and literary grievance concerning a schism in early twentieth-century Western society, in which *el cuerpo de la gente* toils, dies, and then transforms and disappears for the benefit of purported superior beings and loftier economic purposes.

Further addressing this schism, or rift, along with how the corpus is vulnerable to the smothering doctrines of superiority, *River of Angels* forces its reader to witness a gruesome lynching and castration. Occurring amid an enveloping and choking mélange of watery mud and bloody cement, these gruesome acts are enacted upon Albert Rivers, a young, bright, hard-working Mexican American and devoted lover of the young German American girl Louise Keller. Their passionate cross-ethnic/cross-racial/cross-class relationship, marriage, and eventual progeny cause severe dissension among headstrong Keller family members—most notably Louise's incensed uncle Philip. As a steadfast Aryan supremacist he despises Albert, considering him as nothing more than an "mixed lower-race . . . social undesirable" (181). The culmination of this racist hatred results in Albert's grisly beating and laceration at the hands of Philip and his outraged fellow sectarians:[5]

> Three faucets leaked badly, dripping water onto the small concrete platforms in front of each water basin. He reached over to the first faucet and turned it shut. His hand moved over to the second and turned, when a heavy object struck his back and knocked him down to the cement slab. His body rolled

to one side, only to be punched and kicked from many directions. Sharp sudden pain entered his ribs for an instant, shutting down his breathing. Albert's hand scraped mud from his eye that had closed after the blow to his back. A few more sharp kicks to his chest and shoulder brought him around on his back where he could not scream, not say a word. (215)

Against an unambiguous watery backdrop, Albert's body is knocked down and violently shoved from side to side, pummeled, and suffocated. Like Ernest's Mexican worker, Albert becomes a voiceless being, unaided and plunged into darkness. It is here that Morales suddenly veers his novel's established third-person descriptive narration head-first toward a hallucinatory free-indirect discourse. He unveils the continuation of the Mexican American's thrashing by blending the voices of the enraged Aryans with the thoughts of the helpless Albert, resulting in a remarkable narrative singularity. Weaving a sensuous, kaleidoscopic rhetoric that teems with eddies of hate and rapid violence, as well as overlapping currents of voices and thought, Morales stitches together numerous elliptical caesuras to unite the discourses and allow for the dynamic passage of time and movement between word and action. It is an extraordinary passage that must be considered in its full length:

> Albert tried to respond, help me, he thought, maybe three, four voices screamed, hands grabbed at his body, ripping his shirt off . . . back to Mexico . . . pulling at his shoes, his pants down . . . half-breed . . . a knife cut through his pants . . . the belt . . . warm liquid, blood covered his arms . . . Albert felt for his nose . . . he sensed laughter . . . flat nose against his mouth . . . you won't fuck . . . the voices dragged his body half way off the cement slab . . . white girl again . . . voices grabbed his legs . . . a voice cut off Albert's underwear . . . this knife on my hogs . . . laughter . . . loud laughter . . . Albert twisted his shoulders violently . . . get up, get up . . . several hands fondled his genitals . . . it all off . . . only his balls . . . just like your pigs . . . the voices broke out in great laughter . . . a celebration . . . his balls . . . pain . . . terrible pain . . . he lost his breath . . . his hands clutched his penis . . . blood came from below . . . he screamed . . . the voices kicked him again and again . . . you ain't going to sin anymore boy . . . no more mongrel moron children . . . he won't run . . . just to make sure . . . several boards crushed a knee . . . opened his eyes . . . only mud . . . crawled through the mud . . . pushed damp mud between his legs . . . cool relief . . . under the leaky pipes . . . dripping

water valves ... stuffed mud into his crotch ... screamed ... screamed again ... mud-smeared eyes widened ... felt light ... floating away ... short breath ... breathing ... pain faded ... into mud. (215–16)

Morales strategically inserts these chilling, seemingly empty caesuras to signify a sense of the quick-moving, lung-collapsing, bone-crushing, skin-tearing, and near-deafening vortex of being beaten. They also suggest a sense of being engulfed and drowning in the fast, pre-concrete Los Angeles River rapids. In the most ferocious rapids there is at all times a boiling interplay between the velocity of the water, the surface of the riverbed, the shape of the channel, and the amount of mineral or arboreal debris present. There is a dynamic interplay of the disoriented senses of hearing, seeing, smelling, and touching. Morales captures in this passage the act of falling victim to harsh water forces, replicating what Bell and Lyall describe as being thrust into a "dynamic" and "accelerated" violent terrain. In *Accelerated Sublime*, they consider how many landscapes maintain exceedingly "kinetic" and "immersive" properties that involve rapidity, flow, steep falls, rises, declinations, rush, and power (2002, 60). Bell and Lyall classify the relationship between the body and the landscape as "dangerous, not only because of the forces brought to bear on the body ... but also because dynamic systems are inherently unstable" (61).

This corresponds both in rhetorical terms and in meaning to poor Albert's beating, for his is an episode ingeniously crafted to fling the reader into the blend of sequence and simultaneity; we are tossed into the whirlwind ferocity of elemental liquidity. This ferocious beating reminds us that though a water current has a sequence and progression, in its uncontrollable destructive state all movement or directive flows become haphazardly overlapping and simultaneous. Thus, Morales skillfully transcribes the multidimensional phenomenon of liquid force onto a flat two-dimensional page—an aesthetic folding technique or rhetorical origami transforming his book's pallid sheet of paper into a bloody-muddy dimensional form. Morales' endeavor to simultaneously represent Albert's fluidic bodily ooze, his mental sensations, and emotional dynamism is successful beyond doubt. The lengthy passage plays with our sense of time and sequence, transcending both movement *and* moment within the slowing overlapping action. Albert Rivers cannot escape. He is rupturing and drowning.

Such a bodily-mental rhetorical interplay of a hatred that injures and drowns, of the disorientation and resultant dynamism of chaotic movement, is affirmed by an analogue from Ambrose Bierce's "An Occurrence at Owl Creek Bridge"

([1890] 1989). In this tale, through inner fantasy, the forsaken prisoner of war Peyton Farquhar escapes a hostile Union lynching party and firing squad by dropping into a river. Dodging bullets and enduring punishing currents, he is swept away by harsh rapids from homicidal men who seek to catch him and hang him for his seemingly illicit deeds:

> Keen, poignant agonies seemed to shoot from his neck downward through every fiber of his body and limbs. These pains appeared to flash along well-defined lines of ramification and to beat with an inconceivably rapid periodicity. They seemed like streams of pulsating fire heating him to an intolerable temperature. As to his head, he was conscious of nothing but a feeling of fullness—of congestion. These sensations were unaccompanied by thought. The intellectual part of his nature was already effaced; he had power only to feel, and feeling was torment. He was conscious of motion. . . . he swung through unthinkable arcs of oscillation, like a vast pendulum. Then all at once, with terrible suddenness . . . a frightful roaring was in his ears, and all was cold and dark. (13–14)

Bierce's and Morales' stories share thematic configurations of sociocultural conflict, loathing, and warped ideological superiority. They both reveal how contradictory currents collide (an Aryan force hunting down Mexicans, a Union Army force hunting down Confederates), the way undercurrents of time get distorted through trauma, and how those abstract and elemental forces pummel and play havoc on the human senses. Peyton's and Albert's capacity to think is compromised, so that they can now pretty much only feel. What the reader witnesses in these portrayals are brilliantly explicative representations of the blunt-force simultaneity and disarray that accompany a lynching (in Peyton's case it is a literal and inevitable hanging). Yet Morales differentiates himself from his predecessor by taking us further, to the extent that his description of Albert's execution also becomes its form. He formally portrays on the page—that is, folds onto it—a rippling psychosomatic rhetoric that is *broken-up* (as are Albert's skin and bones), *convoluted* (as are Albert's awareness and feelings), *continuous* (as are the tortuous beatings and insults to Albert's body), *overlapping* (as are Albert's sensations and the voices of his hangmen), and *flowing* (as are the muddy water and Albert's blood).

These rhetorical patterns, however, go further still as Morales gathers all the forces brought to bear on Albert's body and describes its beating through not so much an aural but a verbal onomatopoeia. Equal to and yet beyond Bierce's word patterns, Morales imitates the prevailing "kinetic" and "immersive" movements and senses of the terrible racist assault itself. We may discern his rhetorical arrangement in Bruce Dean Willis' terms as a "kind of radical onomatopoeia, expanded beyond the rage of mere sound such that the word is the image" (2013, 11). In the cited passage from *River of Angels*, word formations act as structural imagery exposing the anguish or vertigo of the Mexican corpus hit by a devastating force of Anglo-Aryan odium. Our author summons all his innovative power to essentially mimic the "occurrence" that he describes, evoking near drowning and suffocation, thereby making said description much more interactive and intense for the increasingly uneasy reader.

This metaphorical interconnection of life, landscape, and senses, of the feeling of being beaten, buried, and submerged, is profound. Ironically, Albert studies design engineering and construction at a prominent local university, but Morales twists his character out of order, deconstructs him and violently submerges him in the elements so that his bodily integrity is disintegrated to the point that he is virtually liquefied—or in Dyens' terms, rendered (59) into his surroundings. The effects of xenophobic antipathy are figuratively measured through the lessening of bodily and landscape cohesion and through an image of sorrowful disintegration. What is more, as Albert's anguished body is disintegrated among the elements it lies upon (and within), his body in turn objectively measures the desperate moral disintegration of the Aryans themselves. This collision-disintegration metaphor, where the Mexican body is battered by Anglo force, richly correlates to Arturo Islas' *The Rain God* (1984)—specifically, to the character of Felix, whose fear of desert canyon sandstorms always "made him feel buried alive" (136). At one point in Islas' tale, Felix is in fact buried alive, not by some literal sandstorm but by forces of fear and hatred. Driving in the desert with no storm in sight, Felix tries to seduce a young white midwestern soldier from a nearby camp:

> "Ah don't think ah want to go into the canyon," the boy said.
> "Oh, come on, only for a few minutes. It's real nice in there."
> Felix took the boy's silence as an indication of consent and he began the slow drive up the canyon road. . . .
> Felix said and put his hand on the boy's knee. The boy sat rigidly on his side staring at the windshield and not the landscape. Felix sensed his preoccupation with the hand as it stroked his thigh.

"Don't do that," the boy said in a quiet, even tone.

"Don't be scared. I'm not going to hurt you. Let's have some . . ." The blows began before he finished. They were a complete surprise to him, and the anger behind them stunned and paralyzed him. He began to laugh as he warded off the attack. . . .

"Hey, come on. I was just kidding." He was vaguely aware that he spoke through a mouthful of stones. It did not occur to him to struggle or to fight back. He forced his door open and fell to the ground, kicked sharply in the kidneys from behind. (136–37)

Here Felix is also being beaten to death. In the story, he sexually exploits young men who have entered the country illegally to work, requiring them to have "physical examinations" that he tenderly performs when they first arrive at their jobs. Yet Felix is now paying for these manipulations with his life. Like Morales and Bierce, Islas intermingles previous elements of a character's life, the terrain they fall upon, their senses, and the robust liquid element. Islas' scene, in other words, depicts the occurrence of being trampled, choked, and submerged into the rough desert sand and into abstract fluidity:

The stones in his mouth looked like teeth as he spat them out, and he turned to avoid the blows to his back. The boy stood over him. The kicking continued and he felt great pain in his groin and near his heart. Then his mouth was full of desert and then it was not. He could no longer see the boy. The pain in his loins and along his side seemed distant . . . He tasted the dust. . . .

The biting ache began to recede and it seemed odd to be falling from a great height while lying on the desert floor. The sound of walking on stones puzzled him because he was surrounded by water. Its reflection and the luster of the boots flashed before him in an irregular, rhythmic motion . . . Felix had time to be afraid before he heard his heart stop.

The desert exhaled as he sank into the water. (137–38)

Islas describes Felix fighting "irregular, rhythmic" motions and currents, "falling from a great height" that does not exist in physical actuality. His description captures the aforesaid violent dynamics of landscape and force and the resulting disorientation of a sensual vertigo. Though one could reasonably argue that the frightened young man was defending himself from Felix's sexual assault, he nonetheless murderously pummels a pitiable man into the tough desert topography. Laying there, Felix transitorily feels enveloped in a bizarre runny realm. This metaphorical illustration of landscape and senses, of the perception of being enshrouded and submerged, signifies both consequence and confluence of sociocultural conflict, clashing identities, and revulsion against the sexual, political, or cultural Other.

While Bierce's prisoner of war and Islas' sexually conflicted man die on the spot, Albert in fact survives the beating and castration, if only barely.[6] Like Felix, Albert is not prepared for the attack. Like Felix, he finds himself stunned and suffocating within the filthy mineral setting. Albert's unbelievably vile assault, however, is taken to a higher level than Felix's. Alex submerges into something fluid and viscous, ending up swollen, broken, and cut, but it is only as he lays stricken at hospital that the reader comes to understand the increasingly figurative enormity of his assault:

> Mr. Rivers, your son was severely beaten. He sustained a broken nose, several broken ribs and his right knee is swollen to the point that we cannot assess the damage. And he suffered a glancing blow to the head. Whatever they hit him with struck him mostly in the back . . .
>
> Mr. Rivers, the cowards that did this to your son, Albert, also attempted to castrate him . . .
>
> They tried, but they did a bad job of it. There's no other way to say this but to tell you that your son lost one of his testicles. The other one is slightly damaged. They cut one testicle out and slightly cut the other one. (2014, 219)

Albert Rivers thus becomes a particular text to be read in the context of passive Mexican ethnicity and violent white dominion. He is a character-maneuver employed by Morales to exemplify the brutal dialectical collision between these two entities. In this fictional story, just as they do in actual reality, Aryans hold an excessively credulous belief in their own superiority (peruse pages 181 through 183 in the novel). They maintain a widely held and near-superstitious belief in causation leading to unwanted consequence that must be stopped by any means: the miscegenation and wholly damaging dilution of their race *and* their city by lesser bloodlines.

The attack on poor Albert is a culmination of these pairings and conflicts, of these vicious contests for control and separation. For Morales, lynching and castration are a legible aesthetic-rhetorical trope for the reality of racial confrontation and struggle within Los Angeles. In employing it in the novel he substantiates Melissa Stein's principle that "lynching and castration served the same ideological and practical functions: intimidation, containment, and social control" (2015, 239). In *Measuring Manhood—Race and the Science of Masculinity*, Stein demonstrates how this manner of assault powerfully symbolizes white supremacy in its agenda to thwart crossbreed, immigrant, biologically inferior, and low-morality peoples (239). What Stein claims and how she claims it are apposite to Morales' novel. When the unreasonable Aryan mob cuts Albert, the victim clutches at his bloody genitals, screaming until he loses his breath. He is punished by the mob for his immorality ("you ain't going to sin anymore boy"), kicked in the groin to thwart copulation ("you won't fuck"), and thrashed to the point of permanently stopping his ability to generate "mongrel moron children." Preventing procreation, putting a violent halt to the ability to have sex in any form and with anyone, does not stem merely from a general "anxiety" about the ethnic body; rather, according to Catherine Clinton and Michele Gillespie it is a control mechanism over what they fittingly call a "bonded labor force" (1997, 82). Though considered in respect to ownership, sex, generation, and cost burden, Clinton and Gillespie stress that castration is ultimately a "means of retribution and punishment" (78). It is a sick, hostile rite connected to a certain division of people, by a certain division of people, and woefully done to a certain division of people.

So we must consider these connotative maneuvers of lynching, punishing assault, and bloody slicing as enhanced Moralesian attempts to provoke his reader. Such attempts not only succeed at doing so—they underscore a wholesale ethnic, political, geo-cultural (and in some respects, sexual) rivalry taking place in the city of Los Angeles. This rivalry reflects past outcries over the supposed threat to pure American homogeneity by the representative dirty Mexican (Gómez-Quiñones 1994, 65), and as we have seen, the novel chronicles this with a variety of figuratively laden connotative scenarios. The drama composed in *River of Angels* is real, and its author prompts the reader to recall that many industries like Ernest's construction company historically sought to maximize profits by bringing in Mexican labor, even though there were countervailing efforts to eventually suppress, deport, and repatriate the migrants (Gómez-Quiñones 65). Indeed, the novel reminds us how immigrants were "forced into cycles of movement based on their economic need that place them into a bare life that renders them invisible with respect to rights then marks them as criminals whose bodies need to be eradicated from the land while they are also being sought for their labor" (Manzella 2018, 157). Such efforts to eradicate the Mexican body are darkly portrayed in *River of Angels*, whether by unsafe working conditions, by indifferent and dismissive attitudes as seen with the smothered and entombed unnamed Mexican worker, or by hateful racist violence represented by the attack on poor Albert.

The connotative depictions of the submerged, flattened, and wounded racial-ethnic body within elemental textures of tough cement, oozing immersive mud, drips and splotches of water, and an enveloping blood are powerful and revealing. But in the novel these depictions pertain to others as well. For instance, further indications of being emblematically beaten, broken, submerged, bloody, and delirious are unearthed when the "mean" and "hard-headed" Philip Keller falls victim to the 1929 stock market crash (145). Badly hurt by this nationwide disaster, something awful befalls this terrible character before he is found by his nephew Ernest, face-down in in his bedroom. Cautiously, Ernest comes upon his uncle, who was somehow assailed and injured and is now lying in vomit, blood, shit, and urine:

> Ernest walked into the bedroom. Uncle Philip, wearing a shirt and nothing else, lay face down in the middle of his bloodied bed. The stench was even more repulsive. At the side of the bed on an expensive Indian rug, Ernest found a pan half-filled with urine and lumps of feces.
>
> "Uncle Philip," Ernest called in a whisper to his uncle, but there was no response. He moved closer. "Uncle Philip?" He lay in a puddle of vomit and urine.
>
> Ernest turned him over. What he saw horrified him. His uncle's face was unrecognizable. His left ear was hideously enlarged, his nose flattened, his eyes swollen shut, his lips split open. But he was breathing. (146)

This moment is a flawlessly expressive one and not devoid of striking imagery. It is disturbing to read. There is nonetheless metaphorical import as Keller lies (deservedly) immobile, drenched in his own fluids—an anguished living carcass altered into a trodden and twisted pile of goo. Bodily transformation of this sort once again verifies Dyens' idea regarding the materiality of the body, how our frail physical being at all times remains malleable and ultimately transformable (58). While we acknowledge this frightening scene as an exquisitely connotative moment, we become sensitized not just to its visuality but to the manner in which Keller's puddling excrement, vomit, and blood associate with abject violence, failure, and isolation—a violence, failure, and isolation that he is plainly drowning in:

Ernest jumped on the bed, crouched behind him and wrapped his arms under Uncle Philip's armpits. His uncle yelled when Ernest pulled him up. Ernest was finally able to button the shirt and put a jacket over Uncle Philip's shoulders. With a soaked cloth he gently wiped the sweat from Uncle Philip's face. His uncle winced with pain every time Ernest dabbed at the crusted blood. Ernest stopped when a trickle of blood ran from a deep cut on his cheek. Ernest noticed that many deep cuts covered Uncle Philip's face, as if his face had been slashed repeatedly with a sharp object. (147)

River of Angels aesthetically bonds Keller's body to forces of intolerance, fear, class, race, geography, and insensitive business. Morales superimposes figurative imagery and connotative devices onto these forces as follows: (1) Keller is fully immersed in his hideous racist beliefs, so he is portrayed suffocating in his own vomit and feces; (2) Keller is full of uncontainable anxiety and fear, so he is portrayed incontinent and submerged in his own urine and blood; (3) the man reeks of a nasty dogma, so he is portrayed surrounded by and emitting a stinking odor; (4) he is a sadistic Aryan bully who is guilty of beating others to a bruised and bloody condition, so he is portrayed beaten, bruised, and blanketed in blood; (5) Keller is a chauvinistic and sometimes ruthless businessman, so he is portrayed in the very state of the early twentieth-century municipal and national economy—that is, warped, slashed, and flattened.

Thus, as he lies there petrified and secluded in his filthy bed, Philip Keller becomes an allegorical personification on the written page. What is more, he presents a lesson in the dynamics of choking and liquefaction. To choke is to be deprived of air, to become constricted and obstructed by an intractable force. With liquefaction, a solid is made liquid in response to an applied stress or shock. Whether caused by an acute collapse of solidity, a drowning, or subsequent necrosis of landscape and bodily structure, liquefaction and choking operate as emblematic constructs in Morales' novel to portray the wholesale breakdown of a guilty man's mind and body. If we liken this to "A Subtle Plague" by Alejandro Murguía (1992), we grasp a comparative portrayal of the breakdown of one man's avarice and his contemptable chauvinistic business tactics. Murguía's character John Shaker, a corporate developer long coveting the sacred homeland ranch of the very old Mexican citrus farmer José García, takes over all of the parcels surrounding García's land, Rancho Maravilla. Shaker's eventual takeover of Rancho Maravilla occurs after the old farmer's mysterious death. Arrogantly inspecting his newly acquired property, Shaker inventories what must be discarded and torn down to make way for the inevitable condominiums to be built. He walks all around the Mexican farmer's home, where his sense of smell is assaulted by an unbearable hidden force:

> While standing on the porch admiring the site, Shaker noticed the overpowering army of smells assaulting him from within the house. The stink of pungent Mexican cigarettes permeated the walls; the smell of grease and chilies and jerked deer meat stormed from the kitchen, and emanating from the bedroom came the sad odor of loneliness and stale farts. (322)

The horrendous smells entering Shaker's nose start to grow into something more material. With every step he takes from the porch and inward through the rows of citrus trees, he is overtaken by an odd "white dust" made entirely, he realizes, of "minute, triangular-shaped white flies" (322). Growing thicker, the wave smothers Shaker, blinding his eyes and clogging his nose. Running back and forth in the yard and then into the García house, frightened and panicked, the selfish developer finds himself trapped. The flies, along with a hurricane wind forming in that space, force him to flee from what he realizes must be a curse. Making a desperate rush to escape the ghostly force into his parked car he descends into more dust:

> By the time he reached his car, the white powder was up to his waist and the door handles were buried and impossible to reach. He flailed at the mounds of white but succeeded only in stirring up the flies. Turbulent clouds of white rose up against him and clogged his ears, blinded his eyes, choked his throat. Shaker stumbled through the moonlit orchards in a blind rage—howling, spitting, choking, and lost . . . they found Shaker lying in a mud puddle face down in the turkey water. A grotesque, agonized expression of terror twisted his stiff features. (324)

Murguía executes a figuration of the collision of class struggle, personal ownership, and unfriendly business—and a haunting retribution for the contempt one character in his story displays for another family's venerable abode. Undeniably, there is pain in José García losing Rancho Maravilla to Shaker, so the author creates a fantastic suffocating vengeance for its takeover. This pain is represented by the elemental textures of a choking matter, in addition to an encasing muddy water that creates image-driven connotations of a justifiable punishment.[7] Still, though "A Subtle Plague" also employs the device of a man found face-down in a puddle, and though both Shaker and Philip suffer artistic measures of the same relative fate (isolated, in agony, smothered, face-down, punished, and discovered by others), it is Morales' dramatic flesh-and-blood details that augment the explicit racist ethos of Philip Keller.

Unlike Murguía with Shaker, Morales highlights not so much Keller's overly avaricious or tyrannically self-seeking traits but rather his Aryan racist character—one that despises nonwhites, the members of the Mexican Rivers family in particular. An intolerant xenophobe, he angrily thinks of the Riverses as low and essentially "mongrel." We have already observed how, when his niece Louise falls in love with Albert, Keller fiercely attempts to prevent the two families from ever coming together by directing wild rapids of aggression and violence against Albert. In doing so, Keller shields both himself and his heirs from proximate racial mixing and degenerative social flux. His aggressive hatred for Albert is both as silent as a shallow brook and as savage as a river torrent, setting up significant tensions and wholesale dissension within the novel as a whole. All of his words and deeds, in fact, directly lead to significant strife and resulting tragedies. It is remarkable, then, that in this scene Uncle Philip Keller himself becomes the ugly, paralyzing, foul-smelling manifestation of strife and tragedy.[8]

The reader thus registers both revulsion and curiosity at seeing him laying glued to his bed, at witnessing him submerged and nearly drowned in his own swollen flesh, blood, and waste matter. Is this the result of a savage beating meted out by his fellow Aryans for failing to tear down Albert and Louise's bond? Was the assault committed by despicable bankers, cruel mobsters, or merciless creditors to whom he owed money when the market crashed? Some common wretched home-invading robbers, perhaps? Did Uncle Philip perhaps do this to himself as self-flagellation or maybe an abortive suicide? Is this an act of revenge? The reader will come to agree that the reason for the beating, exactly who did it and how, is not made clear by Morales. What is clear is that a hypergraphic flesh-and-blood moment such as this is, in a way, a microcosm of the initially seeping, then overrunning effects of the 1929 stock market crash and the resulting national depression.[9]

Indeed, the crash was earth-shattering and far-reaching, fascinatingly described by historian Howard Zinn with this curiously relevant diction:

> The capitalist system was by its nature unsound: a system driven by the one overriding motive of corporate profit and therefore unstable, unpredictable, and blind to human needs. The result of all that: permanent depression for

many of its people, and periodic crises for almost everybody. Capitalism, despite its attempts at self-reform, its organization for better control, was still in 1929 a sick and undependable system. [. . .] After the crash, the economy was stunned, barely moving. Over five thousand banks closed and huge numbers of businesses, unable to get money, closed too. Those that continued laid off employees and cut the wages of those who remained, again and again. (2001, 387)

Zinn's progression of select words attach fittingly to Philip Keller's beaten, bleeding, and prostrate self. The historian employs such evocative words as "unsound," "driven," "unstable," "blind," "crises," "sick," "stunned, barely moving," "unable" and "cut . . . again and again" (387). In the novel Keller is a singularly *driven* ideological man, mentally *unsound* as well as emotionally *unstable*, somewhat *blind* to the unstoppable realities of the multicultural realm of Southern California. He is deep in fiscal and personal *crises*, physically *sick*, lying there on the bed *stunned, barely moving*, obviously *unable* to protect himself—and most assuredly and brutally *cut again and again*. Thus, how the historian Zinn literally describes the event of the market crash coincides with how the novelist Morales describes the event of Keller's near-death state. In both Zinn's representative rhetoric and in Morales' representative imagery the crashed economy *and* the crushed man become emblematically connected in a most amazing way. Such is the unmistakable relevance of Alejandro Morales' well-conceived, innovative literature to various episodes of human history and society.

All in all, to probe the ways in which Morales painstakingly grafts connotative devices and rhetorical figurations onto torrents of history, racial enmity, and disposals of human rights and life is necessary to help his reader better comprehend particular intangibilities in particularly tangible ways. Call it his style of artistically criticizing early Los Angeles' social injustices and controls in addition to racist dogmas. In this regard, Melanie Pooch is spot-on when she declares, in "The Poetics of DiverCity," that "stylistic devices, such as metaphor, irony, alliteration, simile, or parody, are often used as a tool to overtly or covertly criticize certain ideologies or conventions" (2016, 58). Yet, Morales' artistic style comes at a price, for it produces very severe sprains in an otherwise stable novel, and these sprains elicit undeniable reactions and tense emotions from the reader. Because of this, critics who may regard *River of Angels* as an affirmative or optimistic turn away from his past works of death, pain, and decay will find themselves mistaken. This novel lays bare numerous thematic ideas, but it especially lays bare its author's conception of ethnic stratification and social animosity not as a natural phenomenon but as a contrivance—just like the controlled "man-made" Los Angeles River itself.

It therefore may be the model Chicano novel in that it portrays the sadly all-too-human states of intolerance, fear, and sociocultural fracture while attempting to set the record straight regarding the value of the Mexican, which Morales confesses is the very motivation for writing the book: "to show the reader that Mexican labor, not the U.S. Army Corps of Engineers, not history, not Los Angeles, was responsible for building the bridges over the L.A. River. *They* did it and have a right to be recognized" (Morales 2020). All things considered, we are left with an arguably menacing literary testimony, with a rhetorically charged, aesthetically emotive rendering of bodies that are submerged, broken, entombed, suffocated, lacerated, and liquefied. It is through such testimonial rendering that the reader may better fathom the fierce conflicts that develop when racialist Anglo discrimination and its often horrific and hegemonic social rites angrily collide with Mexican cultural ethnicity and its self-determinant rights.

NOTES

1. *Connotation* is a slippery term, complicated by critical conceptions and esoteric theoretical revisions. In its basic sense, connotation means a semantic phenomenon involving perceived ideas, emotions, and relative interpretations of word or phrase. Frye et al. consider it in an emotive context as ideas, attitudes, or emotions associated with a word in the mind of the reader, a range of "feelings aroused by the word" (1977, 127). Muffin and Ray explain it as associations evoked by a word beyond a literal intention, a word-driven reflection of recognized or understood "broad cultural associations" (2009, 73). I prefer Barthes' consideration, in which he puts forth that illustrative imagery or narrative moments in a text can indeed be connotative—what he calls an "aesthetic signified" that suggests a broader range of interpreted possibility (1997, 34–35). What I interpret in Morales' novel, then, involves ideas, emotions, senses, and associations arising out of particular acts: occurrences in his novel must be read for their overtones, emotional coloring, tenor, and sudden figurative import.

2. Ernest is an anagram for *resent*, employed conceivably to signal his annoyance with his responsibilities or circumstances, or perhaps indignation at having (for financial reasons) to deal with these people. Though indifferent here, Ernest ultimately comes to represent principled tolerance and friendship later in the novel.

3. The novel also references the disposal of bodies, along with the disposal of objects, via the asphyxiating encasements of children in a junkyard. The childrens'

deaths are prevented by the River Mother, a mystical descendant of the indigenous Tongva culture and Yangna settlement that was to become Los Angeles. She keeps a vigilant watch for children who become trapped in old ice boxes at the junkyard: "Several men finished loading old rusty ice boxes. The River Mother had the doors removed before sending the boxes to the metal chopper. She had dealt with too many tragedies concerning abandoned ice boxes with doors that locked playing children inside to suffocate. Few paid much attention to these killers of children" (Morales 2014, 175). A domestic container becomes a deadly coffin in this instance, a terrifying suffocation made all the more heartbreaking due to human life prematurely shortened.

4. Some old castles in Japan are also connected to hitobashira: Maruoka Castle in Fukui Prefecture is said to contain a hitobashira in its pillar, and Matsue Castle in Shimane prefecture is said to contain one buried under its stone wall. Matsue Ohashi Bridge is believed to have human sacrifices built into its base, as is the Hokkaido Jomon tunnel, located on the Sekihoku Main Line. In the aftermath of a 1968 earthquake, several skeletons were said to be found buried upright in the walls of that tunnel. For additional information online, see Matthew Meyer's *Illustrated Database of Japanese Folklore* and *Online Database of Japanese Ghosts and Monsters* (yokai.com/hitobashira/); Lafcadio Hearn's *Unfamiliar Glimpses of Japan*, 142–43 (http://www.gutenberg.org/ebooks/8130?msg=welcome_stranger); and *SlappedHam*'s "Creepiest Urban Legends Around the World" (slappedham.com/creepiest-urban-legends/2).)

5. Note that this is actually the second time that Albert Rivers is beaten by Philip and his xenophobe comrades. His first beating is relatively short and quite violent, but meant only as a warning (Morales 2014, 204–6). This subsequent attack and beating is planned, prolonged, and much worse.

6. Only to sadly die later on in the novel by direct, willful murder (238–37).

7. Though Shaker goes on to perish, note a less lethal retribution for incursion into a venerable abode that transpires in Morales' tale after the matriarch Toypurina's death: "Oakley's parents' home, for at least four or five years, had one renter after another and not one stayed a year. The last renter stayed for only two weeks. It was Toypurina, according to Sol, who returned to make life miserable for the renters. She haunted every room, every object that was in the house. It happened over and over again: pots and pans rattling, chairs levitating, babies moved at night, ice freezes in the middle of warm rooms, bed covers torn off the bed while the renters made love, screams and sighs coming from within the walls, dishes and glasses falling off shelves and tables. The last renters complained about not being able to get out of their clothes, then their rooms, then the house. The renters left when the house finally allowed them to leave" (Morales 2014, 57).

8. A manifestation, that is, until the novel's surprising conclusion, where Uncle

Philip undergoes what can only be described as an evolution of conscience. The reader encounters in the book's final pages a changed Keller who seeks to atone for his sinful words and deeds. Finding God, his change is personal, social, geographic, religious, financial, and legalistic—and generational, as descendants of the Rivers family are positively affected by the alteration in more ways than one.

9. See my book *The Flesh-and-Blood Aesthetics of Alejandro Morales* (2014) for compelling explications of Morales' visceral, hypergraphic representation and its artistic metaphorical significance in nearly all of his works to date.

WORKS CITED

Aston, William George. 1905. *Shinto: The Way of the Gods.* ATLA monograph preservation program. Issues 1188–92 of *Western Books on Asia: Japan.* London: Longmans, Green.

Atwood, Margaret. 2001. *The Blind Assassin—A Novel.* New York: Random House.

Barthes, Roland. 1977. *Image/Music/Text.* Translated by Stephen Heath. New York: Hill and Wang.

Bell, Claudia, and John Lyall. 2002. *The Accelerated Sublime: Landscape, Tourism, and Identity.* Westport, CT: Praeger.

Bierce, Ambrose. 1989. "An Occurrence at Owl Creek Bridge." In *The Collected Writings of Ambrose Bierce*, 9–18. New York: Citadel Press.

Blake, Beverley. 1902. "Every-Day Japan." *Chautauquan Magazine* 35, no. 1 (April): 582–89.

Branch, Edgar M., and Robert H. Hirst, eds. 1979. *Twain's Early Tales and Sketches, 1851–1864.* Berkeley: University of California Press.

Clinton, Catherine, and Michele Gillespie. 1997. *The Devil's Lane: Sex and Race in the Early South.* New York: Oxford University Press.

Dyens, Ollivier. 2001. *Metal and Flesh—The Evolution of Man.* Translated by Evan J. Bibber and Ollivier Dyens. Cambridge, MA: MIT Press.

Frédéric, Louis. 2005. *The Japan Encyclopedia.* Translated by Kathe Ross. Cambridge, MA: Belknap.

Frye, Northrup, Sheridan W. Baker, George B. Perkins, and Barbara M. Perkins. 1997. *The Harper Handbook to Literature.* 2nd ed. New York: Longman.

Gómez-Quiñones, Juan. 1994. *Mexican American Labor.* Albuquerque: University of New Mexico Press.

Kozaki, Fumito. 1973. *Iwarenaki Miike tanko no hitobashira.* Edited by Massaki Hiraoka. Tokyo: Ushio Shuppansha-Showa.

Manzella, Abigail G. H. 2018. *Migrating Fictions: Gender, Race, and Citizenship in U.S. Internal Displacements.* Columbus: Ohio State University Press.

Mitchelhill, Jennifer. 2003. *Castles of the Samurai: Power and Beauty*. Tokyo: Kodansha International.

Morales, Alejandro. 2014. *River of Angels*. Houston: Arte Público Press.

——— . 2020. Guest lecture presentation for the course Chicano Authors (Chicano Studies 182). University of California, Santa Barbara, February 4, 2020.

Muffin, Ross C., and Supryia M. Ray, eds. 2009. *The Bedford Glossary of Critical and Literary Terms*. 3rd ed. Boston: St. Martin's Press.

Munro, Neil Gordon. 1908. *Prehistoric Japan*. Yokohama. eBook.

Murguía, Alejandro. 1992. "A Subtle Plague." In *Mirrors beneath the Earth: Short Fiction by Chicano Writers*, edited by Ray González, 321–25. Willimantic, CT: Curbstone Press.

Pooch, Melanie U. 2016. "The Poetics of DiverCity." In *DiverCity–Global Cities as a Literary Phenomenon: Toronto, New York, and Los Angeles in a Globalizing Age*, 57–78. Bielefeld, Germany: Transcript Verlag. eBook.

Stein, Melissa N. 2015. *Measuring Manhood: Race and the Science of Masculinity, 1830–1934*. Minneapolis: University of Minnesota Press.

Tsuda, Nortake. 1918. "Human Sacrifices in Japan." *Open Court—A Monthly Magazine* 32, no. 740 (January): 760–67.

Willis, Bruce Dean. 2013. *Corporeality in Early Twentieth-Century Latin American Literature: Body Articulations*. New York: Palgrave-Macmillan.

Zinn, Howard. 2003. *A People's History of the United States: 1492–Present*. Updated edition. New York: HarperCollins.

TWO / The Analogous Correspondence of an Extreme Poetics between Stanley Kubrick's *A Clockwork Orange* and Alejandro Morales' *Barrio on the Edge* / FRANCISCO A. LOMELÍ

> Utopia is a place where everything is good; dystopia is a place where everything is bad; heterotopia is where things are different.
> —Walter Russel Mead, "Trains, Planes, and Automobiles," 1995

The novelist, short story writer, poet, and essayist Alejandro Morales is considered something between an anomaly and a rarity within the field of Chicano/a letters. He has penned a sizable production of eight landmark novels, one collection of short stories, various theoretical essays, and several poems, yet he has, almost inexplicably, not been regarded as a trendsetter or innovator. Morales has certainly embarked on a broad variety of provocative as well as sophisticated narrative techniques, approaches, and experimentations that well illustrate a fiercely independent originality and uncanny inventiveness in broaching what might be considered unorthodox, even odd ideas. His work often tackles controversial and taxing subjects head-on, such as diseases, plagues, monstrosities, and hyper-real depictions. It is difficult to point out any direct disciples of Morales, although the argument could be made that he launched the subgenre of the hard-core barrio novel with *Caras viejas y vino nuevo* (1975) and its translation *Barrio on the Edge* (1998),[1] which other authors such as Luis J. Rodríguez, Yxta Maya Murray, and Danny Santiago later refashioned.[2] In other words, he introduced the barrio theme to the Chicano novel after it had already become widespread in poetry, theater, and to some degree in short stories as a reflection of protest and social angst. Morales' main contribution consists of interrogating the barrio as a permanent element of the Chicano lifestyle, inviting the reader to examine and decode it in order to better understand its predicaments, entrapments, and shortcomings. Per Morales, Chicanos have had to confront their demons and the corrosive nature of the barrio, which has lost its way (or has it been subverted?) from a pastoral setting to a degenerative, death-filled, and alienating milieu comprising a series of symbolic and ambiguous inversions. The gnawing issue remains: how to survive, change, or transcend such a place that also functions as home?

Morales' signature aesthetics stands out for its narrative innovations, its thematic audaciousness (another form of extreme poetics), its boundary-breaking topics, and its eerie intimations about disease, antihistory, and the future. Specifically, he dedicates considerable attention to the interpretation or revisionism of intrahistory among Chicanos/as in relation to how their respective social sphere establishes and lives by its own rules. Morales indeed stands out as an author profoundly committed to the act of writing: not simply for exploring new topics but for engaging with a wide array of subjects that more often than not rattle entrenched or complacent sensibilities. His writings are self-referential, often constructed as an antiesthetic that goes against the grain of the mainstream American canon while also challenging the trends of Chicano/a writings in vogue since the mid-1970s.[3] His place in the field has been well chronicled in terms of not necessarily conceding to strictly favorable representations of the people and environments he portrays.[4] Succinctly put, he advances various works with a rawness and sometimes crudeness of unorthodox ruminations, as Marc García-Martínez (2014) compellingly proves, thereby offering visceral and unfiltered depictions.[5] A number of critics, including the novelist himself in his critical essays, have stipulated that his aesthetic project corresponds well with the social order of a heterotopia, as originally proposed by Michel Foucault in "Different Spaces" (1998), given that the Chicano writer often harnesses reigning hegemonic circumstances, forcing characters to confront or oppose the status quo's legitimacy. Others argue that Morales is well rooted in conceptualizing what Edward Soja terms a "thirdspace" or Homi Bhabha calls a "hybrid zone," in which invented space fuses with reality.[6] The metonymic barrio in *Barrio on the Edge*, a unique Chicano construction, unfolds as ripe with an underground swell of dissent and bottled-up rage, in the process becoming a contorted representation of a heterotopia uneasy with its own social conditions and raison d'être.

I still recall my first reading of *Caras viejas y vino nuevo* in 1976 as a venture into a dark, sordid style, since most of the novel takes place at night and discernible descriptions and movements are blurred or indistinct. Greatly influenced by an all-encompassing neorealism, the most advanced style par excellence of the latter part of the twentieth century—with repeated hints of an extreme surrealism—every page is contoured by way of airbrushing characters with imprecise features, much like an incomplete graffiti mural; at the same time, the narrative anecdote figures in a minimalist rather than mechanistic manner. Its neonaturalist bent suggests a distinct dystopia, seen via Morales' intrepid and honest efforts to capture what hard-core barrio life is like for forsaken characters who are not only trapped in their environment but also molded and defined by it. They are essentially trapped within an environment driven by vices and self-negation. Ultimately, the internal structural elements of the novel are brought together by a definite neobaroque impulse that encapsulates the spirit of the milieu, the arrangement of the components of the action within a kaleidoscopic simultaneity, and the multiplicity of layers of meaning inherent to a cross-sectional narrative. Here we encounter a complex web of interconnected elements that defy simplicity for the sake of emphasizing underlying connotations of chaos and disorder. The work disrupts any sense of an orderly aesthetics appropriate to an unfinished modernity. This discourse of rupture corresponds well to a literary enterprise that captures marginalized characters ensnared (and perhaps victimized) in vices that are either self-created or assimilated from the surrounding environment. The almost absent central plot is characterized by impressionable flurries of backward action as if deliberately designed inside out. Furthermore, the novel suggests much more than it actually tells, enhanced by qualities of ambiguity, fragmentary internal and external structures, dreamlike iterations, and calculated disfigurements that put a premium on deciphering and connecting floating dots—notice, for example, the extensive use of semicolons to stitch predicates and clauses as jointed sentence fragments. At times, the novel appears to present a radiographic or X-ray image of a barrio environment more than the barrio itself. Here we encounter a carefully articulated representation of an atavistic social setting driven by habit and preconditioned practices that only an extreme poetics can capture in order to personify the visceral nature of such an intense place.

With these preliminary observations, I attempt to unpack and then confront a nagging concern about genealogy or origins in certain enigmatic pages of *Barrio on the Edge*. The novel seems to appear out of nowhere in 1975—in Spanish, which contributed to its prolonged imperceptibility—because no one before Morales had focused on the barrio as a viable subject within narrative fiction. He essentially undermined prevalent idealizations of this milieu to remind us of its complications and the need to confront its negative baggage. A philosophical question seemed to haunt readers at the time: Why write about a barrio in the first place? For one, the Chicano publishing company Quinto Sol located in Berkeley, California, led by editor Octavio Romano-V., rejected the manuscript of *Caras viejas y vino nuevo*, proving that even Chicanos at the height of the cultural nationalist Chicano Movement were not prepared for portrayals of a hard-core barrio in the face of the long-standing history of social stigma, stereotyping, and vexing views of their community. With the exception of John Steinbeck's *Tortilla Flat* (1935), which touched on subaltern populations, mainstream American literature up through the 1970s did not consider the barrio a relevant or worthy topic of representation; it was simply either a nonsubject or an invisible one— although most Chicanos were fully cognizant of living a version of it every day. For that reason, Morales opted to target the Mexican mainstream publishers Fondo de Cultura Económica and Siglo Veintiuno and the unconventional publisher Joaquín Mortiz as possible venues, but they in turn found the novel too unusual, even exotic, bizarre, and somewhat strange. These publishers sympathized with a youthful generation of Mexican literature from the 1960s known as La Onda, which attempted to "modernize" the previously mythologized trends of Mexican nationalism into a more experimental, craft-oriented, and concerted search for renovating thematics. Finally, Joaquín Mortiz proved willing to gamble on such an obscure and risqué subject matter, attracted by the novel's unconventional syntax and convoluted style. The abstruse subtextual underpinnings of Morales' work probably reminded Mortiz of both the linguistic and political reverberations of other short Latin American text packed with connotations, for example the interpersonal and disparaging violence in Mario Vargas Llosa's *La ciudad y los perros* (1967), the deep-rooted sense of despair in Juan Carlos Onetti's *El pozo* (1939), the interior action and overriding moral crisis in Alejo Carpentier's *El acoso* (1957), and perhaps hints of the stark alienation and psychologically entrapped characters in Ernesto Sábato's *El túnel* (1947).

While we can directly detect in Morales the compelling influence of such *Nouveau roman* aesthetics that had in great part helped shape the Latin American literary boom as a school of fiction dedicated to style and especially craft, in his work this acquires a new function and purpose. Laying out the novel's basic plot in reverse serves as a brilliant technique to challenge readers who might wish to find facile social renderings or solutions to hard-core barrio predicaments, while reminding us that complexity and intertwining factors characterize postmodern reality. In fact, Morales' barrio becomes a central metonymic metaphor in the Chicano novel, similar to how authors such as Alurista, Rodolfo "Corky" Gonzales, and Ricardo Sánchez had earlier established it as a common trope in poetry, except that Morales does not mythologize or romanticize. This is because he does not view it as a redemptive aspect of Chicano life but sees it rather as the cross to bear and an experiential motive to overcome. The barrio for him is our best friend—if we understand it as community—but also our worst enemy, which functions as a framework of encirclement, entrapment, and cannibalization that turns inhabitants into interchangeable objects. The natural conclusion is that the barrio falls under what sociologists Tomás Almaguer (1994) and Mario Barrera (1979) classify within the framework of dependency theory as an internal colony in terms of its marginal condition and degree of exploitation.[7] Frankly stated, the barrio was both cruel and merciless, in fact a pivotal marker in 1960s and '70s Chicano life of our underprivileged and underclass social conditions, requiring deep reflection, interrogation, and possibly doing something to at least overcome or, better yet, transcend it.[8] The novel's central action confirms that this story is no boy scout or girl scout outing, with death flanking it in the beginning and the end: this is harsh, graphic, unsentimental, violent, oppressive, eschatological, fanatically obsessive, pent-up anger and subjacent rage that is easy to penetrate but difficult to escape. In many ways, this kind of representation embodied what Chicanos saw as their inevitable sociohistorical backdrop, or as their main experience in negotiation with their relegated urban environments that typically ended in either bare survival or being swallowed up by them. The fact that the repeated references to the outside world ("over there" or "on the other side") seem obscure and almost unidentifiable speaks to the barrio's insularity, lost within an urban jungle. Morales captured it in a timely fashion to try to rescue both this environment and its inhabitants from themselves.

By focusing on the second narrative fragment of the novel, which consists of only three pages near the "beginning" (out of a total of thirty-four segments that resemble chapters), we discern that this cutting-edge work, which initially caught us off guard, has more influences and intertextual points of contact than it lets on. Indeed, its publication by Joaquín Mortiz in Mexico City subtly decoded and consequently cloaked it within the Latin American Boom. There is something highly intuitive about the way the story unfolds, in that the beginning is really the end and the end is really the beginning of this cumulative chaos that moves like the collision course of a train wreck. Interestingly, there is a gap, a pause, a ventriloquism of introspective flashes that resemble attitudes and images out of such a seemingly dissimilar work as Stanley Kubrick's 1971 film *A Clockwork Orange*—and probably older antecedents such as Luis Buñuel and Salvador Dalí's *Un Chien Andalou* (1929) and José Camilo Cela's *La familia de Pascual Duarte* (1942)—suggesting a social time bomb ticking in the midst of unbridled violence around the world or at least insinuating an extreme environment of inverted values of contradictions and paradoxes.[9] These works encompass or reflect violent times of the twentieth century as lived during the Great Depression, World War II, the turbulent period of the civil rights struggle of the 1960s, and the period of intense sociocultural experiments of the 1970s. They hint in each case at historical watershed moments when aesthetic niceties or decorum become targets of an affront, with each attempting to reach out to the viewer/reader to shock, alarm, and leave an unforgettable impression. Likewise, in *Barrio on the Edge* something is clearly off kilter, as if the barrio were an incongruous and isolated social ambience, precariously devoid of a destiny, as an anonymous narrator observes: "Here only the lights tried to shine, sparkling as if the stars had disappeared" (Morales 1998, 34).

Barrio on the Edge advances as if in a gestational state, open to possibilities and intertextual renderings in search of an extreme form and content. In the novel's second narrative fragment, we find some odd references peppered with critical assessments about the development of the modern world in a cryptic and enigmatic prose. Instead of discovering the natural evolution of progress, the reader encounters the exact opposite. Should we presume that there is a secret coded message embedded as a cautionary tale with numerous reverberations throughout the murky narrative of disjointed objects? If not, why are there repeated peculiar and discordant allusions to objects that appear hidden as if inert in dark closets, such as the 1968–1969 calendar within a grungy bathroom; the confusion between sirens as ambulance alarms, *lloronas*, or wailing women and mythological figures who mesmerized sailors; the bonfires around which the barrio men congregate to warm up but which seem to multiply exponentially from a rooftop view; a crucifix that sometimes suggests something beyond religiosity; and the drug hallucinations that directly affect both the narrative style as well as the perception of reality for most characters? Certain allegorical qualities seep through the text by assembling counterpoints of meaning: for example, through the contrast of the calloused, self-destructive, and self-indulgent drug-alcohol-sex addict named Julián (a budding Julius Caesar, potentially capable of exerting power and leadership, but who goes awry) to Mateo, who symbolically functions as a disciple of an indirect religiosity or social order, signaling a fundamental change from this tawdry Chicano Sodom and Gomorrah; the bus driver with his Jewish medallion as a sign of committing to a specific religion and the prevalence of the mystical number "3" throughout the novel; Christmas time, which marks the birth of a savior in contrast to the barrio's many deaths; and finally the issue of a mystical experience to reach a higher level of transcendence (be it God or a pseudogod), but which metamorphoses into what I call "mystical realism." The latter implies the portrayal of an environment consisting of distortions via stimulants, sexual encounters, hallucinations, rage, and unidentified sentiments that overwhelm characters, illustrating their fallibilities and vulnerabilities. Even the father, Edmundo, a misguided family figurehead, echoes the "world" ("*mundo*" in his name) while the mother, Margo (short for "*amargo*," or sour), reflects bitterness as a mother and wife. Then we have the Buenasuerte brothers, who hold the keys to perdition by serving as the drug suppliers for the barrio inhabitants—hardly representing good luck or good fortune, in ironic contrast to their last name.

After describing in considerable detail the failed, rampantly decadent landscape of a barrio surrounded by "famished dogs" and "mangled automobile carcasses," rotted or "skeletal" structures, "threatening warehouses," crying children, and "foreboding black lethal chimneys [that] puff pollution into the air," Morales equates Western civilization to an enslaving orgasm, wherein "the crucifix is both used as a cane and a condom through youth's delirium" and "strange familiar sounds . . . [blend] with the jungle" [an urban one?] (34). The analogy between *Barrio on the Edge* and *A Clockwork Orange* is not found in explicit terms related to the physical landscape as described in Morales' novel, but rather in the social depravity that exists within this urban space of aimless characters. Extreme descriptions of endless ruins abound and populate the landscape like ominous reminders of their predictable and exorable corrosion.

The barrio is a Chicano ground zero of a degenerating urban jungle situated in plain view, that is, a place that is fast regressing backward to the point of self-ruin—in parallel to the way the story unfolds. A clarification is required: this is hardly the stuff of a cultural nationalist literary agenda, which up until the mid-1970s preferred culturally positive and near-sanitized representations of Chicanos. On the contrary, we encounter a disturbing setting on the verge of bursting at the seams, that is, an environment that cannot take the pressures hinted at by Morales any longer. Morales creates a Chicano *Guernica*, echoing one of Picasso's maximum cubist expressions that deals with its own horrors from an undeclared war within an unspecified cause-and-effect framework. The barrio landscape resembles an outright war zone, except that the bombs and artifices of war are not easily discernible because they are multidirectional. Yet the effects of evoking what *Guernica* connotes are comparable: human and social tragedies seem to accumulate exponentially due to invisible forces that have exerted their might and dominance over this Chicano space, seen as a dumping ground of humanity where people are barely remnants of themselves, as effectively represented in the cubist style. At the same time, the barrio is a bastion of insularity (a lost urban island), a singularity and the "last" line of defense for its inhabitants, who are unable to escape the onslaught of outside forces, many of which have been internalized—a sense of quick gratification via drugs or sex, male prowess as the ruling social order over women, poverty and its social symptoms, education as a futile exercise, religion as a questionable vehicle for spiritual renewal, and sanctified cultural archetypes (family, church, kinship) as worthless and ineffectual sources of community cohesion. This *Guernica*-like space also provides the inhabitants with a semblance of a fortress of temporary protection, which then becomes a mirage or what Morales calls "un mundo torcido" (a twisted world) (17).[10] The tone that reigns is logically one of desolation, gloom, and hopelessness, suggesting the barrio is at a point of no return when it comes to seeking redemption from its own self-destruction. A foreboding ambiance is consequently emerging that appears to presage either a collapse or a reckoning.

Hints of *A Clockwork Orange*'s bizarre and sometimes wacky but opaque morality narrative begin to surface in Morales' text, making themselves manifest through obscure tropes and stylistic devices. They take on a visceral quality in the second narrative fragment (or chapter?) of the novel, while historically placing the action in 1968 and 1969 when Chicano barrios were historically on the brink of exploding in the midst of a social movement slowly transitioning from a rural to an urban setting, that is, from a labor movement of human rights to a student movement of civil rights. In the novel, an anonymous, freewheeling narrator with a dystopian lens (who seems to be oblivious to the characters' actions) pauses to pontificate, criticize, and indict in vague terms: "The fires of people burning the past, protesting the present, and fornicating the future can be heard in the streets of the nation" (36). The fires are both signs and harbingers of things as they were, have been, and will become. We detect a veiled call to arms, or a rallying cry to face the full spectrum of history and what it has done to the barrio itself as a Chicano space and its people as victims. The surroundings indicate a boiling point of no return, expressed by a place raging with anguish and on the brink of exploding. The barometric pressure of this barrio appears to be intensifying.

In a parallel but conspicuously distinctive fashion, the film *A Clockwork Orange* raises the ante by exhibiting gratuitous violence to an extreme, for example, when Alex and his three "droogs" or delinquents wander the streets of London in the form of tricksters, always ready to mischievously or subversively carry out—in their minds—half-hearted cruel "jokes" by beating a homeless tramp and then later gang-raping the wife of a writer while "innocently" singing "I'm Singing in the Rain." In contrast to the zany and sensationalized sense of unbridled brutality toward defenseless victims in *A Clockwork Orange*, in Morales' novel brutality takes on a more serious note due to the effects of the oppression of modern society in a Chicano barrio; there is no gaiety here, but rather muffled thoughts and muted actions. In the film, the first home invasion appears to be a sardonic game of sexual assault in which the perpetrators prance to Beethoven's music in the background while using phallic-shaped masks with a mindful justification of participating in what are purportedly young men's playful pranks. In a second home invasion, Alex indiscriminately kills a woman by smashing her head with a giant-sized penis sculpture. We witness the use of violence for violence's sake as a subversive weapon against the social establishment, supposedly "acting" playfully while harboring antisocial hostilities in the form of farcical or eccentric revelry. Alex is later arrested and subjected to behavioral conditioning in a rehabilitation center, with the objective of recovering a sense of social morality, except that he learns to fake his cure in front of psychologists. At one point he admits to his inherently violent tendencies by ironically acknowledging "I want to do good," which sounds disingenuous and vacuous when uttered. On another occasion, he notes, "My mind is blank," a symbolic statement that indicates the degree of his hollowness. He is essentially an empty individual devoid of well-intentioned sentiments, for whom morality is a foreign concept (reminding us of Julián in Morales' novel). At the end of the film, Alex confesses, "I was cured all right," after dreaming of a sexual rendezvous with a nude woman—the moral message being that he cannot heal because he doesn't have anything inside to mend. Kubrick's 1971 film, based on Anthony Burgess' homonymous novel from 1962, had a more lasting influence than the book, by capturing a historical juncture of intense sociocultural tensions and bizarre behavior as the norm through inversions. The film operates between a parody and a satire while implying a definite ethical overtone in trying to purge the protagonist's twisted sense of behavior and social order. It also depicts an impression of the modern world gone askew, thanks to unbridled violence, a decaying social fabric, and arbitrary actions against others—the very world narrated in *Barrio on the Edge*. Both Morales and Kubrick, therefore, offer correspondences aimed at shocking their respective social sensibilities, but the latter also intends to insult by hyperbolizing the droogs' actions to an extreme point. The Chicano author, on the other hand, leans more toward a subtle commentary on social conditioning and scruples, even suggesting that drug- or sex-induced actions become akin to a religious or mystical experience. Morales strategically prefers to unveil the complexities of his main characters as they struggle with a sense of fate gone astray while at the same time posing a stinging denunciation of the way the barrio has deteriorated. Either way, both works are clear expressions of a hyperpoetics aimed at rattling the senses. María Herrera-Sobek points out this particular effect in *Barrio on the Edge:* "The society in which they live has usurped their soul, their spirituality and left them bereft of any tender human feeling. The man and woman in this society, aware of this horrendous vacuum, seek to fulfill themselves through alcohol, drugs, sex and violence. In this state of 'numbness' they 'forget' some of the pain" (1977, 149).[11]

The second narrative fragment of Morales' novel contains an exceptionally enigmatic paragraph worth examining in order to fully establish its correlation with *A Clockwork Orange* and other comparable texts. Only in this way can we confirm the presence of an extreme poetics that serves to contextualize, and by extension, rationalize the Chicano characters' predicament. The first part of the paragraph, serving almost as a preamble or quasi manifesto, consists of a series of extraneous reflections by an omniscient narrator who makes value judgments about contemporary life in metaphorical terms, alluding to modernity as "the menstrual period of time" (using "period" as a double entendre) and society as the "jackass of humanity." The nihilistic overtones are inevitably comparable to *A Clockwork Orange*'s overt anarchism, with both fostering a sense of an underlying rebellion. This is followed by references to explicit sexual acts and power differentials in relation to countries that succumb, acquiesce, or surrender to greater nations or authorities:

> Padded with sanitary napkins for negotiating the menstrual period of the time, the bloody jackass of humanity appeared last night on television. In countries inundated with mouths, the cock is apt to be eaten. And in still others we can see silk ties on top of gorged bellies supported by leather belts. (36)

Later in the same the paragraph, descriptions become appraisals and beliefs more than judgments, expressly articulated through a free-flowing surrealism of uninhibited associations aimed at provoking more than explaining while situating the action historically at the end of the l960s. The "bull testicles" conjure up the emblematic image of the cubist representation of the bull in *Guernica*, invoking bottled-up sentiments of apprehension, sexual suppression, and a beheaded nation that treats its minorities and other countries similarly via a system of impositions. In other words, these are efforts to capture what is almost ineffable and certainly difficult to articulate. Here we also find explicit sexual references so prevalent in *A Clockwork Orange*, such as the incongruous, yet abstract, correlation between a clitoris and revolutions. The sentence "Films show erections of breasts and trouser flies" smacks of numerous scenes in Kubrick's film, where the droogs not only use pointy masks in the form of erections but also wear conspicuous plastic jock straps to conceal what would be equivalent to their "trouser flies." In addition, while a comment about pornography is inserted to reinforce the idea of 1968 as a year of historical changes, the year 1969 can be understood as a masked symbol of the conversion of hypersensibilities: extreme social tensions related to the Vietnam War, the exploding hippie movement, and the open generational and cultural conflicts. The year "nineteen sixty-nine" could also suggest a symbolic pun and covert reference to rampant sexuality (again, something common in both the film and the novel):

Art expresses the yanking out of bull testicles with which to illustrate the school-like lessons of how to suck the clitoris of modern revolutions. Films show erections of breasts and trouser flies. The year nineteen sixty-eight is not so significant, but in nineteen sixty-nine more pornography will be sold. (36)

In addition, the reference to pornography here conveniently corresponds to the year "sixty-nine," which in part applies to elements in both works by Kubrick and Morales if viewed superficially and with a decontextualized lens. Sexuality as an uninhibited form of expression here parallels what in the 1950s was called the "pornography of violence."[12] The overt sexual acts or references correspond more to expressions of personal validation, a desperate reaching out for companionship and potential affection, which the characters seem to lack in their respective ambience. However, their self-indulgence does not permit them to make authentic connections with others because of their obsession with immediate self-gratification; their actions ultimately appear as sensationalized acts of violence that do not pretend to stimulate erotic feelings. In both cases, sex is utilized as a weapon of conquest, victory, and subjugation, not as the mutual communion of spirits but simply as temporary carnal imposition.

The paragraph in question continues with provocative statements that go unqualified and would appear to be more bizarre than some of the scenes in *A Clockwork Orange*. The narrator's utterance "Psychiatrists masturbate horses and scream: The Russians are coming!" (36) is as striking as Luis Buñuel and Salvador Dalí's iconic scene in *Un Chien Andalou* in which someone cuts across a large eye with a blade in full view, with blood gushing out. The objective is to evoke actions that evoke strange deeds. The first part of the sentence suggests a hypersexualized act committed by scientists—an explicitly exaggerated or irrational action leaning toward sensationalism—but the second part embodies a slogan from the height of the Cold War warning Westerners of a Russian invasion. Incompatible ideas are somehow fused together as if their connections were seamless, but the opposite is true. The interpretation can be left to the eye of the beholder. The point is that the references initially seem nonsensical, except that their disparate nature lends itself to greater connotation for a shock effect into disbelief. Given the explosive content of *Barrio on the Edge,* these free associations of disconnected realities further suggest a surrealistic composition, which at times is enhanced by cubist synecdoches that figure as fragments of abstract movements in the dark tinged with nihilistic overtones (e.g., hands that strike, arms that flail, feet that move into a room, "mouths with bites and painful grimaces," that is, parts of the body acting and reacting independently as if they have a mind of their own). Consequently, the paragraph reads more like a codex meant to be deciphered about a place and characters that share acute issues, thanks in great part to the stream of metaphors that give a restrained impression of existing social tensions without providing specificities. As depicted in the paragraph, Morales' expressive violence cannot be reduced to ideology, as the various fragments speak for themselves. At the same time, such violence can be subtle, overt, sublime, arbitrary, or take the seductive form of counteracting inhibitions—but the degree of sensationalism here does not match *A Clockwork Orange*, where it is in fact the norm and arguably the ultimate goal. Nonetheless, both texts leave decidedly long-lasting impressions.

In addition to echoing *A Clockwork Orange*, the central ideas in the paragraph intertextually bring to mind other works with a strong surrealistic bent influenced by the inherent skepticism of nihilism, such as Buñuel and Dalí's